STAGE FOUR

Longman Mathematics
New Metric Edition

A. E. Howard, C.B.E., B.Sc.
HEADMASTER, WANDSWORTH SCHOOL

W. Farmer, B.Sc.
HEADMASTER, CATFORD SCHOOL

R. A. Blackman, B.Sc.
HEADMASTER, LANFRANC HIGH SCHOOL

LONGMAN

Longman Mathematics

A five-year course

A graded series to cover the requirements of O level in Stage Five. Stage Four reaches the standard required for the Certificate of Secondary Education.
Stages One, Two and Three are provided with a separate combined answer book.
Stages Four and Five are published with answers.

LONGMAN GROUP LTD
London

Associated companies, branches and representatives throughout the world

© *A. E. Howard, W. Farmer and R. A. Blackman 1965*
New Metric edition © *Longman Group Ltd 1970*

All rights reserved. No part of this publication may be reproduced, stored in a retrieval system or transmitted in any form or by any means, electronic, mechanical, photocopying, recording, or otherwise, without the prior permission of the Copyright owner.

First published 1965
New Metric edition 1970
Third Impression 1973

ISBN 0 582 20868 8

Printed in Great Britain by Western Printing Services Ltd, Bristol

Contents

		PAGE
	Introduction	iv
1	Powers, Roots and Reciprocals	1
2	Trigonometry	14
3	A New Geometry	42
4	Mappings and Matrices	54
5	Space and Time	69
6	Similar Figures	84
7	Civic Arithmetic	94
8	Statistics	103
9	Algebra	118
10	The Sphere	134
11	Practical Applications of Trigonometry	153
12	Sets	175
13	Geometry	191
14	Series	213
15	The Number System and Fields	227
16	Chance in Mathematics	234
17	Revision Exercises	238
	Answers	290

Introduction

The authors of these books have written them with two main ideas in mind. The first is, that mathematics is indivisible; it contains all the elements we know of arithmetic, algebra, geometry and trigonometry and each of these branches of the subject is dependent on all the others. For this reason we believe that all secondary school pupils should be taught *mathematics*. Furthermore, we believe that most secondary school pupils, even those less academically inclined, can learn mathematics provided that the emphasis is placed on the results and uses of the subject rather than the abstract reasoning behind the various processes. We have, therefore, concentrated on the application of mathematics to the solution of many practical problems in order to show its value to the pupils, and we have endeavoured to avoid the traditional 'academic' approach to the teaching of this subject.

Our second idea is this. We do not believe that pupils in secondary schools are particularly interested in the methods of teaching mathematics. They require a textbook to direct them to perform certain operations with clearly set out diagrams and worked examples for reference. A large number of graded questions is obviously necessary. On the other hand, we firmly believe that many teachers of mathematics will welcome a book which gives well-tried methods of teaching the various aspects of the subject, including some parts with which they are not so familiar or which their pupils have not attempted before.

Stage 4 of *Longman Mathematics* contains the remaining material which will be required for pupils taking the Certificate of Secondary Education Examination (15+ age group). We have assumed that in most cases the syllabuses for this examination will contain a common core of mathematics together with certain optional topics which may be chosen by individual schools.

Our series of books contains therefore a considerable amount of 'modern mathematics', statistics, elementary surveying and extended graphical work as well as the more familiar portions of the subject. We hope in this way to give pupils a wide choice of the topics they study.

Although we would not wish to impose our views on any teacher we suggest that the chapters be worked through in order, for they are arranged in a carefully considered sequence. The work on

INTRODUCTION

'Modern Mathematics' has been so devised that it follows naturally the topics already considered in Stage 3 and does not require any particular background knowledge by any teacher as yet unacquainted with these concepts.

The following detailed suggestions may be helpful to you:

Chapter 1: A slide rule should be constructed by each member of the class. Schools having the advantage of well-equipped workshops will probably choose the method which involves cooperation between the departments but the simple method using cardboard is quite satisfactory to enable pupils to learn the principles.

Chapter 2: The graph should be drawn by all the pupils as it is fundamental to the work which follows.

Chapters 3, 4 and 15 should be covered in this order (not consecutively). Completely new work is introduced in these chapters, and, as with the introduction of any new ideas or concepts, this needs to be carefully worked through in class by the teacher and pupil together.

Chapters 3 and 4 introduce new technical vocabulary as the work proceeds. These terms are always carefully explained and their use should arise naturally.

Chapter 7: In each part of this chapter situations as they exist have been included. Because of this some of the numbers involved are slightly more difficult than if fictitious amounts had been introduced. The examples have been devised, however, so that long and complicated computation is not necessary.

Chapter 12 is a continuation of the work on sets started in Stage 3.

Chapter 16: This introduction to the theory of Probability should be considered as a series of practical experiments to be undertaken by the pupils. There is plenty of opportunity for group work.

Revision Exercises

Some of the papers are specifically designed to be revision of arithmetic already considered in the previous books. The others contain general questions covering the whole field.

The books are designed for pupils in all secondary schools, particularly for those who appreciate the non-traditional approach to mathematics. If we succeed in widening the opportunities of learning this most fascinating of subjects to many boys and girls then we shall feel our efforts have been well rewarded.

                      A. E. HOWARD   W. FARMER   R. A. BLACKMAN

Note about this Edition

In view of the adoption of decimal currency and the progressive introduction of metric units, most examining boards are introducing these changes into their O-level papers in 1970–71. Accordingly, this book employs decimal currency and metric units exclusively.

The opportunity offered by the new edition has been taken to make some modifications to the contents and arrangement of the books. Stages 1 and 2 have been slightly expanded by the inclusion of 'modern' topics and new material has been introduced in Stages 4 and 5 to accommodate syllabus changes.

Stages 1, 2 and 3 are published without answers and a combined answer book is provided for teachers; Stages 4 and 5 include answers.

A.E.H.
W.F.
R.A.B.

Acknowledgements

We are indebted to the Associated Examining Board for the General Certificate of Education, the University of Cambridge Local Examinations Syndicate, The College of Preceptors, the Union of Educational Institutions, the Joint Matriculation Board of the Universities of Manchester, Liverpool, Leeds, Sheffield and Birmingham, the Senate of the University of London, the Oxford Delegacy of Local Examinations, and the Royal Society of Arts for permission to reproduce questions from various past examination papers.

We are indebted to the following for permission to reproduce copyright material:

Associated Examining Board for questions from G.C.E. Mathematics examinations, November 1967, June 1967, May 1968 and June 1969; Joint Matriculation Board of the Universities of Manchester, Liverpool, Leeds, Sheffield and Birmingham for questions from June 1968 and June 1969 Mathematics examinations; Metropolitan Regional Examinations Board for questions from 1966, 1967 and 1969 C.S.E. Mathematics examinations.

1 Powers, Roots and Reciprocals

We have already seen how logarithms can help us with many complicated calculations concerning multiplication and division, and we must now investigate how the same idea can simplify even more difficult calculations.

Powers

x^2 is the 'shorthand' method of writing $x \times x$
x^3 is the 'shorthand' method of writing $x \times x \times x$
x^4 is the 'shorthand' method of writing $x \times x \times x \times x$ and so on.

Thus the *index* ('2' in the case of x^2, '4' in the case of x^4 etc.) tells us how many x's are to be multiplied together.

Example

Find the value of $13\cdot29^4$.

To solve this problem we need to find the value of
$$13\cdot29 \times 13\cdot29 \times 13\cdot29 \times 13\cdot29$$
First find an approximate answer (or rough check).

$13\cdot29 \simeq 13$
$13\cdot29^4 \simeq 13^4$ i.e. $13^2 \times 13^2 = 169 \times 169 \simeq 170 \times 170$
$\therefore (13\cdot29)^4 \simeq 28\,900$

Using logs:

Number	Log.
13·29	1·123 5
13·29	1·123 5
13·29	1·123 5
13·29	1·123 5
Add	4·494 0

Antilog. $4\cdot494\,0 = 31\,190$

$\therefore (13\cdot29)^4 = 31\,190$

Since these logs are all the same there is no need to perform this

1

addition sum, all we need do is write the log. once and *multiply by 4*. Thus,

Number	Log.
13·29	1·123 5
	4
(13·29)⁴	4·494 0

Antilog. 4·494 0 = 31 190

$\therefore (13 \cdot 29)^4 = 31\ 190$

Similarly, find the value of (0·069 23)³

Rough check

$$0 \cdot 069\ 23 \simeq 0 \cdot 07$$
$$\therefore (0 \cdot 069\ 23)^3 \simeq (0 \cdot 07)^3$$
$$\simeq \frac{7}{100} \times \frac{7}{100} \times \frac{7}{100}$$
$$\simeq \frac{343}{1\ 000\ 000}$$
$$\therefore (0 \cdot 069\ 23)^3 \simeq 0 \cdot 000\ 343$$

Using logs:

Number	Log.
0·069 23	$\bar{2}$·840 3
	3
(0·069 23)³	$\bar{4}$·520 9

(*Note:* In this case the 'carrying figure' is +2, thus the 'whole' number part of the log. becomes −6+2=−4)

Antilog. $\bar{4}$·520 9 = 0·000 331 8

$\therefore (0 \cdot 069\ 23)^3 = 0 \cdot 000\ 331\ 8$

Exercise 1a

Using logs find the value of

1. 8·263²
2. (16·96)³
3. (3·656)⁵
4. (194·6)²
5. (0·584 3)⁴
6. (0·091 63)²
7. (0·001 250)²
8. (0·916 4)³
9. (0·059 05)⁴

POWERS, ROOTS AND RECIPROCALS

10. The area of a circle is given by the formula πr^2. Find the area of a circle whose radius r is (a) 2·5 cm, (b) 0·575 cm.

Roots

Using the same method find the value of $(9 \cdot 000\ 0)^{\frac{1}{2}}$.
Using logs. In this case we shall need to find the log. of 9·000 0 and multiply it by *one half*.

Thus

Number	Log.
9·000 0	0·954 2
	$\frac{1}{2}$
$(9 \cdot 000\ 0)^{\frac{1}{2}}$	0·477 1

(*Note:* Multiplying by $\frac{1}{2}$ is the same as dividing by 2)

Antilog. 0·477 1 = 3·000 0

$\therefore (9 \cdot 000\ 0)^{\frac{1}{2}} = 3 \cdot 000\ 0$

But we already know that $3 = \sqrt{9}$ (the square root of 9)

Hence $9^{\frac{1}{2}}$ is the index method of writing $\sqrt{9}$.

We can prove this fact in another way. If x is any number then by the laws of indices $x^{\frac{1}{2}} \times x^{\frac{1}{2}} = x^{\frac{1}{2}+\frac{1}{2}} = x^1 = x$, or $x^{\frac{1}{2}}$ is that number which if multiplied by itself gives the original number x.

$\therefore$ By definition $x^{\frac{1}{2}} = \sqrt{x}$

Similarly $x^{\frac{1}{3}} = \sqrt[3]{x}$ (i.e. the cube root of x)

and $x^{\frac{1}{6}} = \sqrt[6]{x}$ (i.e. the sixth root of x)

Using logs we have a simple method of determining roots of numbers —all we need do is *find the log. of the given number and divide it by the root concerned* (2 for square root, 3 for cube root etc.). The antilog. of the answer will give the root required.

Thus find $\sqrt{184 \cdot 6}$.

(*Note:* Finding a 'rough check' in this case is difficult unless we happen to know the value of a perfect square near the given number. When finding roots it is better to follow the given procedure and check *afterwards* that the answer is of the correct order.)

Using logs:

Number	Log.
184·6	2·266 2
$\sqrt{184·6}$	$\dfrac{2·266\ 2}{2} = 1·133\ 1$

Antilog. 1·133 1 = 13·58

$$\therefore \sqrt{184·6} = 13·58$$

(Check 13·58 ≃ 14 and $14^2 = 14 \times 14 = 196$)

Similarly: Find $\sqrt[3]{39\ 620·0}$

Using logs:

Number	Log.
39 620·0	4·597 9
$\sqrt[3]{39\ 620·0}$	$\dfrac{4·597\ 9}{3} = 1·532\ 6$ (correct to 4 dec. places)

Antilog. 1·532 6 = 34·09

$$\therefore \sqrt[3]{39\ 620·0} = 34·09$$

(34·09 ≃ 30 and $30^3 = 900 \times 30 = 27\ 000$)

Exercise 1b

Using logs find the value of

1. $\sqrt{5·638}$
2. $\sqrt[4]{984·7}$
3. $\sqrt[3]{18·69}$
4. $\sqrt{896·2}$
5. $\sqrt[5]{4\ 567·0}$
6. $\sqrt{8·000\ 0}$
7. $\sqrt[3]{222·0}$
8. $\sqrt{981}$
9. $\sqrt[4]{66·84}$

10. A circle has an area of 65 cm². What is its radius? (*Hint:* Area of circle $A = \pi r^2$; $\therefore r^2 = \dfrac{A}{\pi}$ and $r = \sqrt{\dfrac{A}{\pi}}$; first use logs to find the value of $\dfrac{A}{\pi}$)

POWERS, ROOTS AND RECIPROCALS

Roots of numbers less than 1·000 0

The same method is used when we wish to find the root of a fractional number. Extra care is required with these numbers, however, because part of the log. is negative and part positive.

Example

Find $\sqrt{0\cdot075\ 21}$

Taking logs we get

Number	Log.
0·075 21	$\bar{2}$·876 3
$\sqrt{0\cdot075\ 21}$	$\dfrac{\bar{2}\cdot876\ 3}{2}$

In this case we can proceed quite easily because the negative part of the log. i.e. ($\bar{2}$) is exactly divisible by 2

Hence log. $\sqrt{0\cdot075\ 21} = \dfrac{\bar{2}\cdot876\ 3}{2} = \bar{1}\cdot438\ 2$ (to 4 dec. places)

$\therefore \sqrt{0\cdot075\ 21} = 0\cdot274\ 3$ (Check $0\cdot274\ 3 \simeq 0\cdot3$; $(0\cdot3)^2 = 0\cdot09$)

Supposing, however, that we had required to find $\sqrt{0\cdot752\ 1}$

Proceeding as before and taking logs:

Number	Log.
0·752 1	$\bar{1}$·876 3
$\sqrt{0\cdot752\ 1}$	$\dfrac{\bar{1}\cdot876\ 3}{2}$

Dividing by 2 in this case produces no useful result as the 'negative part' of the log. must be a whole number to establish the position of the decimal point in the antilog.

A negative *whole number* must therefore be added to the negative part of the log. which makes it *exactly divisible by 2 and produces a whole number answer* and, in order not to alter the value of the original log., *a corresponding positive whole number be added to the positive part of the log.*

Thus $\bar{1}\cdot876\ 3 = \bar{2} + 1\cdot876\ 3$

(*Note:* Add the lowest possible whole number in each case.)

5

LONGMAN MATHEMATICS

Dividing by 2, $\dfrac{\bar{1}\cdot 876\,3}{2} = \dfrac{\bar{2}+1\cdot 876\,3}{2} = \bar{1}\cdot 938\,2$ (to 4 dec. places)

∴ log. $\sqrt{0\cdot 752\,1} = \bar{1}\cdot 938\,2$

Hence $\sqrt{0\cdot 752\,1} = 0\cdot 867\,4$ (using antilog. tables)

(Check $0\cdot 867\,4 \simeq 0\cdot 9$ and $(0\cdot 9)^2 = 0\cdot 81$)

Similarly: Find $\sqrt[3]{0\cdot 521\,9}$

Number	Log.
$0\cdot 521\,9$	$\bar{1}\cdot 717\,5$
$\sqrt[3]{0\cdot 521\,9}$	$\dfrac{\bar{1}\cdot 717\,5}{3}$

But $\bar{1}\cdot 717\,5 = \bar{3} + 2\cdot 717\,5$

(In this case the lowest possible whole number to add to each part of the log. is 2.)

∴ $\dfrac{\bar{1}\cdot 717\,5}{3} \quad \dfrac{\bar{3}+2\cdot 717\,5}{3} = \bar{1}\cdot 905\,8$

∴ $\sqrt[3]{0\cdot 521\,9} = 0\cdot 805\,0$

(Check $0\cdot 805\,0 \simeq 0\cdot 8$ and $(0\cdot 8)^3 = 0\cdot 8 \times 0\cdot 8 \times 0\cdot 8 = 0\cdot 64 \times 0\cdot 8$
$= 0\cdot 512$)

Exercise 1c

Using logs find the value of

1. $\sqrt{0\cdot 032\,51}$
2. $\sqrt{0\cdot 981\,6}$
3. $\sqrt[3]{0\cdot 008\,1}$
4. $\sqrt[3]{0\cdot 500\,0}$
5. $\sqrt{0\cdot 001\,025}$
6. $\sqrt[4]{0\cdot 061\,92}$
7. $\sqrt[3]{0\cdot 01}$
8. $\sqrt{0\cdot 333\,3}$

9. The formula for the volume of a cube is $v = x^3$ (x = side of cube). Find the side of a cube whose volume is $7\cdot 5$ cm³.

10. The time of swing of a simple pendulum is given by the formula

$$T = 2\pi \sqrt{\dfrac{l}{g}}.$$

Find T if $l = 52$ and $g = 981$.

POWERS, ROOTS AND RECIPROCALS

Reciprocals

According to the *Oxford Dictionary*, the *Reciprocal* of a function or expression is defined as being 'the function or expression so related to one another that their product is unity' (thus $\frac{1}{5}$ is the reciprocal of 5). Another way of stating this is 'The reciprocal of a given number is *one* divided by that number'. In many cases the reciprocal of a number can be found by inspection thus:

the reciprocal of 12 is $\frac{1}{12}$

the reciprocal of $\frac{1}{4}$ is $\dfrac{1}{\frac{1}{4}} = 1 \times \dfrac{4}{1} = 4$ etc.

Where this is not possible, reciprocals can easily be found by using logs thus:

Find the reciprocal of (a) 7·231 (b) 0·085 61

(a)
Number	Log.
1·000 0	0·000 0
7·231	0·859 2
Subtract	$\bar{1}$·140 8

Antilog. $\bar{1}$·140 8 = 0·138 3

∴ Reciprocal of 7·231 = 138 3

(Check 7·231 ≃ 7·00 ∴ Reciprocal ≃ $\frac{1}{7}$ = 0·142 9)

(b)
Number	Log.
1·000	0·000 0
0·856 1	$\bar{2}$·932 6
Subtract	1·067 4

Antilog. 1·067 4 = 11·68

∴ Reciprocal of 0·085 61 = 11·68

(Check 0·085 61 ≃ 0·09 = $\dfrac{9}{100}$

and Reciprocal of $\dfrac{9}{100}$ is $\dfrac{1}{\frac{9}{100}} = \dfrac{100}{9} = 11\cdot1$)

7

Exercise 1d

Find the reciprocals of

1. 6·38   **2.** 0·25   **3.** 104·6   **4.** 0·001 064

5. Find the value of R if

$$\frac{1}{R} = \frac{1}{r_1} + \frac{1}{r_2} \text{ and } r_1 = 8·5, r_2 = 25·75$$

6. The formula given in question 5 is that used to find the total resistance of two electrical resistances connected in parallel. Find the total resistance when two resistances 1·5 ohms and 36·5 ohms are connected in parallel.

The Slide Rule

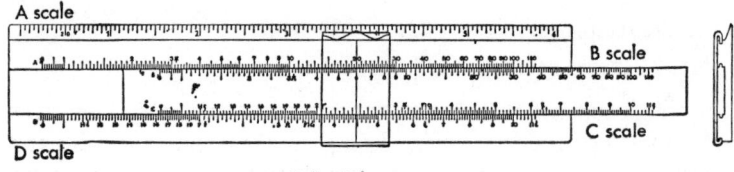

Slide Rule.
Fig. 1-1

The slide rule is a portable set of log. tables, and for this reason is very popular among engineers, architects and surveyors. The simplest way to learn how to use a slide rule is to make one for yourself.

A slide rule consists of 3 separate parts,
  (i) a fixed frame
  (ii) a slide
  (iii) an additional movable frame called a cursor held in position on the face of the rule by sliding in two grooves.

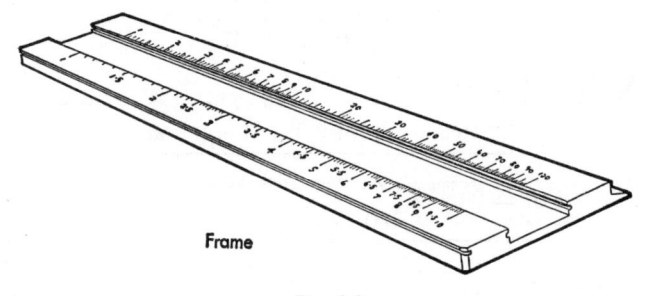

Fig. 1-2

POWERS, ROOTS AND RECIPROCALS

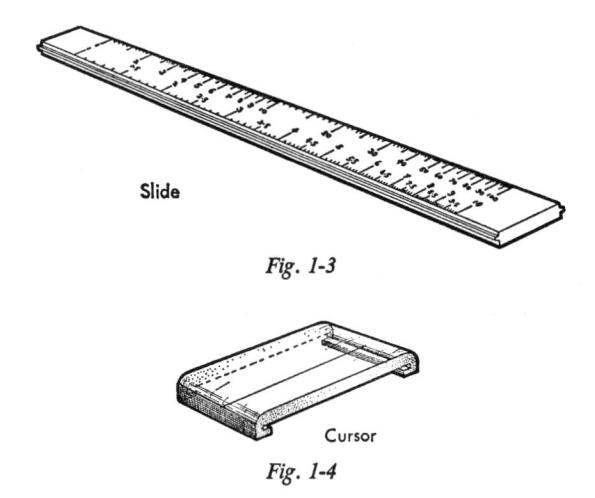

Fig. 1-3

Slide

Fig. 1-4

Cursor

Construction of a Slide Rule

The frame consists of 3 pieces of wood, one 20 cm long, 3 cm wide and 5 mm thick and two similar pieces each 20 cm long, 1 cm wide and 2 mm thick. The two smaller pieces are attached to the base of the frame to fit exactly along the two edges leaving a groove 1 cm wide 2 mm thick in the middle to receive the slide.

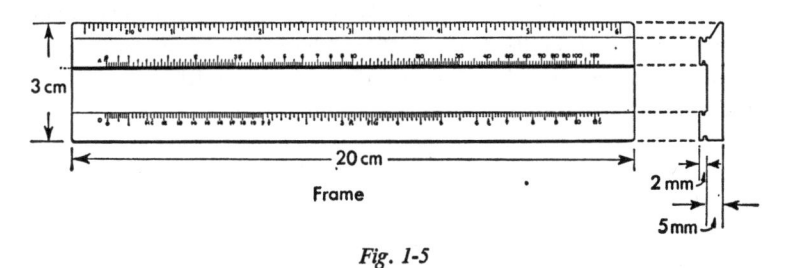

Fig. 1-5

Frame
20 cm
3 cm
2 mm
5 mm

The slide is a piece of wood 22 cm long, 1 cm wide and 2 mm thick.

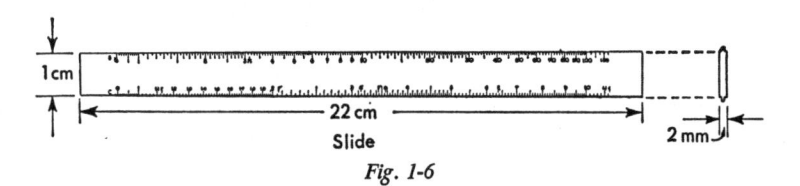

Fig. 1-6

Slide
22 cm
1 cm
2 mm

The cursor, which is merely a device to get a movable line perpendicular to the scales on the rule, may be simply made by soldering a piece of thin wire 3 cm long to two pieces of tin and bending these to fit over the rule.

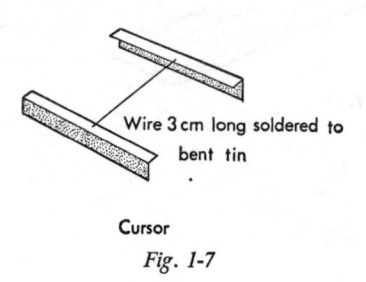

Wire 3 cm long soldered to bent tin

Cursor

Fig. 1-7

Note. The frame and slide may be made of stiff cardboard of approximately the same thicknesses if there is any difficulty in obtaining wood. In this case three pieces of cardboard will be required, one 20 cm long, 3 cm and 'chocolate box' thickness, and two similar pieces each 20 cm long, 1 cm wide and the same thickness as before. The smaller pieces should be attached to the base by an adhesive to fit exactly along the edges leaving a groove 1 cm wide in the middle to receive the slide.

The slide is a piece of cardboard 22 cm long, 1 cm wide and 'chocolate box' thickness. In this case the cursor can be a piece of thin string or a thin elastic band fitting tightly round the slide rule.

Graduating the Slide Rule

The slide rule (which is a portable set of log. tables) is based on the theory that multiplication of numbers can be performed by *adding distances* and that division of numbers can be performed by *subtracting distances*. Since this is precisely the same operation which we have already done using log. tables it follows that the distances we add or subtract must be proportional to the logarithms of the numbers.

The log of 1·000 0 is 0·000 0 and the log. of 10·000 0 is 1·000 0 but if we made our scale from 0 to 1 cm the distances for numbers in between would be so small that they would be difficult to read and small inaccuracies would become greatly magnified in calculations. We shall therefore base our scale on a length of 20 cm. Four scales are needed.

Scale A. On a piece of white drawing paper draw a line exactly 20 cm long. At the left-hand end put the number 1 and at the right-hand end the number 10. Now, using your log. tables find the log. of 2·000 0.

POWERS, ROOTS AND RECIPROCALS

Log. 2·000 0 = 0·301 0. Multiplying 0·301 0 by 20 we get 6·020.
Starting from the left-hand end (the figure 1), measure a distance 6·02 cm as accurately as possible and mark this point 2.
Similarly from the log. tables log. 3·000 0 = 0·477 1.
Multiplying 0·477 1 by 20 we get 9·542.
Starting from the left-hand end (the figure 1), measure a distance 9·542 cm as accurately as possible and mark this point 3. Repeat this process for all the whole numbers from 4 to 9. You now have the whole number part of Scale A, and by further using the log. tables in the same way as described above you can measure distances proportional to the logs. of 1·1, 1·2, 1·3 etc., up to 9·9 (remember to multiply by 20 each time!), and only mark the points 1·5, 2·5, 3·5

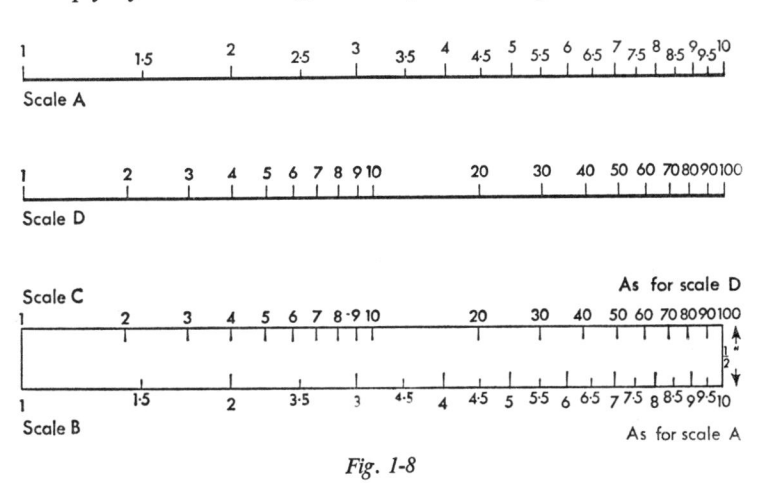

Fig. 1-8

etc., or you will find it impossible to read. You should also mark the position of π.

Scale D is exactly half the size of Scale A, so that the number 10 is 10 cm from the left-hand end. The remaining 10 cm is divided into exactly the same distances as the first 10 cm but the points are marked with the numbers 20, 30 . . . 100.

Scale B is an exact copy of *Scale A* and *Scale C* of *Scale D*, but note these two scales must be drawn 1 cm apart so that this strip can be cut out to fit on the slide.

Scale A is then attached to the bottom of the frame, Scale D to the top and Scales B and C to the slide. (*Note:* When the slide is placed in position Scales A and B and Scales C and D should coincide.)

11

When the cursor is placed in position your home-made Slide Rule is complete.

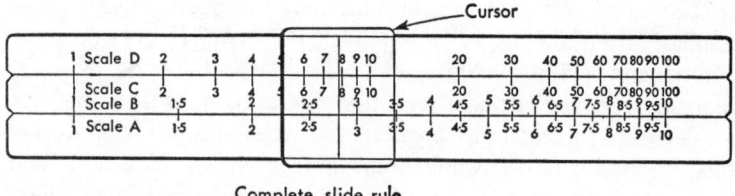

Complete slide rule

Fig. 1-9

Using the Slide Rule

As with any other device, practice makes perfect, so get as much practice as possible. Basically, movement to the right performs multiplication and movement to the left performs division.

Thus using Scales A and B.

Move the slide so that the 1 of Scale B coincides with the 2 of Scale A. Move the cursor until it coincides with the 3 of Scale B. The corresponding reading on Scale A is 6. Thus we have performed the operation $2 \times 3 = 6$.

Similarly move the slide so that the 2 on Scale B coincides with the 9 on Scale A. Move the cursor to the 1 on Scale B and the corresponding reading on Scale A is 4·5.

Thus we have performed the operation $\frac{9}{2} = 4\cdot5$.

All other multiplications and divisions are merely extensions of this method. (*Note:* In order to ensure the correct *order* of your answer, it is essential to obtain an approximate answer first.) Scale D gives the square of numbers on Scale A and likewise Scale A gives the square-root of numbers on Scale D, thus it is simple to make calculations involving squares and square-roots.

Thus, find the area of a circle whose radius is 1·5 cm.

Area of circle $= \pi r^2$.

(Approx. Ans. $1\cdot5^2 = (1\tfrac{1}{2})^2 = \frac{9}{4}$; Area $\simeq \frac{22}{7} \times \frac{9}{4} \simeq \frac{99}{14} \simeq 7\cdot0$)

Make the 1 of Scale B coincide with 1·5 of Scale A. Move the cursor until it coincides with π on Scale C. The corresponding reading on Scale D gives the required area 7·1 cm².

Similarly, find the radius of a circle whose area is 35 cm².

POWERS, ROOTS AND RECIPROCALS

Radius = $\sqrt{\dfrac{\text{Area}}{\pi}}$

(Approx. Ans.) $\sqrt{\dfrac{35}{\pi}} \simeq \sqrt{\dfrac{35}{\frac{22}{7}}} \simeq \sqrt{\dfrac{35 \times 7}{22}} \simeq \sqrt{\dfrac{36}{3}} \simeq \sqrt{12} \simeq 3\cdot5$)

Make the π on Scale C coincide with 35 on Scale D. Move the cursor to coincide with the 1 on Scale B. The corresponding reading on Scale A is the required radius (3·32 cm).

Try as many different kinds of operations as you can with your home-made Slide Rule until you become confident in its use. You will be then well advised to purchase a good machine-graduated Slide Rule, which need not be expensive and is well worth having.

Exercise 1e

Use a Slide Rule to find as accurately as you can:

1. $\dfrac{2 \times 3}{4}$
2. $\dfrac{5 \times 25}{130}$
3. $\dfrac{125 \times 0\cdot75}{5\cdot25}$
4. $45\cdot8 \times 3\cdot5 \times 1\cdot25$
5. $\dfrac{24\cdot5 \times 3\cdot5}{0\cdot75}$
6. $38\cdot25 \times 0\cdot126$
7. $\dfrac{0\cdot587\,5}{0\cdot007\,2}$
8. $\dfrac{56\cdot7 \times 0\cdot812}{35\cdot5}$
9. $\dfrac{26\cdot28 + 104}{19 \quad 25}$

(In every case find an approximate answer first.)

10. The total surface area of a cylinder is given by the formula
$$A = 2\pi rh + \pi r^2 \begin{cases} r = \text{radius of base} \\ h = \text{height} \end{cases}$$
Find the total surface area of a cylinder whose radius is 1·25 cm and height 15·5 cm.

11. Find the radius of a circle whose area is 384 cm².

12. Given that the formula for the volume of a cylinder is $V = \pi r^2 h$, find the volume of the cylinder whose base radius is 2·25 cm and height is 7·5 cm.

2 Trigonometry

The Sine of an Angle

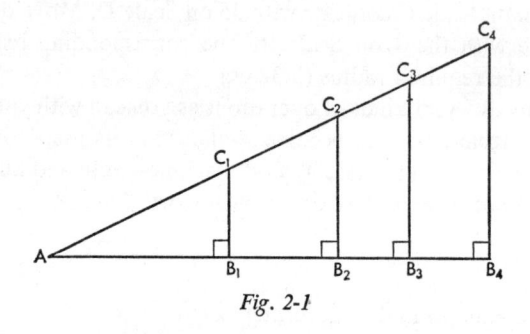

Fig. 2-1

This figure was studied in Stages One and Three.

It was found that $\dfrac{B_1C_1}{AB_1} = \dfrac{B_2C_2}{AB_2} = \dfrac{B_3C_3}{AB_3} = \dfrac{B_4C_4}{AB_4} = \tan A$

It can also be shown that $\dfrac{B_1C_1}{AC_1} = \dfrac{B_2C_2}{AC_2} = \dfrac{B_3C_3}{AC_3} = \dfrac{B_4C_4}{AC_4}$

(see Stage Three, Chapter 6).

The value of this ratio, like the first, depends only on the size of the angle A and is called the sine of angle A, or, for short, sin A. AC, the side opposite the right angle, is called the hypotenuse of the triangle ABC and so

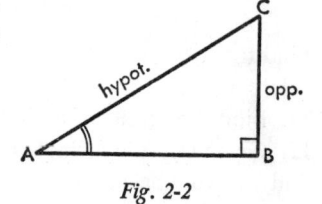

$\sin B\hat{A}C = \dfrac{\text{opp.}}{\text{hypot.}}$

$= \dfrac{BC}{AC}$

Fig. 2-2

Something to do

On a piece of graph paper, Fig. 2-3, draw a quadrant of a circle centre A radius 4 cm. With your protractor mark off angles at intervals of 10°, as shown.

Set up a pair of axes Ox and Oy, and let Op = 1 unit on Oy = 4 cm.

TRIGONOMETRY

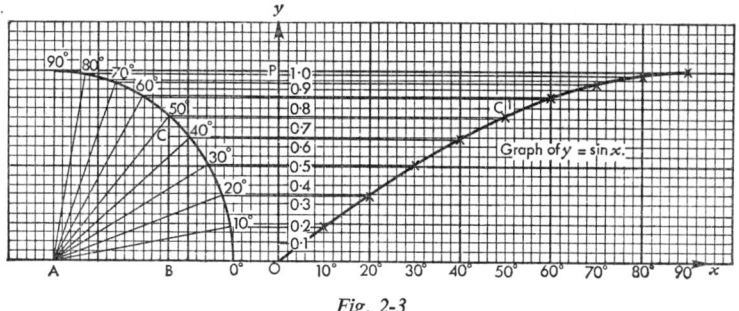

Fig. 2-3

Mark the x axis from $0°$ to $90°$ ($10° = 1$ cm).
The radius of the circle can be regarded as 1 unit. Why?
In the right-angled triangle ABC

$$\sin 50° = \sin \hat{BAC} = \frac{BC}{AC}$$

But $AC = 1$ unit

$$\therefore \sin 50° = BC \text{ numerically}$$

Draw a parallel CC' to Ox to obtain the point C' where $x = 50°$.
Repeat the process for all the angles from $0°$ to $90°$ and draw the graph of $y = \sin x$. The scale is small but you will be able to build up an approximate table of sines from the graph.

The word 'sine' has an interesting history. It is derived from the latin 'sinus' (a fold) which was a mistaken translation of the Arab word for a half chord, e.g. BC, Fig. 2-3.

Important

As x increases from $0°$ to $90°$, $\sin x$ increases from 0 to 1.
Natural sine tables are read in the same way as natural tangent tables.

Exercise 2a

1. From your graph of $y = \sin x$ make up a table of sines for angles from $0°$ to $90°$ at $10°$ intervals. Estimate the values of $\sin 15°$, $\sin 28°$ and $\sin 36°$ and find the approximate values of the angles whose sines are 0·3, 0·7 and 0·8.

2. Using the sine table write down the sines of the following angles. (Each answer should be written in the form: $\sin 23° = 0·390\ 7$.)

15

27°, 75°, 45°, 13°, 30°, 87°, 64°, 16°, 18°,
69°6′, 54°24′, 37°54′, 63°24′, 63°30′, 35°42′,
31°15′, 74°50′, 35°4′, 4°39′, 53°17′, 71°43′.

3. Using the sine table in reverse write down the angles which have the following sines. (Each answer should be written in the form: If $\sin x° = 0.981\ 6$, $x = 79°$.)

0·707 1, 0·275 6, 0·992 5, 0·656 1, 0·017 5, 0·231 7,
0·989 5, 0·818 1, 0·007 0, 0·516 5, 0·757 4, 0·121 5,
0·535 1, 0·980 5, 0·932 2, 0·255 8, 0·879 0, 0·482 9,
0·165 2, 0·572 8.

Examples

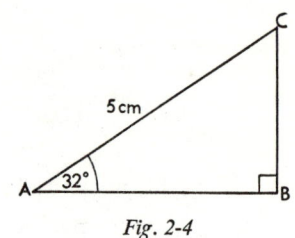

Fig. 2-4

In the triangle ABC, $\hat{ABC} = 90°$, $\hat{CAB} = 32°$ and AC = 5 cm. Find BC.

$$\frac{BC \text{ (opp.)}}{AC \text{ (hypot.)}} = \sin \hat{BAC}$$

$$\therefore \frac{BC}{5} = \sin 32°$$

$$\therefore BC = 5 \sin 32°$$
$$= 5 \times 0.529\ 9$$
$$= 2.649\ 5$$

$\therefore$ $\underline{BC = 2.65 \text{ cm}}$ (3 significant figures)

Further

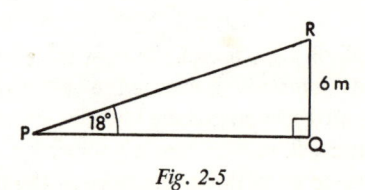

Fig. 2-5

$\hat{PQR} = 90°$; $\hat{QPR} = 18°$; QR = 6 metres. Find PR.

TRIGONOMETRY

$$\frac{QR \text{ (opp.)}}{PR \text{ (hypot.)}} = \sin Q\hat{P}R.$$

$$\therefore \frac{6}{PR} = \sin 18°$$

or $\quad PR = \dfrac{6}{\sin 18°}$

Number	Log.
6	0·778 2
sin 18°	$\bar{1}$·490 0
PR	1·288 2

$= 19·42$

$\therefore PR = \underline{19·4 \text{ metres}}$ (3 sig. figs.)

The value of the log of sin 18° is obtained directly from the LOG SINE table, which is read in the same way as the sine table. Take care to read the characteristic properly and also to subtract it correctly.

Exercise 2b

In the triangle ABC, $A\hat{B}C = 90°$. Give your answers correct to 3 sig figures, using logs where necessary.

1. Find BC if AC = 10 cm and $C\hat{A}B = 73°$.
2. Find BC if AC = 7 m and $C\hat{A}B = 25°$.
3. Find BC if AC = 12 cm and $C\hat{A}B = 27° 30'$.
4. Find BC if AC = 3·7 cm and $C\hat{A}B = 31° 14'$.
5. Find BC if AC = 582 mm and $C\hat{A}B = 37° 51'$.
6. Find AC if BC = 4 m and $C\hat{A}B = 81°$.
7. Find AC if BC = 26·2 cm and $C\hat{A}B = 14° 30'$.
8. Find AC if BC = 467 mm and $C\hat{A}B = 47° 8'$.
9. Find AC if BC = 6·34 cm and $C\hat{A}B = 63° 15'$.
10. Find AC if BC = 12·9 m and $C\hat{A}B = 76° 37'$.
11. A kite flies at the end of a string which makes 37° with the horizontal. If the string is 50 m long find the height of the kite.
12. A straight stretch of railway line is half a kilometre in length and it rises at an angle of 5° to the horizontal. What is the difference in vertical height between the two ends? (*Answer in metres.*)

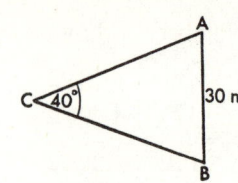

13. Fig. 2-6 shows the section of a tapered wedge. If AB = 30 mm and $A\hat{C}B = 40°$ find the length of the sloping face AC. *Note:* AC = BC. (*Hint:* Bisect $B\hat{C}A$.) (The wedge is symmetric.)

Fig. 2-6

14. The cable of a mountain railway makes an angle of 12° with the horizontal. Between two supports it drops a distance of 20 m. How long is the cable between the supports?

15. The width QR of a rectangle PQRS is 4 cm. If $R\hat{P}Q = 36°$ find the length of the diagonal PR. Use Pythagoras' theorem to find the length of the side PQ.

16. A tangent PT is drawn to a circle centre O of radius 6 cm from a point P outside it. If $T\hat{P}O = 27°$ calculate the distance OP.

Examples

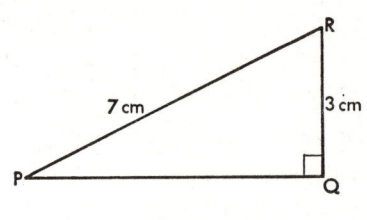

Fig. 2-7

In the triangle PQR, $P\hat{Q}R = 90°$, QR = 3 cm, PR = 7 cm. Find the angle $Q\hat{P}R$.

$$\sin Q\hat{P}R = \frac{QR \text{ (opp.)}}{PR \text{ (hypot.)}}$$

$$= \tfrac{3}{7}$$

$$= \frac{3\cdot000\ 0}{7}$$

$$= 0\cdot428\ 57\ldots$$

$$= 0\cdot428\ 6 \text{ (correct to 4 decimal places)}$$

$\therefore Q\hat{P}R = 25°\ 22'$ using the sine table in reverse.

Note: In order to obtain the value of the sine to 4 decimal places it is first calculated to 5 decimal places by division and then corrected to 4 decimal places.

TRIGONOMETRY

Further

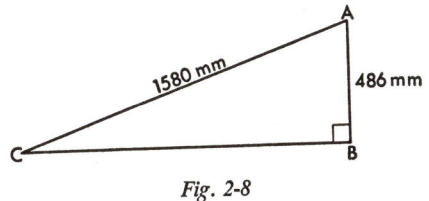

Fig. 2-8

In a triangle ABC, $\widehat{ABC} = 90°$, AB = 486 mm and AC = 1 580 mm. Calculate $\widehat{ACB}$.

$$\text{Sin } \widehat{ACB} = \frac{AB \text{ (opp.)}}{AC \text{ (hypot.)}}$$

$$= \frac{486}{158\ 0}$$

$$\therefore \widehat{ACB} \quad 17° 55'$$

Number	Log.
486	2·686 6
1 580	3·198 7
sin $\widehat{ACB}$	$\bar{1}$·487 9

Note: Here the division is done by using logarithms. The size of the angle was obtained directly from the logarithm by using the log-sine tables in reverse. There is no need to take the anti-log, and then use the sine-tables in reverse.

Exercise 2c

In the triangle ABC, $\widehat{ABC} = 90°$.

1. If BC = 3 cm, AC = 4 cm, calculate $\widehat{CAB}$.
2. If BC = 7 cm, AC = 9 cm, calculate $\widehat{CAB}$.
3. If AB = 6 m, AC = 11 m, calculate $\widehat{ACB}$.
4. If AB = 3·8 cm, AC = 10 cm, calculate $\widehat{ACB}$.
5. If BC = 47·8 mm, AC = 73·2 mm, calculate $\widehat{CAB}$. (Use logs.)
6. If AC = 14·6 cm, AB = 9·37 cm, calculate $\widehat{ACB}$.
7. If BC = 376 mm, AC = 492 mm, calculate $\widehat{CAB}$.
8. If AC = 10·3 cm, BC = 4·897 cm, calculate $\widehat{CAB}$.
9. If AC = 14·9 cm, BC = 11 cm, calculate $\widehat{CAB}$.

10. If AB = 436 m, AC = 621 m, calculate $A\hat{C}B$.

11. A hill has a gradient of 1 in 7. What angle does it make with the horizontal?

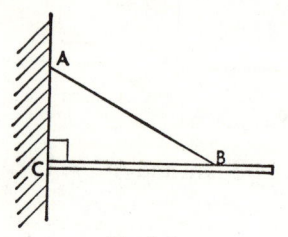

Fig. 2-9

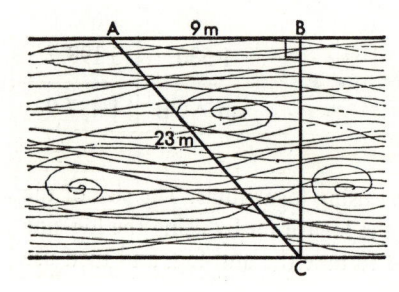

Fig. 2-10

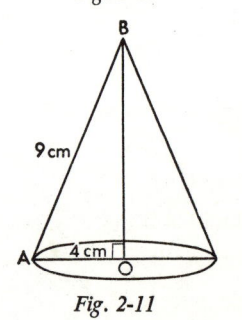

Fig. 2-11

12. A beam hoist CB has a stay AB 5 m long. If AC = 3·5 m, what angle does AB make with the beam? (Fig. 2-9.)

13. In a rectangle ABCD, the side AB is 8 cm long and the diagonal AC is 12·6 cm long. Calculate the angle $A\hat{C}B$. Hence find $C\hat{A}B$ and use the tangent of $C\hat{A}B$ to calculate the length of BC.

14. A and B are points on the bank of a river and C is a point on the opposite bank such that $A\hat{B}C$ is a right angle. AC is a bridge across the river and is 23 m long. If AB = 9 m, calculate angle $A\hat{C}B$ and hence the width of the river BC, Fig. 2-10.

15. A cone has a base radius of 4 cm and a slant height of 9 cm. Calculate the semi-vertical angle of the cone ($A\hat{B}O$) and the perpendicular height, Fig. 2-11.

The Cosine of an Angle

In Fig. 2-1 it also follows that

$$\frac{AB_1}{AC_1} = \frac{AB_2}{AC_2} = \frac{AB_3}{AC_3} = \frac{AB_4}{AC_4}$$

As before the value of this ratio depends on the size of angle A and is called the cosine of angle A, or for short, cos A.

TRIGONOMETRY

In Stage Three the side containing the angle with the hypotenuse was called the adjacent side.

Hence $\cos \text{BAC} = \dfrac{\text{adj.}}{\text{hypot.}} = \dfrac{\text{AB}}{\text{AC}}$

Fig. 2-12

Something to do
As with the sine of an angle it is quite simple to draw a graph of the values of the cosine angles of between 0° and 90°.

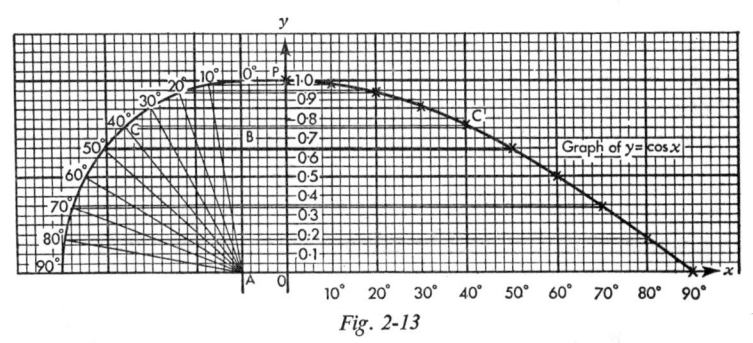

Fig. 2-13

On a piece of graph paper draw a quadrant of a circle centre A, radius 4 cm, as shown. Mark off angles at 10° intervals and set up axes Ox, Oy. Let OP = 1 unit on Oy. The radius of the circle is 1 unit.

In the right-angled triangle ABC
$$\cos 40° = \cos \text{BAC} = \dfrac{\text{AB}}{\text{AC}}$$
But $\qquad\qquad\quad$ AC = 1 unit
$$\cos 40° = \text{AB numerically}$$
Draw CC′ parallel to Ox to obtain the point C′ where $x = 40°$. By this process draw the graph of $y = \cos x$ as shown. Note how the quadrant is 'turned' so that AB is parallel to Oy.

Important
Look at your graph and notice that $\cos 0° = 1$ and $\cos 90° = 0$.
∴ As x increases from 0° to 90°, $\cos x$ *decreases* from 1 to 0.

This is different from sin x, and great care must be taken in reading the natural cosine table. Numbers in the difference columns must be *subtracted*. This line is taken from the natural cosine table.

NATURAL COSINES   SUBTRACT

	0′	6′	12′	18′	24′	30′	36′	42′	48′	54′	1′	2′	3′	4′	5′
54°	·5878	5878	5850	5835	5821	5807	5793	5779	5764	5750	2	5	7	9	12

Fig. 2-14

e.g. To find cos 54° 22′

$$\cos 54° 18' = 0.583\ 5$$
$$\cos 54° 24' = 0.582\ 1$$

Note that cos 54° 24′ is *less* than cos 54° 18′.
54° 22′ lies between 54° 18′ and 54° 24′.
∴ cos 54° 22′ is *less* than cos 54° 18′.
∴ cos 54° 22′ = 0·583 5 − 0·000 9 (Subtract 0·000 9—the difference for 4′)
        = 0·582 6

In a similar way care must be taken when using the Cosine Table in reverse to find an angle whose cosine is known.
e.g. If cos x = 0·575 9, find x.
Look for the nearest number in the body of the tables *greater than* 0·575 9. It is 0·576 4 = cos 54° 48′.
The necessary difference is 0·576 4 − 0·575 9 = 0·000 5 which represents 2′ since the angle we are seeking is *greater* than 54° 48′.
∴ If cos x = 0·575 9
     x = 54° 48′ + 2′
        <u>54° 50′</u>

Exercise 2d

1. From your graph of $y = \cos x$ make up a table of cosines for angles from 0° to 90° at 10° intervals. Estimate the values of 34°, 58° and 73°. Find the approximate values of the angles whose cosines are 0·2, 0·3 and 0·6.

2. Find from the Cosine Table the cosines of the following angles. (Write your answer in the form cos 18° = 0·951 1.)

TRIGONOMETRY

69°, 88°, 60°, 3°, 16° 12′, 32° 48′, 73° 6′, 49° 54′,
7° 36′, 83° 42′, 31° 8′, 45° 50′, 75° 23′, 19° 32′,
40° 19′, 77° 47′, 2° 3′, 86° 23′, 49° 57′, 38° 1′.

3. Use the Cosine Table in reverse to find the angles which have the following cosines. (Write each answer in the form: If cos $x = 0.104\ 5$, $x = 84°$.)

0·951 1, 0·707 1, 0·850 8, 0·235 1, 0·516 5, 0·066 3,
0·999 1, 0·130 5, 0·112 9, 0·366 0, 0·963 7, 0·207 3,
0·525 8, 0·791 9, 0·917 0, 0·209 1, 0·880 4, 0·523 2,
0·114 5, 0·579 6.

Examples

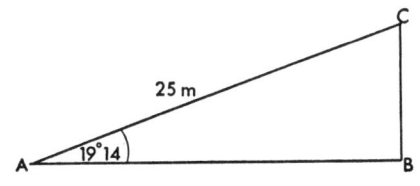

Fig. 2-15

In the triangle ABC, $A\hat{B}C = 90°$, $C\hat{A}B = 19°\ 14'$ and AC = 25 metres. Find the length of AB.

$$\frac{AB}{AC}\frac{\text{(adj.)}}{\text{(hypot.)}} = \cos B\hat{A}C$$

$$\therefore \frac{AB}{25} = \cos 19°\ 14'$$

$$\therefore AB = 25 \cos 19°\ 14'$$
$$= 25 \times 0.944\ 2$$
$$= \frac{94.42}{4} \text{ (Note method of multiplying by 25)}$$
$$= 23.605$$
$$\therefore AB = 23.6 \text{ metres (3 sig. fig.)}$$

Further

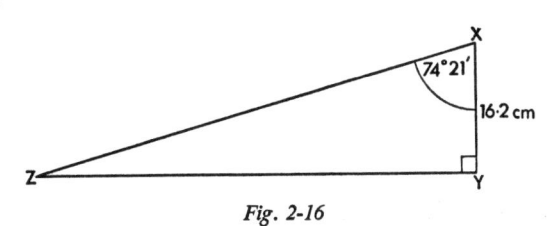

Fig. 2-16

In the triangle XYZ (Fig. 2-16) $X\hat{Y}Z = 90°$, $Y\hat{X}Z = 74°\,21'$ and $XY = 16\cdot2$ cm. Calculate the length of XZ.

$$\frac{XY\ (\text{adj.})}{XZ\ (\text{hypot.})} = \cos Y\hat{X}Z$$

$$\therefore \frac{16\cdot2}{XZ} = \cos 74°\,21'$$

$$\therefore XZ = \frac{16\cdot2}{\cos 74°\,21'}$$

$$= 60\cdot06$$

$$\therefore XZ = 60\cdot1 \text{ cm (3 sig. fig.)}$$

Number	Log.
16·2	1·209 5
cos 74°21'	$\bar{1}$·430 9
XZ	1·778 6

The logarithm of cos 74° 21' was found directly in the LOG COS table. This is read in the same way as the cosine table and care must be taken to *subtract the numbers in the difference columns* because the logarithms of the cosines of angles between 0° and 90° *decrease* as the angle *increases* from 0° to 90°.

Exercise 2e

In the triangle PQR, $PQR = 90°$. Give your answers correct to 3 significant figures using logs where necessary.

1. Find QR if PR = 10 cm and $P\hat{R}Q = 37°$.
2. Find QR if PR = 12 cm and $P\hat{R}Q = 28°\,24'$.
3. Find QR if PR = 2·5 cm and $P\hat{R}Q = 48°\,27'$.
4. Find QR if PR = 5·9 cm and $P\hat{R}Q = 78°\,4'$.
5. Find QR if PR = 17·6 m and $P\hat{R}Q = 53°\,57'$.
6. Find PQ if PR = 14 cm and $Q\hat{P}R = 14°\,19'$.
7. Find PR if QR = 20 cm and $Q\hat{R}P = 27°\,35'$.
8. Find PR if QR = 13·7 m and $Q\hat{R}P = 63°\,17'$.
9. Find PR if QR = 732 mm and $Q\hat{R}P = 20°\,14'$.
10. Find PQ if PR = 196 m and $Q\hat{P}R = 39°\,42'$.
11. A ladder 6 m long leans against a vertical wall, with its base on horizontal ground. If the ladder makes an angle of 75° with the ground, how far is the bottom end from the wall?

TRIGONOMETRY

12. O is the centre of a circle radius 7 cm. PQ is a chord subtending the angle $P\hat{O}Q = 152°$. Calculate the length of the perpendicular ON. Find $O\hat{P}N$ and hence calculate the length of the chord PQ.

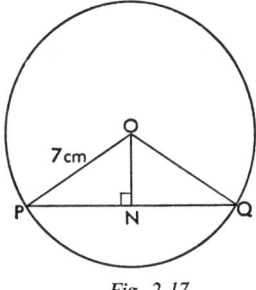

Fig. 2-17

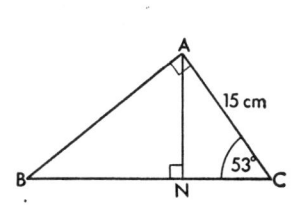

Fig. 2-18

13. In triangle ABC, $B\hat{A}C = 90°$ and AN is perpendicular to BC. If AC = 15 cm and $A\hat{C}N = 53°$, calculate the lengths of BC and NC and hence find the length of BN.

14. The track of a mountain railway makes 24° with the horizontal. Between two certain points the *horizontal* distance is 175 metres. Calculate the length of the track between these two points.

15. A and B are two towns 31 kilometres apart and B is on a bearing 053° (N 53° E) from A. Calculate how far B is East of A.

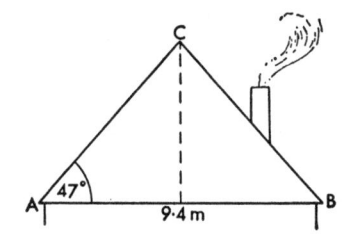

Fig. 2-19

16. The roof of a house makes 47° with the horizontal. If AB = 9·4 metres, calculate the length AC of the roof given that AC = BC.

Example

In a triangle XYZ, $X\hat{Y}Z = 90°$, YZ = 17·2 cm and XZ = 21·8 cm. Calculate $X\hat{Z}Y$.

Fig. 2-20

25

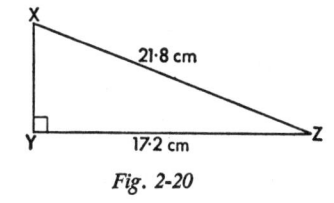

$\cos X\hat{Z}Y = \dfrac{YZ \text{ (adj.)}}{XZ \text{ (hypot.)}}$
$= \dfrac{17\cdot 2}{21\cdot 8}$
$\therefore X\hat{Z}Y = 37° 55'$

Number	Log.
17·2	1·235 5
21·8	1·338 5
$\cos X\hat{Z}Y$	$\bar{1}\cdot 897\ 0$

The division cannot be done simply, and so logarithms are used. The value of the angle is read directly from the log. cosine table, remembering that the differences must be *subtracted*.

Exercise 2f

Only use logarithm tables where necessary.

In the triangle ABC, $A\hat{C}B = 90°$

1. If BC = 5 cm, AB = 7 cm, calculate $A\hat{B}C$.
2. If BC = 17 mm, AB = 20 mm, calculate $A\hat{B}C$.
3. If AC = 2·1 cm, AB = 4·9 cm, calculate $B\hat{A}C$.
4. If AC = 3·67 cm, AB = 5·9 cm, calculate $B\hat{A}C$.
5. If BC = 14·78 m, AB = 19 m, calculate $A\hat{B}C$.
6. If BC = 5·65 cm, AB = 7·03 cm, calculate $A\hat{B}C$.
7. If AB = 236 mm, AC = 147 mm, calculate $B\hat{A}C$.
8. If AB = 3·437 cm, BC = 2·018 cm, calculate $A\hat{B}C$.

9. A ladder 8·5 m long stands against a wall and its bottom end is 3 m from the wall. Calculate the angle which the ladder makes with the ground.

10. A cone 14 cm high has a slant height of 23 cm. Calculate its semi-vertical angle.

11. A road on a hillside is such that for every 100 m of roadway the *horizontal* distance travelled is 85 m. What angle does the road make with the horizontal?

12. Two towns A and B are 43 km apart and A is 28 km west of B. Find the bearing of A from B, if B is to the north of A.

13. ABCD is a trapdoor held by a tie PQ. If PQ = 3 m and AB is 2·5 m, calculate the angle $A\hat{Q}P$ if AQ is two-thirds of AB, Fig. 2-21.

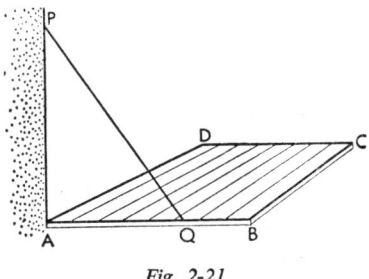

TRIGONOMETRY

Fig. 2-21

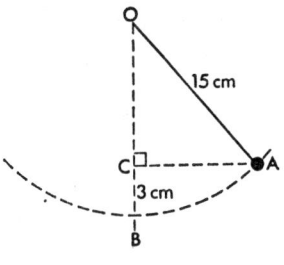

Fig. 2-22

14. A pendulum OA length 15 cm, is swinging as shown. Calculate the angle $A\hat{O}C$ when A is 3 cm vertically above B (i.e. BC = 3 cm).

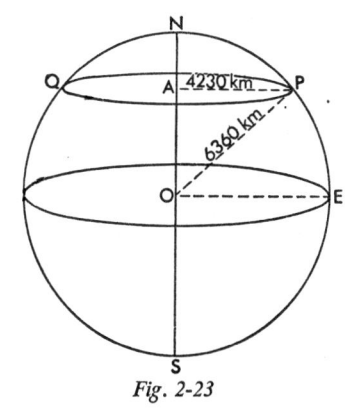

15. The figure represents the Earth. O is the centre and OE lies in the equatorial plane. PQ is a circle of latitude and its radius PA = 4 230 km. Angle $P\hat{O}E$ is the angle of latitude and AP is parallel to OE. If the radius of the earth is 6 360 km, calculate the latitude of the point P.

Fig. 2-23

Summary

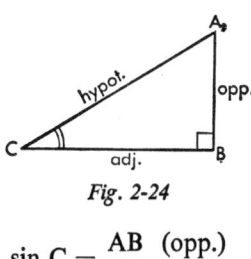

Fig. 2-24

$$\sin C = \frac{AB}{AC} \frac{\text{(opp.)}}{\text{(hypot.)}}$$

$$\cos C = \frac{BC}{AC} \frac{\text{(adj.)}}{\text{(hypot.)}}$$

$$\tan C = \frac{AB}{BC} \frac{\text{(opp.)}}{\text{(adj.)}}$$

LONGMAN MATHEMATICS

A useful Mnemonic (*memory jogger*)

Some Officers Have Curly Auburn Hair Till Old Age.
I   P   Y   O   D   Y   A   P   D
N   P   P   S   J   P   N   P   J

This sentence will help you to choose the right ratios for the work which follows. Regard it only as a prop which you can discard as soon as you are able to write down the correct ratios at sight.

Two useful triangles

1.

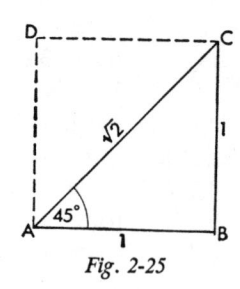

Fig. 2-25

ABCD is a square and side AB = 1 unit
$\therefore$ BC = 1 unit
and $AC^2 = AB^2 + BC^2$ (Pythagoras' theorem)
         $= 1^2 + 1^2$
$\therefore AC^2 = 2$
$\therefore AC = \sqrt{2}$ units

Angle $B\widehat{A}C = 45°$.
From triangle ABC

$$\sin B\widehat{A}C = \frac{BC}{AC} \text{ i.e. } \sin 45° = \frac{1}{\sqrt{2}}$$

$$\cos B\widehat{A}C = \frac{AB}{AC} \text{ i.e. } \cos 45° = \frac{1}{\sqrt{2}}$$

$$\tan B\widehat{A}C = \frac{BC}{AB} \text{ i.e. } \tan 45° = 1$$

TRIGONOMETRY

2.

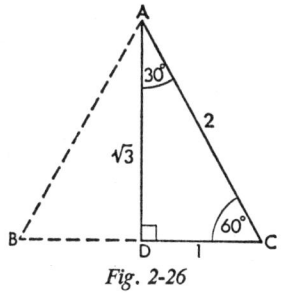

Fig. 2-26

ABC is an equilateral triangle.
Side AB = BC = AC = 2 units.
Draw AD perpendicular to BC
Then D is the mid-point of BC and DC = 1 unit

$$AD^2 = AC^2 - DC^2 \text{ (Pythagoras' theorem)}$$
$$= 2^2 - 1$$
$$= 4 - 1$$
$$\therefore AD^2 = 3$$
$$\therefore AD = \sqrt{3} \text{ units}$$

Angle $A\hat{C}B = 60°$ and angle $C\hat{A}D = 30°$

$$\sin A\hat{C}D = \frac{AD}{AC} \qquad \sin 60° = \frac{\sqrt{3}}{2}$$

$$\cos A\hat{C}D = \frac{DC}{AC} \qquad \cos 60° = \frac{1}{2}$$

$$\tan A\hat{C}D = \frac{AD}{DC} \qquad \tan 60° = \sqrt{3}$$

$$\sin C\hat{A}D = \frac{DC}{AC} \qquad \sin 30° = \frac{1}{2}$$

$$\cos C\hat{A}D = \frac{AD}{AC} \qquad \cos 30° = \frac{\sqrt{3}}{2}$$

$$\tan C\hat{A}D = \frac{DC}{AD} \qquad \tan 30° = \frac{1}{\sqrt{3}}$$

Note that sin 60° = cos 30°. Can you spot other pairs of equal ratios?
When solving problems involving angles of 45°, 30° and 60° it is often useful to use these ratios and to leave the answers in surd form. Surd, short for absurd, is the name given to quantities like $\sqrt{2}$, $\sqrt{3}$

LONGMAN MATHEMATICS

etc., where the number under the square root sign is *not* a perfect square. To the mathematicians of ancient Greece such numbers appeared to be impossible and were therefore considered absurd. Such numbers are also called irrational.

Example

A ladder leans against a wall making an angle of 60° with the ground. The height of the top of the ladder from the ground is 6 metres. Calculate the length of the ladder and the distance of its bottom end from the wall.

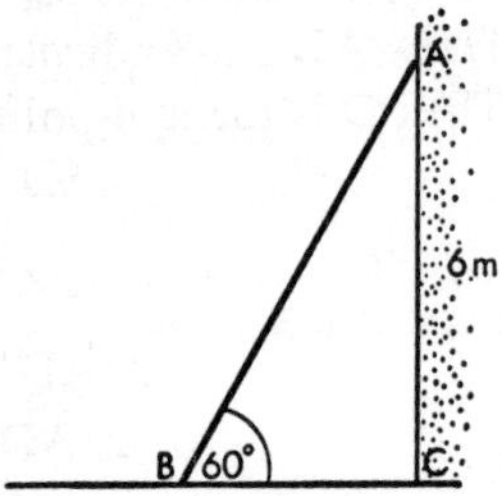

$$\frac{AC}{AB} = \sin A\hat{B}C$$

$$\frac{6}{AB} = \sin 60°$$

$$\therefore AB = \frac{6}{\sin 60°}$$

$$= \frac{6}{\sqrt{3}/2}$$

$$= 6 \times \frac{2}{\sqrt{3}}$$

$$= \frac{12}{\sqrt{3}} \times \frac{\sqrt{3}}{\sqrt{3}}$$

$$= \frac{12\sqrt{3}}{3}$$

(Multiply by $\frac{\sqrt{3}}{\sqrt{3}}$ to clear the 'bottom' of surds)

Fig. 2-27

$$\therefore AB = 4\sqrt{3} \text{ metres}$$

$$\frac{BC}{AC} = \tan B\hat{A}C$$

$$\therefore \frac{BC}{6} = \tan 30°$$

$$BC = 6 \tan 30°$$

$$= \frac{6}{\sqrt{3}} \cdot \frac{\sqrt{3}}{\sqrt{3}}$$

$$= \frac{6\sqrt{3}}{3}$$

$$\therefore BC = 2\sqrt{3} \text{ metres}$$

TRIGONOMETRY

Note: The lengths of AB and BC are left in surd form, but the surds appear only in the 'top' of the fractions. The denominators are said to be rationalized.

Exercise 2g

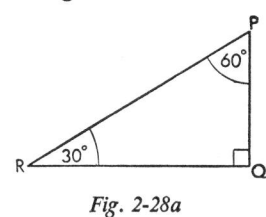

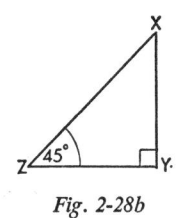

Fig. 2-28a *Fig. 2-28b*

In the triangle PQR, $P\hat{Q}R = 90°$, $Q\hat{R}P = 30°$ and $R\hat{P}Q = 60°$.
In the triangle XYZ, $X\hat{Y}Z = 90°$ and $X\hat{Z}Y = 45°$.
Leave the answers to the following questions in surd form, clearing the denominators of surds.

1. If PR = 30 m, find PQ and QR.
2. If XZ = 14 cm, find XY.
3. If PR = 10 cm, find PQ and QR.
4. If QR = 5 cm, find PQ and PR.
5. If XY = 7 cm, find XZ.
6. If PQ = $\sqrt{3}$ m, find PR and QR.
7. If PR = $6\sqrt{3}$ cm, find PQ and QR.
8. If XZ = $5\sqrt{2}$ m, find XY.
9. If QR = $7\sqrt{3}$ cm, find PQ and PR.
10. If PQ = $\sqrt{6}$ cm, find PR and QR. (*Note:* $\sqrt{6} = \sqrt{2} \times \sqrt{3}$.)

Exercise 2h

Miscellaneous examples using sine, cosine and tangent ratios.
Use logarithms only where necessary.
Examples 1 to 10 refer to the triangle DEF in which $D\hat{E}F = 90°$, Fig. 2-29, p. 32.

1. If EF = 7 cm, FD = 10 cm, find $E\hat{F}D$ and ED.
2. If ED = 3 m, DF = 4 m, find $E\hat{F}D$ and EF.

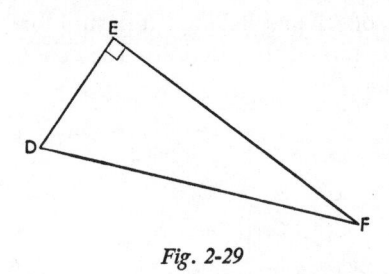

Fig. 2-29

3. If DE = 4 cm, EF = 9 cm, find $E\hat{F}D$ and DF.
4. If $E\hat{F}D$ = 62° 30′ and EF = 5 cm, find DE.
5. If $E\hat{F}D$ = 47° 21′ and DE = 10 m, find EF. (Find $E\hat{D}F$ first.)
6. If $E\hat{D}F$ = 37° 14′ and DF = 36 mm, find DE.
7. If FD = 14·2 cm and $E\hat{D}F$ = 73° 14′, find EF.
8. If DE = 721 mm and EF = 837 mm, find $E\hat{F}D$ and $E\hat{D}F$.
9. If EF = 4√3 cm and DF = 8 cm, find $E\hat{F}D$ without using tables.
10. If ED = EF and DF = 16√2, find ED without using tables.
11. The elevation of a church tower from a point on the level 71 metres from its base is 22° 30′. Calculate its height.
12. A is 12 km South and 20 km West of B. Calculate the bearing of B from A and the distance AB.

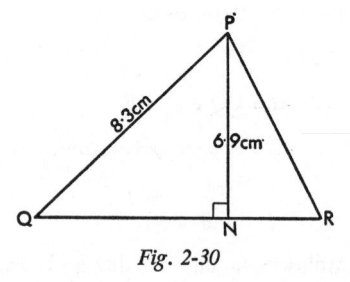

Fig. 2-30

13. If PN = 6·9 cm and PQ = 8·3 cm, calculate $P\hat{Q}N$. If $Q\hat{P}R$ = 80°, find $P\hat{R}N$ and hence find the length of NR.
14. When a field in the shape of a trapezium was surveyed it proved impracticable to measure the side DC because of an obstacle. The following measurements were made. AB = 95 m, AD = 70 m.

TRIGONOMETRY

$\hat{ADN} = 61°$ and $\hat{BCM} = 82°$. Using these dimensions calculate the area of the field.

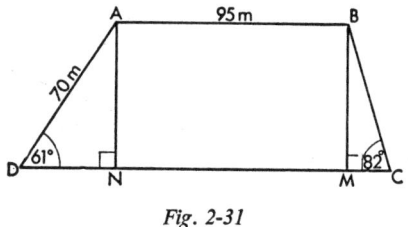

Fig. 2-31

15. A telegraph pole is supported by a tie AC. If AB = 6 metres and $\hat{ACB} = 67°$, calculate the length of the tie AC and the distance BC.

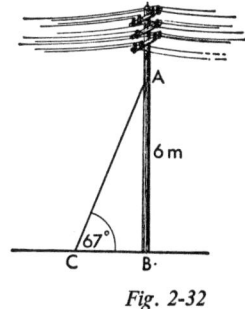

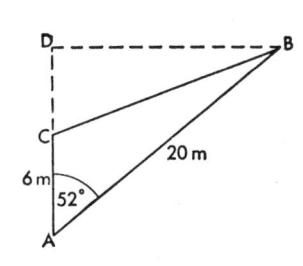

Fig. 2-32   *Fig. 2-33*

16. The jib AB of a crane is 20 m long and it makes an angle of 52° with the vertical. The cable BC is attached so that AC = 6 m. Calculate BC, the length of the cable. (*Hint:* Find AD, DC and DB and then use Pythagoras' theorem.)

17. A ladder PQ is 11 metres long and rests against a wall AB such that the distance PA = 3 metres. If $\hat{APB} = 58°$ 30′, find BQ.

Fig. 2-34

33

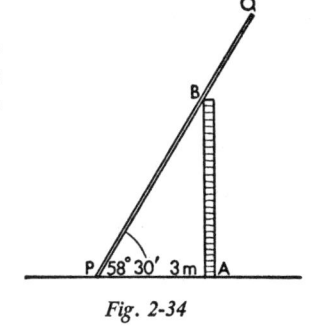

18. Town P is 4·5 km North and 5·25 km West of town Q. Calculate the bearing of P from Q and the distance between the towns.

19. AB and BC are sections of a hillside track. AB is inclined at 7° to

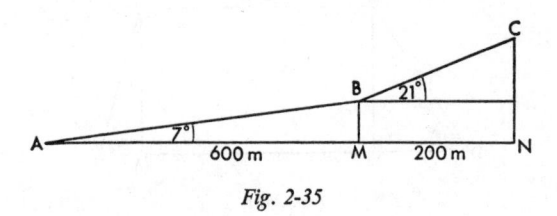

Fig. 2-35

the horizontal and BC at 21° to the horizontal. BM and CN are perpendicular to the horizontal through A. If AM = 600 metres and MN = 200 metres, calculate the lengths of AB and BC, the heights of B and C above A and the angle of elevation of C from A.

20. Fig. 2-36 represents a roof truss for a factory building.

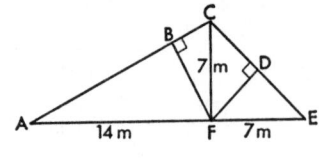

Fig. 2-36

AF = 14 m, FE = 7 m and CF = 7 m. Without using tables find the angles $C\hat{A}F$ and $C\hat{E}F$. Calculate, using square root tables only, the lengths of AC, EC, BF and FD.

21. In an isosceles triangle ABC, $A\hat{B}C = A\hat{C}B = 14°$ and BC = 7·4 cm. Calculate the lengths of AB and the length of the perpendicular from A to BC. Hence find the area of the triangle.

The Sine Rule

ABC is an acute-angled triangle. Draw CD perpendicular to AB, and let CD = h.

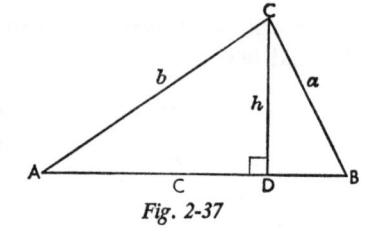

Fig. 2-37

TRIGONOMETRY

In triangle ADC

$$\frac{CD}{AC} = \sin C\hat{A}D$$

or

$$\frac{h}{b} = \sin A$$

$$\therefore h = b \sin A \qquad (1)$$

Similarly in the triangle BDC

$$h = a \sin B \qquad (2)$$

From (1) and (2)

$$h = b \sin A = a \sin B$$

$$\therefore \frac{b}{\sin B} = \frac{a}{\sin A}$$

(Can you see why this is so?)
By drawing a perpendicular from B to AC, it can similarly be shown that

$$\frac{a}{\sin A} = \frac{c}{\sin C}$$

$$\therefore \frac{a}{\sin A} = \frac{b}{\sin B} = \frac{c}{\sin C}$$

This result is known as the Sine Rule and it applies to all acute-angled triangles.

Example

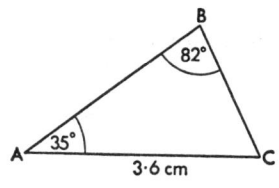

Fig. 2-38

In the triangle ABC, AC = 3·6 cm, $C\hat{A}B = 35°$ and $A\hat{B}C = 82°$. Calculate the length of AB.

$$A\hat{C}B = 180° - (C\hat{A}B + A\hat{B}C)$$
$$= 180° - (35° + 82°)$$
$$= 180° - 117°$$
$$\therefore A\hat{C}B = 63°$$
$$\therefore \hat{C} = 63°, \hat{B} = 82° \text{ and } b = 3·6 \text{ cm}$$

By the Sine Rule

$$\frac{c}{\sin C} = \frac{b}{\sin B}$$

$$\therefore \frac{c}{\sin 63°} = \frac{3\cdot 6}{\sin 82°}$$

$$\therefore c = \frac{3\cdot 6 \sin 63°}{\sin 82°}$$

$$= 3\cdot 239$$

$$= \underline{3\cdot 24 \text{ cm } (3 \text{ sig. fig.})}$$

Length	Log.
3·6	0·556 3
sin 63°	$\bar{1}$·949 9
	0·506 2
sin 82°	$\bar{1}$·995 8
C	0·510 4

Note the direct use of the log. sine tables.

Never use the Sine Rule in a right-angled triangle.

$$\frac{b}{\sin B} = \frac{c}{\sin c}$$

$$\therefore \frac{b}{\sin B} = \frac{c}{\sin 90°}$$

But $\sin 90° = 1$

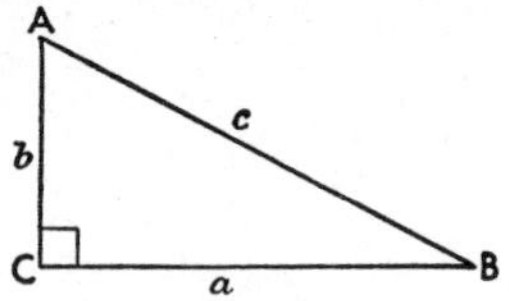

$$\therefore \frac{b}{\sin B} = c$$

or $\underline{b = c \sin B}$

Fig. 2-39

This result is easily obtained by using the ordinary result

$$\sin B = \frac{AC}{AB} = \frac{b}{c}$$

Exercise 2i

Express all answers correct to three significant figures.

1. In the triangle ABC, BC = 17 cm, $\widehat{ABC} = 47°$, $\widehat{ACB} = 78°$. Calculate the lengths of AB and AC.

2. In the triangle ABC, AB = 2·4 cm, $\widehat{ABC} = 53°\ 10'$, $\widehat{ACB} = 71°\ 43'$. Calculate the lengths of BC and AC.

3. In the triangle PQR, PQ = 108 mm, $\widehat{PQR} = 75°\ 14'$, $\widehat{PRQ} = 65°\ 10'$. Calculate the lengths of QR and PR.

TRIGONOMETRY

4. In the triangle XYZ, XY = 7·83 cm, $Z\hat{X}Y = 76° 48'$, $Z\hat{Y}X = 53° 32'$. Calculate the lengths of YZ and XZ.

5. In the triangle BCD, BD = 4·76 cm, $B\hat{C}D = 79° 26'$, $B\hat{D}C = 63° 34'$. Calculate the lengths of BC and CD.

6. In the triangle PQR, PQ = 6·73 cm, $P\hat{Q}R = 27° 14'$, $R\hat{P}Q = 81°$. Calculate the lengths of PR and QR.

7. In the triangle ABC, AC = 432 mm, $A\hat{C}B = 65° 37'$, $A\hat{B}C = 62° 47'$. Calculate the lengths of AB and BC.

8. In the triangle LMN, LM = 29·37 m, $L\hat{M}N = 78° 31'$, $N\hat{L}M = 43° 28'$. Calculate the lengths of LN and MN.

9. A town X lies due East of a town Y and it is 37 km from X to Y. A third town Z has a bearing 027° (N 27° E) from Y and a bearing of 335° (N 15° W) from X. Calculate the distances XZ and YZ and the perpendicular distance of Z from XY

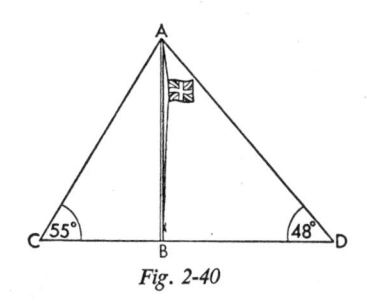

Fig. 2-40

10. AB is a flag-pole. The angles of elevation from C and D are 55° and 48° respectively. If CD = 20 m calculate the height of the flag-pole. (*Hint:* Find AC first.)

11. In the quadrilateral ABCD, AB = 6·5 cm, $A\hat{B}C = 75°$,

Fig. 2-41

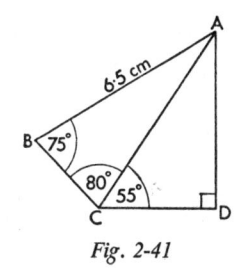

$A\hat{C}B = 80°$, $A\hat{C}D = 55°$ and $A\hat{D}C = 90°$. Calculate the length of AD.

12. In a survey to find the width of a river a point C was sighted from two points A and B, 23 m apart on the opposite bank. If $B\hat{A}C = 79° 30'$ and $A\hat{B}C = 64° 50'$, calculate the width of the river CN.

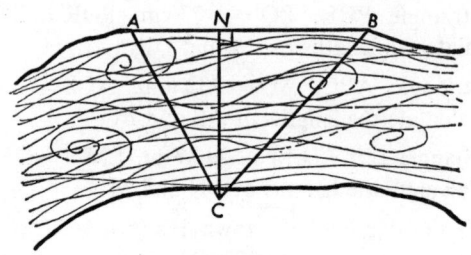

Fig. 2-42

13. A builder wishes to erect a house such that QP makes 37° with the horizontal and QR makes 60° with the horizontal.
If PR = 9·4 m calculate the lengths of the timbers PQ and QR correct to the nearest cm.

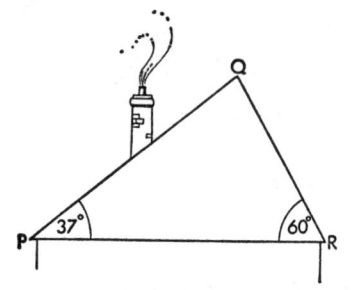

Fig. 2-43

14. In a parallelogram ABCD, AB = 5·6 cm, $B\hat{A}D = 62°$ and DBA = 42°. Calculate the lengths of side AD and the diagonal BD. Calculate also the area of ABCD.

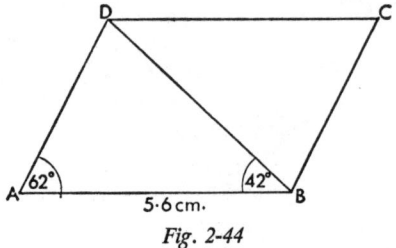

Fig. 2-44

TRIGONOMETRY

15. In a quadrilateral ABCD, AB = 343 mm, $\widehat{ABC} = 65°$, $\widehat{BAC} = 73° 30'$, $\widehat{ACD} = 25°$ and $\widehat{ADC} = 81°$. Calculate the lengths of the sides BC, CD and DA and of the diagonal AC.

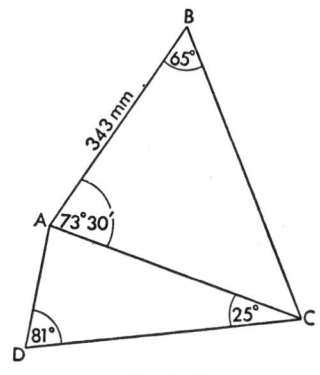

Fig. 2-45

16.

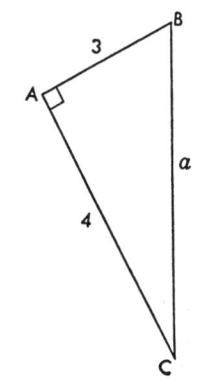

Fig. 2-46

ABC is a triangle, right-angled at A. Say whether the following statements are TRUE or FALSE.
(i) If $c = 3$, $b = 4$ then $a = 5$
(ii) $\cos C = \frac{4}{5}$
(iii) $\tan B = \frac{3}{4}$
(iv) $\sin C = \frac{5}{3}$
(v) $\cos B = \frac{3}{5}$
(vi) $C = 36° 57'$

17.

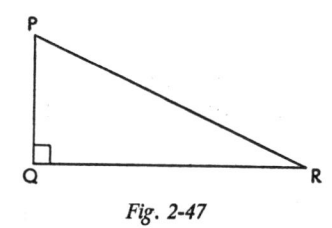

Fig. 2-47

PQR is a triangle right-angled at Q and $\cos P = 0.414\,2$
Which of the following statements are TRUE and which are FALSE?

(i) P = 65° 32'   (ii) R = 15° 28'   (iii) tan R = 0·258 0
(iv) sin R = cos P = 0·414 2
(v) If PQ = 10 then PR = 41·42
(vi) If PQ = 10 then QR = 19·77

18. Which of the following statements are TRUE and which are FALSE?

   (a) If acute angle A is less than acute angle B:
      (i) sin A is less than sin B
      (ii) cos A is less than cos B
      (iii) tan B is less than tan A
   (b) If A + B = 90°
      (i) sin A = cos B
      (ii) sin B = cos A
   (c) If A = 30° and B = 60°
      (i) sin A = 2 sin B
      (ii) cos B = $\dfrac{1}{\sqrt{3}}$
      (iii) tan B = $\sqrt{3}$
      (iv) tan 2A = tan B
      (v) cos B = 2 cos A

19.

AB is a cliff 30 m high and there is a boat at C. $\beta = 20°14'$. Select the correct answer to each statement.

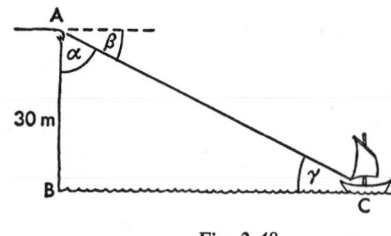

Fig. 2-48

   (a) The angle of elevation of A from C is (i) α (ii) β (iii) γ.
   (b) The length of BC is (i) 30 cos α (ii) 30/sin α (iii) 30 sin β (iv) 30 tan α.
   (c) The distance BC is (i) 81·3 m (ii) 114·8 m (iii) 51·4 m (iv) 97·0 m.
   (d) The distance AC is (i) 81·6 m (ii) 70·9 m (iii) 92·5 m (iv) 86·7 m.

TRIGONOMETRY

20.

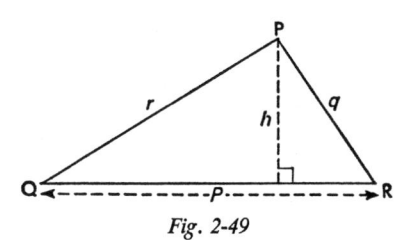

Fig. 2-49

Say whether the following statements concerning Fig. 2-49 are TRUE or FALSE.

(i) $p = r \cos Q + q \cos R$
(ii) $h = r \sin Q\widehat{P}R$
(iii) $p = \dfrac{r \sin Q}{\sin P}$
(iv) Area of $\triangle$ PQR $= \frac{1}{2} ph$
(v) Area of $\triangle$ PQR $= \frac{1}{2} rp \sin Q$
(vi) If $q = 100$ m, $R = 59°$ and $Q = 27° \ 15'$ then $r = 187$ mm.

3 A New Geometry

One of the most important of the many tasks that mathematicians undertake is that of 'classification'. That is, dividing things, numbers, problems, etc., into sets, so that members of a set all have some important fact in common. A simple example of this is the classification of books in a library. Find out what you can about this subject.

Classification is really another way of talking about 'sets', and is obviously of great importance in practical situations such as library-work and store-keeping; it has also proved useful in studying Mathematics. Having found that a particular problem, for example, belongs to a particular set of problems, then the solution of one might well lead to the solution of other problems in the set. This is one of the objects of the study of sets and groups and one which has been very profitable.

The same study has been applied in the field of geometry and is part of a study called TOPOLOGY. Topology includes the study of '*basic*' shapes, that is, it does not worry about faces, sides, corners, edges, or regularity, but it attempts to study the properties of the shape even when the shape has been completely deformed! Because of allowing the shape to be deformed, Topology is sometimes called 'rubber sheet geometry'. As an example consider the shape in Fig. 3-1. If this shape was made of rubber it could easily be deformed into any of the shapes

Fig. 3-1

Fig. 3-2

A NEW GEOMETRY

in Fig. 3-2, on the condition that it is kept flat. Thus in Topology all these shapes are considered *to be the same*. Now look at Fig. 3-3. Would it be possible, without cutting or tearing the rubber, to deform this shape into any of those in Fig. 3-2? Similarly you can deal with solids; a large inflated balloon might be pressed into a wide variety of shapes, a sausage, an octahedron, or a sphere. It is, however, impossible to shape it into a hollow cylinder or an inner tube (the inner tube shape has the mathematical name TORUS, Fig. 3-4).

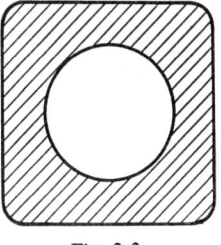

Fig. 3-3

While there are many similar qualities between the sphere and the Torus, they must have some essential character difference in their solid shape since one cannot be deformed into the other. This essential character is known as the 'connectivity' of the shape, and this remains

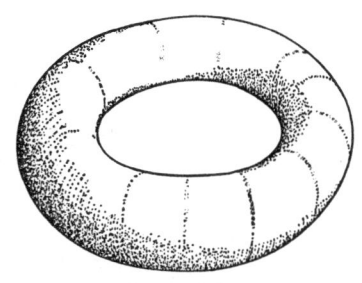

Fig. 3-4

unaltered no matter how the shape is deformed. 'Connectivity' can be thought of simply as the ways in which any two points can be connected. The 'connectivity' will only alter if either

(a) the surface is cut, or

(b) if two or more points, previously not touching, are brought into contact.

For the purpose of classification, discs, as in Fig. 3-2, are treated separately from solids.

Connectivity

The connectivity of a shape is determined by the greatest number of similar complete rings that can be drawn on the surface of the shape without dividing all the surface points into two distinct sets which cannot be connected without crossing a ring. On a sphere, for example, EVERY simple closed curve will divide the surface into two distinct sets of points, Fig. 3-5. The Torus can, however, take one 'harmless' complete curve without dividing the surface points into two distinct sets, Fig. 3-6a. Any further complete curve would divide the Torus into two distinct sets of points, Fig. 3-6b. The solid in Fig. 3-7 will take two complete 'harmless' curves. Draw out the shape and draw in suggested curves. For classication the sphere is class O (no curves), the Torus is

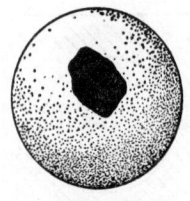

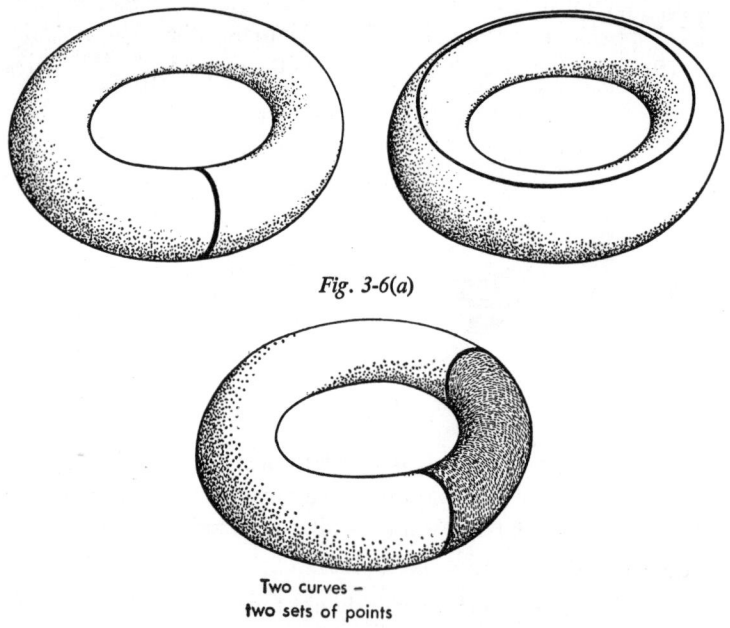

Fig. 3-5

Fig. 3-6(a)

Two curves –
two sets of points
Fig. 3-6(b)

class 1 (one curve) and the shape in Fig. 3-7 is in class 2. [It is worth noting here that Euler's formula about the relation of edges, corners and faces applies only to simple solids, i.e. solids with no 'holes'. Fig. 3-8 shows a 'non-simple' solid. Show that Euler's rule does not apply. See Stage 3 for Euler's formula.]

A NEW GEOMETRY

You have been shown that if a closed curve is drawn on a sphere, the curve will divide the surface area into two distinct parts. These parts

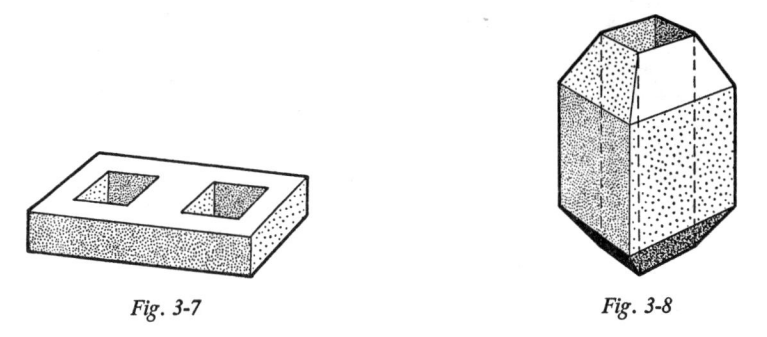

Fig. 3-7

Fig. 3-8

will always remain distinct, no matter how the shape is deformed, and a point 'inside' the curve will always remain 'inside' the curve, while a point 'outside' the curve will always remain 'outside', Fig. 3-9.

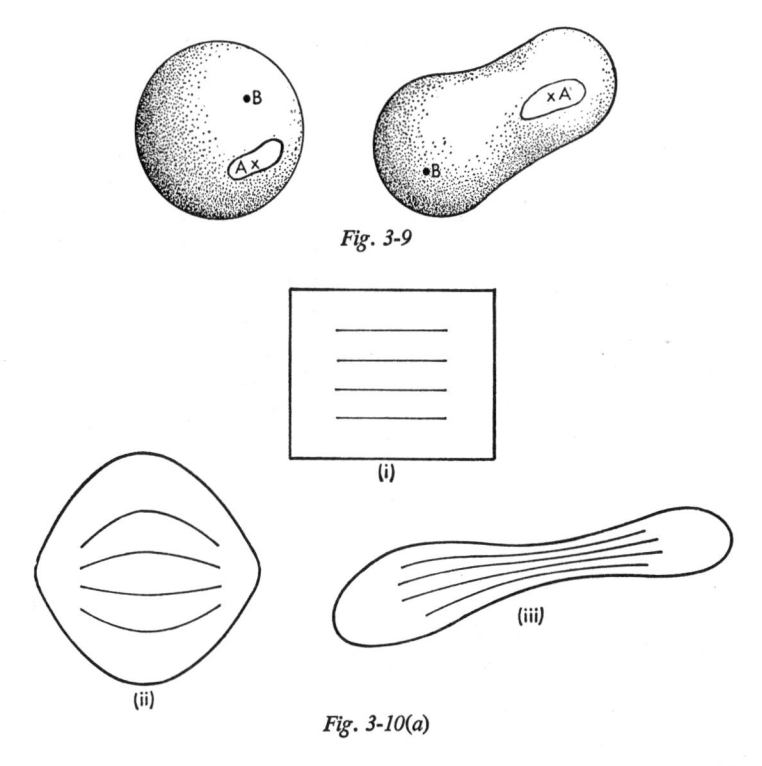

Fig. 3-9

(i)

(ii)

(iii)

Fig. 3-10(a)

45

LONGMAN MATHEMATICS

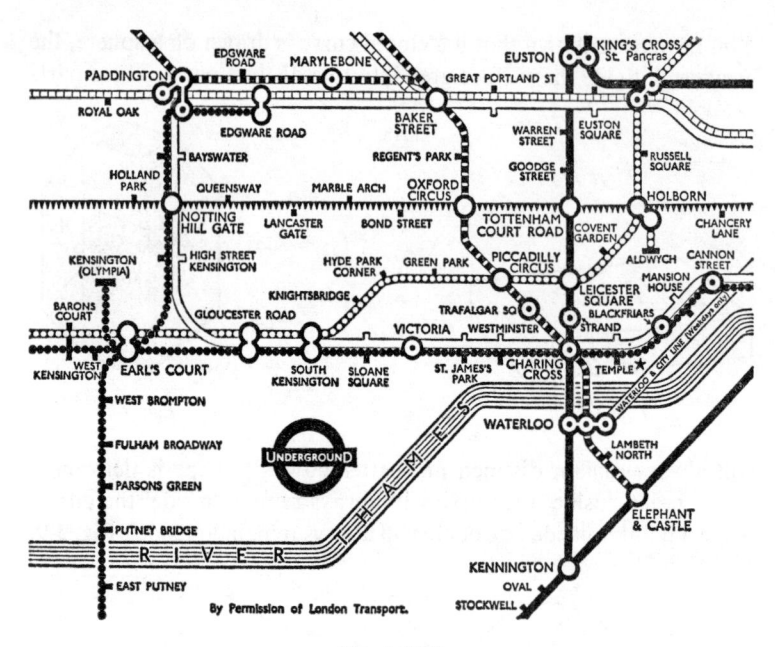

Fig. 3-10(b)

Adjacent sets of points forming lines illustrate another facet of connectivity. If several distinct and non-intersecting lines are drawn on a surface, then no matter how the surface is distorted these lines will always remain distinct and can never be made to intersect, Fig. 3-10a. London Underground map shown in Fig. 3-10b is a good example of a topological distortion showing how connectivity (i.e. connections between stations) is maintained. All maps are actually topological distortions since it is impossible to draw accurately a spherical map (which our Earth is) on a flat or plane surface.

Exercise 3a

1. Cut several strips about 10 cm wide from the length of a newspaper. Take one strip and paste or clip the ends together to form a shallow cylinder, Fig. 3-11. How many surfaces has this shape?

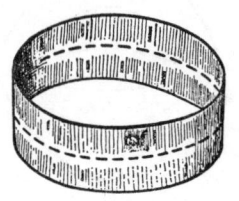

Fig. 3-11

46

A NEW GEOMETRY

What would happen if you were to cut the cylinder centrally around the length? (Along the dotted line.)
Cut your strip to check your suggestion.

2. Take a second strip, twist one end through 180° (one twist) and secure the two ends together.
How many surfaces has this shape?
Check by drawing a line on each surface.
Are there the same number as you expected?
This strip is known as a MOBIUS strip after A. C. Mobius (1790–1868) who was the first to analyse it mathematically. Both the first strip and the MOBIUS strip were formed from a stretched-out disc, but no amount of stretching or deforming can turn one into the other —they are topologically different!
What would you expect to happen if you cut the Mobius strip down the middle?
Cut your strip and check your guess.
What can you say about the resultant strip?

3. Take the resultant strip from No. 2 above and cut this down the centre as before.
Before cutting the strip can you make a guess at the end result?
Describe the result exactly.
If you can, try cutting the above result down the centre again.

4. Take a fresh strip and twist one end twice (i.e. through 360°) before joining the two ends.
What sort of solid have you now?
Has it one surface or two?
Cut the strip down the centre and describe the result.
Cut the resultant down the centre.

5. Form a Mobius strip and cut down the length of the strip but not in the centre this time, but one-third of the distance across the width of the strip. Describe the result.

6. Try various experiments of your own, starting either with the results obtained above or with strips having three or four twists.

Mathematical Knots

The idea of connectivity has been extended to the forms taken by the edges of discs or sheets. The edges can be looked upon as closed curves which separate the points on one side of a disc or shape from the points on the other side. The edges when considered separately from the disc or sheet lead to the study of knots. Consider first the edges of the cylindrical strip formed in Exercise 3*a* 1. They form two distinct closed curves.

Exercise 3b

Take a Mobius strip and sketch the edge showing how or if it interlocks.
Does the edge form one curve or two?
Is the curve closed?
Can the curve be pulled to form a simple closed curve, or is it knotted? If a Mobius strip is cut down the centre a 2-sided strip will be formed, the edges of this strip form two closed curves, neither curve is knotted but they are interwoven together. One of the most well known knots studied is the clover leaf or trefoil, Fig. 3-12. No amount of deforming will transform the left trefoil into the right trefoil, they are thus fundamentally different knots. The edge of a band twisted three times will be in a form similar to the left-hand type of trefoil in Fig. 3-12.

Fig. 3-12

Pathways

The idea of connectivity faced Euler when he tried to solve an ancient problem connected with the city of Konisberg. In the eighteenth century the city had seven bridges joining two islands to each bank, Fig. 3-13. The problem was to find a route so that a pedestrian, starting at any point and finishing at any point, could cross all seven bridges without crossing any bridge twice. Euler solved the problem in 1736 by showing that it was impossible.

The problem can be seen more clearly if the diagram is simplified to the figure in Fig. 3-14 consisting of 4 points joined by seven paths.

A NEW GEOMETRY

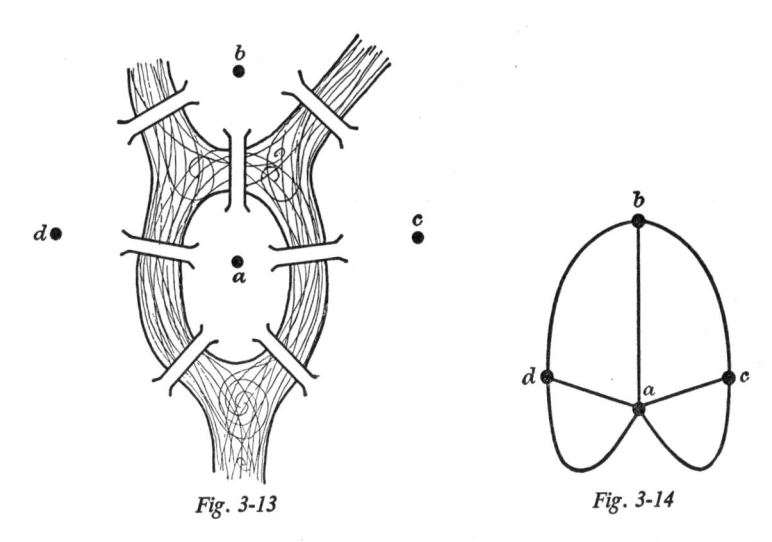

Fig. 3-13

Fig. 3-14

The question then becomes: can we trace these paths with a pencil without either lifting the pencil from the paper, or without going over any line twice? Try it—you will find Euler was right!

Diagrams which can be drawn under the above conditions are known as 'EULERIAN CHAINS or CYCLES'.

Now try the following:

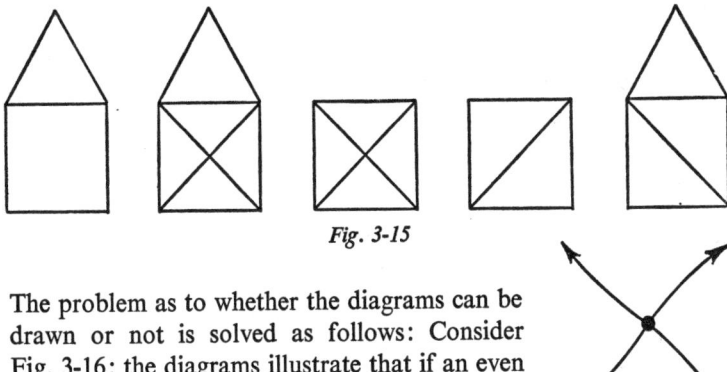

Fig. 3-15

The problem as to whether the diagrams can be drawn or not is solved as follows: Consider Fig. 3-16; the diagrams illustrate that if an even number of paths emanate from a point or vertex the point can be considered as a 'crossroad'. Thus if a figure has only even-numbered vertices and the paths are continuous then it forms an Eulerian Chain, Fig. 3-17, and the diagram can be started from any point.

Fig. 3-16

49

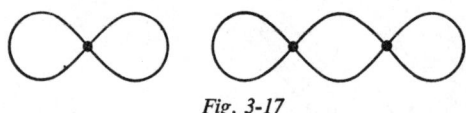

Fig. 3-17

Now consider Fig. 3-18; the diagrams here illustrate that if an odd number of paths emanate from a vertex then the vertex must be either a starting point or a finishing point. An Eulerian Chain can only have two odd vertices—why? Count the vertices in Fig. 3-15 and check your results.

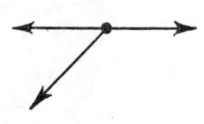

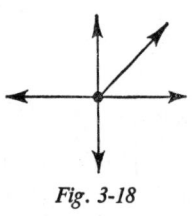

Chains and Networks

The mathematics of chains, or networks, as they are usually called, plays a very important part in some advanced problems. They can be applied to problems of traffic flows; transportation; factory layout; telephone and communication systems; nerve networks in animals; organization charts; electronic computers; chemical compositions, etc.

Fig. 3-18

A very interesting theorem shown by Euler in his study shows that if the number of vertices is V, the number of paths E, and the number of regions into which the network has divided the plane is F, then $V - E + F = 2$. Check this in Fig. 3-19. Compare this to Euler's theorem concerning solid figures.

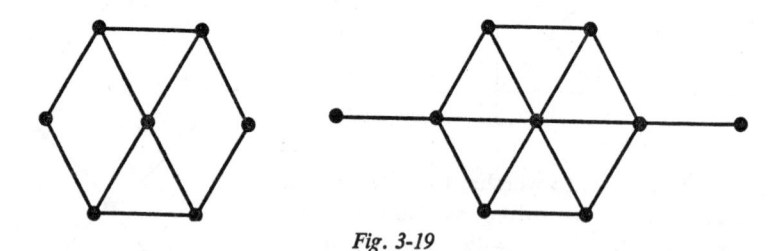

Fig. 3-19

It is necessary, however, to be able to convert a network diagram into a mathematical form that can be analysed and used by computers. Consider Fig. 3-20 where we have four points and five 2-way lines of communication between them. To describe this mathematically it is

A NEW GEOMETRY

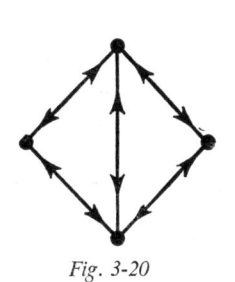

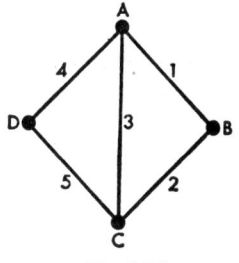

Fig. 3-20

Fig. 3-21

necessary to number the lines of communication as in Fig. 3-21. The diagram can then be fully represented by a table as in Fig. 3-22. This table is more suitable for use in a computer if instead of ticks and

	A	B	C	D
1	✓	✓		
2		✓	✓	
3	✓		✓	
4	✓			✓
5			✓	✓

Fig. 3-22

	A	B	C	D
1	1	1	0	0
2	0	1	1	0
3	1	0	1	0
4	1	0	0	1
5	0	0	1	1

Fig. 3-23

blanks a binary system is used as in Fig. 3-23, '1' being used where there is a connection and '0' where there is no connection.

Exercise 3c

1. Consider the table in Fig. 3-23.

(*i*) Add up the columns. What does each sum represent?
(*ii*) Add up each row. What does each sum represent?
(*iii*) Can a row have a sum of 1? If so, explain.
(*iv*) Can a row have a sum greater than 2? Explain why.
(*v*) Can a column have a sum 1? Explain.

The 2-way communication system as above has many drawbacks and cannot be used if 'one-way' lines of communication exist. To overcome this and to show 'flow' direction a table similar to the one in Fig. 3-25 is used. This table is read as follows: Starting *from* the point

51

indicated at the *top* of the column, and moving *to* the point indicated at the side of a row, a 1 is placed at the intersection of row and column if it *is* a line of communication, and 0 is used if there is *no* line of communication. Compare the graph and the table in Figs. 3-24 and 3-25.

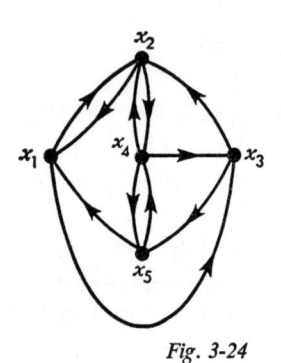

	x_1	x_2	x_3	x_4	x_5	
	0	1	0	0	1	x_1
	1	0	1	1	0	x_2
	1	0	0	1	0	x_3
	0	1	0	0	1	x_4
	0	0	1	1	0	x_5

Fig. 3-24   Fig. 3-25

Exercise 3d

1. Add up each column in Fig. 3-25. What does each total represent?
2. Add up each row in Fig. 3-25. What does each total represent?
3. Why is the diagonal from top left to bottom right a line of 0's?
4. Could this diagonal contain 1's? Explain.

The sort of table used in Fig. 3-25 appears in many different branches of mathematics, and is usually simplified and written with a pair of straight or square brackets only as in Fig. 3-26. This form is known

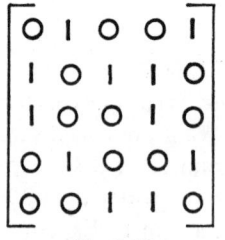

$$\begin{bmatrix} 0 & 1 & 0 & 0 & 1 \\ 1 & 0 & 1 & 1 & 0 \\ 1 & 0 & 0 & 1 & 0 \\ 0 & 1 & 0 & 0 & 1 \\ 0 & 0 & 1 & 1 & 0 \end{bmatrix}$$

Fig. 3-26

as a MATRIX, and can be written with or without the x's. A shorthand way of indicating a particular path is by writing x_3^2 for the path *from* 2 to 3, and x_2^3 for the path from 3 to 2.

A NEW GEOMETRY

Exercise 3e

1. Write out the matrix for the graph in Fig. 3-27. Call this matrix A.
2. What are $x_1\underset{5}{;}\ x_5\underset{1}{;}\ x_3\underset{1}{;}\ x_1\underset{1}{;}\ x_1\underset{2}{;}\ x_2\underset{1}{;}$?

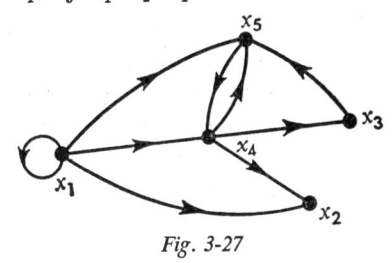

Fig. 3-27

3. The 'transpose' of a matrix is a second matrix obtained from the first by either interchanging rows and columns or by reflecting the matrix about its main diagonal (the diagonal from the top left to bottom right). See the example in Fig. 3-28. Write out the transpose of matrix A. Call this matrix A*.

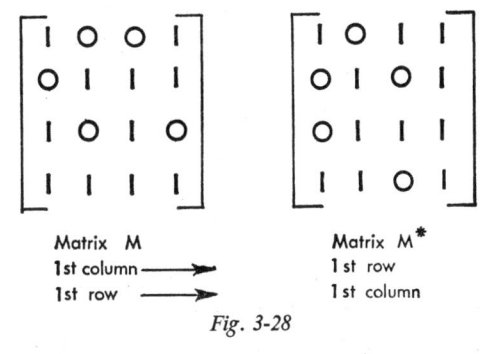

$$\begin{bmatrix} 1 & 0 & 0 & 1 \\ 0 & 1 & 1 & 1 \\ 1 & 0 & 1 & 0 \\ 1 & 1 & 1 & 1 \end{bmatrix} \qquad \begin{bmatrix} 1 & 0 & 1 & 1 \\ 0 & 1 & 0 & 1 \\ 0 & 1 & 1 & 1 \\ 1 & 1 & 0 & 1 \end{bmatrix}$$

Matrix M
1st column ⟶
1st row ⟶

Matrix M*
1st row
1st column

Fig. 3-28

4. Draw the graph A*. Can you find a connection between the graph A and the graph A*?
5. Make up a graph of your own for x_{1-6}. Call the associated matrix B. Form B* and draw the graph. Is the connection found in question 4 still applicable? Will this always be true?
6. A 2 × 2 matrix is a matrix with 2 rows and 2 columns. Form a 2 × 2 matrix C so that C = C*. Use at least one 0 and one 1. Form a 3 × 3 matrix D so that D = D*. When this condition holds, a matrix is said to be symmetric. From your matrices drawn the corresponding graphs. When does a graph give a symmetric matrix? Why is the matrix said to be '*symmetric*'?

4 Mappings and Matrices

In previous work you have seen that a point can be defined by a pair of numbers which are given in a definite order, e.g. (3, 6). The point defined by this pair of numbers is distinct from the point given by the same numbers but in a different order, i.e. (6, 3). The pair of numbers are thus referred to as an ORDERED PAIR. In this chapter certain mathematical operations are going to be applied to ordered pairs to produce new ordered pairs.

Example 1

Consider the point (x, y) where $x = 3$ and $y = 6$: a new point and thus a new ordered pair (x_{new}, y_{new}) can be obtained by taking some combination of the old ordered pair.
e.g. if $x_{new} = 2x + 3y$
and $y_{new} = 3x + 2y$, then the new point is (24, 21).
Mathematically it is said that the point (3, 6) has been MAPPED into the point (24, 21) by the mapping:
$$\left. \begin{array}{l} x_n = 2x + 3y \\ y_n = 3x + 2y \end{array} \right\} \text{ (writing } x_n \text{ for } x_{new}\text{)}$$

Example 2

Map the point (3, 6) by the following mappings, and show the mappings by plotting the points on 2 axes:
(i) $x_n = x + 2y$ (ii) $x_n = 2x + y$ (iii) $x_n = 0x + y$
    $y_n = x - y$ $y_n = 3x - 3y$ $y_n = x + y$
The mappings are thus:
  (i) $x_n = 3 + (2 \times 6) = 15$ (ii) $x_n = 6 + 6 = 12$
     $y_n = 3 - 6 = -3$ $y_n = 9 - 18 = -9$
(iii) $x_n = 0 + 6 = 6$
    $y_n = 3 + 6 = 9$
(see Fig. 4-1).

Exercise 4a

1. Map the point (3, 6) into new points by the following mappings

MAPPINGS AND MATRICES

and plot them on 2 axes drawing arrows as in Fig. 4-1 from the original point to the new points.

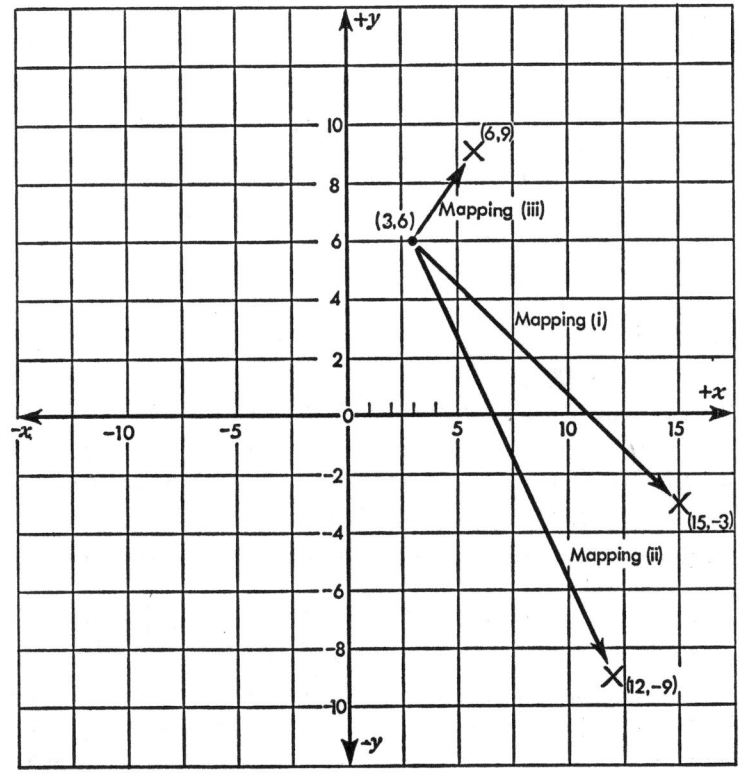

(i) $x_n = x + 2y$
$y_n = 2x + 2y$

(ii) $x_n = 2x + y$
$y_n = 3x + 2y$

(iii) $x_n = 2x + 0y$
$y_n = 3x - y$

(iv) $x_n = 0x - y$
$y_n = -3x + y$

(v) $\left. \begin{array}{l} x_n = 2x + 0y \\ y_n = 0x + 2y \end{array} \right\}$ Call this, mapping A.

Fig. 4-1

2. Find the new ordered pairs when mapping A is applied to:
(i) (1, 1)   (ii) (−1, 1)   (iii) (−1, −1)
(iv) (1, −1)

Draw 2 axes, put in the original points and the new points drawing lines with arrow-heads to show the mappings. Discuss the mapping.

3. Repeat question 2 with the following points:

(*i*) (0, 1)   (*ii*) (2, 2)   (*iii*) (4, 3)
(*iv*) (6, 4)   (*v*) (8, 5)   (*vi*) (10, 6)

What can you say about the set of points (*i*)–(*vi*)?
What can you say about the set of new points?
If another point was added to the original set having the same characteristic as the others, would its mapping be added to the set of new points?
Mapping A is an example of a type of mapping called LINEAR MAPPINGS or LINEAR TRANSFORMATIONS. Why do you think the word LINEAR was chosen?

4. What is the equation of the line on which points (*i*)–(*vi*) lie?
Let T be the set of ALL points on this line.

5. Plot the points (*i*)–(*vi*) in question 3 and the points obtained by the following mappings:

(*a*) $\left.\begin{array}{l} x_n = x - y \\ y_n = x + y \end{array}\right\}$ B   (*b*) $\left.\begin{array}{l} x_n = 2x - 3y \\ y_n = x + 2y \end{array}\right\}$ C   (*c*) $\left.\begin{array}{l} x_n = x + 2y \\ y_n = 2x - y \end{array}\right\}$ D

(*d*) $\left.\begin{array}{l} x_n = 0x + 0y \\ y_n = x + 3y \end{array}\right\}$ E   (*e*) $\left.\begin{array}{l} x_n = -3x + y \\ y_n = 0x + 0y) \end{array}\right\}$ F

Are the mappings B to F all linear mappings?
From your graphs can you find a point in set T that is mapped *into itself* by (*i*) mapping B, (*ii*) mapping C, (*iii*) mapping D, (*iv*) mapping E, (*v*) mapping F, (*vi*) mapping A?

6. Form two mappings of your own (*Note:* Do not use high numbers as this makes the points more difficult to plot), plot the points (*i*)–(*vi*) and their mappings and find points in set T that are mapped into themselves. (If there are any!)

7. By considering mappings E and F, can you find a mapping that will map ALL points in set T into one single point? What point would you pick? Would this mapping map every point in the plane into the same point?

In the above example you have been studying the effect of various random mappings on several points all lying on a straight line. The mapping can of course be applied to EVERY point in the x–y plane. What exactly is the effect of each mapping on the whole plane? This can be a little more clearly seen in the following exercise.

MAPPINGS AND MATRICES

Exercise 4b

1. plot the points (1, 1), (0, 1), (−1, 1), (−1, 0), (−1, −1) (0, −1), (1, −1), (1, 0). (Use scale 1 cm:1.) Join these points to form a square. Now apply mapping B, drawing arrows from the original point to the new point. Join the new points—in a different colour if possible. What figure is formed? Does it bear any relation to the original figure? What effect has the mapping had? Is there any special point in this mapping? Are the sides still straight?—parallel? —equal?

2. Repeat the above question using mapping C, then using mapping D. Are these mappings similar in their effects? If not what new operation has been introduced? Discuss these mappings fully.

3. Repeat question one with mappings E and F. In what way are these mappings different? In what ways are these the same?

The mappings which you have used obviously combine various mathematical operations; e.g. stretching, rotating, reflecting, etc. It is neccesary to investigate exactly how and why each of these operations becomes effective. Before doing this however it would be helpful to introduce a simplified method of writing out the mapping. In the chapter on Topology the idea of a matrix array was introduced, and the mappings A to F can easily be put into this form:

$$A = \begin{bmatrix} 2 & 0 \\ 0 & 2 \end{bmatrix} \quad B = \begin{bmatrix} 1 & -1 \\ 1 & 1 \end{bmatrix} \quad C = \begin{bmatrix} 2 & -3 \\ 1 & 2 \end{bmatrix} \quad D = \begin{bmatrix} 1 & 2 \\ 2 & -1 \end{bmatrix}$$

$$E = \begin{bmatrix} 0 & 0 \\ 1 & 3 \end{bmatrix} \quad F = \begin{bmatrix} -3 & 1 \\ 0 & 0 \end{bmatrix}$$

In order to map the point (3, 6) into the point (6, 12), (see Exercise 4a, no. 1 (v)), the matrix A has to be multiplied by the point matrix (3, 6), i.e.

$$\begin{bmatrix} 2 & 0 \\ 0 & 2 \end{bmatrix} \times \begin{bmatrix} 3 \\ 6 \end{bmatrix}.$$

The multiplication of matrices must be done in a particular way.

Multiplication of Matrices

Point 1. When two matrices are *multiplied* together the ROWS of one are combined with the COLUMNS of the other.

Point 2. In order to combine a row and a column each must have the same number of 'elements'.

Point 3. The method of combining a row and a column is as follows: Multiply element one in the row by element one in the column; multiply element two in the row by element two in the column; multiply element three in the row by element three in the column. Continue this until all pairs of elements have been multiplied together, then add together these products.

Example 1

$$[2, 3, 4, 5] \begin{bmatrix} 3 \\ 6 \\ 2 \\ 4 \end{bmatrix} = [(2 \times 3) + (3 \times 6) + (4 \times 2) + (5 \times 4)]$$

$$= 6 + 18 + 8 + 20$$
$$= 52$$

In the above example the matrices are single rowed and single columned, but matrices A to F above have two rows. This means that each row must be combined with the column separately as follows:

Example 2

$$\begin{bmatrix} 2, 3, 4, 5 \\ 1, 0, 4, 2 \end{bmatrix} \begin{bmatrix} 3 \\ 6 \\ 2 \\ 4 \end{bmatrix} = \begin{bmatrix} (2 \times 3) + 3 \times 6) + (4 \times 2) + (5 \times 4) \\ (1 \times 3) + (0 \times 6) + (4 \times 2) + (2 \times 4) \end{bmatrix}$$

$$= \begin{bmatrix} 52 \\ 19 \end{bmatrix}$$

(b)

A. $\begin{bmatrix} 3 \\ 6 \end{bmatrix} = \begin{bmatrix} 2 & 0 \\ 0 & 2 \end{bmatrix} \begin{bmatrix} 3 \\ 6 \end{bmatrix} = \begin{bmatrix} (2 \times 3) + (0 \times 6) \\ (0 \times 3) + (2 \times 6) \end{bmatrix}$

$$= \begin{bmatrix} 6 \\ 12 \end{bmatrix}$$

(Note that the matrix of the point is put as a column matrix so that multiplication is possible.)

Compare the working to that in Exercise 4a 1 (*v*).

MAPPINGS AND MATRICES

Exercise 4c

(1) Multiply matrices B to F by the matrix $\begin{bmatrix} 3 \\ 6 \end{bmatrix}$, as in Example 2b above.

(2) Multiply the matrices A to F by the matrices of the points (*i*) to (*vi*) in Exercise 4a, no. 3.

Matrix Transformations

In the following exercises simple matrix transformations will be applied to several points in order to investigate more closely what mathematical operation they represent.

Exercise 4d

1. Multiply out the following:

(*i*) $\begin{bmatrix} 1 & 0 \\ 0 & 1 \end{bmatrix} \begin{bmatrix} 3 \\ 6 \end{bmatrix}$ (*ii*) $\begin{bmatrix} 1 & 0 \\ 0 & 1 \end{bmatrix} \begin{bmatrix} 2 \\ 1 \end{bmatrix}$ (*iii*) $\begin{bmatrix} 1 & 0 \\ 0 & 1 \end{bmatrix} \begin{bmatrix} 4 \\ 5 \end{bmatrix}$

What effect has the transformation matrix $\begin{bmatrix} 1 & 0 \\ 0 & 1 \end{bmatrix}$?

Compare this matrix and its effect, with multiplying by one in a product, or adding 0 in a sum.
This matrix is the IDENTITY matrix.
Discuss why this is the identity matrix.

2. In Exercise 4a you applied the matrix transformation $\begin{bmatrix} 2 & 0 \\ 0 & 2 \end{bmatrix}$ to a number of points. Remind yourself of the effect of this mapping. What effect did the mapping have on
(*i*) The distance between the points
(*ii*) The distance of the points from the origin?
What effect do you think the mapping $\begin{bmatrix} 3 & 0 \\ 0 & 3 \end{bmatrix}$ will have?
Applying the mapping to the points (1, 1), (−1, 1), (1, −1) (−1, −1) and check your guess.
How has the distance of each point from the centre been affected?
How has the distance of each point from other points been affected?

3. Plot the following points (−2, −1) (−1, 0), (0, 1) (1, 2) (0, 3), (−1, 4), (−2, 5), (−2, 3), (−2, 1). Join them up in order to form a triangle.

59

Pre-multiply each by the transformation matrix $\begin{bmatrix} -1 & 0 \\ 0 & 1 \end{bmatrix}$.

Plot the new points and join them up in order.
What effect does this mapping have?
What can be said about the 'y' axis in the mapping?
Can you see from your matrix multiplication why this mapping has this particular effect?

What would the mapping $\begin{bmatrix} -2 & 0 \\ 0 & 2 \end{bmatrix}$ do to the above points?

Map the above nine points after transformation by this matrix and check your guess.

4. What effect do you think the transformation matrix $\begin{bmatrix} 1 & 0 \\ 0 & -1 \end{bmatrix}$ will have on the points in a plane? Why?

Transform the last seven points in Question 3 above by this matrix. Plot the original points and their mappings. Join each set to form quadrilaterals.

What would the mapping $\begin{bmatrix} 2 & 0 \\ 0 & -2 \end{bmatrix}$ do to the points?

Question 3 above illustrates that the matrix $\begin{bmatrix} -1 & 0 \\ 0 & 1 \end{bmatrix}$ reverses the sign of the x component and leaves the y component unchanged. Thus all points on the right of the y axis (i.e. x +ve) are rotated to the left of the y axis (x −ve) and the points on the left of the y axis are mapped into the right of the y axis.

Similarly Question 4 illustrates that the matrix $\begin{bmatrix} 1 & 0 \\ 0 & -1 \end{bmatrix}$ reverses the sign of the y component but leaves the x component unchanged; thus all +ve values of y become −ve and all −ve values become +ve, i.e. all points are rotated about the x axis. The effective parts of these matrices are obviously the (−1) elements.

What effect do you think the transformation matrix $\begin{bmatrix} -1 & 0 \\ 0 & -1 \end{bmatrix}$ will have on points in the plane?

Taking a general point may help you to guess the answer.

e.g. $\begin{bmatrix} -1 & 0 \\ 0 & -1 \end{bmatrix} \begin{bmatrix} x \\ y \end{bmatrix} = \begin{bmatrix} -x \\ -y \end{bmatrix}$ i.e. $x_{new} = -x_{old}$
$y_{new} = -y_{old}$

Thus points in the 1st quadrant (x +ve, y +ve) will go to the 3rd quadrant (x −ve, y −ve) and vice versa; while points in the 2nd

MAPPINGS AND MATRICES

quadrant (x −ve, y +ve) will interchange with points in the 4th quadrant (x +ve, y −ve).

5. Plot the following points joining them in order to form a triangle, (0, 0), (2, 1), (4, 2), (3, 3), (2, 4), (1, 5), (0, 6), (−1, 7).
Find the mappings of these points when they are transformed by the matrix $\begin{bmatrix} -1 & 0 \\ 0 & -1 \end{bmatrix}$.
What effect does this matrix have on points?
What effect will the matrix $\begin{bmatrix} -2 & 0 \\ 0 & -2 \end{bmatrix}$ have on the seven points?
Plot the mappings to check your guess.

Summary

It is important that the work so far covered should be seen as a whole.

Matrix I = $\begin{bmatrix} 1 & 0 \\ 0 & 1 \end{bmatrix}$ is the *Identity* matrix, leaving all points as they were originally.

Matrix II = $\begin{bmatrix} -1 & 0 \\ 0 & 1 \end{bmatrix}$ will rotate all points about the y axis.

Matrix III = $\begin{bmatrix} 1 & 0 \\ 0 & -1 \end{bmatrix}$ will rotate all points about the x axis.

Matrix IV = $\begin{bmatrix} -1 & 0 \\ 0 & -1 \end{bmatrix}$ will rotate all points through 180° about the centre, OR can be said to rotate points about the x axis and y axis simultaneously.

You have also seen that by replacing the '1' by some numbers, we can also stretch the distance between the points.

From the above summary it would appear that by applying matrix IV the same result is obtained as by applying matrix II and matrix III in any order, i.e.

$$\begin{bmatrix} x_n \\ y_n \end{bmatrix} = \begin{bmatrix} -1 & 0 \\ 0 & 1 \end{bmatrix} \begin{bmatrix} 1 & 0 \\ 0 & -1 \end{bmatrix} \begin{bmatrix} x_0 \\ y_0 \end{bmatrix} = \begin{bmatrix} -1 & 0 \\ 0 & -1 \end{bmatrix} \begin{bmatrix} x_0 \\ y_0 \end{bmatrix}$$

Thus $\begin{bmatrix} -1 & 0 \\ 0 & 1 \end{bmatrix} \begin{bmatrix} 1 & 0 \\ 0 & -1 \end{bmatrix} = \begin{bmatrix} -1 & 0 \\ 0 & -1 \end{bmatrix}$. It would seem obvious that combining two operations produces a third operation; hence combining two transformation matrices produces a third operation matrix. The method of combining two matrices is an extension of the method you have used for mapping a point. The same rules apply, i.e. rows combine with columns by summing the products of the elements. Since in our example each matrix has 2 rows and 2 columns, the product of rows and columns will produce 4 results, i.e. the four elements of the resultant matrix. The position of each element is of course vital. This positioning is given as follows:

(a) When the 1st row $\begin{bmatrix} ---- \end{bmatrix}$ combines with the 1st column

$\begin{bmatrix} \vdots \end{bmatrix}$ the resultant is placed where these two lines

meet $\begin{bmatrix} *--- \\ \vdots \end{bmatrix}$

(b) When the 2nd row $\begin{bmatrix} ----- \end{bmatrix}$ combines with the 1st column

$\begin{bmatrix} \vdots \end{bmatrix}$ the resultant is placed where these two lines

meet $\begin{bmatrix} \vdots \\ * --- \end{bmatrix}$

(c) When the 1st row $\begin{bmatrix} ---- \end{bmatrix}$ combines with the 2nd column

$\begin{bmatrix} \vdots \end{bmatrix}$ the resultant is placed where these two lines

meet $\begin{bmatrix} ---* \\ \vdots \end{bmatrix}$

(d) When the 2nd row $\begin{bmatrix} ---- \end{bmatrix}$ combines with the 2nd column

$\begin{bmatrix} \vdots \end{bmatrix}$ the resultant is placed where these two lines

meet $\begin{bmatrix} \vdots \\ ---* \end{bmatrix}$

whence $\begin{bmatrix} r_1 \times c_1 & r_1 \times c_2 \\ r_2 \times c_1 & r_2 \times c_2 \end{bmatrix}$ where r = row c = column.

Example

$$\begin{bmatrix} 2 & -3 \\ 1 & 2 \end{bmatrix} \begin{bmatrix} 1 & 2 \\ 2 & -1 \end{bmatrix} = \begin{bmatrix} (2 \times 1) + (-3 \times 2) & (2 \times 2) + (-3 \times -1) \\ (1 \times 1) + (2 \times 2) & (1 \times 2) + (2 \times -1) \end{bmatrix}$$

$$= \begin{bmatrix} -4 & 7 \\ 5 & 0 \end{bmatrix}$$

MAPPINGS AND MATRICES

Exercise 4e

1. Referring to matrices A, B, C, D, E and F (after Exercise 4b) find:

(*i*) AB   (*ii*) BA   (*iii*) BD   (*iv*) DB
(*v*) BE   (*vi*) EB   (*vii*) CD   (*viii*) DC
(*ix*) EF   (*x*) FE   (*xi*) AD   (*xii*) DA

Is matrix multiplication commutative?

You have studied the effect of four transformation matrices on points in a plane, the following exercise is to show their effect on other matrices

Matrices I, II, III and IV in the following questions refer to those given in the summary above.

2. Multiply out the following:

(*i*) I × A   (*ii*) I × B   (*iii*) I × C   (*iv*) I × D
(*v*) I × E   (*vi*) I × F

In transforming a point, the matrix I was the *Identity* matrix. Is this still true when it is multiplied by another matrix?
Multiply out:

(*vii*) I × I   (*viii*) B × I   (*ix*) C × I   (*x*) D × I

Is multiplication by the identity matrix commutative?

3. Multiply out the following:

(*i*) A × II   (*ii*) B × II   (*iii*) C × II   (*iv*) D × II
(*v*) E × II   (*vi*) F × II   (*vii*) II × A   (*viii*) II × B
(*ix*) II × C   (*x*) II × D   (*xi*) II × E   (*xii*) II × F

Is multiplication by $\begin{bmatrix} -1 & 0 \\ 0 & 1 \end{bmatrix}$ commutative?

What effect does pre-multiplying by II have on a matrix?
What effect does post-multiplying by II have on a matrix?

4. Repeat Question 3 above using matrix III.

5. Repeat Question 3 above using matrix IV.

6. Form a multiplication table for the four matrices I to IV.
Are these multiplications commutative? Check the requirements for a group and show that these four matrices form a group under multiplication.

The four matrices investigated so far have been special matrices in

LONGMAN MATHEMATICS

that all elements other than those in the leading diagonal have been zeros. The following matrices will now be investigated:

$$V = \begin{bmatrix} 0 & 1 \\ 1 & 0 \end{bmatrix} \quad VI = \begin{bmatrix} 0 & -1 \\ 1 & 0 \end{bmatrix} \quad VII = \begin{bmatrix} 0 & 1 \\ -1 & 0 \end{bmatrix} \quad VIII = \begin{bmatrix} 0 & -1 \\ -1 & 0 \end{bmatrix}$$

Exercise 4f

1. Plot the following points:
$(-10, -10)$ $(-9, -10)$ $(-7, -10)$ $(-5, -10)$ $(-4, -8)$ $(-3, -6)$ $(-2, -4)$ $(-1, -2)$ $(0, 0)$ $(1, 2)$ $(2, 4)$ $(3, 6)$ $(4, 8)$ $(5, 10)$ $(7, 10)$ $(8, 11)$ $(9, 10)$ $(10, 10)$. Join up in order.

Transform each point by pre-multiplying by the matrix $\begin{bmatrix} 0 & 1 \\ 1 & 0 \end{bmatrix}$

What effect has the mapping $\begin{bmatrix} 0 & 1 \\ 1 & 0 \end{bmatrix}$?

Can you give a reason for this effect?
Is there symmetry? If so about which line or point?

What effect do you think the matrix $\begin{bmatrix} 0 & 2 \\ 2 & 0 \end{bmatrix}$ will have?

Check your guess by mapping on the same axis as above the points:
$(-9, -10)$ $(-5, -10)$ $(-4, -8)$ $(-2, -4)$ $(0, 0)$ $(2, 4)$ $(4, 8)$ $(5, 10)$ $(9, 10)$ when pre-multiplied by $\begin{bmatrix} 0 & 2 \\ 2 & 0 \end{bmatrix}$.

2. Plot the following nine points:
$(3, 0)$ $(4, 1)$ $(5, 1)$ $(5, 2)$ $(6, 3)$ $(5, 4)$ $(4, 3)$ $(3, 2)$ $(2, 1)$. Join up in order.

Transform these points by pre-multiplying by the matrix $\begin{bmatrix} 0 & 1 \\ 1 & 0 \end{bmatrix}$ and plot the points on the same axes as above.

Now transform the original nine by pre-multiplying by the matrix $\begin{bmatrix} 0 & -1 \\ 1 & 0 \end{bmatrix}$, plotting the transforms on the same axes as above.

What effect has this transformation had on the set of eight points?
Is there any bi-linear symmetry between the original points and their final mappings?
Is there rotational symmetry? If so, about what line or point?
Can the symmetry be expressed as the result of two operations? If so which two? Explain why the matrix has this effect.

What effect would the matrix $\begin{bmatrix} 0 & -a \\ a & 0 \end{bmatrix}$ have on a set of points?

MAPPINGS AND MATRICES

3. From the knowledge you have already gained about the transformation matrices previously mentioned can you guess the result when a set of points is pre-multiplied by the matrix $\begin{bmatrix} 0 & 1 \\ -1 & 0 \end{bmatrix}$? Using the same axes as for question 2, plot the mappings when the nine points in question 2 are pre-multiplied by (*i*) the matrix $\begin{bmatrix} 0 & 1 \\ -1 & 0 \end{bmatrix}$ (*ii*) the matrix $\begin{bmatrix} 0 & -1 \\ -1 & 0 \end{bmatrix}$.

Mark each set of points with its matrix.

4. Plot the points:
(1, 2) (2, 4) (3, 6) (4, 8) (5, 10) (7, 10) (9, 10) (10, 10). Join them in order.

On the same axes plot the resulting points when the above points are transformed by pre-multiplying by the matrix $\begin{bmatrix} 0 & -1 \\ -1 & 0 \end{bmatrix}$. Describe the transformation as the sum of *two* operations.

5. Copy out and fill in the multiplification table in Fig. 4-2 for the matrices I to VIII, where each space is given by row × column.

	I	II	III	IV	V	VI	VII	VIII
I								
II								
III								
IV								
V								
VI								
VII								
VIII								

Fig. 4-2

LONGMAN MATHEMATICS

Is the multiplication always commutative? If not when?
Is there an identity element? If so what is it?
Is there an inverse for each element? If so list them.
Is this set of matrices a group?

6. Draw two lines, one from (10, 1) to (10, 7) and the second from (8, 5) to (12, 5).
SKETCH the results, without any working out, when the set of points defined by the above two lines is pre-multiplied by matrices I to VIII, marking each transformation with the associated matrix number.

7. Transform the set of points that forms the square with corners at (2, 1) (3, 0) (4, 1) (3, 2) by pre-multiplying by matrices I to VIII. What factors are unaltered by the transformation? Length? Angles? Area? When any of the above eight mappings are applied to a point, one, and only one, new point is defined. From the multiplication table, Fig. 4-2, an inverse for each mapping can be applied which will reverse the mapping back to the original point. This mapping of one point into one point is an example of a very important mathematical relationship known as a 'one-to-one correspondence'. Not all matrix transformations are one-to-one correspondences. Those that are, are the most important. An example of a 'many-to-one' is $\begin{bmatrix} 0 & 0 \\ 0 & 0 \end{bmatrix}$ which maps EVERY point in the plane into the origin. This matrix has been called the 'annihilator'—an apt term! Two matrices in Exercise 4a question 5 are examples of mappings in which all points in the plane are mapped into a straight line. Discuss these two matrices, E and F, and why they map all points into the axes. In each case give 2 points which are mapped into the same new point.

Exercise 4g

1. In the following exercise each question should have full class discussion. Consider the transformation IX $= \begin{bmatrix} 1 & 1 \\ 1 & 1 \end{bmatrix}$
Take three points in each of the four quadrants, transform them by pre-multiplying by matrix IX. Discuss the result.
Why does this particular mapping arise?
Is this a one-to-one relationship?

MAPPINGS AND MATRICES

2. Divide a plane into eight sections by the lines $y = 0$, $x = 0$, $x = y$, $x = -y$.

By taking two or three examples of points in each section, show where all points in each section are mapped by matrix IX, giving reasons for your results.

3. Repeat Question 1 above with matrix $X = \begin{bmatrix} -1 & -1 \\ -1 & -1 \end{bmatrix}$

4. Repeat Question 2 using matrix X

5. Repeat Questions 1 and 2 using matrix $XI = \begin{bmatrix} -1 & 1 \\ 1 & -1 \end{bmatrix}$

6. Repeat Questions 1 and 2 using matrix $XII = \begin{bmatrix} 1 & -1 \\ -1 & 1 \end{bmatrix}$

In this chapter you have studied some elementary matrix transformations. Not only has the development of this subject led to the solution of many difficult problems but it means many geometrical problems can be stated in a number form and thus fed into a computer. Whilst all the matrices discussed have mapped straight lines into straight lines, there are many transformations which will map straight lines into curves or circles, and circles or curves into straight lines.

As an example of how transformations have simplified a very difficult problem consider Fig. 4-3. This shape is known as an 'aerofoil'

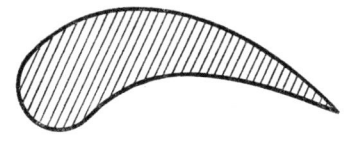

Fig. 4-3

and is of great importance in the study of aerodynamics, and fluid dynamics. The equations which give the pressures at the various points of the perimeter and the equations of the flow of air or fluids around an aerofoil are almost impossible to handle. A fairly simple transformation, however, can be applied to the aerofoil which will map it into a circle. The equations of pressure and flow are then easily worked out and these are then transformed back into the results required for the aerofoil.

LONGMAN MATHEMATICS

Corresponding Points

In Exercise 4a, no. 5 the mapping $\begin{bmatrix} 0 & 1 \\ 1 & 3 \end{bmatrix}$ was used to transform the points on a straight line. Use the matrix to transform the points (4, 3) (1, 4) (−2, 5) (−5, 6) (−8, 7). Plot the points and their transforms.

What is special about the transformation and the resultant points? What is the connection between the original set of points?

Find two other points which can be added to the original set. Transform these by the above matrix. Are the results consistent?

How many points are there in the plane that have the same characteristic?

Repeat the whole of the above section using the same mapping on the following points: (−2, 4) (1, 3) (4, 2) (7, 1) (10, 0).

The above mappings are examples of 'many-to-one' mappings or correspondences, for under the transformations each set of points is mapped into one single point

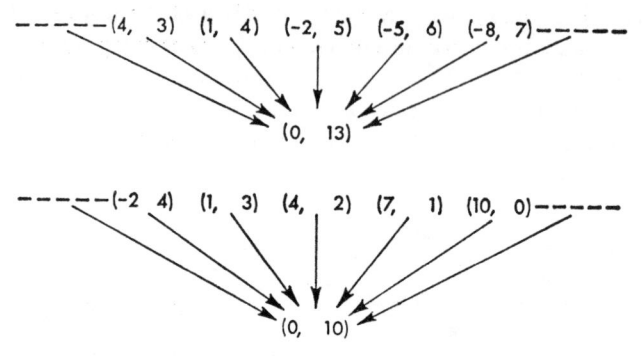

```
-----(4, 3)  (1, 4)  (-2, 5)  (-5, 6)  (-8, 7)-----
              \   \    |    /    /
               \   \   |   /    /
                \   \  |  /    /
                 (0, 13)
```

```
-----(-2, 4)  (1, 3)  (4, 2)  (7, 1)  (10, 0)-----
              \   \    |    /    /
               \   \   |   /    /
                \   \  |  /    /
                 (0, 10)
```

If the whole plane of points is transformed by the matrix $\begin{bmatrix} 0 & 0 \\ 1 & 3 \end{bmatrix}$, what is the result?

Now consider matrices I to IV. Do the mappings obtained lead to 'many-to-one' correspondences? If not, why not and what sort of correspondences, if any, are obtained? Discuss this in class.

5 Space and Time

Pure Mathematics is the study of mathematics which is concerned with mathematical principles; Applied Mathematics, sometimes called Mechanics, is the study of the application of mathematical principles to the solution of problems dealing with space and time. Many great mathematicians have given special thought to the problem of Applied Mathematics, particularly Newton who lived from 1642 to 1727 and Einstein who lived from 1879 to 1955. Both of them were particularly concerned with the problems of motion, an aspect of applied mathematics which has become of increasing importance in this century where travel by land, sea and air has now become commonplace and where 'Space Travel' is just around the corner.

Distance, Time and Speed

When we say that a car is travelling at 50 km/h we mean that if the car continued to travel at this speed for 1 hour it would cover a distance of 50 km, for 2 hours it would travel 100 km and so on. Such a journey can be pictorially represented on a graph, Fig. 5-1. The horizontal axis (abscissa) represents time and the vertical axis (ordinate) represents distance.

The graph is the simplest form of linear relationship which would be represented by an equation of the first degree whose form would be $d = mt + c$ where $d =$ distance, $t =$ time, m is the slope or gradient of the line and c is the intercept on the vertical axis.

In fact m, the gradient of the line, measures the speed (or velocity) which is verified by reference to the well-known formula

$$\frac{\text{Distance}}{\text{Time}} = \text{Speed}$$

It is very unlikely that a car travelling say for 4 hours will keep up a continuous speed of exactly 50 km/h, but this does not make the principle wrong. Another way of looking at this problem is that if the car travels 200 km in 4 hours then its *average speed* is 50 km/h and this is quite a usual occurrence.

Distance–Time graph showing a journey at a constant speed of 50 km/h.

Fig. 5-1

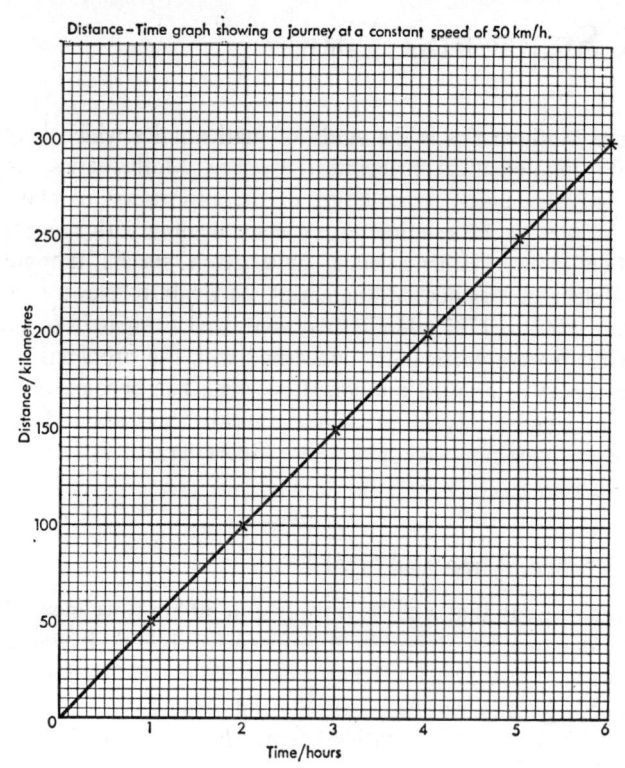

Thus the formula given above is more correctly stated as

$$\text{Average Velocity} = \frac{\text{Distance}}{\text{Time}}$$

A complete pictorial representation of a journey is, however, more likely to be as shown in Fig. 5-2.

OABC shows the journey made by a car during a 4-hour period. The line OA shows a journey of 45 km made in first $1\frac{1}{2}$ hours.

$\therefore$ average velocity for OA $= \dfrac{45}{1\frac{1}{2}} = 30$ km/h

The *horizontal* line AB shows that the car has not moved forward during the next $1\frac{1}{2}$ hours.

Hence average velocity in second $1\frac{1}{2}$ hours $= 0$ km/h
(i.e. the car was at rest)

The line BC shows the return journey of 45 km in the last 1 hour.

Hence average velocity in last 1 hour $= \dfrac{45}{1} = 45$ km/h

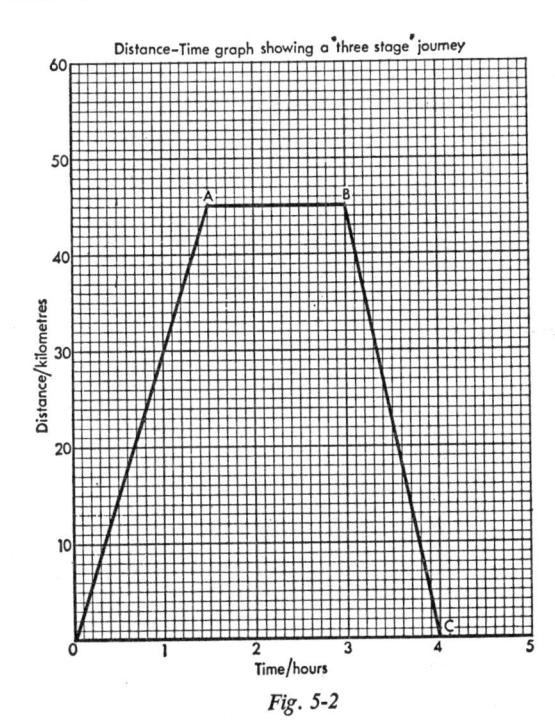

SPACE AND TIME

Distance-Time graph showing a 'three stage' journey

Fig. 5-2

Exercise 5a

Draw the distance-time graphs for the following journeys and calculate the average velocities of the various parts of the journeys.
1. 30 km in 2 hours, ½ hour rest and return journey in 2½ hours.
2. A 12-km walk in 3 hours, ¾ hour rest and the return journey in 4½ hours.
3. 60 km in 1½ hours, the next 30 km in 1 hour, 2 hours rest and the return journey in 2½ hours.
4. 40 km in 1¼ hours, return journey in 1 hour, ½ hour rest and another outward journey of 75 km in 1½ hours.

All the above examples assume that the velocity is *uniform* throughout each of the parts of the journey. In practice, however, such conditions are rarely true. For example a motor car usually starts from rest (i.e. zero velocity), gradually increases its velocity up to a certain cruising speed and when it comes near to its stopping place the velocity decreases gradually to zero again when it comes to rest.

LONGMAN MATHEMATICS

Even when the car is travelling at its cruising speed, the velocity will vary from instant to instant because the road will not always be equally level and will certainly not be straight.

We must therefore investigate the *velocity at a particular instant* (more often called *instantaneous velocity*).

Consider the following example:

A boy slides down a chute 15 m in length, and the distance he has travelled measured each second is given in the following table:

Time/seconds	0	1	2	3	4	5
Distance/metres	0	0·6	2·4	5·4	9·6	14·8

Plotting these points on a distance-time graph we get the following diagram.

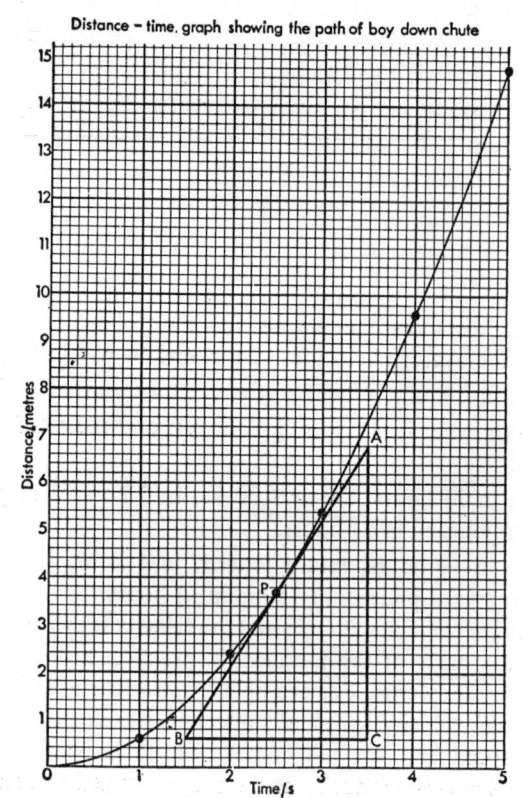

Fig. 5-3

Distance – time. graph showing the path of boy down chute

72

SPACE AND TIME

The *gradient* of this graph will give the instantaneous velocity at any particular time. To find this gradient we must draw the tangent to the curve at the instant chosen. Thus to find the velocity after $2\frac{1}{2}$ s draw the tangent at P. Choosing suitable points A and B on this tangent complete the right-angled triangle ABC by drawing AC parallel to the vertical axis and BC parallel to the horizontal axis. The instantaneous velocity at P is then given by dividing the distance AC by the time BC, each being measured to scale

$$\therefore \text{Velocity of boy after } 2\tfrac{1}{2} \text{ s} = \frac{\text{AC (measured in m)}}{\text{BC (measured in s)}}$$

$$= \frac{6\cdot 2}{2} = 3\cdot 1 \text{ m/s}$$

Exercise 5b

1. Using the table given above, draw the graph and find the velocity of the boy after $1\frac{1}{2}$ s and after 4 s.
What will his velocity be when he comes to the end of the chute?

2. The height of a cricket ball thrown vertically upwards measured at half-second intervals is given in the following table:

Time/seconds	0	$\frac{1}{2}$	1	$1\frac{1}{2}$	2	$2\frac{1}{2}$
Height/metres	0	4·8	7·2	7·2	4·8	0

Draw the distance-time graph and from it estimate the velocity of the ball after $\frac{1}{2}$ s and after 2 s. What can you say about these two velocities?

3. A stone falls from the roof of a building 45 m high. The distances it has fallen are measured at half-second intervals and are given in the following table:

Time/seconds	0	$\frac{1}{2}$	1	$1\frac{1}{2}$	2	$2\frac{1}{2}$	3
Distance/metres	0	1·2	4·8	10·8	19·2	30·0	43·2

Draw the distance-time graph and estimate the velocity of the stone after (a) $1\frac{1}{2}$ s; (b) 3 s.

Acceleration

Examples like these above where the distance-time graph is a curve, show a body moving with a variable velocity.

The *rate of change* of velocity of the body is called the acceleration.

Hence   Average Acceleration = $\dfrac{\text{Increase in Velocity}}{\text{Time}}$

Consider the following example.

In an advertisement for a certain make of car it is stated that after starting from rest the car can reach a speed of 48 km/h after 10 s. What is the average acceleration of the car?

We must keep all measurements of time in the same units.

∴ We first change the speed in kilometres per hour to metres per second

$$48 \text{ km/h} = \frac{\overset{8}{\cancel{48\,000}}}{\cancel{60} \times \cancel{60}} \text{ m/s}$$

$$= \frac{80}{6} = 13{\cdot}33 \text{ m/s}$$

∴ average acceleration $= \dfrac{13{\cdot}33}{10}$ metres per second per second

$= 1{\cdot}33$ metres per second per second

(*Note:* The unit in which this acceleration is measured, i.e. metres per second per second is usually written m/s².)

Exercise 5c

1. An aeroplane reaches its 'flying speed' of 240 km/h in 6 s. What is its average acceleration in m/s²?

2. A motor car changes its speed from 16 to 64 km/h in 3½ s. What is its average acceleration (*a*) in m/s²; (*b*) km/h²?

3. A railway train travelling at 96 km/h slows down to stop at a station in 16 s. Assuming the retardation is constant, what is the average retardation in m/s²?

(*Note:* Retardation means *negative* acceleration.)

The Velocity-Time Graph

Using the same principles as we did in drawing the distance-time

SPACE AND TIME

graph to enable us to find velocity, we can also draw the velocity-time graph to find acceleration.

Referring back to the car which reached a speed of 48 km/h in 10 s with uniform acceleration we can plot the velocity-time graph as follows, Fig. 5-4.

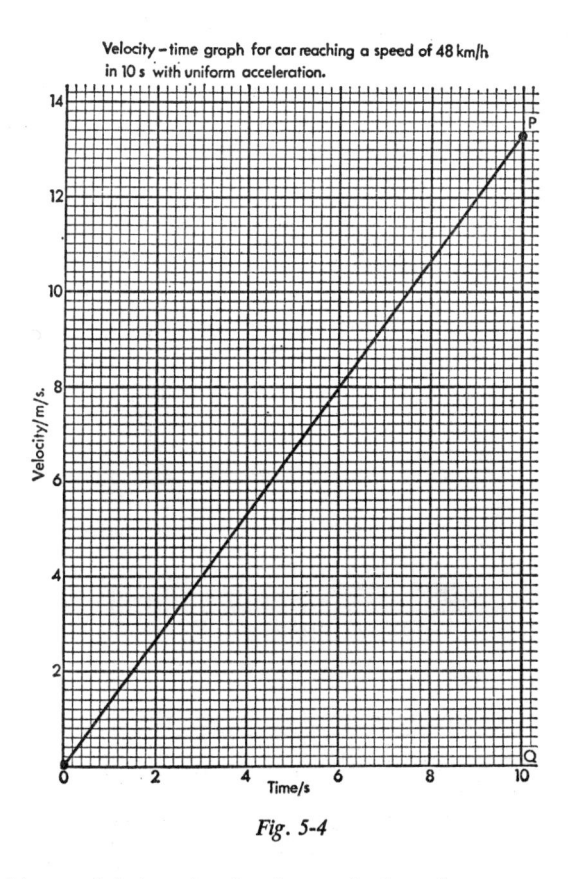

Velocity-time graph for car reaching a speed of 48 km/h in 10 s with uniform acceleration.

Fig. 5-4

Using this graph it is quite simple to calculate the average acceleration by measuring the velocity at P (i.e. the ordinate PQ) in m/s and dividing this amount by the time (i.e. the abscissa OQ) in s. Not all moving bodies move with uniform acceleration, but we can still use the velocity-time graph to find the acceleration at any given instant by calculating the *gradient* of the graph at the required instant.

75

Example

A motor car starting from rest was observed to have the velocities shown in the following table at nine one-second intervals. Find the acceleration of the car at the 6th second after the start.

Time/s	0	1	2	3	4	5	6	7	8
Velocity/m/s	0	0·17	0·7	1·5	2·7	4·17	6·0	8·17	11·0

Using this table draw the velocity-time graph thus, Fig. 5-5.

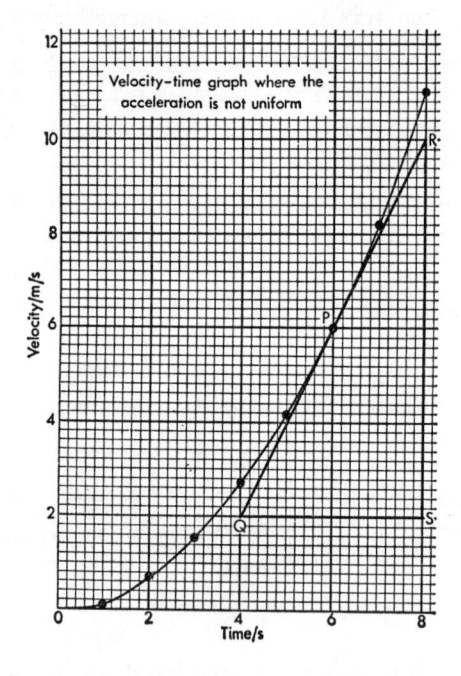

Fig. 5-5

At the point P where the abscissa is 6 draw the tangent to the curve QPR. Complete the right-angled triangle QRS making QS a convenient length for calculation purposes. Measure RS.

Then Gradient of graph $= \dfrac{RS}{QS}$

(where RS and QS are each measured to scale)

$$\therefore \text{Gradient} = \frac{8}{4} = 2$$

∴ Acceleration at 6 s after start is 2 m/s²

Exercise 5d

1. A railway train starting from rest and travelling with uniform acceleration reaches a speed of 96 km/h in 20 s. Draw the velocity-time graph and find the average acceleration during this period.

2. A racing motorist covers the first lap of the race track at an average speed of 144 km/h in 50 s. Draw his velocity-time graph assuming that his acceleration is uniform throughout and find what his average acceleration is during this period.

3. The log book of a journey made by a motorist shows that during a period of 30 s, his speed increased from 32 km/h to 80 km/h whilst during the next 20 s his speed decreased to 48 km/h. Draw the velocity-time graph for these two periods, using the same axes for both and find

(1) his average acceleration during the first period.

(2) his average retardation during the second period.

Assume that both the acceleration and retardation were uniform.

4. A motor car starts from rest, and its velocities during the first 10 s are given in the following table:

Time/s	0	1	2	3	4	5	6	7	8	9	10
Velocity/ m/s	0	0·5	2·0	4·5	8·0	12·5	18·0	24·5	32·0	40·5	50·0

Draw the velocity-time graph and find the acceleration at 5 s after the start.

5. An aeroplane 'touches down' with a ground speed of 288 km/h and finally comes to rest 20 s after touch down. The readings on the air speed indicator are taken at 2-s intervals and are given in the following table:

Time/s	0	2	4	6	8	10	12	14	16	18	20
Velocity/ km/h	288	233·3	184·3	141·1	103·7	72	46·1	25·9	11·5	2·9	0

Draw the velocity-time graph and find the retardation (*a*) 5 s; (*b*) 16 s after touch down.
Give your answers in kilometres per hour per second.

Another Use of the Velocity-Time Graph

The fundamental relationship between distance, time and speed is given by the formula $\dfrac{\text{Distance}}{\text{Time}} = \text{Speed}$

This formula could be re-written as Distance = Speed × Time; or as we would prefer to write it Distance = Average Velocity × Time. Refer back to Fig. 5-4 which showed the velocity-time graph for a car which reached a speed of 48 km/h (i.e. 13·33 m/s) in 10 s.
In this case the car started from rest so its initial velocity was 0 and its final velocity was 13·33 m/s.

$$\therefore \text{ average velocity} = \frac{0 + 13{\cdot}33}{2} \text{ m/s} = 6{\cdot}66 \text{ m/s}$$

∴ distance travelled in 10 secs. = 6·66 × 10 m = <u>66·6 m</u>

Drawing a horizontal line on the graph at A where the velocity is 6·66 m/s to meet the ordinate PQ (see Fig. 5-6) this amount is equivalent to the area of the rectangle ABQO. But △AOC and △PCB are congruent for OA = BP (both equiv. to velocities of 6·66 m/s).

$\widehat{OAC} = \widehat{PBC}$ (both right angles)

and $\widehat{ACO} = \widehat{PCB}$ (vertically opposite)

∴ the two triangles are congruent (2 angles and corresponding sides).

Hence △AOC and △PCB are equal in area

∴ Area of rectangle ABQO = Area of △OPQ

SPACE AND TIME

Velocity-time graph with uniform acceleration

Triangles AOC and PCB are equal in area

Av. velocity 6.66 m/s

The area of this rectangle represents the distance travelled at an average speed of 6.66 m/s in 10s.

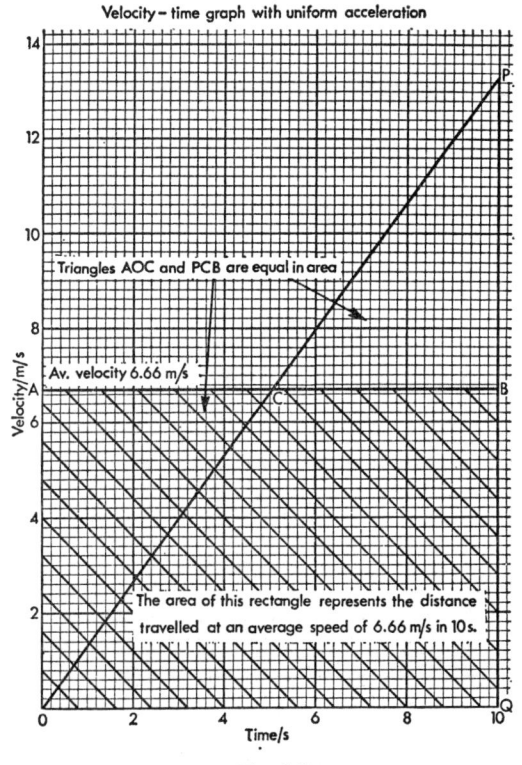

Fig. 5-6

But the area of $\triangle OPQ$ is the area *under the velocity-time graph*. Hence we may conclude that if a velocity-time graph is drawn, the area under this graph will represent the distance travelled at the given velocity in the given time.

Exercise 5e

1. In Exercise 5d Question 2 find from your graph the distance travelled in the first lap of the race.

2. In Exercise 5d Question 3 find from your graph the total distance travelled by the motorist.

It is, of course, a simple matter to calculate distance given time and average velocity without using the velocity-time graph if the acceleration is uniform. The problem becomes much more difficult

LONGMAN MATHEMATICS

when the acceleration is variable. In this case the knowledge that the area under the graph represents the distance travelled is of paramount importance for the problem then becomes merely a matter of finding this area.

Example

Question 5 in Exercise 5d gave the following table of speed readings for an aircraft after 'touch down' at 2-s intervals.

Time/s	0	2	4	6	8	10	12	14	16	18	20
Velocity/km/h	288	233·3	184·3	141·1	103·7	72	46·1	25·9	11·5	2·9	0

Drawing the velocity-time graph from these figures we get the curved line drawn in Fig. 5-7.

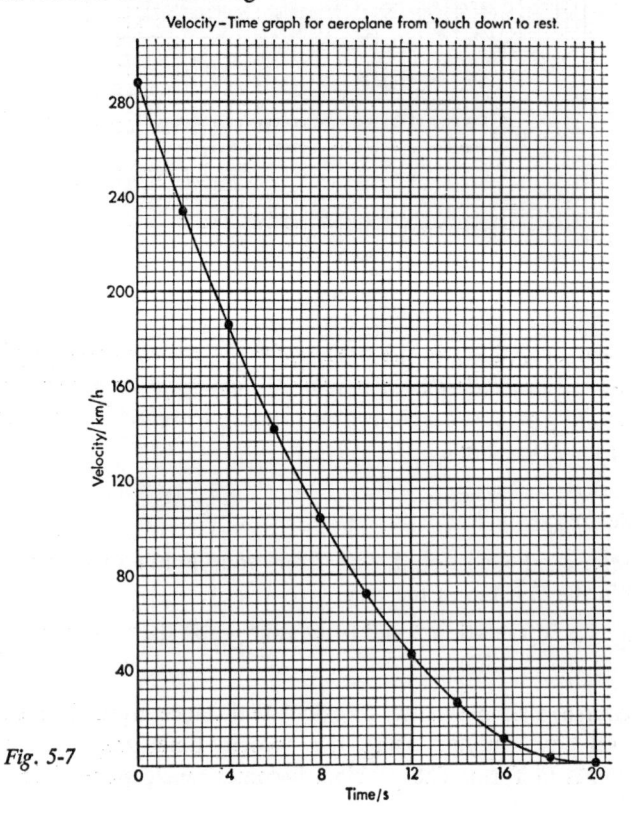

Fig. 5-7

SPACE AND TIME

To find the area under this curve we must divide it up into a number of vertical strips (or elements) find the area of each strip and add them altogether.

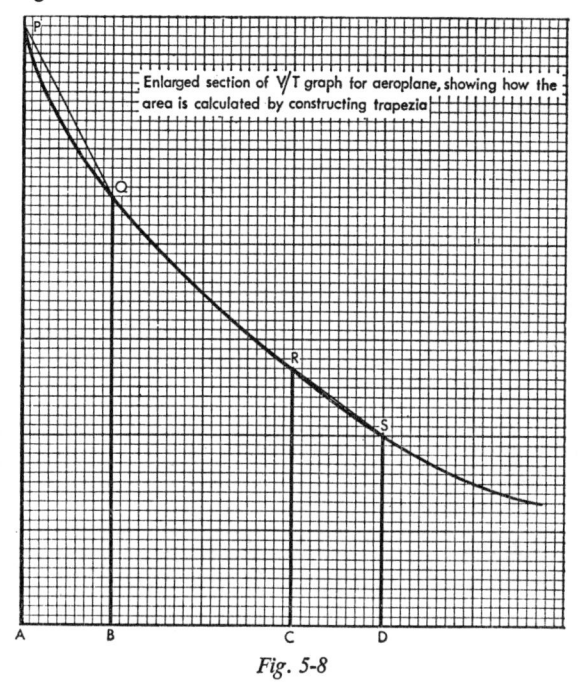

Fig. 5-8

Fig. 5-8 shows part of the graph shown in Fig. 5-7 on a large scale. P, Q, and R, S are typical points on the graph.

PA, QB, RC and SD are the ordinates at P, Q, R and S respectively, and if the points P and Q are joined by a straight line then the area under the curve PQ is approximately equal to the area of the trapezium PQBA. Similarly the area under the curve RS is approximately equal to the area of the trapezium RSDC.

But Area of trapezium = ½ sum of the parallel sides × perpendicular distance between them

∴ Area of trapezium PQBA = ½ (PA + QB) × AB

PA is a typical ordinate of the curve so we will call it y_r, QB is the next ordinate and will therefore be y_{r+1}

Hence if $\qquad AB = h$

$$\text{Area of trapezium PQBA} = h\left(\frac{y_r + y_{r+1}}{2}\right)$$

81

LONGMAN MATHEMATICS

The total area under the graph will be approximately equal to the sum of all such trapezia as PQBA; each trapezium being adjacent to the next.

Thus, if we number the ordinates as follows

$$y_0, y_1, y_2 \ldots y_n$$

then the area under the curve will be given by the formula

$$\text{Area} = h\frac{y_0 + y_1}{2} + h\frac{y_1 + y_2}{2} + h\frac{y_2 + y_3}{2}$$
$$+ \ldots + h\left(\frac{y_{n-1} + y_n}{2}\right)$$

where h is the common interval between the ordinates.

Examining this formula, we see that each ordinate except y_0 and y_r appears *twice* hence the formula may be simplified to read as follows:

$$\text{Area under graph} = h\left(\frac{y_0 + y_n}{2} + y_1 + y_2 + \ldots + y_{n-1}\right)$$

This rule may be expressed as

Area under graph

= (Mean of extreme ordinates + sum of other ordinates)
× by the common distance between the ordinates.

This rule is known as the *Trapezoidal Rule*.

Using this rule to find the distance travelled by the aeroplane after 'touch down' before coming to rest refer back to the table on p. 78. In this case

$$y_0 = 288 \quad y_1 = 233\cdot3 \quad y_2 = 184\cdot3 \quad y_3 = 141\cdot1$$
$$y_4 = 103\cdot7 \quad y_5 = 72 \quad y_6 = 46\cdot1 \quad y_7 = 25\cdot9$$
$$y_8 = 11\cdot5 \quad y_9 = 2\cdot9 \quad y_{10} = 0$$

and $$h = 2 \text{ s} = \frac{2}{60 \times 60}\text{h}$$

(*Note:* We must measure the time in hours since the speeds are given in kilometres per hour.)

∴ Area under graph, by Trapezoidal Rule

$$= h\left(\frac{288 + 0}{2} + 233\cdot3 + 184\cdot3 + 141\cdot1 + 103\cdot7 + 72 + 46\cdot1 + \right.$$
$$\left. 25\cdot9 + 11\cdot5 + 2\cdot9\right)$$

SPACE AND TIME

$$\therefore \text{Area} = \frac{2}{60 \times 60}(144 + 820\cdot8)$$

$$= \frac{2}{60 \times 60} \times 964\cdot8 = \frac{1\,929\cdot6}{3\,600}$$

$$= 0\cdot536\,2$$

Number	Log.
1 930	3·285 6
3 600	3·556 3
Subtract	$\bar{1}$·729 3

Antilog $\bar{1}$·729 3 = 0·536 2

∴ Distance travelled by plane after touch down = 0·54 km

Exercise 5f

1. From the table in Exercise 5d, no. 4 (p. 77) find the distance travelled by the car in 10 s using the Trapezoidal Rule.

2. Draw a semi-circle of radius 50 mm. Draw ordinates at intervals of 5 mm apart (including each end of the diameter) and measure their lengths. Using the Trapezoidal Rule find the area of the semi-circle. Compare your answer with that obtained by using the formula for the area of a circle taking $\pi = 3\cdot14$.

3. At a certain instant a motor car is travelling at 16 km/h, 10 s later its speed is increased to 110 km/h. The speedometer readings at each second are given in the following table:

Time/s	0	1	2	3	4	5	6	7	8	9	10
Velocity/km/h	16	17	19·8	24·6	31·4	40	50·6	63	77·4	93·8	110

Draw the velocity-time graph and find the distance travelled by the car in accelerating from 16 to 110 km/h.

4. The equation connecting velocity (v) in m/s and time (t) in s of a certain moving body is $v = 2t^2$.
Taking values of t from 0 to 10 plot the velocity-time graph and from it find

(1) the acceleration after the first 6 s
(2) the distance travelled in the 10 s

6 Similar Figures

Architects and Engineers make scale drawings (and in some cases scale models) of houses, buildings, motor cars and aeroplanes before the building is built or the machine is put together. The reason for doing this is to enable them to see what the 'finished article' is like at considerably less expense than the final cost and also to provide a series of 'working' drawings.

Exactly the same principle is applied when a map is made of a country or a continent or even when you take a photograph of a view or a person. All these are examples of figures which may be two dimensional (i.e. drawings or pictures), or three dimensional (i.e. models), which are *similar* in shape to the ultimate construction. What do we mean by the word *similar* in this connection? Mathematics is an exact science and we must therefore examine the matter more thoroughly in order to get an accurate definition.

Example

1. A map is drawn to a scale of 1 cm to 1 km. If the distance from London to Manchester is 294 km what is the distance between these two towns on the map?
Scale is 1 cm to 1 km.

∴ A distance of 294 km is represented by 294 cm

i.e.   2·94 metres

2. The representative fraction of a map is $\frac{1}{250\,000}$. What is the actual distance which is represented on the map by a distance of 4·5 cm?

Representative fraction $\frac{1}{250\,000}$.

∴ 4·5 cm on the map represents 4·5 cm × 250 000 cm on the ground

$$= \frac{4·5 \times \overset{5}{\cancel{250\,000}}}{\underset{2}{\cancel{100} \times \cancel{1\,000}}} = \frac{22·5}{2}$$

$$= 11·25 \text{ km}$$

SIMILAR FIGURES

These two examples show that there is a direct multiple relationship between scale drawing and actual distance when we are concerned with length.
Another way of stating this is to say that corresponding lengths are proportional.

Areas of similar figures

We must now examine what happens in regard to the relationships of the areas of similar figures.

Example 1

The sides of the square PQRS are three times longer than the sides of the square ABCD. What is the ratio of the area of PQRS to ABCD?

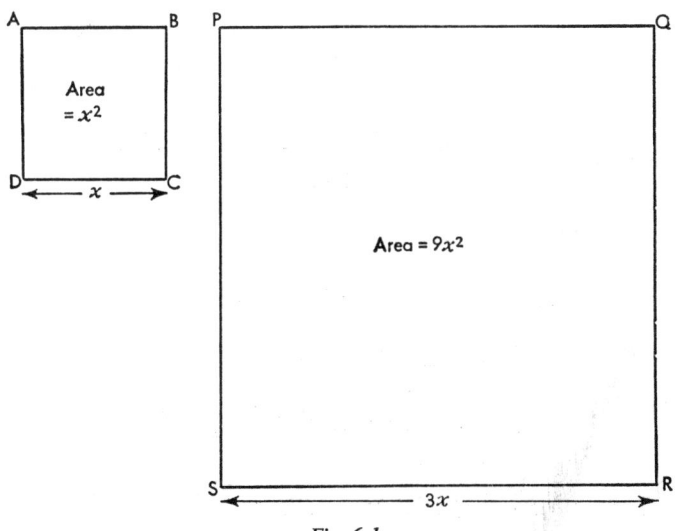

Fig. 6-1

Let the length of each side of the square ABCD be x cm.
Then the area of ABCD $= x \times x = x^2$ cm². Since each side of PQRS is three times as long as each side of ABCD the length of each side of the square PQRS is $3x$ cm.
∴ The area of PQRS $= 3x \times 3x = 9x^2$ cm².
Hence the ratio of the area of PQRS to ABCD is $9x^2 : x^2$
i.e. $9 : 1$ or $3^2 : 1$

Example 2

The triangles ABC and PQR have $\hat{A} = \hat{P}$, $\hat{B} = \hat{Q}$, $\hat{C} = \hat{R}$ and PQ = 2AB, QR = 2BC, PR = 2AC. Find the ratio of the area of $\triangle$PQR to the area of $\triangle$ABC.

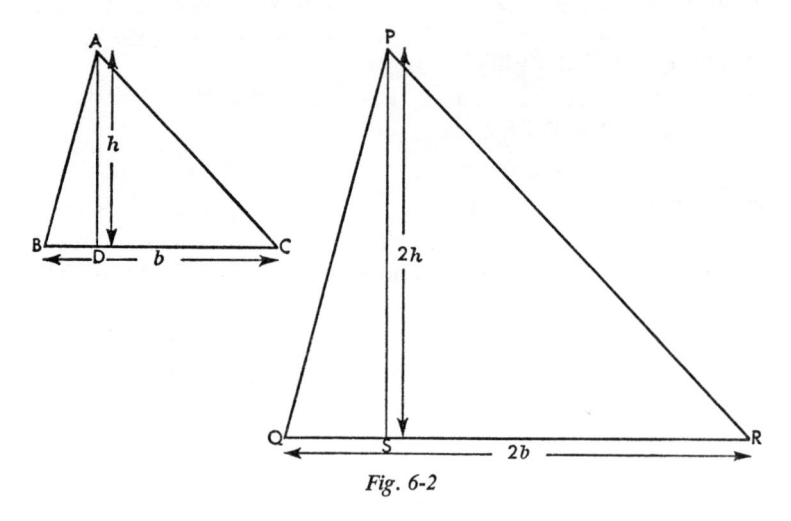

Fig. 6-2

Each of the triangles have the same shape, and when we draw the perpendicular heights PS and AD we find also that PS = 2AD. Let BC = b, AD = h then QR = $2b$, PS = $2h$.

$$\text{Area of } \triangle ABC = \frac{b \times h}{2} = \frac{bh}{2}$$

$$\text{Area of } \triangle PQR = \frac{2b \times 2h}{2} = \frac{4bh}{2}$$

Ratio of area of $\triangle$PQR to $\triangle$ABC is $4\frac{bh}{2} : \frac{bh}{2}$

i.e. $\underline{4:1 \text{ or } 2^2:1}$

Example 3

The circle centre O has a radius of r cm and the circle centre P has a radius of $4r$ cm. What is the ratio of the area of the larger circle to that of the smaller?

SIMILAR FIGURES

Area of circle centre O $= \pi r^2$
Area of circle centre P $= \pi \times (4r)^2 = 16\pi r^2$
∴ Ratio of area of larger circle to area of smaller circle is
$16\pi r^2 : \pi r^2$ i.e. 16:1 or $4^2 : 1$

These three examples show that if we have two figures having the same shape *whose linear dimensions are in a given ratio, then the areas of these figures are proportional to the squares of this ratio.*

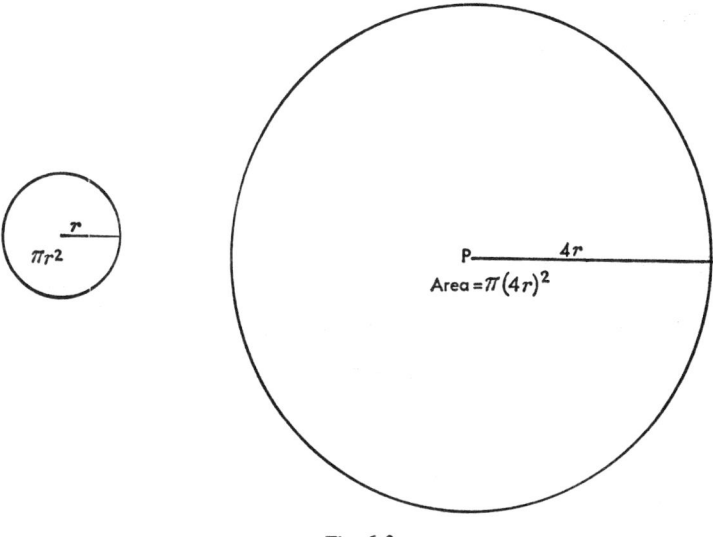

Fig. 6-3

(*Note* particularly Example 2. Every polygon (or multisided figure) can be split up into a number of triangles. Since we have proved the rule for triangles we have therefore proved it to be true for polygons.)

Exercise 6a

1a. The area of a certain triangle is 4·8 cm². What is the area of a triangle with the same shape whose sides are four times the length of the given triangle?

b. The area of a certain triangle is 36 cm². The length of its base is 8 cm. What is the length of the base of a triangle having the same shape whose area is 9 cm²?

2. Draw a circle of radius 50 mm. By stepping out distances on the circumference equal in length to the radius construct a regular hexagon ABCDEF. If O is the centre of the circle, join OA, OB.

(1) What kind of triangle is AOB?

(2) Bisect AB at P and join OP. Measure OP and calculate the area of $\triangle$AOB.

(3) Calculate the area of the hexagon ABCDEF.

3. Using the values obtained in Question 2 above, write down the area of

(1) A regular hexagon whose sides are 25 mm long.

(2) A regular hexagon whose sides are 100 mm long.

4. A film transparency 35 mm by 20 mm is projected on a screen.

(*a*) If the size of the picture on the screen is 1·75 m by 1·0 m what is the magnification of the projector?

(*Hint:* Magnification is measured by comparing areas.)

(*b*) What are the dimensions of the picture if the magnification is 1 100?

5. On squared paper draw the following irregular pentagon ABCDE. AB = 5 cm, $B\hat{A}E$ = 90°, AE = 4 cm, $A\hat{E}D$ = 120°, ED = 5 cm, $E\hat{D}C$ = 130°, DC = 3 cm.

Take a point O inside the pentagon and join OA, OB, OC, OD, OE. Produce OA to OA^1 so that $OA^1 = 20A$. Produce OB to OB^1 so that $OB^1 = 20B$, and continue this process until all the points A^1, B^1, C^1, D^1, E^1, are determined. Join $A^1B^1C^1D^1E^1$ to form a pentagon.

(*a*) Measure the lengths of the sides A^1B^1 and AB and calculate the ratio of these lengths. Repeat this process for the other sides of each of the pentagons.

(*b*) Measure the angles $O\hat{A}B$ and OA^1B^1. What can you say about the sides AB and A^1B^1? Give your reasons. Is the same fact true about all the other corresponding sides of the pentagons?

(*c*) By counting squares or by drawing and measuring appropriate lines in each of the triangles, find the ratio of the areas of the pentagons ABCDE and $A^1B^1C^1D^1E^1$. Is this the result you would have expected?

(*Note:* This exercise shows the basic principle of all projection machines where every part of the figure is projected outwards from a fixed point, i.e. the point where the source of light is placed.)

SIMILAR FIGURES

Volumes of Similar Solids

Example

1. A rectangular block is 4 cm long, 3 cm wide and 2 cm deep. Find the ratio of the volume of this block to a block having the same shape but whose linear dimensions are twice as large.

Volume of original rect. block $= 4 \times 3 \times 2$ cm$^3 = 24$ cm^3

Volume of rect. block whose linear dimensions are twice as large
$$= 8 \times 6 \times 4 \text{ cm}^3 = 192 \text{ cm}^3$$

∴ Ratio of volumes is 192:24 or 8:1, i.e. $2^3:1$

2. A triangular prism (or wedge) Fig. 6-4 has an end section with the shape of a right-angled triangle and the dimensions as shown in diagram. Find the ratio of the volume of this wedge to a wedge of a similar shape whose linear dimensions are *three* times as large.

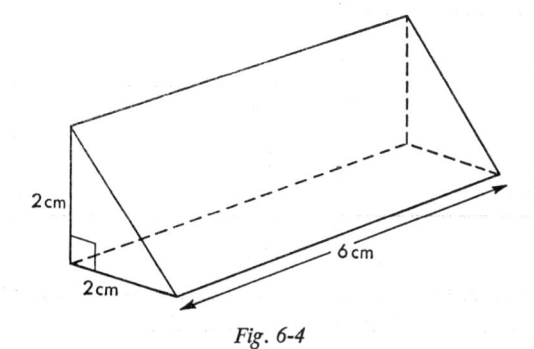

Fig. 6-4

1st Wedge

Area of end section $= \dfrac{2}{2 \times 2}$ cm$^2 = 2$ cm^2

Length of wedge $= 6$ cm

∴ Volume of wedge $= 2 \times 6 =$ <u>12 cm^3</u>

2nd Wedge

Area of end section $= \dfrac{6 \times 6}{2} = 18$ cm^2

Length of wedge $= 18$ cm

Volume of wedge $= 18 \times 18 =$ <u>324 cm^3</u>

∴ Ratio of volumes is 324:12 or 27:1, i.e. <u>$3^3:1$</u>

From these two examples we see that when we have two solids having the same shape *whose linear dimensions are in a given ratio then the volumes of these solids are proportional to the cubes of this ratio.*

Definition—Similar Polygons

Two polygons are *similar* if (*a*) they have equal angles and (*b*) corresponding sides are proportional.
Note: Both conditions are necessary for it is possible to have two polygons which have their angles equal but they are *not* similar.
For example, the square ABCD and the rectangle PQRS (see Fig. 6-5) have equal angles but they are not similar.

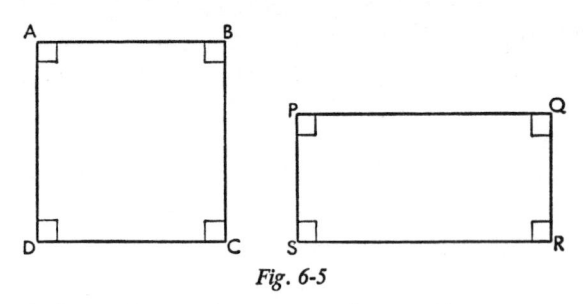

Fig. 6-5

Likewise it is possible to have two polygons whose corresponding sides are proportional but they are not similar.
For example, the square ABCD and the rhombus PQRS (see Fig. 6-6) have corresponding sides proportional but they are not similar.

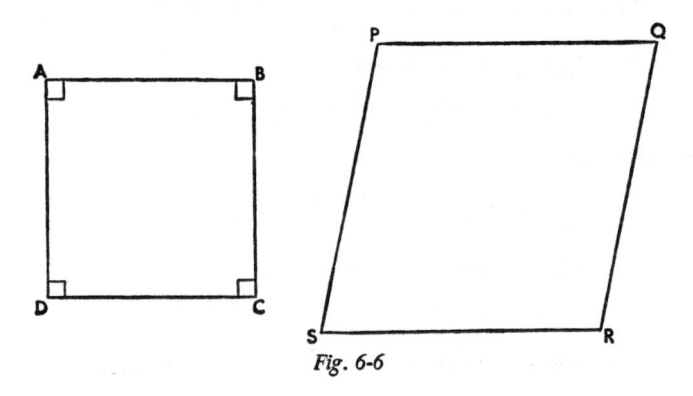

Fig. 6-6

SIMILAR FIGURES

Exercise 6b

1. A model of a boat is made to a scale of 1 to 50 in linear dimensions. If the volume of the model is 6 cm³, what is the volume of the boat? (Ans. to nearest m³.)

2. On squared paper draw a regular hexagon ABCDEF whose sides are 50 mm long. How would you draw a similar hexagon whose sides are 1·5 times as long as those of ABCDEF? Find the area of ABCDEF, and without making any further measurements calculate the area of the larger hexagon. Check your result by measurement.

3. Draw the triangle ABC in which BC = 50 mm, $\widehat{ABC}$ = 64° and $\widehat{ACB}$ = 48°.
Draw also the triangle PQR in which QR = 100 mm, PQR = 64° and $\widehat{PRQ}$ = 48°.
Measure the lengths of the sides AB, AC, PQ, RR, and find the values of the following ratios $\frac{AB}{PQ}, \frac{BC}{QR}, \frac{AC}{PR}$. Are these triangles similar?

4. Draw the triangles ABC, PQR, given that AB = 400 mm, AC = 75 mm, $\widehat{BAC}$ = 60° and that PQ = 50 mm, PR = 37·5 mm, $\widehat{QPR}$ = 60°.
Measure the angles $\widehat{ABC}, \widehat{ACB}, \widehat{PQR}, \widehat{PRQ}$. Are these two triangles similar?

Similar Triangles

Questions 3 and 4 in the above exercise and many others like them show us that in the case of triangles the length of the sides can be decreased or increased in any ratio without altering its angles. Likewise if the sides are proportional then the triangles are equiangular. Thus for triangles *either* of the two conditions for similar polygons are sufficient to prove that they are similar. Hence we may say:
(1) If two triangles are equiangular they are similar.
(2) If the three sides of one triangle are proportional, each to each, with the three sides of another triangle then the two triangles are equiangular and, therefore, similar.

Example

1. In the △ ABC, PQ is parallel to BC. Prove that the triangles ABC, APQ are similar.

Proof: In the △s ABC, APQ, Fig. 6-7,
PQ is parallel to BC.
∴ $A\hat{P}Q = A\hat{B}C$ (corresponding angles)
and $A\hat{Q}P = A\hat{C}B$ (corresponding angles)
and $B\hat{A}C$ is common to both triangles
∴ △s ABC, APQ are equiangular
∴ △s ABC, APQ are similar

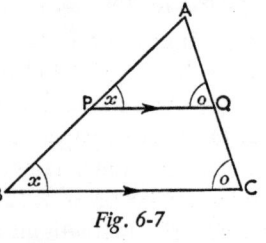

Fig. 6-7

and therefore corresponding sides are proportional

i.e. $$\frac{AP}{AB} = \frac{AQ}{AC} = \frac{PQ}{BC}$$

Exercise 6c

1. Prove that the △s ABC and PQR, Fig. 6-8, are similar, giving reasons for your answer.

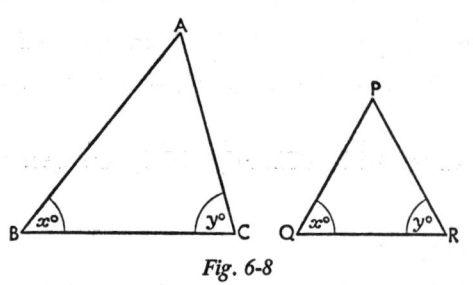

Fig. 6-8

2. Prove that the △s PQR, LMN, Fig. 6-9, are similar, giving reasons for your answer.

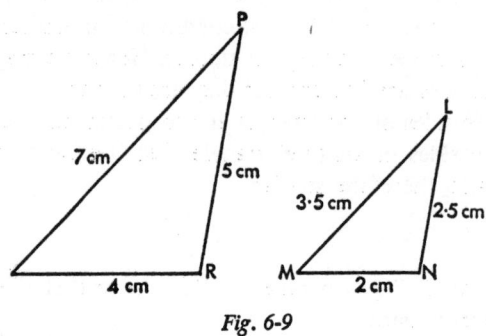

Fig. 6-9

SIMILAR FIGURES

3. In Fig. 6-10 prove that the triangles AOB, COD are similar.

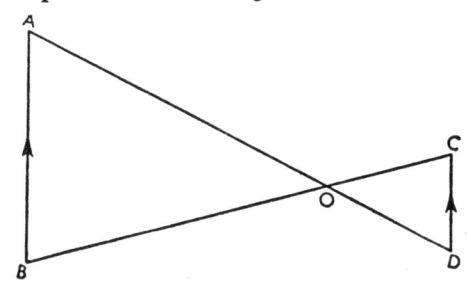

Fig. 6-10

4. In Fig. 6-11 AE = 6 cm, EC = 7·2 cm, and CD = 9 cm. Prove that △s AEB, ECD are similar and calculate the length of AB.

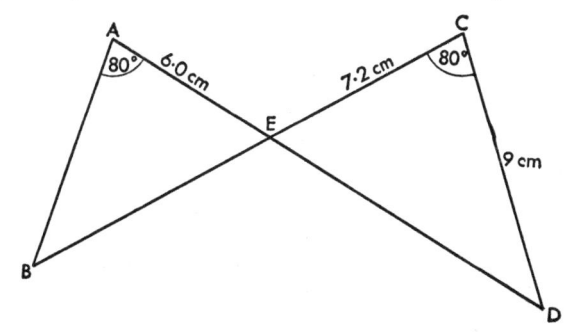

Fig. 6-11

5. At a certain moment a vertical pole 3 m high casts a shadow whose length is 2·5 m. If at the same moment a vertical tower casts a shadow whose length is 15 m, what is the height of the tower?

6. In Fig. 6-12 prove that the △s ABC and ABD are similar. Using this fact complete the ratio

$$\frac{BC}{AB} = \frac{AB}{?}$$

Prove also that the △s ABC, ACD are similar and complete the ratio

$$\frac{BC}{AC} = \frac{AC}{?}$$

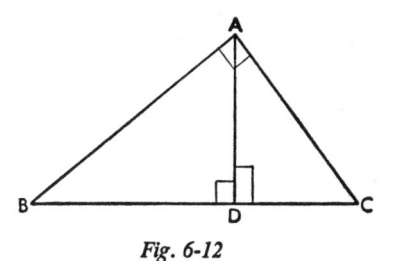

Fig. 6-12

Can you use these results to prove the theorem of Pythagoras?

7 Civic Arithmetic

We all pay rates and taxes. What are these? why do we pay them? and how are they collected?

In general terms, taxes are levied by Her Majesty's Government. Each year the Chancellor of the Exchequer is faced with certain bills which will have to be paid. Thus he receives estimates from, e.g. the Minister of Defence, the Secretaries of State for Social Services and for Education and Science, giving him details of the expected cost of the Armed Services, the provision and maintenance of hospitals and other aspects of the National Health Scheme, the provision and maintenance of schools and colleges. The Chancellor knows also that a certain amount of money will be necessary to pay the interest on National Savings and other forms of public investment. From all the information he receives the Chancellor produces, usually early in April each year, his Annual Budget. On one side of this account he shows how much money will be required to meet all the estimates, on the other he shows the method by which this money will be raised. (The following work is based on taxes in force in 1969/70.) Taxes are of two kinds.

(1) *Direct Taxes.* Every person who earns over a certain amount in salary, wages or fees must pay Income Tax. This is a tax levied on each individual's earnings and is a direct tax.

(2) *Indirect Taxes.* When you buy certain items, e.g. motor cars, leather goods, television sets, a certain percentage is added to the basic price in the form of what is called Purchase Tax. If you buy petrol, tobacco, certain kinds of sweets and chocolate and many other commodities the price you pay includes a certain amount which is repaid to the Government in the form of a sales tax. For example, for each gallon of petrol which costs 34 p to the motorist, 17 p is reclaimed as tax. On commodities which are imported from abroad, e.g. scent or wine, there is an import duty which is contained in the price the customer pays. All these are examples of indirect taxes.

Income Tax

As the law stands at the moment every person who receives an annual income over £255·00 a year must pay Income Tax, but he may claim certain reliefs as follows:

CIVIC ARITHMETIC

(*i*) *Superannuation Payments*, i.e. payments towards a retirement pension.

(*ii*) *Earned Income Allowance*, $\frac{2}{9}$ of first £4 005, and $\frac{1}{9}$ of the next £5 940.

Personal Allowance. If you are a single person, a widow or widower, a personal allowance of £200 will be given.

Married Man's Allowance. £340·00 maximum.

Children's Allowance. An allowance may be claimed for Children as follows.

Under 11	£115·00
11–16	£140·00
Over 16 if still receiving full time education	£165·00

Allowance for Life Insurance Premiums. An allowance according to a scale may be claimed for Annual Life Insurance Premiums.

These are the main 'reliefs' which may be set against 'gross income' and what remains, the 'net income' is subject to tax as follows:

first £260·00 at 30%
(i.e. 30 p in the pound)

the balance (if any) at the 'standard rate' of 41·25% (i.e. 41·25 p in the pound).

Using this information we may now consider some typical examples.

1. Tom Jones, aged $17\frac{1}{2}$ years, earns an average weekly wage of £8·50. If he pays 5 per cent of his wages to a Pension Fund what amount of Income Tax will he have to pay?

Gross Annual Wages $= 52 \times £8·50 = £442·00$

Superannuation at 5 per cent $= £\dfrac{5}{100} \times 442 = £22·10$

∴ Wages after paying superannuation $= £442·00 - £22·10$
$= £419·90$

Reliefs

Earned Income $= £\frac{2}{9} \times 419·90$

$= \dfrac{£839·80}{9} = £93·31$

95

Personal Allowance = £200·00
Total Reliefs = £293·31
∴ Net Taxable Income = £419·90 − £293·31 = £116·59

Income Tax at 30 p in the pound = $£\dfrac{30}{100} \times 116·59$

$= £\dfrac{349·77}{10} = £34·98$

2. Mr Smith is married with two children, one aged 10 years and the other 15 years of age, both attending school. If Mr Smith's annual salary is £2 500 and he pays 5 per cent to a Superannuation Fund what amount of Income Tax will he be liable to pay?

Gross Annual Salary = £2 500
Superannuation at 5 per cent = £ 125
∴ Salary less Superannuation = £2 375

Reliefs

Earned Income = $£\tfrac{2}{9} \times 2\ 375$

$= £\dfrac{4\ 750}{9} = £527·78$

Personal allowance for Mr and Mrs
Smith = £340·00
Children's allowance = £115 + £140 = £255·00
∴ Total Relief = £1 122·78

Hence net taxable income = £2 375·00 − £1 122·78 = £1 252·22

Of this £260 is taxed at 30 p in the pound (30%) and the remainder £1 252·22 − £260·00 = £992·22 is taxed at 41·25 p in the pound (41·25%).

∴ Tax paid is $£260·00 \times \dfrac{30}{100} = £\dfrac{780·00}{10} = £78·00$

$+ £992·22 \times \dfrac{41·25}{100} = £409·29$

∴ Total Tax paid = £487·29

Note: If Mr Smith had taken out a Life Insurance which cost him, for example, £100 a year in premium, he would have reduced his taxable income by $£\tfrac{2}{5} \times 100$, i.e. £40, and since this would be taxed at the standard rate of 41·25 p in the pound, in addition to taking wise precautions for himself and his family it is a good business proposition!

CIVIC ARITHMETIC

Exercise 7a

1. What amount of Income Tax will be paid by a man whose *net* taxable income is £400·00 if the first £260·00 is taxed at 30% and the remainder at 41·25%?

2. Assuming that taxes are levied at the same rate as in Question 1, find the amount of income tax paid by a man whose net taxable income is £700·00.

3. How much tax relief can a man claim if he is
(a) married and has no children;
(b) married and has two children aged 2 years and 8 years;
(c) married and has 3 children aged 7, 11, 16 years all receiving full-time education?
(Refer to the information on p. 93.)

4. What amount of income tax will John Smith have to pay if his annual salary is £750·00? You may assume that the total amount of relief he can claim from every source is £400·00 and that the first £260·00 is taxed at 30% and the balance at 41·25%.

5. Mary Jones, aged 16½ years, earns an annual salary of £360·00 as a typist. Using the information given in this chapter find the amount of Income Tax she pays, assuming that she contributes 5 per cent of her salary towards a Superannuation Fund.

6. Mr Brown is married and earns an annual salary of £1 500·00. He has one son aged 8 years and pays a contribution of 5 per cent towards his Superannuation Fund. Using the information contained in this chapter, how much Income Tax does he pay?

7. You will notice, if you examine the information contained in this chapter carefully, that the first £78·00 of any Income Tax paid represents £260·00 of taxable income. All other tax paid is assessed at the rate of 41·25 p in the pound. If
(a) a man pays £390 tax in all, what was the total amount of his taxable income?
(b) a man pays £465 tax in all, what was the total amount of taxable income?

8. Mr Scott is married and has three sons aged 7, 13 and 17 years respectively, all of whom are in full-time attendance at school. After he has paid a contribution to his pension fund his salary amounts to £1 800·00. If he pays an annual Life Insurance Premium of £150·00 on which he can claim two-fifths tax relief, use the information contained in this chapter to calculate his Income Tax.

Calculations of this kind have to be made by Income Tax Inspectors and Accountants. To save work, however, tables are drawn up which give Code Numbers appropriate to certain relief scales and by references to these the Income Tax to be deducted can be found immediately.

Rates

Rates are really local taxes. Every person who owns any property within a town or a country must pay a rate which is assessed according to the floor area which the property occupies. Even if you occupy property which you do not own but for which you pay rent, part of the rent covers the cost of the rates which the property owner has to pay. Rates which are collected are used to pay for local services, e.g. Education, Fire Brigade services, Police, Public Libraries. This amount is calculated in the same way as taxes. The total cost of all public services in a town or county is computed by the Borough or County Treasurer, the rateable values of all properties within the area are assessed by the Valuation Officer. The number and names of all property holders within the area are also registered at the Town or County Hall, and from all this information the Annual Rate in the pound is determined.

Consider the following examples:

1. A man owns a property whose rateable value is £150·00. If the Annual Rate is 45 p in the pound, how much does he pay in rates?

For each £1 of rateable property owned he pays 45 p.

For a property valued at £150·00 he pays $£150 \times \dfrac{45}{100} = £\dfrac{135}{2}$

$= £67·50$

This rate is usually collected in two half-yearly contributions.

CIVIC ARITHMETIC

2. One of the most valuable pieces of information that a Borough or County Treasurer has is what is known as 'The Product of a Penny Rate'. This amount is the total sum of money which would be collected if each ratepayer paid one penny in the pound on all his property at the assessed rateable value.

Consider a man whose house has a rateable value of £134·00. In his case if he were charged a 'penny rate' he would pay 134 pence, i.e. £1·34. This information is not very useful since rates are very much more than one penny in the pound! But the product of a penny rate over the *whole area* is important, e.g. in a certain area of Surrey the product of a penny rate is estimated to be £37 500. If the local rates are 44 p in the pound what is the total amount of rates collected?

Product of a penny rate = £37 500
Annual Rate = 44 p in the pound
∴ Total amount collected in rates = £37 500 × 44
= £1 650 000

3. The product of a penny rate is also used for calculating the actual Annual Rate.

For example, the costs of local services in a certain town were estimated to be £3 250 000. The estimated product of a penny rate is £50 000. What Annual Rate must be levied to cover the cost of local services?

Cost of local services = £3 250 000
Product of penny rate = £50 000

∴ Annual Rate $= \dfrac{3\ 250\ 000}{50\ 000}$

= 65 p
∴ Annual Rate in the pound is 65 p

You will notice that rates are calculated only by reference to the assessed value of the property owned. The number of people residing in the property and their personal incomes in no way affect the rates. Because of this some people think that levying of rates is an unfair way of collecting taxes. Nonetheless most people agree that if services such as Police, Fire Brigade and Education, had to be paid by individuals rather than by the community as a whole it would be more expensive for each individual person.

Exercise 7b

1. In a certain borough the rates are $42\frac{1}{2}$ p in the pound. If a man owns property assessed at £110 000 rateable value, how much does he pay in rates?

2. In a certain district the product of a penny rate is assessed to be £30 000. The local rates are 45 p in the pound of which $37\frac{1}{2}$ p is the 'education' rate. What is
   (a) the total amount of rates collected in the district in one year?
   (b) the total amount of money spent on education during the year?

3. The total cost of all local services in an area during a certain year is £21 000 000. The product of a penny rate is assessed to be £350 000. What rate in the pound will need to be levied to cover the costs?

4. A man pays £4·50 per week in rent and rates. Assuming 50 per cent of his weekly payments are for rates and that the local rate is 45 p in the pound, what is the assessed rateable value of the house he is renting?

5. In 1962 a house was assessed at a rateable value of £62 and the local rates were £1·$12\frac{1}{2}$ in the pound. In 1963 the house was reassessed at £175 and the local rates were 45 p in the pound. In which year did he pay more rates and by how much?

Heating and Lighting

Nowadays most people have electric light, and may heat their houses by gas and electricity. The various Electrical and Gas Boards have arrangements whereby charges are made at the Standard Rate or at Special Tariff Rates.

For example a Gas Board has the following rates:

(1) *Standard Rate*
   Primary Charge 35 p per quarter + Gas at 12 p per therm.
(2) *Two Part Tariff*
   Standard charge £1·$62\frac{1}{2}$ per quarter + Gas at 8 p per therm.
(3) *Special Heavy User Tariff*
   Standing charge £2·60 per quarter + Gas at 7 p per therm.

Example

A man uses 30 therms of gas in a quarter. What amount must he pay per quarter if he is charged

(a) at the standard rate;
(b) at the two part tariff rate?

Standard Rate is 35 p per therm + 12 p primary charge
∴ 30 therms cost 30 × 12 p + 35 p
= 360 + 35 p = 395 p
= £3·95

Two Part Tariff Rate is 8 p per therm + £1·62½ standing charge
∴ 30 therms cost 30 × 8 p + 162½ p
= 240 + 162½ p = 402½ p
= £4·02½

∴ It would pay him to be charged at the Standard Rate.

Exercise 7c

1. If I use 60 therms of gas in a quarter what would be the cost at (a) the standard rate, (b) the two part tariff?

2. A householder uses 180 therms of gas in a quarter. If he is given the chance of paying his bill at either the 'domestic tariff rate' or the 'heavy duties rate' which should he choose? If he chooses this method how much will he save?

Electricity

An Electricity Board has the following choices for domestic use of electricity.

(1) *Two Part Rate*

  (a) A Unit Charge of 0·7 p per unit.

  (b) A Standing Charge for each quarter as follows:

When area of residence does not exceed 80 m² . £1·03
,, ,, ,, ,, ,, ,, ,, 100 m² . £1·19
,, ,, ,, ,, ,, ,, ,, 120 m² . £1·36
,, ,, ,, ,, ,, ,, ,, 140 m² . £1·52
,, ,, ,, ,, ,, ,, ,, 160 m² . £1·68

For each 20 m² (or part thereof) in excess of
160 m², but not exceeding 300 m² . . . . 15 p
For each 50 m² in excess of 300 m² . . . . 31 p

(2) *Flat Rates*

For each unit supplied $2\frac{1}{2}$ p per unit except that for each unit supplied through a separate meter and used for purposes other than lighting 1 p per unit.

Exercise 7d

1. A man whose house has an area of 120 m² uses 300 units of electricity in a certain quarter. How much will he pay if he uses:
(*a*) the Two Part Tariff, (*b*) the Flat Rate Scheme?

2. A man occupies a house whose floor area is 140 m². He uses 650 units of electricity in a quarter. If he uses the two-part tariff scheme how much will he be required to pay?

3. During the summer quarter a man who occupies a flat whose area is 50 m² uses 30 units of electricity, of which 10 units are for heating purposes. Which is the cheaper scheme, the two-part tariff or the flat rate and how much difference is there between the two?

4. At the end of a quarter a man who occupies a house whose floor area is 200 m² receives two accounts as follows:
Amount of electricity consumed = 500 units.
Amount of gas consumed = 100 therms.
If he uses the two-part tariff in each case what total amount must he pay for heating and lighting?

8 Statistics

Statistical Averages

In Stage 3 we saw how to find the first of the statistical averages, the arithmetic mean. We also saw that this average had certain real disadvantages. For example, in the question concerning the number of goals scored by teams in the First Division at the end of the 1968/69 season the arithmetic mean came to 52·9—and no team can score this number of goals.

The greatest disadvantage of the arithmetic mean is, however, that it is unduly affected by extreme items.
Suppose your pocket money for five successive weeks is 70 p, 75 p, 90 p, 85 p, 80 p, then your average pocket money is

$$\frac{70\ p + 75\ p + 90\ p + 85\ p + 80\ p}{5} = \frac{400\ p}{5} = 80\ p$$

Hence arithmetic mean is 80 p.
During the sixth week let us suppose you receive a birthday gift of £2·00 from an uncle, the arithmetic mean for the six weeks would be

$$\frac{400\ p + 200\ p}{6} = \frac{600\ p}{6} = 100\ p$$

But it would be quite wrong to say that your average pocket money was 100 p a week!
Recognizing these disadvantages we must therefore consider other statistical averages which can provide us with more useful information. The first of these is called the *median*. The median is defined as follows. Suppose we have a number of items which are arranged in ascending or descending order then the median is the one which is half way along the series. Thus, in general, there will be equal numbers of items above and below the median. Referring back to the table of English and Mathematics marks for Set B we can rearrange the marks in descending order as in Table 1.
In the Table 1 col. 3 shows the mathematics marks in percentages written in descending order of merit, the figures being taken from col. 2. Since there are 35 items in all the median value is the 18th item (there are 17 items above and 17 items below)

$$\therefore \text{Median Value} = 64 \text{ per cent}$$

LONGMAN MATHEMATICS

Table 1: English Set B

1 ENGLISH % IN ALPHABETICAL ORDER	2 MATHEMATICS % IN ALPHABETICAL ORDER	3 MATHEMATICS % IN DESCENDING ORDER OF MERIT (TAKEN FROM COL. 2)	4 ENGLISH % IN DESCENDING ORDER OF MERIT (TAKEN FROM COL. 1)
35	32	199	
64	52	96	
56	31	95	
63	74	89	
48	58	89	
42	31	89	
64	12	84	
38	89	80	
40	69	78	
33	89	76	
44	75	75	
38	57	75	
35	199	75	
41	84	74	
59	36	69	
46	75	68	
36	64	67	
73	36	64 median value	
55	27	58	
55	30	58	
57	95	57	
51	26	52	
42	67	38	
48	76	37	
46	96	36	
60	37	36	
36	89	32	
31	80	31	
51	78	31	
49	68	30	
51	26	27	
58	17	26	
45	75	26	
57	38	17	
52	58	12	

104

STATISTICS

Table 2: English Set A

1 ENGLISH % IN ALPHABETICAL ORDER	2 MATHEMATICS % IN ALPHABETICAL ORDER	3 ENGLISH % IN DESCENDING ORDER OF MERIT	4 MATHEMATICS % IN DESCENDING ORDER OF MERIT
69	69		
58	25		
61	64		
Abs.	65		
62	80		
66	82		
46	27		
51	96		
54	71		
62	74		
68	70		
78	27		
59	74		
67	80		
64	55		
69	75		
60	33		
66	31		
68	94		
63	100		
72	61		
75	77		
Abs.	80		
68	24		
53	80		
75	97		
74	82		
72	81		
65	91		
58	71		
80	74		
63	95		
55	63		
58	86		

105

Exercise 8a

Complete col. 4 in Table 1 and find the median value for English marks.

We were able to find the exact value of the median from this table because there was an odd number (35) of separate items. If, however, we examine the English and Mathematics marks for set A we find there are even numbers (32 and 34) of separate items. In this case the median is halfway between the two middle items and is found by taking the average of these two.

Exercise 8b

Table 2 shows the English and Mathematics marks for set A. Complete cols. 3 and 4 and find the median values of English and Mathematics marks for set A.

Note: In the case of English the median will be between the 16th and 17th item (when arranged in descending order of merit) and will be the average of these two items. In the case of Mathematics the median will be between the 17th and 18th item (when arranged in descending order of merit) and will be the average of these two items.

Table 3: English Marks for Set A Ranged in Groups of Five Marks

1 MARKS	2 NUMBER IN SET A
45–49	1
50–54	3
55–59	5
60–64	7
65–69	9
70–74	3
75–79	3
80–84	1

STATISTICS

Calculation of the Median

If we have a long list of separate items in any statistical distribution sorting them into descending order or ascending order becomes very laborious so we prefer to find a simple method based on the frequency distribution.

Using the figures for English in set A we found the frequency distribution as shown in Table 3.

From this table we can construct a *cumulative frequency table* by merely adding the items in col. 2 and amending col. 1 to show the number of candidates who scored less than a certain number of marks. The table then becomes:

Table 4: Cumulative Frequency Table

ENGLISH MARKS	NUMBER IN SET A
Not more than 50	1
,, ,, ,, 55	$1 + 3 = 4$
,, ,, ,, 60	$1 + 3 + 5 = 9$
,, ,, ,, 65	$1 + 3 + 5 + 7 = 16$
,, ,, ,, 70	$1 + 3 + 5 + 7 + 9 = 25$
,, ,, ,, 75	$1 + 3 + 5 + 7 + 9 + 3 = 28$
,, ,, ,, 80	$1 + 3 + 5 + 7 + 9 + 3 + 3 = 31$
,, ,, ,, 85	$1 + 3 + 5 + 7 + 9 + 3 + 3 + 1 = 32$

Plot these points as a *cumulative frequency curve* as shown in Fig. 8-1. Since there are 32 items in the above cumulative frequency table the median will occur halfway between the 16th and 17th item. At the point $16\frac{1}{2}$ on the vertical axis draw a line parallel to the horizontal axis to meet the graph. At this point of contact draw a line parallel to the vertical axis to meet the horizontal axis. The reading on the horizontal axis gives the required median. From the graph the median value is 65·5 marks.

Fig. 8-1

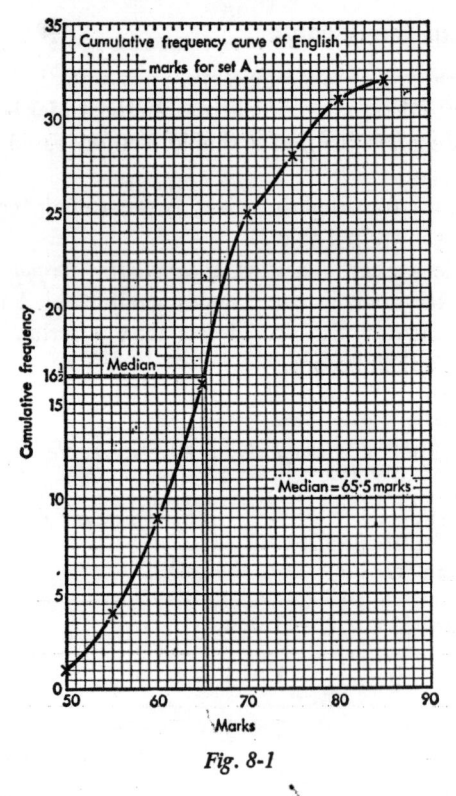

Exercise 8c

1. Using the Mathematics marks for set A (see Table 2, p. 105) draw up
   (a) a frequency table for groups of 5 mark ranges;
   (b) the corresponding cumulative frequency table.
Plot the corresponding cumulative frequency graph and using the graph find the median value of the marks.

2. Using the English and Mathematics marks for set B (see Table 1, p. 104) construct
   (a) a frequency table for groups of 5 mark ranges;
   (b) the corresponding cumulative frequency tables.
Plot the corresponding cumulative frequency graph and using the graph find the median values of the English and Mathematics marks for set A. Compare your results with those obtained by writing the actual marks in descending order of merit.

STATISTICS

3. Define median value. Why is the median more useful than the arithmetic mean for statistical analysis? 100 candidates recently sat for an examination and the frequency distribution in ranges of 5 marks is shown in the following table.

Mark Range	0–4	5–9	10–14	15–19	20–24
Number of Candidates	8	24	38	27	3

Construct the corresponding cumulative frequency table and draw the cumulative frequency graph. From the graph find the median value of the marks concerned.

Using the cumulative frequency curve [sometimes called the ogive (pronounced ojive)] is the simplest way to find the median, though obviously the degree of accuracy obtained depends upon the scale which can be used for the axes of the graph. The larger the scale used the more accurate will be the result. The median can, however, be calculated from the cumulative frequency table using the method of 'proportional variation'. Consider again the cumulative frequency table marks in set A (Table 4, p. 107).

ENGLISH MARKS	NUMBER IN SET A
Not more than 50	1
,, ,, ,, 55	4
,, ,, ,, 60	9
,, ,, ,, 65	16
,, ,, ,, 65	16 >Median occurs at $16\frac{1}{2}$
,, ,, ,, 70	25
,, ,, ,, 75	28
,, ,, ,, 80	31
,, ,, ,, 95	32

Since there are 32 items the median will occur halfway between the 16th and 17th item, i.e. 16½th.

A glance at the table shows that the median value of the marks will be between 65 and 70. The range of the marks is 5 and the interval between the number of items within this range is 9. Moreover, the interval between 16 and 16½ is ½.

∴ To find the median we must increase the value of the mark at the 16th item by $5 \times \frac{\frac{1}{2}}{9}$.

Hence   Median Value $= 65 + 5 \times \frac{\frac{1}{2}}{9}$

$$= 65 + \frac{5}{18} = 65 + 0 \cdot 3$$

$$= 63 \cdot 3 \text{ to one place of decimals}$$

In general it is much easier to find the median by drawing the cumulative frequency graph (or ogive). Notice particularly the characteristic S-shape which is obtained when the ogive is drawn.

The Quartiles

The median is an average or type which depends on its position in the group for its value. Other positions in the group may also be taken as types, the most usual being the *quartiles*. The quartiles divide the group into four equal parts, the *lower quartile* (Q1) being the item which corresponds with the position one quarter of the way along the distribution and the *upper quartile* (Q3) being the item which corresponds with the position three-quarters of the way along the distribution. Once again, these two values are most simply obtained by referring to the cumulative frequency graph (or ogive). Fig 8-2 shows the position of the median and upper and lower quartiles for the distribution above.

In certain cases other position types may be required. These are *deciles and percentiles,* the former divides the group into 10 equal parts and the latter into 100 equal parts. Deciles and percentiles may be obtained from the ogive or calculated by the same method as that used for finding the median or quartiles.

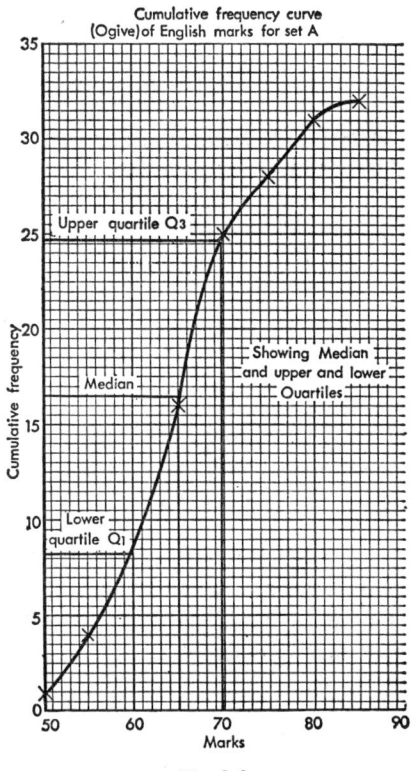

STATISTICS

Fig. 8-2 — Cumulative frequency curve (Ogive) of English marks for set A, showing Median and upper and lower Quartiles.

Exercise 8d

1. In an examination the following frequency distribution of marks was obtained.

Groups	11–15	16–20	21–25	26–30	31–35	36–40
Frequency	5	16	24	39	50	61
Groups	41–45	46–50	51–55	56–60	61–65	66–70
Frequency	68	63	72	65	48	32
Groups	71–75	76–80	81–85	86–90	91–95	96–100
Frequency	25	18	15	9	9	5

111

Construct the cumulative frequency table and draw the corresponding ogive.

Using the graph find (*a*) the median, (*b*) upper and lower quartiles.

2. The results, correct to the nearest centimetre, of measurements of the heights of 100 children are as follows:

Height/cm	150	152	154	156	158	160	162	164	166
Frequency	2	0	15	29	25	12	10	4	3

(*i*) From these figures find the arithmetic mean of the heights.

(*ii*) Construct the cumulative frequency table and draw the corresponding cumulative frequency graph. Using the graph find the median and lower and upper quartiles.

3. An examiner is asked to mark 105 scripts. He submits his results to the Examination Board concerned in the following form. (The pass marks is in the range 40–54, hence the reason for the frequency being given for each mark in this range.)

Marks	0–4	5–9	10–14	15–19	20–24	25–29	30–34	35–39
Number of Candidates	1	2	5	0	2	3	5	6

Marks	40	41	42	43	44	45	46	47	48	49	50	51	52	53	54
Number of Candidates	3	2	4	1	7	3	1	2	2	2	1	2	1	3	0

Marks	55–59	60–64	65–69	70–74	75–79	80–84	85–89	90–94	95–100
Number of Candidates	14	10	10	6	3	2	1	1	0

Rearrange this table in the form of a frequency table in groups of 5 marks 0–4, 5–9, etc. Construct the cumulative frequency table

STATISTICS

and draw the corresponding ogive. Find the median and the upper and lower quartiles.

The Mode

Though the median suffers from less disadvantages than the arithmetic mean it does not always provide the most useful information. For example if you owned a shoe shop and you were required to order a stock of shoes of different sizes, in addition to knowing the range of sizes you require you would particularly want to know what the most popular size is. If you know this you can then plan your order to ensure that more shoes of this size are ordered.

In any distribution the item which occurs most frequently, that is the *most fashionable item, is called the mode*. In many ways the mode gives a better picture of a distribution than either the arithmetic mean or the median.

If the frequency table is given so that each measurement is stated separately with the corresponding frequency, then it is very simple to find the mode.

e.g. *Measurement of height of 100 children.*

Height/cm	150	152	154	156	158	160	162	164	166
Frequency	2	0	15	29	25	12	10	4	3

Examining this table it is immediately obvious that the most popular (or most fashionable) height is 156 cm, as 29 of the hundred children examined have this height.

Hence the Mode of this distribution is 156 cm.

Frequency distributions, however, are not usually given such fine gradings. More often we find the frequencies given or we calculate them over a range. Look at the frequency table for the English marks for set A (Table 5, p. 114).

Examining the table we see that the 'most fashionable' or modal range of marks occurs between 65 and 69 marks. To calculate the actual mode we then proceed by the method of proportional variation. Refer to the frequency table and look particularly at the ranges

113

Table 5: English Marks for Set A Ranged in Groups of 5 Marks.

MARKS	NUMBER IN SET
45–49	1
50–54	3
55–59	5
60–64	7
65–69	9
70–74	3
75–79	3
80–84	1

The 'most fashionable' or ←modal range occurs here.

immediately above and below the modal range as well as the modal range itself. Thus

	MARK	NUMBER IN SET	DIFFERENCE FROM MODAL FREQUENCY
	60–64	7	2
Modal range→	65–69	9	0
	70–74	3	6

The *intervals* between these mark range (60–64, 65–69, etc.) is 4 marks

$$\therefore \text{Mode} = 65 + 4 \times \frac{2}{2+6}$$

$$= 65 + 4 \times \frac{2}{8} = 65 + \frac{4 \times 2}{8} = 65 + \underline{1 = 66}$$

This shows the method of calculating the mode by taking the lowest mark in the modal range and *adding* the proportional variation.

STATISTICS

A similar result will be obtained by taking the highest mark in the modal range and *subtracting* the proportional variation. Thus

$$\text{Mode} = 69 - 4 \times \frac{6}{2+6} = 69 - \frac{4 \times 6}{8} = 69 - 3 = \underline{66}$$

Exercise 8e

1. Using the English and Mathematics of set B (see Table 1, p. 104), construct the frequency distributions in each case for ranges of 5 marks and calculate the corresponding modes.

2. The following table shows the number of flats in a certain block which are to be let at different rents. (The rents are given in ranges as the flats are not identical in each case.)

RANGE OF WEEKLY RENTS IN PENCE	NUMBER OF FLATS
425–429	12
430–434	18
435–439	28
440–444	22
445–449	14
450–454	13
455–460	7

Find (*i*) the average (arithmetic mean) rent, (*ii*) the median, (*iii*) the mode.

Graphical Determination of the Mode

The mode can be estimated by drawing the frequency curve. If this is drawn the mode is the abscissa (i.e. the horizontal reading) corresponding to the highest point of the graph. In some cases a frequency curve may show two modal points. In such cases the

115

frequencies decrease after the first modal value and then increase for a time for the second modal value. A glance at the graph will show which is the more important value of the two.

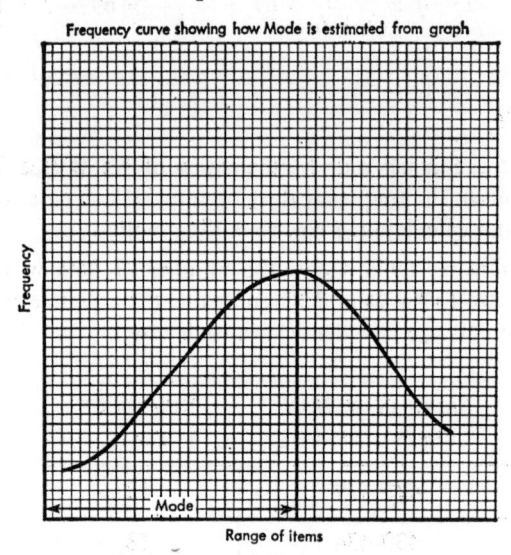

Frequency curve showing how Mode is estimated from graph

Fig. 8-3

Frequency curve showing two Modal points

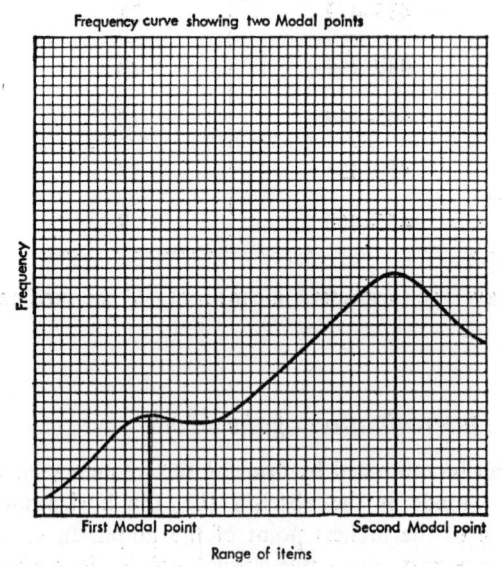

Fig. 8-4

The accuracy of estimating the mode from the frequency curve depends upon the scale which can be used.

Uses of Statistical Averages

Statistical averages, (i.e. the arithmetic mean, the median and the mode) are calculated to enable us to find certain information about a distribution of statistical data or to compare one distribution with another. Which of the averages is the most useful depends upon the nature of the enquiry. The arithmetic mean suffers from the disadvantage that it is unduly affected by extreme items and if a distribution contains such an item then the median is likely to give a better picture of the information. If the most typical item is required the mode is the average which must be found.

9 Algebra

Revision Exercise

Exercise 9a

Solve and check the following equations:

1. $4(x - 1) - 3(x - 2) = 5$
2. $3(y - 1) + 5(2 - y) = 11$
3. $\dfrac{x - 5}{2} + \dfrac{3x + 4}{3} + 2\tfrac{2}{3} = 0$
4. $\dfrac{4x - 1}{2} - \dfrac{6x - 5}{5} = \dfrac{17}{10}$
5. $\dfrac{3}{4}(1 - x) + \dfrac{4x}{7} = 2$
6. $\dfrac{b}{9} + \dfrac{b}{2} - \dfrac{5b}{6} = 2$
7. $\dfrac{5}{6}(3y - 4) - \dfrac{3}{2}(3 - 4y) = \dfrac{2}{3}$
8. $\dfrac{x + 1}{2} + \dfrac{x + 2}{3} + \dfrac{3 - x}{4} = \dfrac{3}{4}$
9. $\left.\begin{array}{l} x - 3y = 7 \\ x + y = -1 \end{array}\right\}$
10. $\left.\begin{array}{l} 6x - 3y = 2 \\ 8x + 9y = 7 \end{array}\right\}$
11. $\left.\begin{array}{l} 3x + 2y = 3 \\ 5y - 7x = 22 \end{array}\right\}$
12. $\left.\begin{array}{l} 3a + 2b = 1 \\ 4b - 9a = 12 \end{array}\right\}$
13. $\left.\begin{array}{l} \dfrac{c}{3} + \dfrac{d}{4} = 7 \\ \dfrac{c}{2} - \dfrac{d}{16} = 4 \end{array}\right\}$
14. $\left.\begin{array}{l} \dfrac{x}{6} + \dfrac{y}{2} = 3 \\ \dfrac{2x}{3} - \dfrac{y}{8} = 3\tfrac{1}{2} \end{array}\right\}$
15. $\left.\begin{array}{l} 3(x - y) - 2(2x + y) = 17 \\ 5(2x - y) + 3(x + y) + 20 = 0 \end{array}\right\}$

Expand the following and collect terms where possible:

16. $(a - 3)(2a + 7)$
17. $(a^2 + b^2)(a - b)$
18. $(3p - 4q)(6p - 7q)$
19. $(x + y + 7)(2x - 3)$
20. $(a + 2b + 3c)(a - b - c)$

Factorize the following expressions:

21. $y^2 + 10y + 25$
22. $a^2 + 4a - 21$
23. $x^2 + 3xy + 2y^2$
24. $70 - 9a - a^2$
25. $2x^2 - 17x - 9$
26. $30y^2 + 49y + 6$
27. $48a^2 - 3b^2$
28. $225 - 9m^2$

ALGEBRA

29. $6x^2y^2 - 216a^4b^4$
30. $a^2 - 18b - 6a + 3ab$
31. $3x - 7y + xy - 21$
32. $2bx - 15ay + 6ax - 5by$
33. $14x^2 - 69xy + 27y^2$
34. $2p^2 + 37pq - 60q^2$
35. $3x^3 - 4y^2 + 3x^2y - 4xy$

Solve the following quadratic equations:

36. $x^2 - 12x + 35 = 0$
37. $2y^2 + 19y - 33 = 0$
38. $6a^2 + 29a - 16 = 0$
39. $(p + 2)(8p + 3) = 2p(p + 3)$
40. $x^2 = \dfrac{13x + 5}{6}$
41. $27x^2 - 9x = 0$
42. $15a^2 = 75a$
43. $3x(7x + 9) = 34x$
44. $(2x + 3)(3x + 5) = (2x + 3)(x + 2)$
45. $p^2 + \dfrac{1}{2} = \dfrac{51p}{14}$
46. $\dfrac{3}{x} + \dfrac{5}{x + 2} - 2$
47. $\dfrac{5}{x + 1} + \dfrac{3}{x - 1} = 2$
48. $\dfrac{4}{x} + \dfrac{7}{5 - x} = -1$
49. $\dfrac{3}{2x - 1} - \dfrac{1}{x + 1} = \dfrac{5}{2}$
50. $\dfrac{10}{x - 1} - \dfrac{7}{x} = 2$

Use Algebraic methods to solve the following problems:

51. I think of a number, double it and add 3. When the resulting number is square the result is 81. Find the original number.

52. The difference between two numbers is 4. Their product is 117. Find the numbers.

53. 4 bars of chocolate and 3 ice creams cost $21\frac{1}{2}$ p. 3 bars of chocolate and 5 ice creams cost 23 p. Find the separate costs of a bar of chocolate and an ice cream.

54.

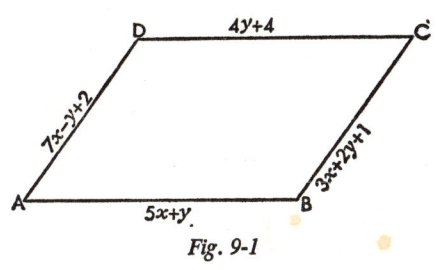

Fig. 9-1

ABCD is a parallelogram. Find the values of x and y.

55.

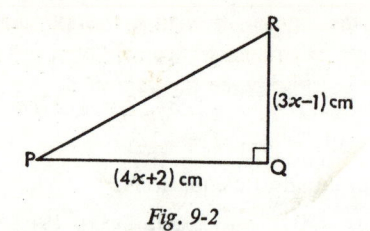

Fig. 9-2

The area of triangle PQR is 56 square centimetres. Find the value of x.

56.

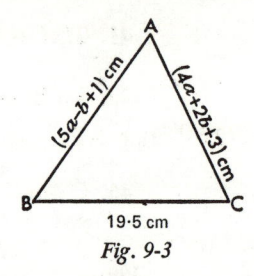

Fig. 9-3

In the triangle ABC, AB = BC and 2BC = AC. If BC = 19·5 cm, find a and b.

×**57.** The base of a triangle is greater than its perpendicular height by 7 cm. The area of the triangle is 39 cm². Find the height.

×**58.** The sum of two numbers is 23. If four times the smallest is subtracted from four times the largest the result is 6. Find the numbers.

59. Divide 16 into two parts so that the sum of their squares is 146.

60. x is the middle number of three consecutive whole numbers. Write down the other two in terms of x.
Show that the difference of the squares of the largest and smallest numbers is always four times the middle number.

Transposition of Formulae

In Stage Three the formula for Simple Interest was given.

$$I = £\frac{PRT}{100}$$

In this form I can be calculated provided the values of P, R and T are known (in the correct units). I is said to be the *subject* of the formula.

ALGEBRA

It is necessary to transpose (or change round) this formula so that, for example, P can be calculated from known values of I, R and T. In other words P is to be made the *subject* of the formula.

$$I = \frac{PRT}{100}$$

Multiply both sides by 100

$$\therefore 100I = PRT$$

Divide both sides by RT

$$\therefore P = \frac{100I}{RT}$$

Now consider another example.

Make g the subject of the formula $T = 2\pi\sqrt{\dfrac{l}{g}}$

Transposition is basically the same process as solving equations.

Consider the equation $5 = 2\pi\sqrt{\dfrac{20}{g}}$, which is similar to the original formula, except that T and l have been replaced by numbers.

g appears under the square root, so square both sides first to remove the square root

$$25 = 4\pi^2 \frac{20}{g} \text{ since } \left(\sqrt{\frac{20}{g}}\right)^2 = \frac{20}{g}$$

Multiply both sides by g

$$25g = 4\pi^2\, 20$$

Divide both sides by 25

$$g = \frac{4\pi^2\, 20}{25}$$

from which g can be calculated.

Now consider the original formula and follow the same steps.

$$T = 2\pi\sqrt{\frac{l}{g}}$$

Square both sides

$$T^2 = 4\pi^2\, \frac{l}{g}$$

Multiply both sides by g
$$T^2\textcircled{g} = 4\pi^2 l$$
Divide both sides by T^2
$$g = \frac{4\pi^2 l}{T^2}$$

Note: It is useful, at first, to ring the required subject in order to pick it out clearly from the other symbols.

Further. Make F the subject of the formula $C = \frac{5}{9}(F - 32)$.

Find F if $C = 100$
$$C = \frac{5}{9}(\textcircled{F} - 32)$$

Multiply both sides by 9
$$9C = 5(\textcircled{F} - 32)$$

Divide both sides by 5
$$\frac{9C}{5} = \textcircled{F} - 32$$

giving
$$F = \frac{9C}{5} + 32$$

If $C = 100$

$$F = \frac{9 \times \overset{20}{\cancel{100}} + 32}{\underset{1}{\cancel{5}}}$$

$$= 180 + 32$$
$$\therefore F = 212$$

Exercise 9b

1. If $A = LB$, make L the subject of the formula.
2. If $V = LBH$, make H the subject of the formula.
3. If $z = 3 - (x - y)$, express y in terms of x and z.
4. If $\frac{a}{2x} = \frac{3b}{5y}$, make y the subject of the formula.

ALGEBRA

5. Make m the subject of the formula $y = mx + c$.

6. If $\dfrac{a}{x-a} = b$, express x in terms of a and b.

7. If $P = 2(L + B)$, make B the subject of the formula.

8. If $A = \dfrac{h}{2}(x + y)$, make h the subject of the formula.

9. Make x the subject of the formula in Question 8.

10. If $L = X(1 + aT)$ express a in terms of L, X and T.

11. If $s - a = \dfrac{b + c - a}{2}$, find s in terms of a, b and c. Find also the formulae for $(s - b)$ and $(s - c)$.

12. If $A = \pi r^2$, make r the subject. Using logarithm tables find r if $A = 2\cdot 67$ and $\pi = 3\cdot 142$.

13. If $V = \dfrac{1\pi r^2 h}{3}$, make h the subject of the formula. Also make r the subject.

14. If $T = 2\pi\sqrt{\dfrac{I}{Mgh}}$, make h the subject of the formula.

15. If $v = u + ft$, express f in terms of v, u and t.

16. If $s = ut + \dfrac{1}{2}ft^2$, make f the subject of the formula.

17. If $A = 2\pi r(r + h)$, find h in terms of A, π and r.

18. If $\triangle = \tfrac{1}{2}bc \sin A$, make c the subject of the formula.

19. If $S = \dfrac{t}{2}(u + v)$, make u the subject of the formula.

20. If $E = \dfrac{m}{2}(v^2 + 2gh)$, find h in terms of E, m, v and g, and then find v in terms of E, m, g and h.

21. If $y = \dfrac{3 + x}{2 - x}$, find x in terms of y.

If $y = 6\cdot 5$, calculate x.

22. Make v the subject of the formula $\dfrac{1}{v} + \dfrac{1}{u} = \dfrac{1}{f}$.

(*Hint:* Find $\frac{1}{v}$ first but do not invert until the expression on the right-hand side has been simplified into *one fraction*.)

23. If $\frac{1}{R} = \frac{1}{R_1} + \frac{1}{R_2}$, find R_1 in terms of R and R_2.

24. If $V = \frac{4}{3}\pi r^2(2r - h)$, make h the subject of the formula.

25. Make $\cos A$ the subject of the formula
$$a^2 = b^2 + c^2 - 2bc \cos A$$
If $a = 6$, $b = 9$, $c = 10$, calculate the value of A in degrees and minutes. (You will need your tables.)

26. Find l in terms of u and h if $u = \dfrac{h}{\sqrt{l^2 - h^2}}$.

27. If $E = \dfrac{P}{2}(x + y)$, make y the subject of the formula.

28. If $M = \dfrac{w(l - x)^2}{2}$, make x the subject of the formula.

(*Hint:* Isolate $(l - x)^2$ and then take the square root.)

29. Express l in terms of M, I and r if
$$I = M\left(\frac{l^2}{12} + \frac{r^2}{4}\right)$$

30. If $x = \dfrac{a^2}{6(2h + a)}$ express h in terms of x and a.

31. If $x^2 + y^2 = \left(\dfrac{v^2}{g} - y\right)^2$, find y in terms of x, V and g.

(*Hint:* Expand the right-hand side.)

32. $T = \left(\dfrac{3\pi}{2} + 2\right)\sqrt{\dfrac{a}{g}}$. Find an expression for g in terms of T, π and a. Simplify your answer as far as possible so that it can be used for calculation.

33. If $R = \sqrt{\dfrac{3M + m}{3M}}$, make M the subject of the formula.

34. If $H = \dfrac{(T_1 - T_2)V}{33\,000}$, make T_2 the subject of the formula. Calculate the value of T_2 when $H = 85$, $V = 2\,500$ and $T_1 = 1\,870$.

ALGEBRA

35. Make p the subject of the formula $F_1\dfrac{\pi d^2}{4} = F_2(p - d)t$.
Calculate p when $F_1 = 80$, $F_2 = 16$, $d = 13$, $t = 2\cdot 5$.

Problems on Time and Speed
Basic formulae
Average Speed

$$\text{Speed} = \dfrac{\text{Distance}}{\text{Time}}$$

or
$$\text{Distance} = (\text{Speed}) \times (\text{Time})$$

or
$$\text{Time} = \dfrac{\text{Distance}}{\text{Speed}}$$

What is meant by average speed?
ABCD is a square of side 10 km.
A car drives along AB at 10 km/h,
along BC at 20 km/h, along DC at
30 km/h and along DA at 40 km/h.
What is the car's average speed for
the whole journey?

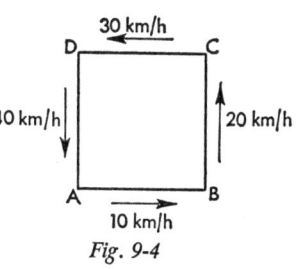

Fig. 9-4

At first sight the average speed would appear to be the average of
10, 20, 30 and 40, i.e. 25 km/h. Is this correct?
Let us look at the problem from a different point of view.

Time taken along AB $= \dfrac{10}{10} = 1$ hour

„ „ „ BC $= \dfrac{10}{20} = \dfrac{1}{2}$ hour $= 30$ minutes

„ „ „ CD $= \dfrac{10}{30} = \dfrac{1}{3}$ hour $= 20$ minutes

„ „ „ DA $= \dfrac{10}{40} = \dfrac{1}{4}$ hour $= 15$ minutes

The total time taken $= 1$ hour $+ 30$ minutes $+ 20$ minutes $+$
15 minutes
$= 2$ hours 5 minutes
$= 2\tfrac{1}{12}$ hours

125

The total distance travelled = 40 km

$$\text{Average speed from A to D} = \frac{\text{Total distance travelled}}{\text{Total time taken}}$$

$$= \frac{40}{2\frac{1}{12}}$$

$$= 40 \div \frac{25}{12}$$

$$= \overset{8}{\cancel{40}} \times \frac{12}{\underset{5}{\cancel{25}}}$$

$$= \frac{96}{5}$$

∴ Average speed = $19\frac{1}{5}$ km/h

This result does not agree with the first value obtained. If the average speed had been taken as 25 km/h then the time for the journey

$$= \frac{\text{Distance}}{\text{Speed}}$$

$$= \frac{\overset{9}{\cancel{40}}}{\underset{5}{\cancel{25}}}$$

$$= 1\frac{3}{5} \text{ hours}$$

$$= 1 \text{ hour } 36 \text{ minutes}$$

This does not agree with the time of 2 hours 5 minutes calculated from the times over the separate sections. Hence we cannot find average speeds in the same way as the averages of ordinary quantities. This is because speeds are *rates* involving two quantities, distance and time. *Always* use the result.

$$\text{Average speed} = \frac{\text{Total distance travelled}}{\text{Total time taken}}$$

Hence in the above example the correct answer is $19\frac{1}{5}$ km/h.

The term 'average speed' is a useful mathematical idea (or concept) but from a practical point of view it has little meaning.

A train travels from town A to town B at an average speed of 100 km/h. Imagine that you are sitting in the train at station A when the guard blows his whistle.

ALGEBRA

Immediately you are travelling at 100 km/h. The train then continues at a steady speed of 100 km/h uphill, downhill, round curves and over points, ignoring signals until it arrives at station B. On arrival it stops *immediately* from 100 km/h to rest. The effects of such a sudden stop (or sudden start) on the train and its passengers defy imagination. The human frame could not stand such acceleration! From this imaginary journey you will understand that the term 'average speed' is not a practical possibility, but just a useful concept. A real train would, of course, start and stop slowly, obey signals and other warnings, possibly stopping occasionally, and at other times travelling at speeds well above 100 km/h in order that the result of dividing the total distance by the total time should equal 100 km/h.

Exercise 9c

1. A car travels 52 km in 45 minutes and a further 68 km in 55 minutes. Find the average speed in km/h for the whole journey.

2. How long will an aircraft take for a journey of 750 km at an average speed of 225 km/h?

3. A train travels between two towns 200 km apart at an average speed of 80 km/h. How long will it take? If a second train takes 30 minutes less than the first train for the journey, find its average speed.

4. A car travels for $1\frac{1}{2}$ hours at an average speed of 72 km/h and then for 1 hour at an average speed of 92 km/h. Find its average speed for the whole journey.

5. A motor rally route takes the form of a triangle ABC where $AB = 60$ km, $BC = 80$ km and $AC = 120$ km. A car travels along AB at 90 km/h, BC at 80 km/h and CA at 80 km/h. Calculate its average speed for the whole journey.

6. A train travels between two towns 200 km apart. It covers the first 120 km at an average speed of 80 km/h. At what speed must it travel the last 80 km in order that its average speed for the whole journey should be 100 km/h?

7. A car travels D km in T hours. Write down an expression for its average speed S. Another car takes $\frac{1}{2}$ hour longer for the same journey. Write down an expression for its average speed V. Find an

127

expression, involving T only, for the ratio of S to V. If $\dfrac{S}{V} = 2$, find T.

8. A man walks x km at 6 km/h and then walks x km back at 8 km/h. Find an expression for (*a*) his total time, and (*b*) his average speed.

9. A man cycles 10 km at x km/h and then 15 km at y km/h. Find an expression for (*a*) his total time, and (*b*) his average speed for the whole journey.

10. A car travels x km at 80 km/h and 60 km at y km/h. Find (*a*) the total distance, (*b*) the total time and (*c*) the average speed for the whole journey.

Algebraic Problems Involving Distance, Time and Speed

Many problems involving distance, time and speed can be solved graphically, but it is useful to be able to do such problems by algebra. e.g. A man cycles a distance of 80 km in 3 hours 40 minutes. He rides part of the distance at 20 km/h and part of the distance at 30 km/h. How far did he ride at 30 km/h?

Let x km $\quad$ = distance ridden at 30 km/h
Then $(80 - x) =\quad$,,$\quad$,,$\quad$,, 20 km/h

Time taken at 30 km/h $= \dfrac{x}{30}$ h

,, ,, ,, 20 km/h $= \dfrac{80 - x}{20}$ h

But the total time $\quad$ = 3 hours 40 minutes
$\qquad\qquad\qquad\qquad = 3\tfrac{2}{3}$ h
$\qquad\qquad\qquad\qquad = \dfrac{11}{3}$ h

$$\therefore \frac{x}{30} + \frac{80 - x}{20} = \frac{11}{3}$$

Multiply both sides by 60.

$$\frac{x}{\cancel{30}} \cdot \cancel{60}^{2} + \frac{(80 - x)}{\cancel{20}} \cdot \cancel{60}^{3} = \frac{11}{3} \cdot \cancel{60}^{20}$$

$$2x + 240 - 3x = 220$$
$$\underline{20 = x}$$

ALGEBRA

Check (in the original problem).

Time to ride 20 km at 30 km/h $= \dfrac{20}{30}$ h $= 40$ minutes

„ „ „   60 km at 20 km/h $= 3$ h

∴ Total time for journey $= 3$ hours 40 minutes

∴ <u>Man rides 20 km at 30 km/h</u>

Some problems of this type require quadratic equations for their solution.

e.g. Two men walk a distance of 40 km. Mr Smith walks 2 km/h *faster* than Mr Jones. Smith covers the distance in 1 hour *less* than Jones. Find their speeds.

Let Jones walk at x km/h

Then Smith walks at $(x + 2)$ km/h

Time taken by Jones $= \dfrac{40}{x}$ h

Time taken by Smith $= \dfrac{40}{x + 2}$ h

But (Jones's time) $-$ (Smith's time) $= 1$ hour

$$\therefore \dfrac{40}{x} - \dfrac{40}{x + 2} = 1$$

Put the fractions on the left hand side over the common denominator $x(x + 2)$

$$\dfrac{40(x + 2) - 40x}{x(x + 2)} = 1$$

Multiply both sides by $x(x + 2)$.

$$40(x + 2) - 40x = x(x + 2)$$
$$\therefore 40x + 80 - 40x = x^2 + 2x$$

Rearranging
$$x^2 + 2x - 80 = 0$$
$$\therefore (x + 10)(x - 8) = 0$$
$$\therefore x = -10 \text{ or } x = 8$$

Reject $x = -10$ because it has no meaning. (Neither man is walking backwards!)

$$\therefore \underline{x = 8}$$

Check

If Jones's speed is 8 km/h, Jones's time $= \dfrac{40}{8} = 5$ hours.

If Smith's speed is 10 km/h, Smith's time $= \dfrac{40}{10} = 4$ hours.

∴ Difference between their times $= 5 - 4 = 1$

∴ Jones walks at 8 km/h and Smith walks at 10 km/h

Note: If you have not already done so it would be useful to work Exercise 9a numbers 46 to 50 before starting Exercise 9d.

Exercise 9d

Use algebraic methods to solve the following problems:

1. A train running at 90 km/h takes $\frac{1}{2}$ hour longer to do a journey than when it runs at 120 km/h. What is the length of the journey?

2. A man walks from one village to another by a roundabout route at 8 km/h. He returns by a more direct route which is 8 km shorter at 6 km/h. His total time is $4\frac{1}{2}$ hours. Find the total distance covered.

3. Two towns A and B are 48 km apart. A cyclist leaves A and cycles towards B at 24 km/h. At the same time a man leaves B and walks towards A at 8 km/h. Where do they meet, and how long have they taken from their respective starting points?

4. A woman sets out along a road at 10.00 walking at 7 km/h. A man sets out from the same point at 10.30 walking at 8 km/h. How far are they from their starting point when the man overtakes the woman? Find also the time at which they meet.

5. A motor cyclist usually rides home from work at an average speed of 80 km/h. If he rides $\frac{1}{4}$ of the distance at 100 km/h and the remainder at 90 km/h he can save 4 minutes on the journey. How far is it from home to work?

6. Two boys start out on a journey at the same time. The first boy, John, rides his bicycle at 24 km/h. The second boy, Tom, walks at 10 km/h. John stops on the way for an hour's rest but arrives at the end 10 minutes before Tom. Find the length of the journey.

7. A girl cycles uphill to school at 10 km/h and she cycles home downill at 30 km/h. If the total journey takes 1 hour 20 minutes how far is it from home to school?

ALGEBRA

8. A car averages x km/h and a bus averages y km/h. If on a journey of 120 km a man travels 80 km by car and 40 km by bus he takes 2 hours for the journey. If he travels half the distance by car and half by bus he takes $2\frac{1}{4}$ hours. Find x and y.
(*Hint:* Write down two simultaneous equations and solve for $\frac{1}{x}$ and $\frac{1}{y}$)

9. A motorist sets off on a journey of 240 km. After covering x km at 120 km/h he stops for a break. He completes his journey at an average speed of 100 km/h. His total driving time is $2\frac{1}{4}$ hours. Find x.

10. Two men A and B cycle a distance of 150 km. B's speed is half as much as A's speed. B leaves the starting point $2\frac{1}{2}$ hours after A and they both arrive at their destination at the same time. Find their speeds.

11. Two men motor a distance of 140 km. Mr Brown drives 10 km/h faster than Mr Black. Mr Black takes 20 minutes longer than Mr Brown. Find their speeds.

12. Two men each walk a distance of 24 km. The sum of their times is 5 hours and the sum of their speeds is 20 km/h. Find their speeds.

13. Two aircraft fly between two cities 1 000 km apart. The difference between their times is $\frac{1}{2}$ hour and the difference between their speeds is 100 km/h. Find their speeds.

14. Two men walk towards each other from two towns 34 km apart. They meet in 2 hours, having started at the same time. If one man walks 1 km/h faster than the other, find their speeds and where they meet.

15. A boy cycles to school on a downhill route and because of the slope his speed on the return uphill journey is reduced by 14 km/h. He takes 28 minutes longer to return from school than he takes to get there. If the distance from home to school is 16 km, find his speed on the way to school.

16. The speeds of two cars are in the ratio 7:5. On a journey of 224 km the faster car takes 48 minutes less to cover the distance. Find the speeds of the cars.

17. Two motor cyclists leave two towns at the same time travelling towards each other. Their speeds are 40 km/h and 24 km/h

131

respectively. If their speeds are *both* increased by 8 km/h they meet $\frac{1}{4}$ hour *sooner* than they would have done at their original speeds. Find the time they take to meet at their original speeds and the distance between the towns.

18. A cyclist leaves a town A and cycles towards another town B 66 km away. A second cyclist, whose speed is 8 km/h less than the first, leaves B $\frac{1}{4}$ hour later and cycles towards A. They meet when the first cyclist has covered 42 km. Find their speeds.

19. The speeds of two motorists differ by 20 km/h. Starting at the same time they drive towards each other from two points 110 km apart. After meeting, the slower car takes 36 minutes to reach the starting point of the first car. Find the speed of each car.

20. A car travelled 160 km at v km/h and a further 90 km at a speed 10 km/h faster. The average speed for the whole journey was $83\frac{1}{3}$ km/h. Find v.

In questions 21 to 24 state whether each statement is TRUE or FALSE.

21. If $a = 6$, $b = -5$, $c = 0$ and $d = 2$

  (i) ab is less than bd (vi) $(a + b)(c - d) = -2$
  (ii) ac is greater than ad (vii) $(ab + cd)(ac + bd) = -300$
  (iii) $abcd = -60$ (viii) $abd^3 = -240$
  (iv) $\dfrac{ad}{b} = -0.24$ (ix) $a^4 b^5 c^6 d^7 = 0$
  (v) $a^2 b^2 = 300$ (x) $a^2 + 2bc - 4ab + d = 148$

22. If $S = \dfrac{7\pi (r-x)^2}{y}$

  (i) $y = \dfrac{S}{7\pi (r-x)^2}$

  (ii) $(r-x)^2 = \dfrac{Sy}{7\pi}$

  (iii) $r-x = \pm\sqrt{\dfrac{Sy}{7\pi}}$

  (iv) $x = -r \pm \sqrt{\dfrac{Sy}{7\pi}}$

  (v) If $x = 4$, $S = 11$ and $y = 8$, then $r = 6$ or 2.

23. Consider the expression $2x^2 - 11x + 21$.

  (i) One of the factors of the expression is $(x + 7)$

ALGEBRA

(ii) The other factor is $(2x + 3)$
(iii) The solutions of the equation $2x^2 - 11x + 21 = 0$ are $x = -7$ and $x = -1\frac{1}{2}$
(iv) If x is greater than 7, $(x - 7)$ is less than 0.
(v) If x is greater than 7, $(2x + 3)$ is greater than 17.
(vi) If x is greater than 7, $2x^2 - 11x + 21$ is positive.

24. Select the correct answers from those given.
  (a) The solution of $3x - 7 = 8$ is:
    (i) $x = \frac{1}{3}$, (ii) $x = -5$, (iii) $x = -\frac{1}{3}$, (iv) $x = 5$
  (b) (b) The solution of $\frac{x}{3} + \frac{x}{12} + 2\frac{1}{2} = 0$ is:
    (i) $x = 15$, (ii) $x = -7$, (iii) $x = -6$, (iv) $x = -35$
  (c) The solutions of $\begin{matrix} 3x + y = -8 \\ 2x + 5y = 1 \end{matrix}$ are:
    (i) $x = 1$, $y = -4$ (ii) $x = -1$, $y = 2$ (iii) $x = 2$, $y = \frac{4}{5}$
    (iv) $x = 3$, $y = -10$
  (d) The solutions of $6x^2 - x - 2 = 0$ are:
    (i) $x = -\frac{1}{2}$ or $-\frac{2}{3}$ (ii) $x = \frac{1}{2}$ or $-\frac{2}{3}$ (iii) $x = -\frac{1}{2}$ or $-\frac{2}{3}$
    (iv) $x = -\frac{1}{2}$ or $\frac{2}{3}$

25. A motorist A leaves a town at 09.30 on a journey of 240 km. A second motorist B leaves the same town at 10.30 on the same journey as A. B's speed is 20 km/h faster than A. They both arrive at their destination at the same time. Are the following statements TRUE or FALSE?
  (i) If A's speed is x km/h then B's speed is $(x + 20)$ km/h.
  (ii) A's time for the journey is $240x$ hours and B's time is $240(x + 20)$ hours.
  (iii) A's time + 1 hour = B's time.
  (iv) $\frac{240}{x} - \frac{240}{x + 20} = 1$
  (v) $x^2 + 20x - 480 = 0$
  (vi) $x = +60$ or -80.
  (vii) A's speed is 80 km/h and B's speed is 60 km/h.
  (viii) A and B both arrive at their destination at 13.30.

133

10 The Sphere

The Sphere is a 'solid of revolution' (mentioned in the chapter on symmetry in Stage 3), i.e. the shape is formed when a plane figure is revolved about an axis.
Which plane figure must be revolved?
About which axis must the figure be revolved?
The sphere is mathematically one of the more difficult solids to investigate. This is mainly because the sphere's surface curves in every direction.
Can you think of any solids where the surfaces curve in some but not all directions?
For a full study of the sphere two branches of developed mathematics are necessary, 'the calculus' and 'spherical trigonometry'.

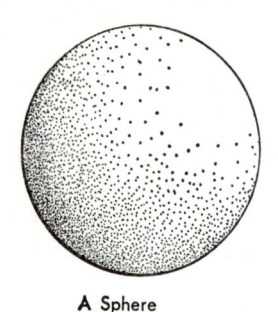

The sphere has two important characteristics; first it gives a maximum volume for a given surface area (compare this to the circle which has a maximum area for a given perimeter); and second, when a sphere is filled with a liquid or gas, the pressure exerted is the same all over the sphere's surface: this is why very large spherical containers are used in the chemical and atomic engineering industries. The same reason produces soap bubbles.

A Sphere
Fig. 10-1

All the solids studied in this series have been developed from plane nets, and have plane surfaces (in one direction at least, for cones and cylinders); the sphere however, because it curves in every direction, *cannot* be developed from a plane net. The reverse process—that of mapping a sphere into a plane—is much more important and many methods have been developed for obtaining close approximations.

Exercise 10a

Measure and draw out on a sheet
    (*i*) a tennis-ball cover panel;
    (*ii*) a football cover panel (more than one type).

THE SPHERE

Sketch how they are fitted and give reasons for their strength.

The most important mapping of a sphere is in the production of maps and atlases of the Earth, since for all practical purposes the Earth can be assumed to be a sphere. If for example an 8 cm diameter sphere represents the earth, the highest mountain and the deepest hole would be about the thickness of a hair.

The easiest method of dissecting a sphere's surface is to dissect it as you would the skin of an orange, Fig. 10-2. The narrower each strip the less will be the curvature, and the nearer it will approach to a plane surface. If the strips are joined along a centre line as in Fig. 10-3 a map with little distortion would be obtained, but it would be of little use as a map!

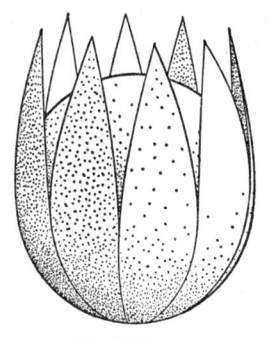

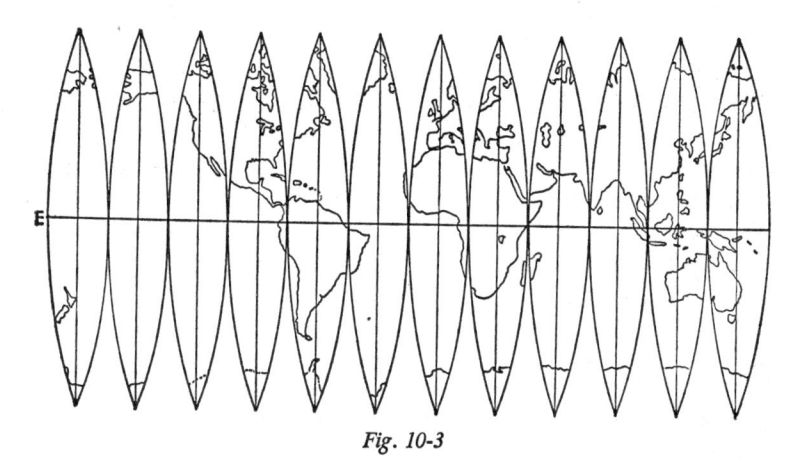

Fig. 10-2

Fig. 10-3

It will be helpful in studying the various methods of mapping a sphere's surface on to a plane if a brief look is taken at the method of dividing up the surface.

The Dissections of a Sphere

When a sphere is cut by a plane what will be the shape of the faces obtained? (Fig. 10-4).

The shape obtained is small when the cut is some way from the sphere's centre, and grows larger as the cuts approach the centre. When will the cut surface be at a maximum?

The largest section obtainable by dissecting a sphere is known as a *great circle*, and sections made by planes which do not pass through

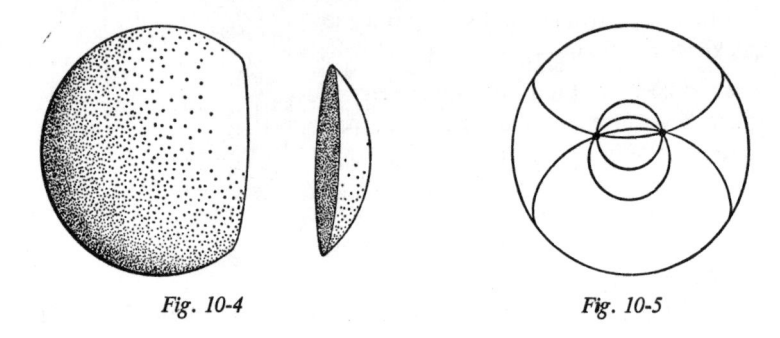

Fig. 10-4   *Fig. 10-5*

the centre of the sphere are sometimes called *small circles*. What will the radius of a *great circle* be?
Is every circle drawn on a sphere either a great or a small circle?
Can a great Circle be drawn through any two points on a sphere?
Fig. 10-5 shows several circles, drawn on a sphere's surface, all passing through two points. Compare the distances from one point to another, moving along the various circumferences.
Which circle gives the longest path?
As the path shortens, what can you say about the circle?
Can you suggest which circle will give the shortest path?

Graphing the Sphere

To position a point on a plane the usual method (but not the only method) is to divide the plane by two sets of lines, one vertical and one horizontal, one of each set being taken as a line of origin, Fig. 10-6. A similar idea of using two sets of lines is used to position a point on a sphere (although again, this is not the only method), Fig. 10-7. 2 points called *poles* are placed diametrically opposite each other, and a set of circles is drawn through these 2 points, Fig. 10-8. Since the points are diametrically opposite what can be said about all of these circles? As many circles as you choose may be drawn through the poles, all the lines being called lines of

THE SPHERE

LONGITUDE. To be precise, a line of longitude is just the semicircle between the poles.

As with the plane coordinate system, a special line is taken as a line of origin, all the other lines being measured from this origin line. An important point of difference is that while lines in the plane

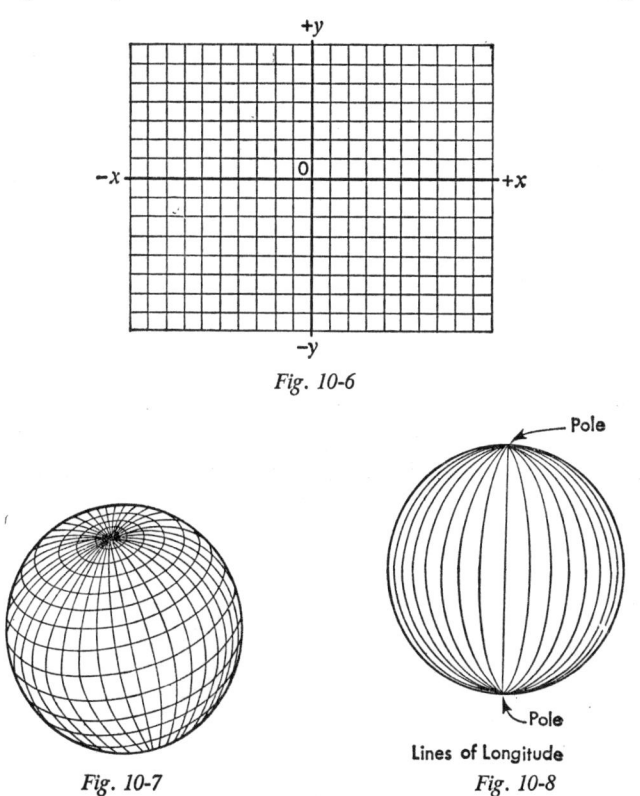

Fig. 10-6

Fig. 10-7

Lines of Longitude
Fig. 10-8

coordinate system are labelled by their *distance* from the origin line, lines of longitude are labelled by their *angle* from the origin line. The angle is obtained in the following way; the sphere is cut in half by a dissection perpendicular to the lines of longitude (the circumference of the circular section being known as an 'equator') and from the centre of the circular section the angles are drawn, with the lines of longitude meeting the angle arms on the equator. The angle of each line of longitude can then be measured round from the origin line, which is at angle 0°, Fig. 10-9. The angles do not move round the circle from 0°–360° but they move from both sides of the 0° line, to the east (right) and to the west (left), meeting on the 180° longitude line (which makes a great circle with the 0° longitude line), Fig. 10-10.

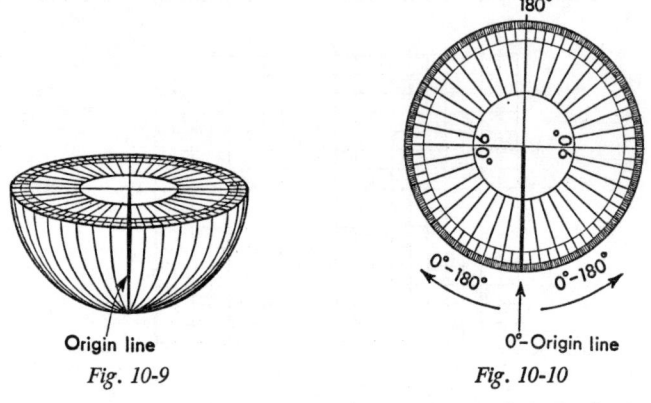

Origin line
Fig. 10-9

0°-Origin line
Fig. 10-10

To complete the coordinate system a second set of circles is drawn parallel to the equator (they are actually perpendicular to the lines of longitude, but perpendicular lines on a sphere have not yet been

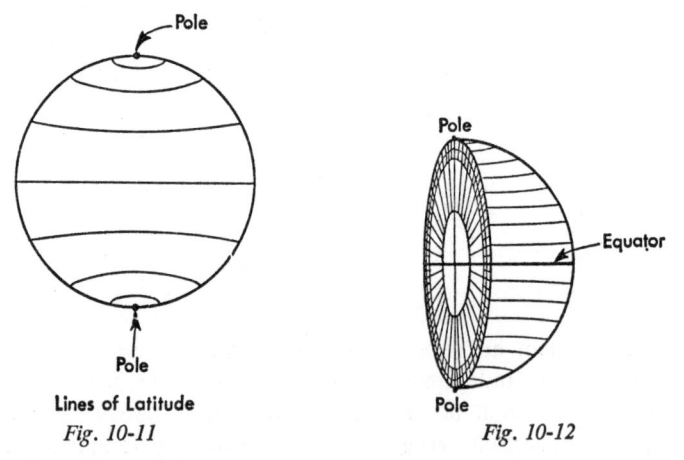

Lines of Latitude
Fig. 10-11

Fig. 10-12

discussed), Fig. 10-11. These lines are called the lines of LATITUDE.
Are all lines of latitude of the same length?
If not is there a smallest? Where?
Is there a longest? Where?
Give another name for lines of latitude.

THE SPHERE

As with lines of longitude, lines of latitude are measured by angular measurement. The angle is obtained in the following way: The sphere is dissected along any line of longitude, thus cutting the sphere in half through its centre, Fig. 10-12. The cross-section circle obtained is then divided into its angular measurement. Once again the angles do not move from 0° to 360° but move from the equator 0° to the poles 90°. Since the equator appears at 2 points the circle is divided up into its quadrants, Fig. 10-13. The whole system is seen best on the following model.

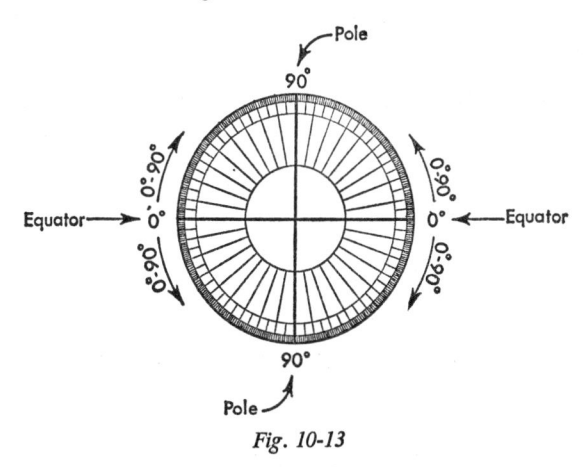

Fig. 10-13

A Model to Show Longitude and Latitude

Cut out in cardboard a circle radius 6 cm. Mark out both sides as in Fig. 10-14, and colour it (using one set of colours on one side and a second set on the other side). This part will represent the equatorial Great Circle.

Make eight 3 cm cuts from the circumference along the lines 0°, 45°E., 45°W., 90°E., 90°W., 135°E., 135°W., 180°.

Make 8 pieces as in Fig. 10-15 (radius 6 cm), each piece to be marked similarly on both sides, colouring the top (northern) half with one of your sets of colours and the lower (southern) half with the other set of colours. A 3 cm cut should be made as indicated along the 0° line. The 9 pieces should be assembled as in Fig. 10-16, and Sellotaped into position. Wire 'small circles' can be also added as required to show lines of latitude, these also being Sellotaped into position.

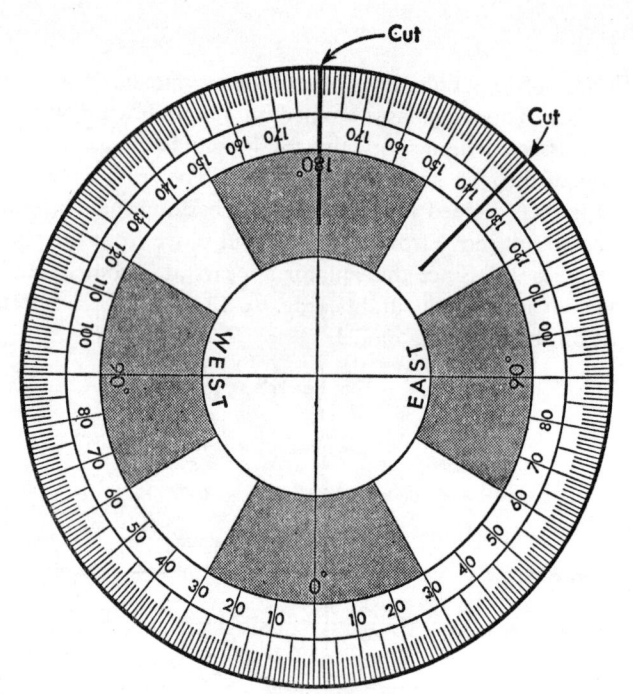

Fig. 10-14

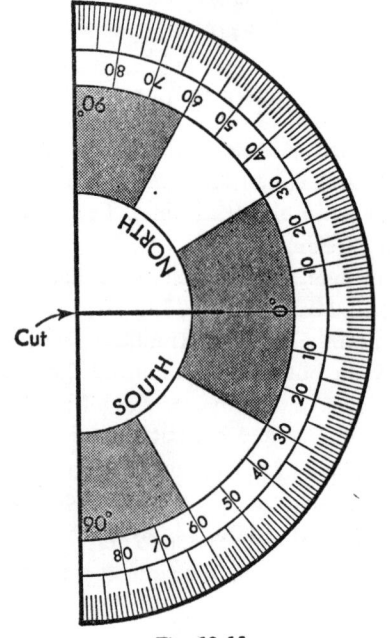

Fig. 10-15

THE SPHERE

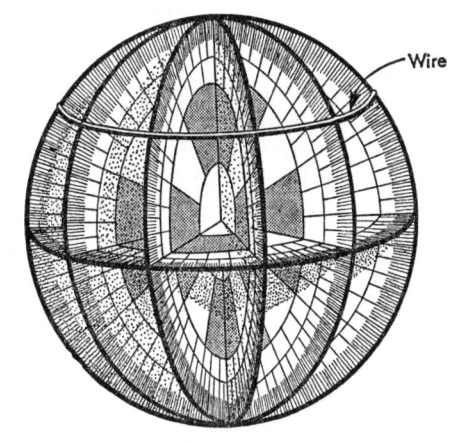

Fig. 10-16

Map Projections

All maps of large areas are really topological maps; i.e. they are distortions of reality. Some maps distort shape but conserve relative areas; others distort areas but conserve shape, others distort both shape and area but conserve certain distances. Look back to Fig. 10-3. This can be made into a map by stretching each strip into a rectangle, Fig. 10-17. This type of map is satisfactory only for

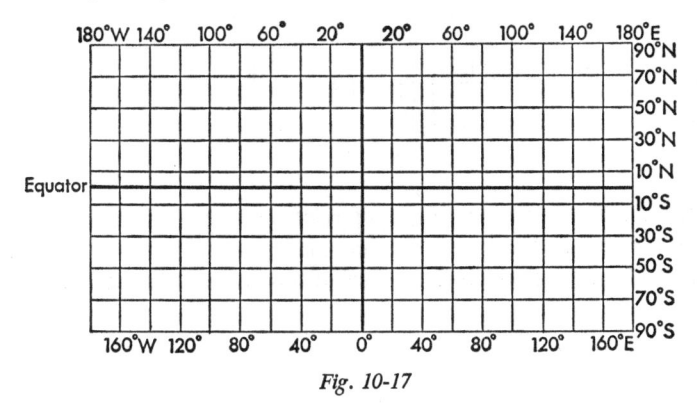

Fig. 10-17

areas fairly close to the centre lines, distances near the poles being stretched in an East–West direction, although the North–South distances would be little affected. The map derived from this dissection is known as the Plate Carrée projection. It is used by the Ordnance

141

Survey for maps of relatively small areas (such as England), the centre line being drawn on a great circle roughly down the centre of the considered area.

The Mercator projection of the world is a similar type of projection to the Plate Caree, except that the North–South distances (i.e. the lines of longitude) are stretched in proportion to the stretching of the latitude parallels, i.e. the nearer to the poles, the greater the

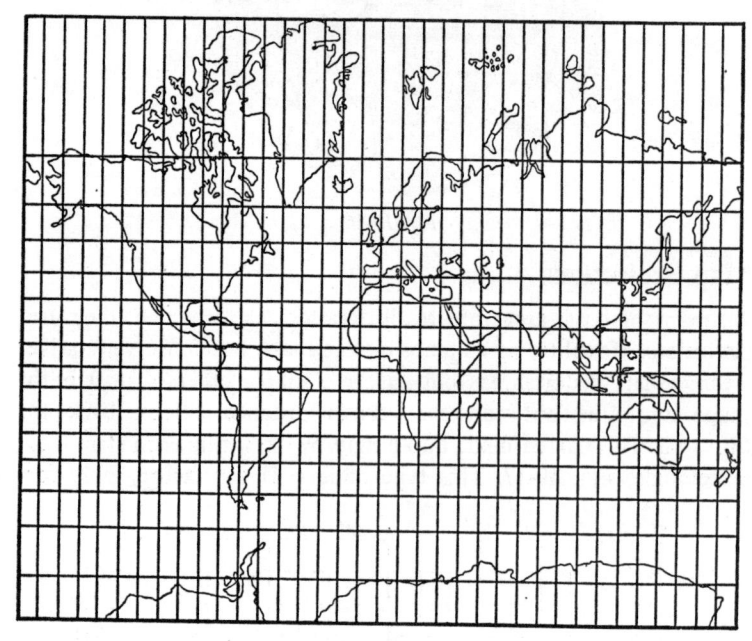

Fig. 10-18

stretching. This preserves *shape* of relatively small areas but area scales vary from the equator to the pole. Compare Fig. 10–18 with Fig. 10-17, both of which show lines of longitude and latitude.

Exercise 10b

On a large Mercator projection of the world find the ratios of Greenland and South America by covering the areas with a set of squares marked on tracing paper and counting the squares. Look up the actual areas in square kilometres and obtain the actual ratios. Compare the two ratios.

THE SPHERE

Area and Volume of a Sphere

The methods of finding the area and volume of a sphere are very old; a manuscript in Moscow seems to show that the Egyptians had

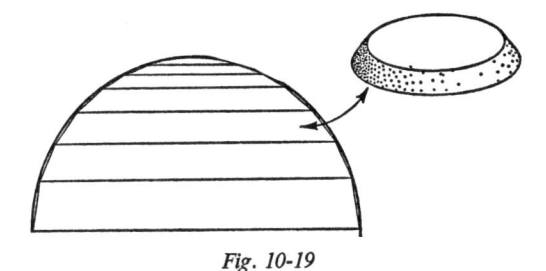

Fig. 10-19

the correct formulae nearly 4 000 years ago. The ancient methods were to split up the figure into a very large number of parallel slices and consider each slice as a slice of a cone, Fig. 10-19. A very similar method is used today, but it is immensely simplified and comes into the field of the calculus. The Greeks, who did a lot of work in this field, showed two useful relationships between the sphere and a cylinder which contains the sphere, Fig. 10-20. These relationships are:

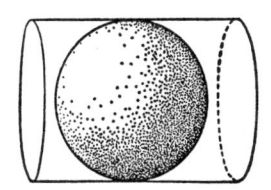

Fig. 10-20

1. The volume of a sphere $= \frac{2}{3} \times$ volume of a containing cyclinder *of the same height.*

2. Two cuts, perpendicular to the cylinder length, will cut off equal areas on the cylinder and on the sphere, Fig. 10-21.

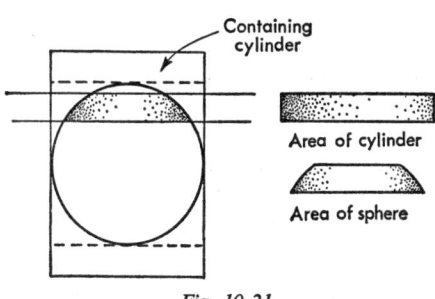

Fig. 10-21

143

Exercise 10c

Derive the volume and area of a sphere in terms of the sphere's radius.

Lambert's equal area projection uses the above fact to obtain a map of the world which shows equal areas. The map is projected *horizontally* out from the centre lines of the sphere onto the containing cylinder which is then unrolled, Fig. 10-22. Compare the lines of longitude and latitude in Figs. 10-17, 10-18 and 10-22.

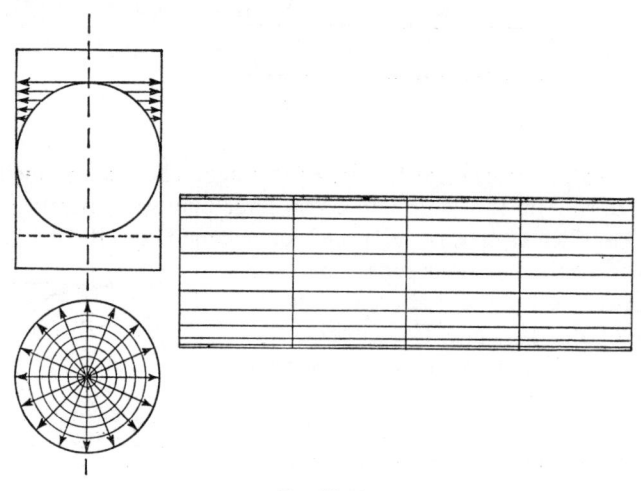

Fig. 10-22

What is the drawback to this projection?

The only other important *cylindrical* projection is Galls projection; the cylinder, instead of containing the sphere, actually intersects it along the 45°N. and 45°S. latitudes. The resulting map is illustrated in Fig. 10-23.

Zenithal or Azimuthal Projections

A different type of projection is obtained from the basic idea of placing the sphere against a plane and projecting parts of the sphere's surface from some point on to the plane. Obviously the whole of the sphere's surface cannot be mapped at one go by this method, Fig. 10-24. Different projection points obviously give slightly different results, and projection points used include the centre

THE SPHERE

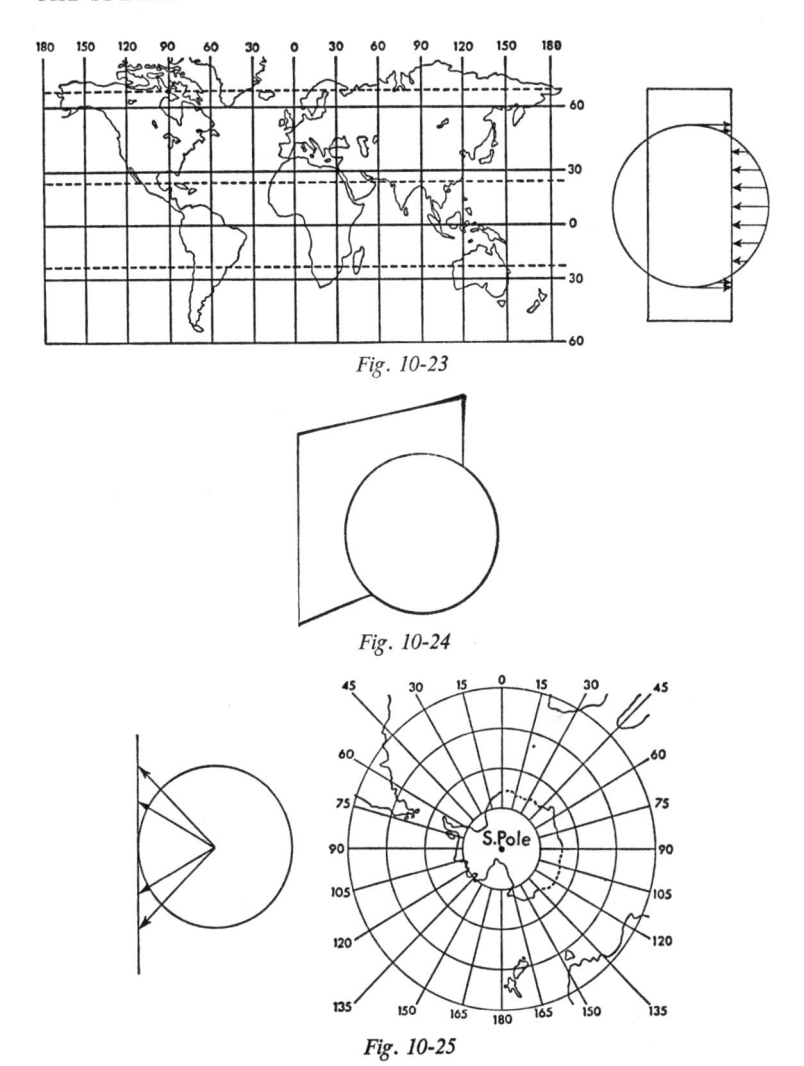

Fig. 10-23

Fig. 10-24

Fig. 10-25

of the sphere for the Gnomonic projection, Fig. 10-25; the point of the surface opposite the point of contact for the Orthomorphic or Stereographic projection, Fig. 10-26; two well-placed points outside the sphere lead to equidistant and equal-area maps, Fig. 10-27; and a point at infinity gives a photograph from a great distance— the Orthographic projection, Fig. 10-28; this is usually used for star charts.

Fig. 10-26   *Fig. 10-27*

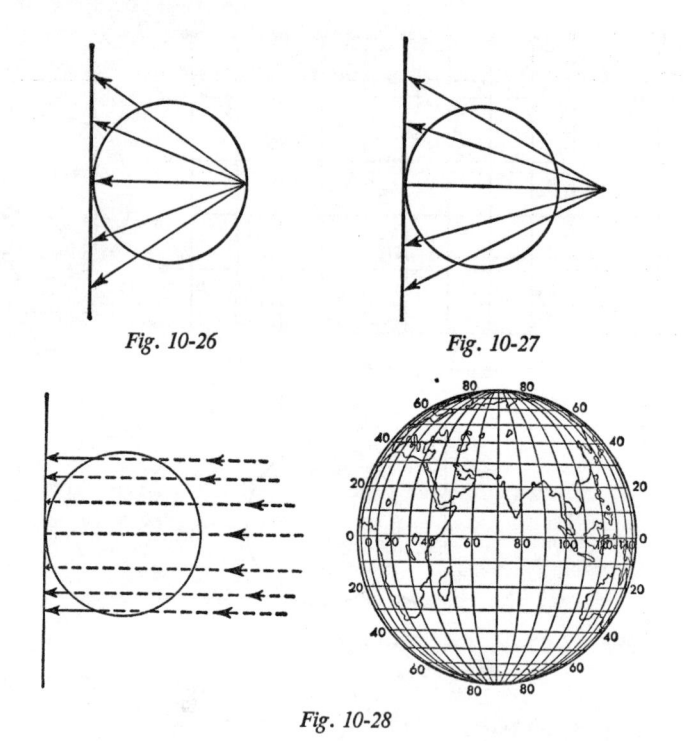

Fig. 10-28

Conical Projection

An important set of maps is obtained by projecting parts of the surface of a sphere on to a cone, which can either touch or cut the sphere. The simplest is shown in Fig. 10-29—the Perspective Conical

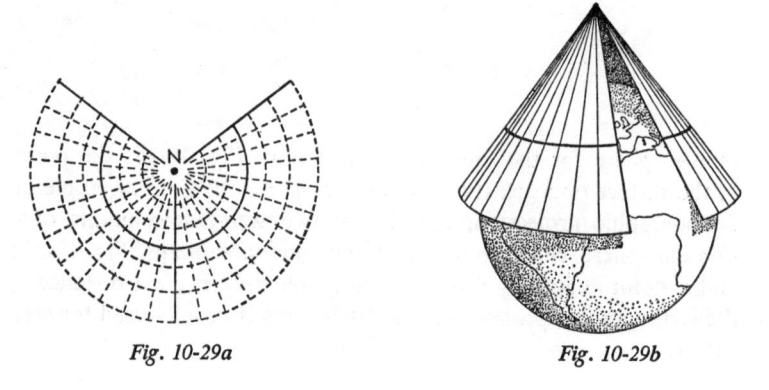

Fig. 10-29a   *Fig. 10-29b*

THE SPHERE

projection. The cone can be made to touch any parallel of latitude chosen. What happens when the chosen latitude is the equator? The conical projection can be modified to give correctly presented

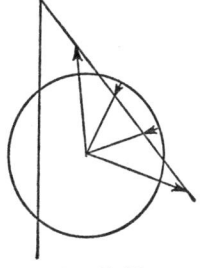

Fig. 10-30

areas. A more accurate map for larger areas is obtained when the cone intersects the sphere, giving perfect accuracy on two lines of latitude, Fig. 10-30. Various modifications can be made to the

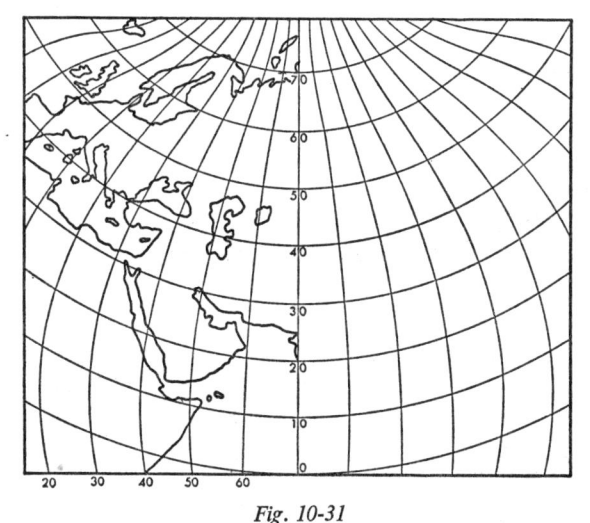

Fig. 10-31

conical projection, such as giving each line of latitude its true length and true spacing. This is Bonnes projection, Fig. 10-31, which gives correct areas but distorts shape.

Special mathematical devices are sometimes used to give a map showing the whole Earth's surface. The sinusoidal projection,

147

LONGMAN MATHEMATICS

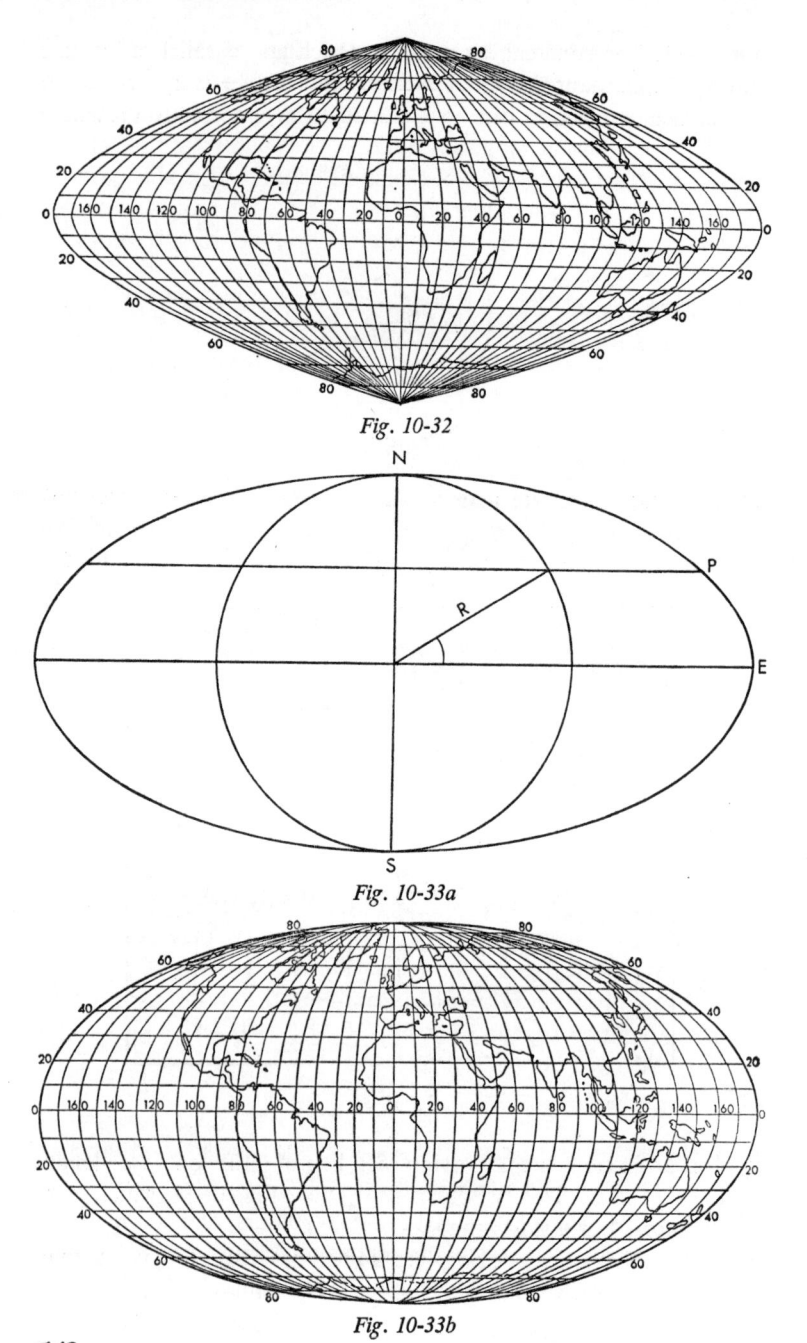

Fig. 10-32

Fig. 10-33a

Fig. 10-33b

148

THE SPHERE

Fig. 10-32, is obtained by drawing the lines of latitude to their correct lengths and correct spacings, and the central vertical line equals one line of longitude (equal to half the length of the equator). All the other lines of longitude intersect the lines of latitude at their correct spacings. These lines of longitude actually form sine-curves— hence the name. Although great distortion occurs, area is preserved. Another equal-area world map is Mollweides, Fig. 10-33b, which has

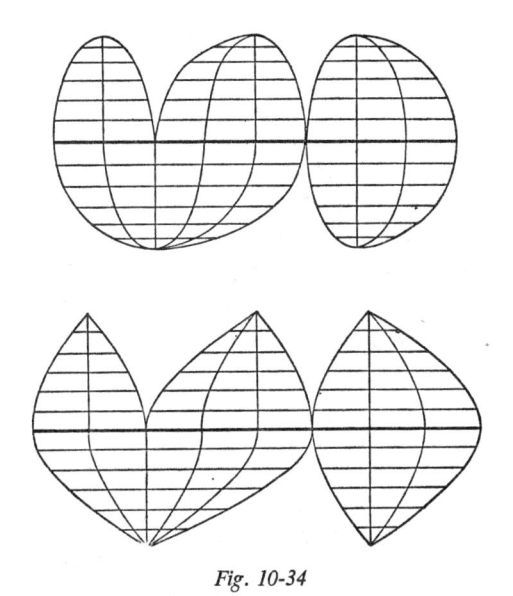

Fig. 10-34

not so great a distortion of shape as the Sinusoidal. The lines of longitude are ellipses, the basic outline being obtained as in Fig. 10-33a, where the area of the ellipse is twice the area of the circle. Less shape distortion is obtained from both the above maps if more than one 'centre' is taken as in Fig. 10-34.

Exercise 10d

1. If the radius of the earth is 6 300 km, what distance on the earth will be measured by 1°, along a great circle?

2. Taking the radius of the earth to be 6 300 km, find to the nearest hundred kilometres the lengths of the following lines of latitude: 0°, 10°, 20°, 30°, 40°, 50°. Study Fig. 10-35.

149

LONGMAN MATHEMATICS

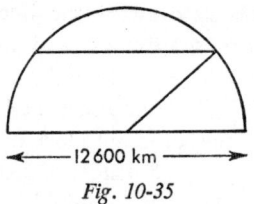

←———12 600 km———→
Fig. 10-35

3. Find the distances between the following towns, each pair being on the same line of longitude:
   (*i*) Malaga (Southern Spain) and Plymouth
   (*ii*) Accra (Gold Coast) and Greenwich
   (*iii*) Scunthorpe and Bordeaux
   (*iv*) Valencia and Guildford
   (*v*) Stockholm and Cape Town

4. A ship, in the Antarctic in a position P 75°S., 170°W., sails due north to latitude 60°S.; then it sails along the parallel 60°S. to a position 10°E. Finally it sails due south to Q, at a latitude 70°S. Calculate
   (*i*) the distance travelled northwards;
   (*ii*) The distance it travels from 170°W. to 10°E. Does it matter whether it travels eastwards or westwards?
   (*iii*) the distance it sails south.
   Take the radius of the earth to be 6 300 km
   (Oxford adapted).

5. Show that the radius of a circle of latitude θ is $r \cos \theta$, when r is the radius of the earth.
   A, B, C and D are four places in the Pacific Ocean. A and D are on the equator and their longitudes are respectively 170°W. and 120°W. B and C are both on latitude 20°N., and their longitudes are respectively 170°W. and 120°W. A ship sails from A due north to B, then due east to C and finally due south from C to D. Calculate to 3 sig. figs. how much farther this journey is than the direct route along the equator from A to D. Take the radius of the earth to be 6 300 km. (Oxford)

6. Calculate the distance a ship travels when sailing due north from a point P, latitude 30°N., longitude 20°W., to a point Q, latitude 45°N., longitude 20°W. If the ship had sailed due west along the parallel of latitude 30°N. from P for the same distance

THE SPHERE

as from P to Q, calculate the longitude of the point reached. Take the radius of the earth to be 6 300 km. (Oxford)

7. A ship is at position A, latitude 30°N., longitude 70°W. It has to sail to a point B, latitude 20°S., longitude 30°W. It first sails along the parallel 30°N. until it is due north of B, then sails due south to B. Calculate to 3 sig. figs. the total distance travelled. Take the radius of the earth to be 6 300 km. (Oxford)

8. A solid geographical globe of radius r cm, is divided into 2 unequal parts by a plane cut through a parallel of latitude in the northern hemisphere. The smaller part is called a spherical cap. If the distance from the north pole of the globe to the centre of the circular section exposed is h cm, then the volume of the spherical cap V in centimetres is known to be given by $V = \dfrac{\pi h^2}{3}(3r - h)$.

Rearrange this formula to give r in terms of V, π and h.

If a spherical cap for which $h = 3$ has a volume of 594 cm^3, calculate (i) the radius of the geographical globe, (ii) the area of the plane base of the cap. (Oxford)

9. From an island, situated latitude 39°S., longitude 62°W., a ship sails eastward for 2 720 km along the parallel of latitude 39°S. to position A. From A it sails due north for 3 840 km to a position B. Taking the earth's radius to be 6 300 km, calculate the latitudes and longitudes of both A and B.

10. Find out all you can about the Bedford Level experiment to measure the diameter of the earth.

A Gnomon

A gnomon is a simple instrument for measuring the angle of the sun's rays. It is simply two pieces of wood at right angles, one piece to lie perfectly horizontal, Fig. 10-36, and marked with a centimetre scale. The height is usually 10 or 20 cm, and the tangent of the angle of the sun's rays, or sun's elevation, would be found by the height of the gnomon divided by the length of the shadow, Fig. 10-37. This gives the tangent of the angle of latitude as the length of shadow divided by the height of the gnomon. Why?

LONGMAN MATHEMATICS

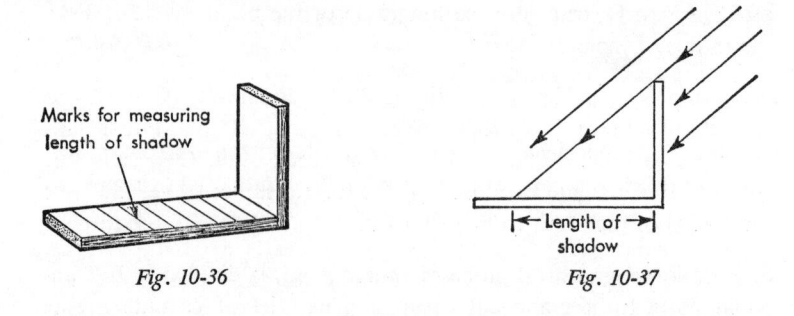

Fig. 10-36

Fig. 10-37

Finding the Latitude of the School

On only two days in the year (equinoxes) the sun shines on one half of the earth from the north pole to the south pole. If the sun

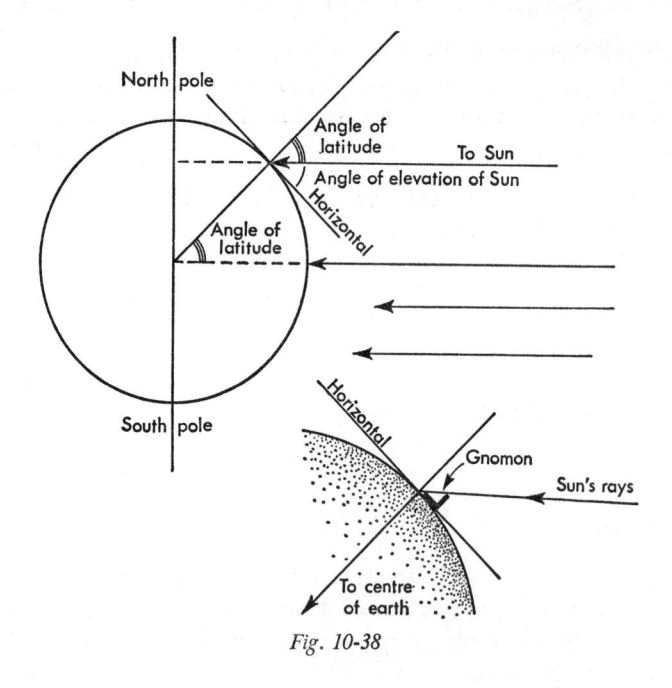

Fig. 10-38

is shining on one of these days then Fig. 10-38 will show why it is possible to find the angle of latitude by using the gnomon. Discuss this with your teacher.

11 Practical Applications of Trigonometry

In Chapter 10 the idea of a line of longitude on the earth's surface was explored. It is a line travelling in a North–South direction and on the earth it is the arc of a circle. It is impossible to represent a curved surface on a flat piece of paper, and map makers have to make certain distortions in the process. A look at an atlas will show this. However, for mapping fairly small areas, there is little distortion involved if a grid of straight lines at right angles is used to represent lines of latitude and longitude. Over fairly small distances such a map can be used for navigation.

The Points of the Compass

A compass used for navigation is an instrument which enables the user to fix the direction in which he is travelling with reference to Magnetic North. This is not true North (i.e. towards the North Pole), but the true direction can be found by making a correction (called the declination) to the reading. This declination can be found in a nautical almanac.

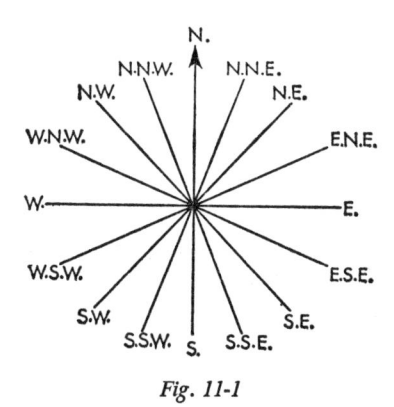

Fig. 11-1

North, South, East and West are the main points of the compass with which you should be already familiar. The direction NE. bisects the right angle between North and East and similar bisections give SE.,

153

SW. and NW. The direction NNE. bisects the angle between N. and NE. The names of the other bisectors can be seen in Fig. 11-1.
Note: Fig. 11-1 can be placed on a map provided that the lines of longitude and latitude are at right angles.
There are two main methods of describing the bearing of one point from another.

True bearings

These are measured in a *clockwise* sense from the true north line and run from 0° to 360°.

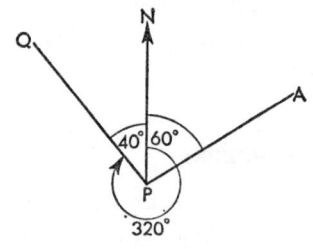

Fig. 11-2

The bearing of A from P is said to be 060°. The 0 is written in front of the 60 so that all true bearings are expressed in three figures. This avoids mistakes when bearings are being signalled by wireless. To find the true bearing of Q from P imagine that you are standing at P facing true North. Then turn clockwise (i.e. to the right) until you are looking along PQ. You have now turned through an angle of 320° (360° − 40°). The true bearing of Q from P is 320°.

Compass bearings

P and Q are two points on a map. If QP makes an angle of 40° with the magnetic north then the bearing of Q from P is said to be N.40°W. or 40°W. of N.
Note: PQ makes an angle of 40° with the line running S. through Q, and so the bearing of P from Q is said to be S.40°C. or 40°E. of S.

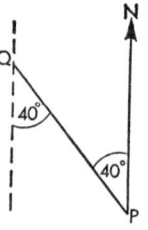

Fig. 11-3

Compass bearings are always measured East to West of North or South.
Study the following example carefully.

PRACTICAL APPLICATIONS OF TRIGONOMETRY

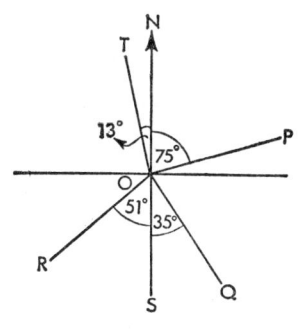

Fig. 11-4

The bearing of P from O is 075° or N.75°E.
The bearing of Q from O is 145° or S.35°E.
The bearing of R from O is 231° or S.51°W.
The bearing of T from O is 347° or N.13°W.

Exercise 11a

1. Express the bearings of A, B, C and D from O as both true

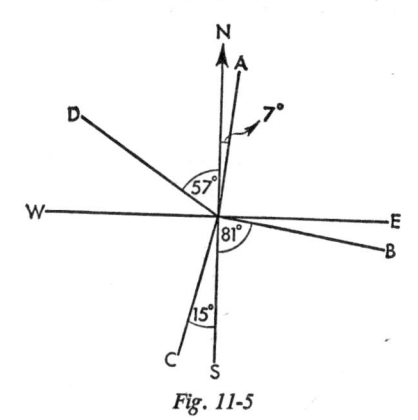

Fig. 11-5

and compass bearings, setting your answers out like the example above. Find the angles between the following bearings. A sketch will help.

2. 113° and 236°.   **3.** 030° and 171°.
4. 115° and 313°.   **5.** 004° and 358°.

155

6. 083° and 272°.
7. 0° and 360°.
8. N.20°W. and N.55°E.
9. N.10°E. and S.72°E.
10. N.47°W. and S.47°E.
11. N.17°E. and N.23°W.
12. S.75°E. and N.21°W.
13. NNE. and ESE.
14. NW. and SSE.
15. N. and SSW.

In the following examples express the final directions both as true bearings and compass bearings:

16. Face N. and turn 70° clockwise.
17. Face N. and turn 50° anti-clockwise.
18. Face E. and turn 95° clockwise.
19. Face W. and turn 87° clockwise.
20. Face S. and turn 210° clockwise.
21. Face S and turn 290° anti-clockwise.
22. Face E. and turn 340° clockwise.
23. Face SE. and turn 17° clockwise.
24. Face NW. and turn 315° clockwise.
25. Face ESE. and turn 30° anti-clockwise.

Examples

A and B are two points 20 km apart. The bearing of B from A is 027° (N.27°E.). Find how far B is North of A and East of A.

Mark point A and through it draw a line going N. Draw a line on the bearing 027° (N.27°E.) and mark B on it so that AB = 20 km. Draw AC due E. and BC due S. Then BC (called the *northing* of B from A) and AC (called the *easting* of B and A) are the required distances.

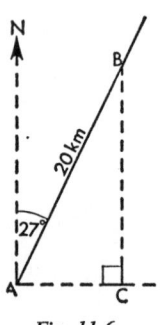

Fig. 11-6

Triangle ABC is right angled at C

$$B\widehat{A}C = 90° - 27°$$
$$= 63°$$

$$\frac{BC}{AB} = \sin B\widehat{A}C$$

PRACTICAL APPLICATIONS OF TRIGONOMETRY

or
$$\frac{BC}{20} = \sin 63°$$
$$\therefore BC = 20 \sin 63°$$
$$20 \times 0{\cdot}891\,0$$
$$= 17{\cdot}82$$
$$\therefore BC = 17{\cdot}8 \text{ km (3 sig. fig.)}$$
$$\frac{AC}{AB} = \cos B\hat{A}C$$
$$\therefore \frac{AC}{20} = \cos 63°$$
$$\therefore AC = 20 \cos 63°$$
$$= 20 \times 0{\cdot}454\,0$$
$$= 9{\cdot}080$$
$$\therefore AC = 9{\cdot}08 \text{ km (3 sig. fig.)}$$
$\therefore$ B is 17·8 km N. and 9·08 km E. of A

Q is 15 km S. and 5 km W. of P. Find the bearing of Q from P and the distance between P and Q.

Construct the figure as shown.
To find the bearing of Q from P it is necessary to find angle $S\hat{P}Q$. But $S\hat{P}Q = P\hat{Q}R$ (alternate angles)

and
$$\tan P\hat{Q}R = \frac{PR}{RQ}$$
$$= \frac{\overset{1}{\cancel{5}}}{\underset{3}{\cancel{15}}}$$
$$= 0{\cdot}3333$$
$$\therefore P\hat{Q}R = 18°\,26' = S\hat{P}Q$$
$\therefore$ Q is 198° 26′ (S.18° 26′W.) from P.

By Pythagoras' theorem
$$PQ^2 = PR^2 + QR^2$$
$$= 5^2 + 15^2$$
$$= 25 + 225$$
$$\therefore PQ^2 = 250$$

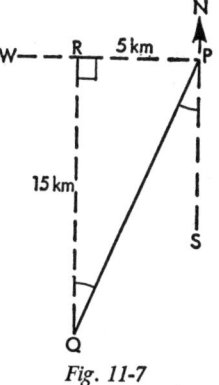

Fig. 11-7

$$\therefore PQ = \sqrt{250}$$
$$= 15\cdot 81$$
$$\therefore \underline{PQ = 15\cdot 8 \text{ km (3 sig. fig.)}}$$

Exercise 11b

Use log. tables *where necessary*.

1. A and B are two points 10 km apart. B lies $067\frac{1}{2}°$ (ENE). from A. Find how far B is E. and N. of A.

2. X and Y are two points 15 km apart. X is 227° (S.47°W.) from Y. Find how far X is S. and W. of Y.

3. P and Q are two ships 18 km apart. The bearing of Q from P is 146°. Find how far Q is S. and E. of P.

4. C and D are two points 1 072 metres apart. The bearing of D from C is 334°. Calculate how far D is N. and W. of C.

5. A is 3 km N. and 4 km E. of B. Find the true bearing of A from B and the distance between A and B.

6. Y is 14 km S. and 8 km. W. of Z. Find the true bearing of Y from Z and the distance YZ.

7. P is 6·7 km W. and 13·2 km N. of Q. Find the true bearing of P from Q and the distance PQ.

8. P is 73 km E. and 47 km S. of O. Find the true bearing of P from O and the distance OP.

9. A destroyer A is 57 km S. and 10 km W. of a point O. A second destroyer B is 33 km N. and 51 km. E. of O. Find the course that each must steam in order to meet at O. Find also the distance each must travel to arrive at O. Find also the true bearing of A from B and the total distance AB.

10. A boat at A is 22 km S. and 10 miles W. of a lightship L. The lightship L is 48 km from a port P on a bearing 117° (S.63°E.). Calculate the bearing of A from P and the distance AP.

(*Hint:* Find the Southing and Easting of A from P.)

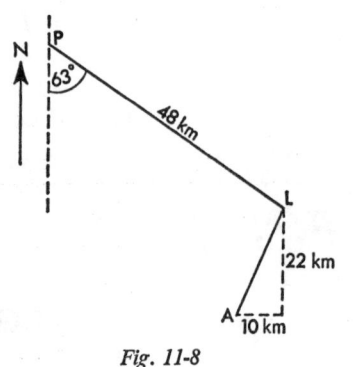

Fig. 11-8

PRACTICAL APPLICATIONS OF TRIGONOMETRY

11. A gunner at point P wishes to hit a target at T. He cannot see T because it lies beyond a hill. A scout moves to a point S, 8 000 metres

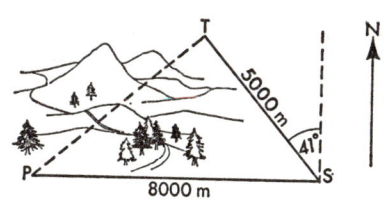

Fig. 11-9

due E. of P, and observes that T is 5 000 metres from S on a bearing 319° (N.41°W.). Find the bearing of T. from P and the range PT.

12. A man wishes to navigate his boat from point P to point Q on

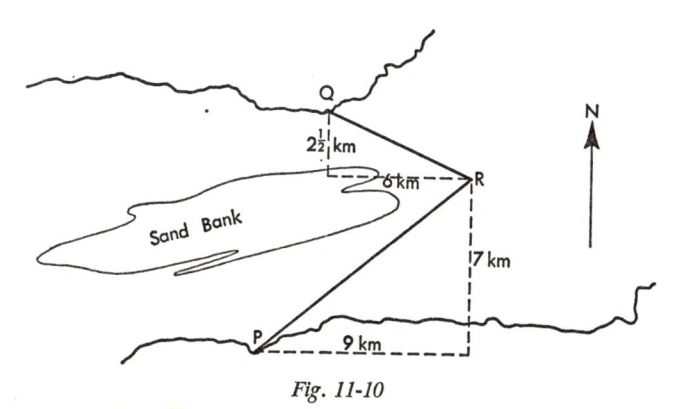

Fig. 11-10

opposite sides of an estuary at low tide. Because of a sand bank he must sail via buoy at R. If R is 7 km N. and 9 km E. of P and 2½ km S. and 6 km E. of Q find the bearings of PR and QR and the total distance PRQ. If he can sail directly from P to Q at high tide, find the bearing of Q from P and the distance PQ.

13. An aircraft flies from an airfield A on a course 235° to an airfield B 100 km from A. It then flies 70 km due S. to an airfield C and finally 200 km due E. to its destination D. Calculate the bearing of D from A and the distance AD.

14. A motor rally route takes the form of a triangle PQR. Q is 10 km from P on a bearing 036° (N.36°E.). R is on a bearing 289°

159

(N.71°W.) from Q and 328° (N.32°W.) from P. Sketch the route and *calculate* the distances QR, RP.
(*Hint:* Use the sine rule.)

15. A boatman intends to sail from A to B, a distance of 26 km in a NW. direction. Because of currents he actually sails a distance of 31 km on a bearing 337° (N.23°W.) to a point C. What course must he now take to sail from C to B? How far is it from C to B?

16. In a yacht race the course is in the form of a quadrilateral ABCD. B is 4 km due W. of A, C is 5 km from B on a bearing 345° and D is 12 km from C on a bearing 075°. Find the distance of the last stage DA and the bearing of A from D.

17. A and B are two points 200 metres apart and the bearing of B from A is 063°. From A the bearing of a point C is 110° and from B the bearing of C is 153°. Calculate the distance AC, the perpendicular distance of C from AB and hence the area of the triangle ABC.

18. A ship is sailing from A to B on a course 153° (S.27°E.) The distance from A to B is 220 km. When it reaches a point C 120 km from A it receives an S O S to go to the help of another ship at a point D which is 150 km from C on a bearing 070° (N.70°E.). On reaching D and giving help the ship sets course for B. On what bearing must it sail, and how far is it to B?

Three-Dimensional Problems

Look carefully at this sketch of a rectangular prism.

An attempt has been made on a flat two-dimensional surface to represent a solid (three-dimensional) object. Does this look solid to you? ABCD is a rectangular base in the *horizontal* plane and AE, BF, CG and DH are *vertical* edges. In such sketches always draw vertical

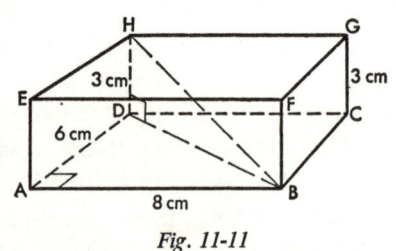

Fig. 11-11

edges at right angles to the bottom of your paper. EFGH is the top rectangular face. One of the difficulties in solving three-dimensional problems is to draw a reasonable sketch so that you can visualize the solid nature of the object.

PRACTICAL APPLICATIONS OF TRIGONOMETRY

If AB = 8 cm, AD = 6 cm and DH = 3 cm calculate the length of BH and the angle $D\hat{B}H$.

It is necessary to connect BH with the other given dimensions. BH is a side of triangle BDH and BD is common to both triangle BDH and triangle ABD. It is helpful to take these triangles from Fig. 11-11 and sketch them in their true shapes. Remember that some right angles do not look like right angles in the sketch of the solid.

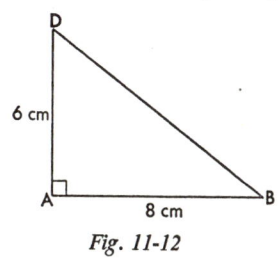

Fig. 11-12

Fig. 11-13

First calculate BD.
In triangle ADB
$$BD^2 = AD^2 + AB^2 \text{ (Pythagoras' theorem)}$$
$$= 6^2 + 8^2$$
$$= 36 + 64$$
$$\therefore BD^2 = 100$$
$$\therefore BD = 10 \text{ cm}$$

Calculate BH and angle $D\hat{B}H$.
In triangle HDB
$$BH^2 = HD^2 + BD^2$$
$$= 3^2 + 100$$
$$= 9 + 100$$
$$\therefore BH^2 = 109$$
$$\therefore BH = \sqrt{109}$$
$$= 10.44 \text{ (from square root tables)}$$
$$\therefore \underline{BH = 10.4 \text{ cm (3 sig. fig.)}}$$
$$\tan D\hat{B}H = \frac{HD}{BD}$$
$$= \frac{3}{10}$$
$$\therefore \tan D\hat{B}H = 0.3$$
$$\therefore \underline{D\hat{B}H = 16° 42'}$$

Two Important Ideas

The angle between a line and a plane.

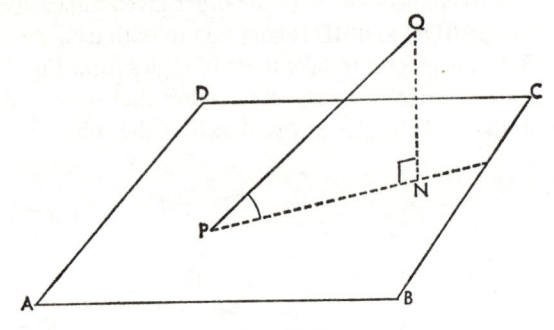

Fig. 11-14

ABCD is a flat surface or a *plane*. PQ is a line which cuts it at P. From Q drop a perpendicular QN on to ABCD. Joint NP. N is called the *projection* of Q on ABCD and NP is called the *projection* of PQ on ABCD.

The angle between PQ and ABCD is *defined* as the angle between PQ and its projection (PN) on ABCD, i.e. angle $Q\hat{P}N$.

In the previous example BD is the projection of BH on the plane ABCD, since HD is perpendicular to ABCD, and the angle $D\hat{B}H$ which was found is the angle between BH and plane ABCD.

The angle between two planes.

Two planes always cut each other along a straight line. Think of a piece of paper folded along AB as in Fig. 11-15. Here are two planes ABCD and ABPQ meeting along AB. Take any point T on AB.

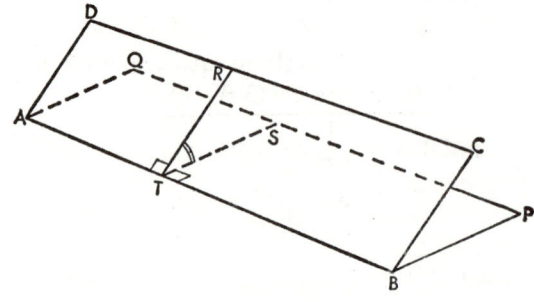

Fig. 11-15

Draw TR in plane ABCD perpendicular to AB and draw TS in plane ABPQ perpendicular to AB. Then the angle between planes ABCD and ABPQ is *defined* as the angle between RT and ST, i.e. angle $R\hat{T}S$. A further example.

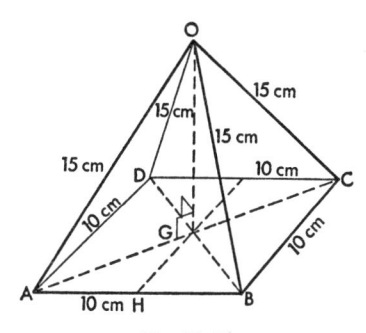

Fig. 11-16

OABCD is a pyramid with vertex O and a square base ABCD of side 10 cm. OA = OB = OC = OD = 15 cm. Find the perpendicular height, the angle that one of the sloping edges makes with the base and the angle between a sloping face and the base.
By symmetry the vertex O is vertically above G, the centre of ABCD (at the intersection of the diagonals)
∴ OG is perpendicular to the base.
∴ OG is the perpendicular height and GA is the projection of OA on the base.
∴ Angle $O\hat{A}G$ is the angle between the sloping edge OA and the base ABCD.
Let H be the midpoint of AB. Join OH and GH.
Now OA = OB (given)
∴ Triangle OAB is an isosceles triangle and AH = HB.
∴ OH is perpendicular to AB.
Similarly triangle AGB is an isosceles triangle since AG = GB.
∴ GH is perpendicular to AB.
∴ Angle $O\hat{H}G$ is the angle between sloping face OAB and the base ABCD.

163

LONGMAN MATHEMATICS

To find OG and angle $O\hat{A}G$.
Angle $O\hat{G}H$ is a right angle in triangle OGH and if AG is known, OG and angle $O\hat{A}G$ can be found.
To find AG.

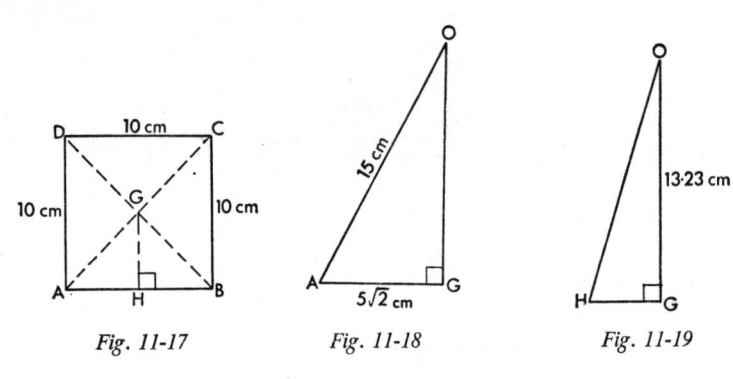

Fig. 11-17   Fig. 11-18   Fig. 11-19

Make true sketches of the base ABCD, triangle OAG and triangle OGH.
In triangle ABC
$$AC = AB^2 + BC^2 \quad \text{(Pythagoras' theorem)}$$
$$= 10^2 + 10^2$$
$$= 200$$
$$\therefore AC = \sqrt{200}$$
$$= \sqrt{10^2 + 2}$$
$$= 10\sqrt{2} \quad (\textit{Note:} \text{ There is no need to work this out.})$$
$$AG = \tfrac{1}{2} AC$$
$$= \tfrac{1}{2} \times 10\sqrt{2}$$
$$= 5\sqrt{2} \text{ cm}$$
In triangle OAG
$$OG^2 = OA^2 - AG^2 \quad \text{(Pythagoras' theorem)}$$
$$= 15^2 - (5\sqrt{2})^2$$
$$= 225 - 25 \times 2$$
$$= 175$$
$$\therefore OG = \sqrt{175}$$
$$= 13 \cdot 23$$
$$\therefore \underline{OG = 13 \cdot 2 \text{ cm}} \text{ (3 sig. fig.)}$$

PRACTICAL APPLICATIONS OF TRIGONOMETRY

$\sin O\hat{A}G = \dfrac{OG}{OA}$ (Use OA, a given length rather than AG which has been calculated.)

$= \dfrac{13 \cdot 23}{15}$

$\therefore \underline{O\hat{A}G = 61° 54'}$ (from Log. Sine tables)

No.	Log.
13·23	1·121 6
15	1·176 1
	$\bar{1}$·945 5

In triangle OGH angle $O\hat{G}H$ is a right angle and OG has been found. If GH is now found angle $O\hat{H}G$ can be calculated.

In Fig. 11-17 in triangle AGH and triangle ACB

$G\hat{A}H = C\hat{A}B$ (common angle)

$G\hat{H}A = C\hat{B}A = 90°$

$\therefore$ Triangle AGH and triangle ACB are similar.

$\therefore \dfrac{GH}{AH} = \dfrac{CB}{AB}$

But $\quad CB = AB$

$\therefore GH = AH = 5 \text{ cm}$

In Triangle OHG

$\tan O\hat{H}G = \dfrac{OG}{GH}$

$= \dfrac{13 \cdot 23}{5}$ (*Note:* The *uncorrected* value of OG is used.)

$\therefore \tan O\hat{H}G = 2 \cdot 646$

$\therefore \underline{O\hat{H}G = 69° 18'}$

This example illustrates many of the methods used when dealing with solid figures. It is important to find the required angles and lengths in the sketch of the solid, then state why they are correct. This statement will be a useful guide to the methods for finding them, and to the triangles which are to be used. These triangles should be sketched in their true shape so as to avoid errors in calculation.

Exercise 11c

1. Fig. 11-20 shows a rectangular prism. AB = 9 metres, AD = 6 metres and AE = 5 metres. Find the length of the diagonal HB and the angle it makes with the base ABCD.

2. In Fig. 11-20 find the angle which plane FGDA makes with the base.

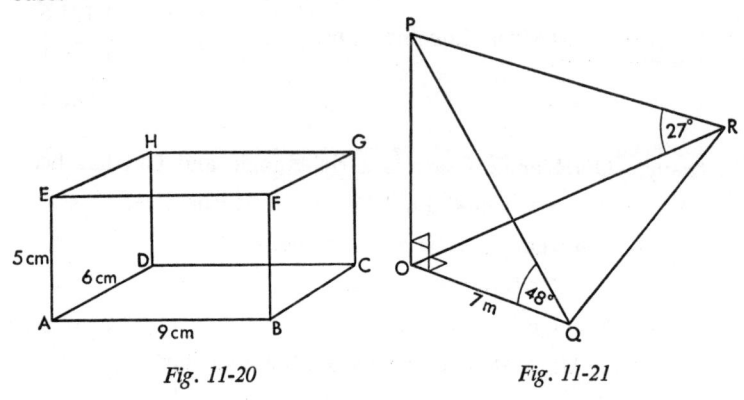

Fig. 11-20

Fig. 11-21

3. In Fig. 11-21 OP is a flagstaff. OQ and OR are lines in the horizontal plane such that angle $Q\hat{O}R$ is a right angle. OQ = 7 metres and the elevation of P from Q is 48°. At R the elevation of P is 27°. Calculate the height of the flagstaff OP, the distances OR and QR.

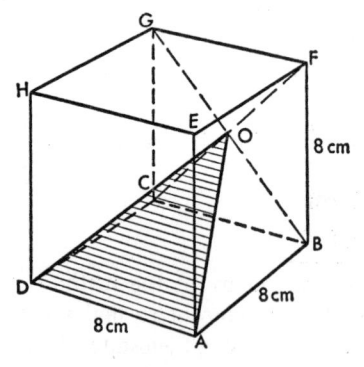

Fig. 11-22

4. Fig. 11-22 shows a cube of side 8 cm. O is the centre of face BCGF. Find the angle which OA makes with ABCD. Find also the angle which plane OAD makes with ABCD.

5. AB is a vertical line and AC and AD are lines through A in the horizontal plane such that angle $C\hat{A}D$ is a right angle. If AB = 6

PRACTICAL APPLICATIONS OF TRIGONOMETRY

metres and BC = BD = 10 metres, find the angle of elevation of B from D and also the angle which face BCD makes with the base ADC.

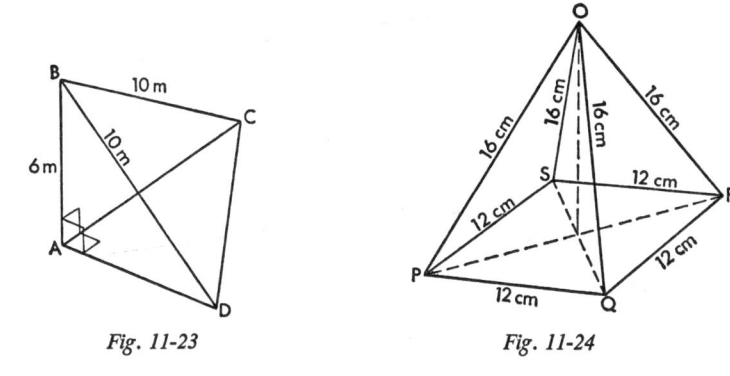

Fig. 11-23

Fig. 11-24

6. Fig. 11-24 shows a pyramid PQRS on a square base PQRS of side 12 cm. OP = PQ = OR = OS = 16 cm. Find the perpendicular height, the angle a sloping edge makes with the base and the angle between a sloping face and the base.

7. OABCD, (Fig. 11-25), is a wedge. BC and BO are perpendicular to each other and to AB. AB = 2 cm, AD = 3 cm and angle $A\hat{O}B = 36°$. Find angle $D\hat{O}C$ and the angle which face OCD makes with face ABCD.

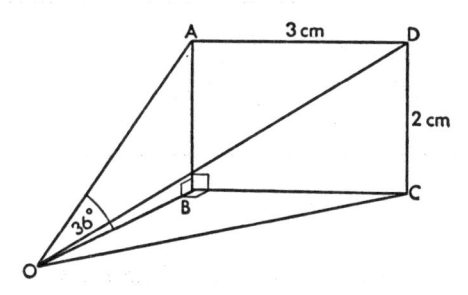

Fig. 11-25

8. ABC represents a hill track. The section AB is in the vertical plane APQR and section BC is in the vertical plane PTSQ which intersects APQR along PQ at right angles. AP = 50 metres and PT = 72 metres. AB makes an angle of 27° with the horizontal and BC makes 31° with the horizontal. Find the vertical height of C above A and the total distance ABC. Also calculate the distance between A and C, Fig. 11-26.

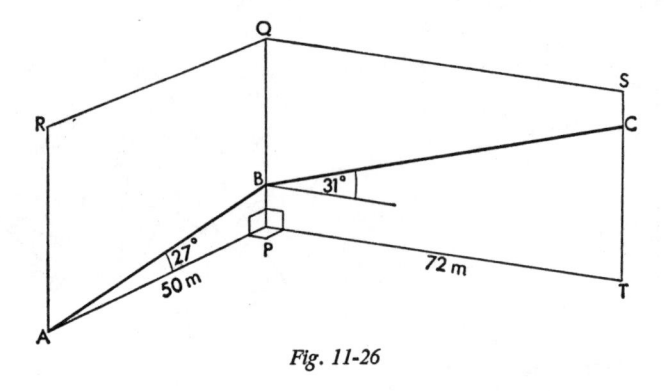

Fig. 11-26

9. Fig. 11-27 shows one end of the roof of a house. The ridge of the roof AE lies symmetrically above BG and CF, and AD is perpendicular to the plane BCFG (i.e. D lies midway between BG and CF). Angle $B\hat{D}C$ is a right angle, AC = 8·5 m, BC = 6 m and angle

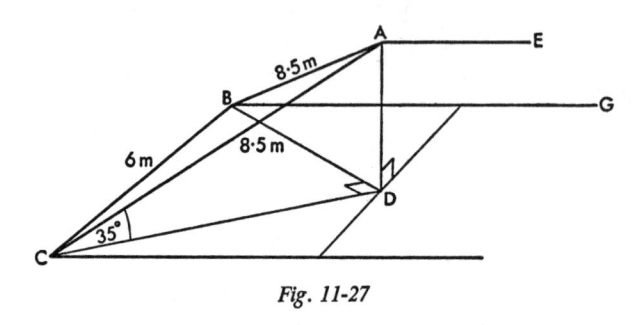

Fig. 11-27

$A\hat{C}D = 35°$. Calculate the height AD and the angle which the sloping roof ABC makes with the horizontal.

10. A man at the top of a cliff 30 metres high at a point A sees two boats C and D out at sea. The angles of depression of D and C are 23° and 51° respectively. Boat D is due N. of A and boat C is due E. of A. Find the distances between the boats and the bearing of C from D, Fig. 11-28, page 169.

PRACTICAL APPLICATIONS OF TRIGONOMETRY

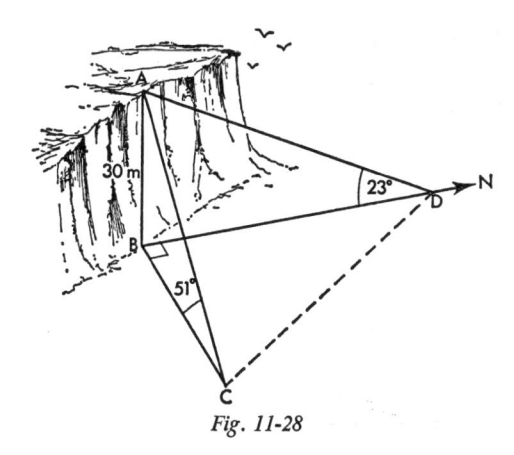

Fig. 11-28

11. An observer at C, Fig. 11-29, 200 metres south of a point A watched an aircraft take off from A and fly upwards along a straight line AB. The angle of elevation of the aircraft at B from C is 35°. It is then vertically over D and D is 450 metres due East of A. Find the height of the aircraft at B and the angle of climb $B\hat{A}D$.

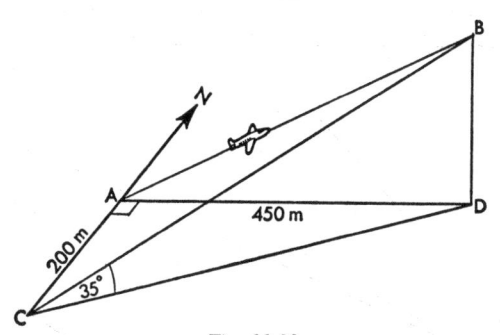

Fig. 11-29

12. Fig. 11-30 represents a rectangular prism. PS = 14 metres, PQ = 18 metres and TS = 10 metres. Find the angle TQ makes with the base PQRS and the angle between plane TQS and the face PSTU.

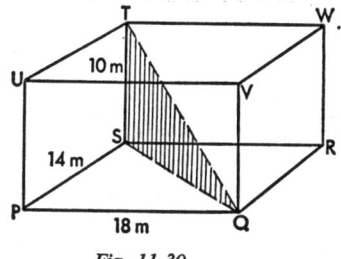

Fig. 11-30

169

LONGMAN MATHEMATICS

13. Fig. 11-31 represents a cube of side 12 cm. Calculate the angle which ABC makes with the base BPCQ and the area of the triangle ABC. (*Hint:* Join PQ to cut BC at R.)

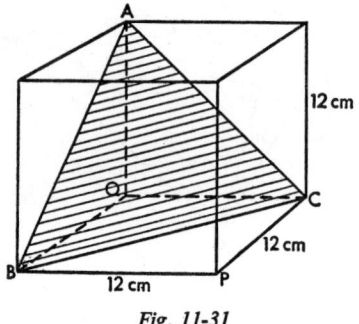

Fig. 11-31

14. Fig. 11-32 represents a sloping hillside, AB and BD are horizontal and D is vertically below C where BC is the line of greatest slope (i.e. BD is perpendicular to ED). Angle DBC = 25° and BC is 50 metres in length. A path AC is 100 metres long. Find the height CD and the angle which AC makes with the horizontal.

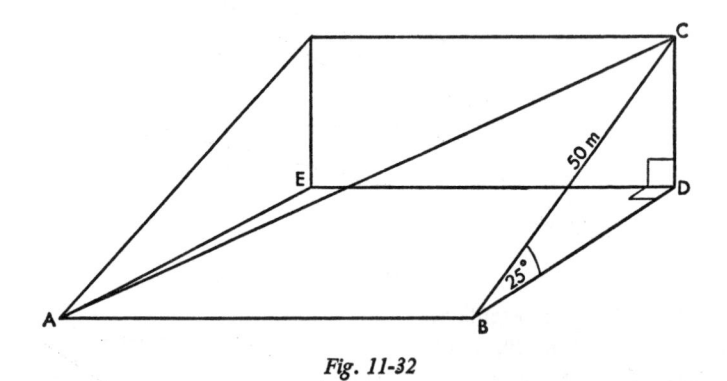

Fig. 11-32

15. Fig. 11-33 shows a sloping hillside. EBA is horizontal and AB is perpendicular to BE. The angle of greatest slope CAB = 21° and AC = 70 metres. A path AD makes an angle of 17° with the horizontal. Find the length of AD and the angle which plane AED makes with the plane BCDE.

PRACTICAL APPLICATIONS OF TRIGONOMETRY

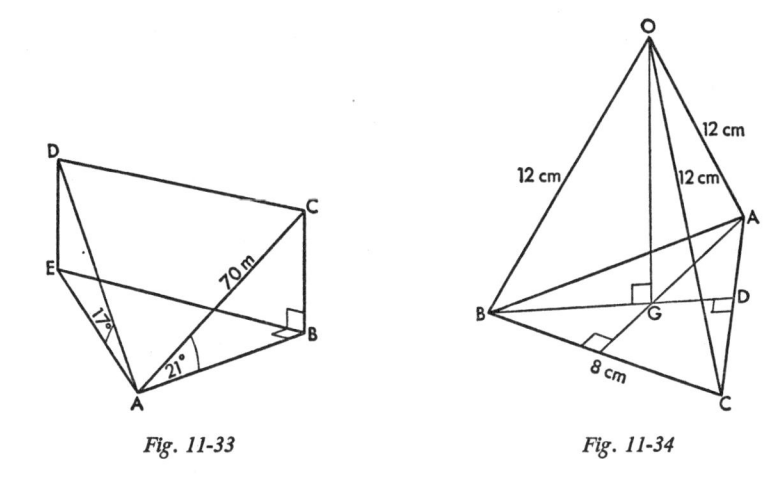

Fig. 11-33

Fig. 11-34

16. OABC, Fig. 11-34, is a tetrahedron. The base ABC is an equilateral triangle of side 8 cm and OA = OB = OC = 12 cm. The perpendicular height is OG. Given that G lies on BD, where D is the mid-point of AC and that BG = $\frac{2}{3}$BD, calculate the height OG and the angle which OB makes with the base ABC. Find also the angle which face OAC makes with the base ABC.

17. The following statements refer to Fig. 11-35. State whether they are TRUE or FALSE.

(*a*) The bearing of P from O is 090°

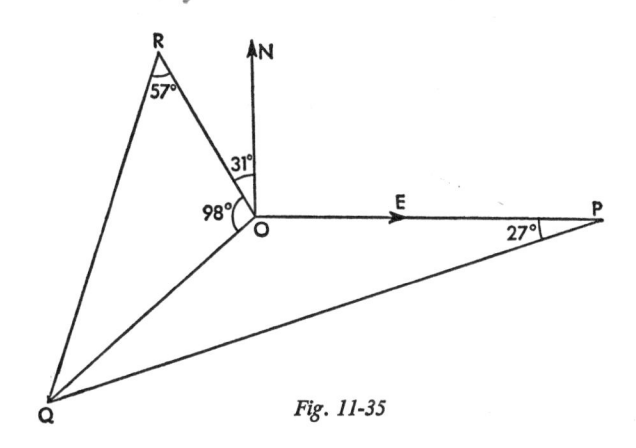

Fig. 11-35

171

(b) The bearing of R from O is N.31°E.
(c) The bearing of Q from R is 196°
(d) The bearing of P from Q is 063°
(e) The bearing of Q from O is 231°

18. A man wishes to sail from A to B across an estuary. Because of the islands he must sail from A to P and from P to B. The bearing of P from A is 229° and AP is 9 km. P is 4 km North and 5 km West of B. Are the following statements TRUE or FALSE?

(a) $A\hat{P}Q = 41°$
(b) $PQ = AP \sin 41°$
(c) $AQ = 5\cdot 90$ km
(d) A is 9·90 km North of B
(e) $BP = \sqrt{41}$ km
(vi) Q is 11·79 km W. of P
(vii) The total distance travelled is 15·40 km
(viii) $\tan B\hat{A}Q = \dfrac{QR}{\text{Northing of A from B}}$
(ix) $B\hat{A}Q = 10° 16'$
(x) The bearing of B from A is 169° 44′

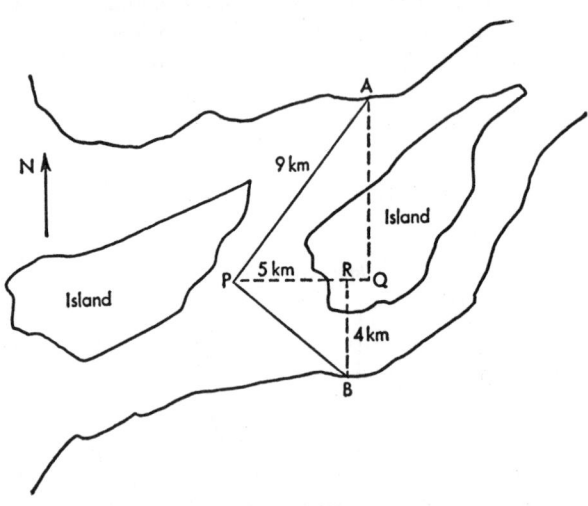

Fig. 11-36

19. A barn, of perpendicular height CD, stands alongside a river. A surveyor makes observations along a horizontal line ABC where AB

PRACTICAL APPLICATIONS OF TRIGONOMETRY

is 12 metres. Angles $D\hat{A}C$, $D\hat{B}C$ are 16° and 25° respectively. Are the following statements TRUE or FALSE?
  (a) The angle of elevation of D from B is 16°
  (b) If BC = x metres then AC = (12 + x) metres
  (c) If DC = h metres then x = h tan 25° metres
  (d) (12 + x) tan 16° = h
  (e) (12 + x) tan 16° = x tan 25°
  (f) $x = \dfrac{3 \cdot 440\ 4}{0 \cdot 179\ 6} = 19 \cdot 15$
  (g) AC = 30·15 m
  (h) DC = 19·15 tan 25°
  (i) The height of the barn is 8·93 metres

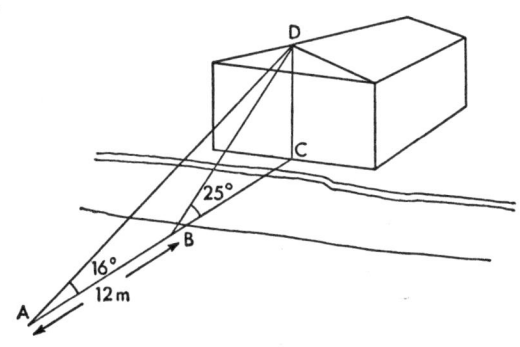

Fig. 11-37

20. PABCD is a right pyramid on a base 4 metres square. The height OP is 4 metres. Select the correct answers in the following statements.
  (a) The length of the diagonal AC is (i) 8 m (ii) $8\sqrt{2}$ m (iii) $4\sqrt{2}$ m (iv) 4 m
  (b) The slant height PB is (i) $4\sqrt{3}$ m (ii) 5 m (iii) $4\sqrt{2}$ m (iv) $2\sqrt{6}$ m
  (c) The tangent of angle $P\hat{B}O$ is (i) $\sqrt{2}$ (ii) $\dfrac{1}{\sqrt{2}}$ (iii) ½ (iv) $\dfrac{4}{5}$
  (d) Angle $P\hat{B}O$ is (i) 26° 31′ (ii) 35° 16′ (iii) 38° 40′ (iv) 54° 44′
  (e) The angle between face PBC and the base ABCD is (i) $P\hat{B}O$ (ii) $P\hat{N}O$ (iii) $P\hat{C}D$ (iv) $O\hat{P}N$

173

(f) The angle between face PBC and the base ABCD is (i) 154° 44′ (ii) 63° 26′ (iii) 37° 59′ (iv) 60°

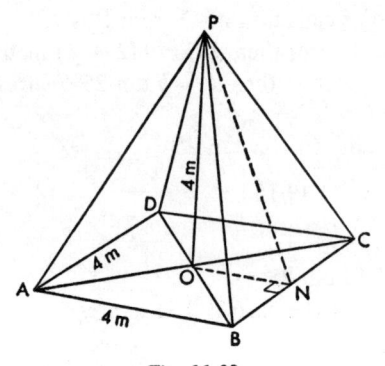

Fig. 11-38

12 Sets

The Number of Elements in a Set

The *number* of elements in a set often needs to be calculated. In order to distinguish between the set itself and the numbers of elements in the set, the latter is written $n(A)$. $n(A)$ is really a *number* and must be treated as a number.
If A and B have no elements in common they are said to be DISJOINT. If A and B are disjoint then $A \cap B = \emptyset$; $n(A \cap B) = 0$; and $n(A \cup B) = n(A) + n(B)$
If however A and B are not disjoint but have some elements in common, $n(A \cup B)$ is a little more complicated to calculate.
From Fig. 12-1

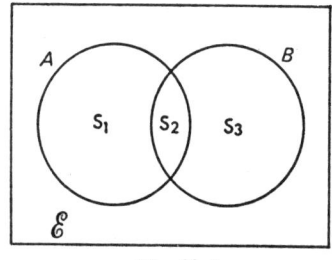

Fig. 12-1

$$n(A \cup B) = n(S_1) + n(S_2) + n(S_3)$$
$$= n(A \cap B') + n(A \cap B) + n(A' \cap B) \quad - \text{(i)}$$
But $\quad n(A \cap B') = n(A) - n(A \cap B)$
and $\quad n(A' \cap B) = n(B) - n(A \cap B)$
substituting these in (i)
$$n(A \cup B) = n(A) - n(A \cap B) + n(A \cap B) + n(B) - n(A \cap B)$$
whence $n(A \cup B) = n(A) + n(B) - n(A \cap B)$
i.e. To find the number of elements in $A \cup B$ we add together the number of elements in A and B; and subtract from this total the number of elements in $A \cap B$. Can you see why this is so?

Example

If in a 6th form, 20 pupils study Mathematics (set M), 15 study Physics (set P), and 8 study both subjects, how many are in the form?

The number required is $n(M \cup P)$
$$n(M) = 20; n(P) = 15; n(M \cap P) = 8$$
Thus $\quad n(M \cup P) = 20 + 15 - 8$
$$= 27$$

Exercise 12a

1. In a class of 31 swimmers, 22 can swim the backstroke and 18 can swim the butterfly. Draw and label a suitable Venn diagram and calculate how many swim both strokes.

2. In a class of 29 girls, 17 were blonde and 16 had blue eyes. If all the girls were in either set how many were blue-eyed blondes? Draw and label a suitable Venn diagram.

3. 96 per cent of people asked could write well with their right hand and 17 per cent could use right or left hands. How many were left-handed?

4. A newsagent had only 2 types of newspapers. 64 people bought *The Daily Telegraph*, 19 bought *The Times*, and 8 bought both. How many people were served?

5. At an Anglo-French Conference 16 Englishmen needed the translators' earphones. If there were 100 delegates present and 47 of these were bilingual, how many present could speak French?

All these above problems can be easily done by ordinary algebraic methods—letting x be the required number, forming an equation and then solving.

Problems involving three sets are however much more difficult by this method than by the use of set theory.

Consider first 3 disjoint sets, as Fig. 12-2,
$$n(A \cup B \cup C) = n(A) + n(B) + n(C)$$

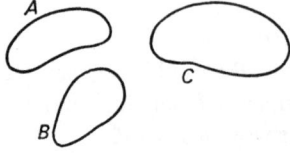

Fig. 12-2 \qquad\qquad Fig. 12-3

If two sets only intersect as in Fig. 12-3,
$$n(A \cup B \cup C) = n(A) + n(B) - n(A \cap B) + n(C)$$

SETS

This follows from the first part of this section.
If the three sets intersect as in Fig. 12-4,
$n(A \cup B \cup C) = n(A) + n(B) + n(C) - n(A \cap B) - n(B \cap C)$

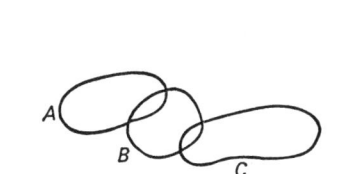

Fig. 12-4

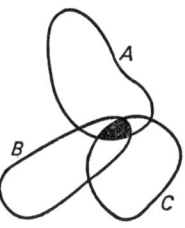

Fig. 12-5

Notice how in the last two examples the intersection sets are subtracted as they have been counted in twice in the summing of the whole sets.

In Fig. 12-5 the shaded part will be counted IN 3 times in $n(A)$, $n(B)$, $n(C)$; it will also be counted OUT in the 3 intersection sets, $n(A \cap C)$, $n(A \cap C)$, $n(B \cap C)$. Thus taking
$n(A) + n(B) + n(C) - n(A \cap B) - n(A \cap C) - n(B \cap C)$
will give us the number of elements in the shaded part of Fig. 12-6. Hence for $n(A \cup B \cup C)$ it is necessary to add in $(A \cap B \cap C)$.
i.e.
$n(A \cup B \cup C) = n(A) + n(B) + n(C) - n(B \cap C)$
$\qquad - n(A \cap C) - n(A \cap B) + n(A \cap B \cap C)$

Fig. 12-6

Example

In a certain science college records showed that 86 students had studied Physics, 43 had studied Chemistry and 94 had studied Mathematics. 34 had studied both Physics and Maths, 21 had studied both Chemistry and Physics, 19 had studied Maths and Chemistry and 12 had taken all 3 subjects. How many pupils were not studying these subjects if the total roll was 210? How many were studying Physics, Chemistry and Mathematics as single subjects?

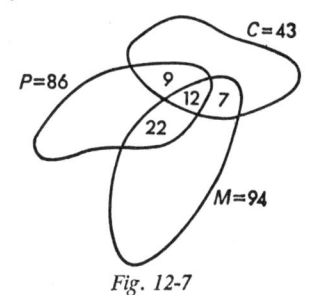

Fig. 12-7

177

Fig. 12-7 gives a picture of all the given information.

From the above formula
$$n(P \cup M \cup C) = 86 + 43 + 94 - 21 - 19 - 34 + 12$$
$$= 161$$

Hence number of students not studying Physics, Maths or Chemistry $= 210 - 161 = 49$

From the diagram

the number studying Physics only $= 86 - (9 + 12 + 22) = 43$
" " " Maths only $= 94 - (7 + 12 + 22) = 53$
" " " Chemistry only $= 43 - (7 + 12 + 9) = 15$

Exercise 12b

1. At a party a number of red, white and blue balloons were released, and prizes were given to all who had one of each colour. 12 people received prizes; 8 people obtained one red and one white balloon; 5 obtained one white and one blue; 7 obtained one blue and one red; 34 obtained nothing, and all the rest obtained one balloon each. If there were 40 balloons of each colour:
How many guests were there?
How many people had one red balloon only? One blue balloon only? One white balloon only?

2. A headmaster called for a report on his Science Sixth Form. He was given the following summary:
46 boys studying Physics; 25 boys studying Chemistry; 27 boys studying Maths; 19 studying Physics and Chemistry; 8 studying Physics and Maths; 10 studying Maths and Chemistry; and 3 studying Physics, Chemistry and Maths.
The headmaster returned the summary as inaccurate. Was he right? Prove your answer.

3. In the Arts Sixth 70 boys were studying English; 40 were studying Languages; 40 were studying History and Geography; 20 studying Languages and English; 15 studying Languages, History and Geography; 25 studying English, History and Geography; 5 studying Languages, English, History and Geography. How many boys were in the Arts Sixth?

4. The following survey shows the percentage of boys reading certain comics.

SETS

60 per cent read *Beano*
50 ,, ,, ,, *Dandy*
50 ,, ,, ,, *T.V. Comic*
30 ,, ,, ,, *Beano and Dandy*
30 ,, ,, ,, *Beano and T.V. Comic*
20 ,, ,, ,, *Dandy and T.V. Comic*
10 ,, ,, ,, *Beano, Dandy and T.V. Comic*

What percentage read only 2 magazines?
What percentage do not read any of the three?
What percentage read only 1 magazine?

5. 160 boys were asked how they travelled to school.
31 always walked; 26 always travelled by bus; 20 always cycled; 23 either cycled or used a bus; 18 either cycled or walked.
If twice as many either walked or used a bus, as used all three methods, how many used all three methods?

6. There are forty girls in a class. Each of them takes French or German or both. Thirty-two of the girls take French and eighteen take German.

(*a*) How many take both French and German?

Seven of the girls in the class take Russian as well. Five of these seven take French and five take German.

(*b*) (*i*) How many girls in the class take all three languages?
(*ii*) How many girls in the class take just one language?

(Met. C.S.E.)

7. Fig. 12-8 represents a universal set ε containing 48 elements. The subsets A, B, and C contain 22, 18 and 20 elements respectively.

The subsets $A \cap B$, $B \cap C$ and $C \cap A$ contain 7, 8 and 10 elements respectively.
If also the number of elements in $(A \cup B \cup C)'$ is 8, find the number of elements in
(*a*) A' (*b*) $A \cap B \cap C$
(*c*) $(A \cap B) \cap C'$.
Find the number of elements in each of the following sets:
(*d*) $(A \cap B)'$ (*e*) $A' \cup B'$.

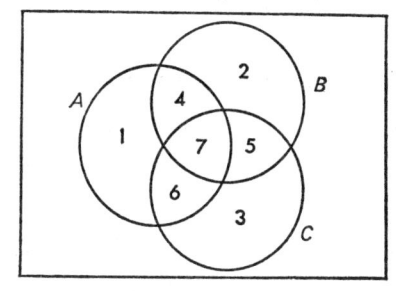

Fig. 12-8

(Met. C.S.E.)

179

8. In a mixed school of 500 pupils, every pupil must play at least one of three sports, football, netball and tennis. None of the boys plays netball and none of the girls plays football, 350 pupils play tennis, 150 play football and 100 play netball. Find the number of pupils who play one sport only. If there are 300 girls in the school, find the number of boys who play tennis only. Explain why the number of boys who play football only cannot be less than 50.
(A.E.B.)

9. A department store has three departments A, B and C. An analysis of 100 shoppers reveals that 52 made a purchase in department A, 23 in department B and 60 in department C. Six shoppers made no purchase at all, the rest made at least one purchase, and 10 made a purchase in all three departments. How many shoppers made a purchase in any two of the departments, but not all three?
(A.E.B.)

10. 675 men were interviewed concerning smoking. 225 did not smoke at all. Of the rest 70% smoked cigarettes, 40% smoked pipes and 24% smoked cigars. Only 2% smoked all three but 10% smoked either cigarettes or cigars. If 18% smoked only pipes how many smoked only cigarettes or only cigars?
How many smoked cigarettes and pipes only?
How many never smoked a cigar?

11. In Fig. 12-1 express S_1, S_2 and S_3 in terms of A, B, A' and B' and in the form $X \cap Y$.

12. In Fig. 12-8 express regions 1–7 in terms of A, B, C, A', B' and C' and in the form $X \cap Y \cap Z$.

The Algebraic Laws of Sets

In the work that you did on sets in Stages 2 and 3, some general results were obtained which were independent of the nature of the set itself. These results show some of the 'operational rules' which all sets obey. The following is a summary of the rules or laws of sets which form the basis for set albegra:

1. (i) $A \cup B = B \cup A$; (ii) $A \cap B = B \cap A$. The commutative law.
2. (i) $(A \cup B) \cup C = A \cup (B \cup C)$; (ii) $(A \cap B) \cap C = A \cap (B \cap C)$. The associative law.

SETS

3. (i) $A \cap (B \cup C) = (A \cap B) \cup (A \cap C)$
   (ii) $A \cup (B \cap C) = (A \cup B) \cap (A \cup C)$ The distributive law.

The above three laws are of course part of the normal number system. The following laws are not:

4. $A \cap \mathscr{E} = A$
5. $A \cap \varphi = \varphi$
6. $A \cup \mathscr{E} = \mathscr{E}$
7. $A \cup \varphi = A$
8. $A \cup A = A$
9. $A \cap A = A$
10. $(A \cup B)' = A' \cap B'$
11. $(A \cap B)' = A' \cup B'$
12. $A \cup A' = \mathscr{E}$
13. $A \cup A' = \varphi$
14. $\mathscr{E}' = \varphi$
15. $\varphi = \mathscr{E}$

Exercise 12c

By using Venn diagrams verify all the above laws.

While Venn diagrams can be used to verify or demonstrate the set laws they are not proofs. Proofs are not required before 6th form level.

Boolean Algebra

If some given operations with specified factors satisfy the rules given above then the algebra is said to be a Boolean algebra, after the mathematician George Boole (1815-64). Many different Boolean algebras have been developed in recent years some of which have become quite important in modern research and technology. One interesting development is the use of Boolean algebra to examine logical problems and logical statements. In this development the ideas of subsets is important and an emphasis has been placed on the link between the operations (', $\cup$, $\cap$) and the ideas behind the words ('not', 'or', 'and') which arise in the definitions of the operations;

A' is the set of elements NOT in A.

$A \cup B$ is the set of elements both in A OR in B.

$A \cap B$ is the set of elements in A AND in B.

In some cases where the factors being dealt with are not sets, and also because of the similarity of some of the laws with those of ordinary arithmetical algebra, then the symbols of ordinary arithmetic are used; $+$ is used for union, $\times$ is used for intersection, the universal set is 1, and the empty set is 0. While the similarities cannot be taken very far they are sufficient to give rise to a number of workable systems.

Exercise 12d

1. Re-write the above laws for Boolean algebra using the symbols $(+, \times, 1, 0)$. Apart from the laws involving complements, which laws do not hold in arithmetical algebra?

2. Complete the following tables for Boolean algebra

∪	0 1
0	
1	

∩	0 1
0	
1	

	′
0	
1	

Compare these tables to similar tables for $+$ and $\times$.

To summarise: A Boolean algebra is a system of elements closed under two operations which are associative (2), commutative (1), and distributive (3). There exist complements (10–15) identities and inverses (4–7) and the elements are idempotent (8 & 9).

One important fact concerning the rules of Boolean algebra is that they are completely symmetrical. Look at the rules 1–15 above; their symmetry leads to the property of duality which you first met in connection with the regular solids (stage 3). That is by interchanging the operations and the identity elements one of the rules becomes transformed into its counterpart.

Boolean Algebra and Switching Circuits

Computers perform their operations mainly by means of electrical pulses. These pulses can be stored, delayed or combined with other material by electronic means. One of the main difficulties is in preparing the problem material into the correct form to feed into the computer, this preparation is called 'programming'. Several methods are then used to change the programmed information into electrical pulses, these include punched cards, paper tape, magnetic tape, printed characters, for optical or magnetic use, etc.

Each electrical impulse takes only about one millionth of a second (a microsecond) to pass with a similar gap between two impulses. Fig. 12-9 illustrates a *regular* stream of pulses. Since at a particular

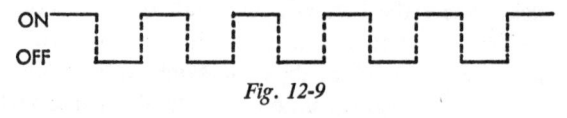

Fig. 12-9

registering point there will be either a pulse or an absence of a pulse, only two symbols are required to represent the flow of the pulses. Since binary arithmetic uses only two symbols, numbers can be

SETS

easily recorded using this method, by taking 1 for the presence of a pulse and 0 when no pulse is present. For example the number 101 101 000 (binary form) will be registered by pulses as in Fig. 12-10.

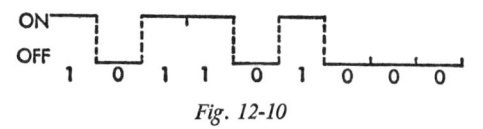

Fig. 12-10

Individual numbers are discernible as all pulse patterns have a fixed length large enough to carry the largest numbers.

Switches

Most of the devices mentioned above for allowing or stopping pulses can be thought of as electrical switches. When a switch allows a pulse to pass through it is said to be CLOSED, and can be illustrated thus →————→. When a switch stops pulses from passing it is said to be OPEN, and can be illustrated thus ————————. As there are only two alternatives for a switch (open or closed) they can be denoted by just two symbols. The two digits 1 and 0 are generally used, 1 when the switch is closed and 0 when the switch is open. It should be noted that in this usage they are not to be considered as numbers.

It is usual to denote a switch by a single letter (a, b, c . . .) and if two or more switches work simultaneously, opening or closing in unison, they are denoted by the same letter. If, however, two switches work in opposition, that is, when one opens the other closes, then they are denoted by a and a' etc. a' is called the *complement* of a.

Switches in parallel and in series

The two switches in Fig. 12-11 are said to be connected IN PARALLEL.

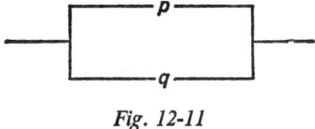

Fig. 12-11

The pulses will flow through this device if p or q or both p and q are closed. A device of this type is called an OR-gate, usually written

183

$p \vee v$ and read as 'p or q'. This always carries the implication of 'one or the other or both' and is derived from the Latin word 'vel'. Tables for the OR-gate can be drawn up as in Fig. 12-12.

p	q	$p \vee q$
0	0	0
0	1	1
1	0	1
1	1	1

(a)

Fig. 12-12a

p \ q

$\vee$	0	1
0	0	1
1	1	1

(b)

Fig. 12-12b

The table on the left is produced by taking all the possible alternatives of the two switches being open or shut.

—p——q—

(a)

Fig. 12-13

Fig. 12-13 shows two switches connected *in series*. Pulses will flow only if both p and q are closed. This type of device is called an AND-gate, usually written $p \wedge q$ and read as 'p and q'.

Exercise 12e

Write out the two tables for $p \wedge q$.
Compare the two (b) tables for $p \vee q$ and $p \wedge q$ with the tables for $\cup$ and $\cap$ in exercise 12d no. 2.
Compare the definitions of $\cup$ and $\cap$ in Boolean algebra with the definitions of $\vee$ and $\wedge$.
Complete the two tables
Table (*i*) for a switch and
Table (*ii*) for Boolean algebra.

a	a'
1	
0	

(i)

	$'$
1	
0	

(ii)

These tables of Boolean functions are quite important and appear in other topics including logical analysis.

SETS

Most electronic devices consist of numerous switches linked in various ways and by using Boolean algebra it is possible to describe the switches in algebraic terms. Consider for example the switching device in Fig. 12-14.

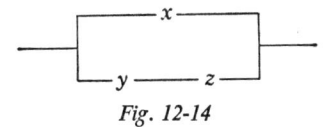

Fig. 12-14

The current has to pass through x or $y \vee z$. Thus the full algebraic function can be written as $x \vee (y \wedge z)$. This expression is known as the Boolean function of the device.

Exercise 12f

1. Draw the circuits with the following Boolean functions:
   (i) $a \vee b$ (ii) $a \wedge b$ (iii) $a \vee b \vee c$
   (iv) $a \wedge b \wedge c$ (v) $a \vee (b \wedge c)$ (vi) $(a \vee b) \wedge c$
   (vii) $a \wedge (b \vee c)$ (viii) $(a \wedge b) \vee c$ (ix) $(a \wedge b) \vee (c \wedge d)$
   (x) $(a \vee b) \wedge (c \vee d)$ (xi) $a \wedge (b \vee a')$
   (xii) $a \vee (a' \wedge b') \vee (a \wedge b)$

2. Write down the Boolean functions for the following devices:

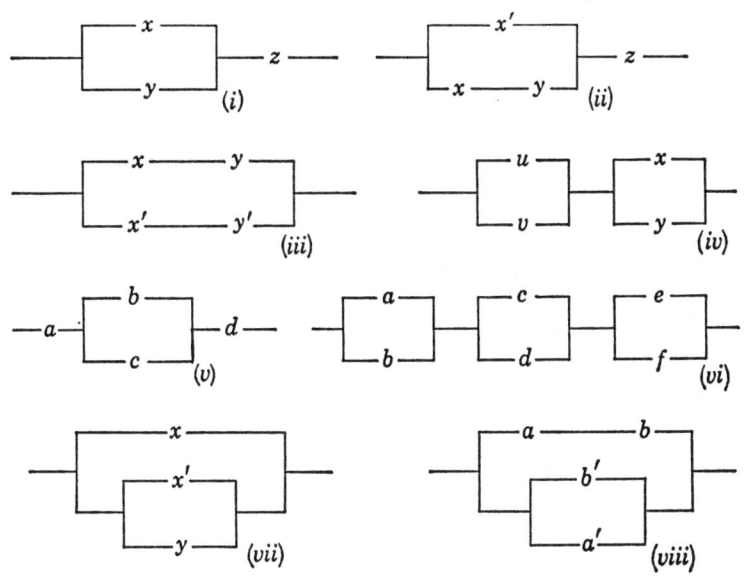

(ix)   (x)

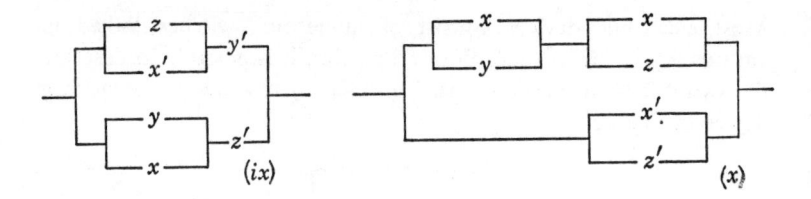

Closure Tables

Tables such as those in Figs. 12-12 (*a*) and Exercise 12e (*a*) can be obtained for all switch devices and are known as *closure tables*. Example 1. Consider Fig. 12-15. The Boolean function is $x' \vee (x \wedge z)$. The closure table Fig. 12-16 is developed by considering what happens when each switch is open or closed. Note: the best method to write down all the possible alternatives is to use the binary notation.

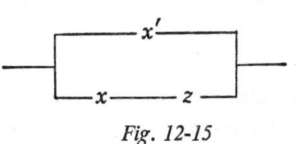

Fig. 12-15

x	z	$x \wedge z$	x'	$x' \vee (x \wedge z)$
0	0	0	1	1
0	1	0	1	1
1	0	0	0	0
1	1	1	0	1

Fig. 12-16

Example 2

Example 2. Obtain the closure table for the circuit in Fig. 12-17.

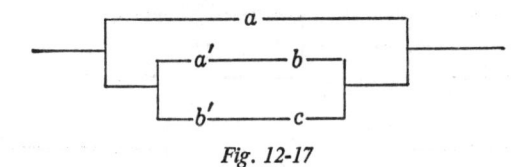

Fig. 12-17

A pulse will flow through a, or through a' and b, or through b' and c. Thus the Boolean function is given by $a \vee (a' \wedge b) \vee (b' \wedge c)$; and the closure table will be:

SETS

a	b	c	a'	b'	$(a' \wedge b)$	$a \vee (a' \wedge b)$	$(b' \wedge c)$	$a \vee (a' \wedge b) \vee (b' \wedge c)$
0	0	0	1	1	0	0	0	0
0	0	1	1	1	0	0	1	1
0	1	0	1	0	1	1	0	1
1	0	0	0	1	0	1	0	1
0	1	1	1	0	1	1	0	1
1	0	1	0	1	0	1	1	1
1	1	0	0	0	0	1	0	1
1	1	1	0	0	0	1	0	1

Fig. 12-18

Exercise 12g

1. Write out the closure tables for all the circuits in Exercise 12f nos. 1 and 2.

Switching Circuits as a Boolean algebra

Switching algebra can be shown to obey the laws of Boolean algebra by the use of closure tables. For example the associative law (no. 2)

p	q	r
0	0	1
0	1	0
1	0	0
0	1	1
1	0	1
1	1	0
1	1	1

$(q \vee r)$	$p \vee (q \vee r)$
1	1
1	1
0	1
1	1
1	1
1	1
1	1

$(p \vee q)$	$(p \vee q) \vee r$
0	1
1	1
1	1
1	1
1	1
1	1
1	1

Fig. 12-19

states that (i) $p \vee (q \vee r) = (p \vee q) \vee r$ and
(ii) $p \wedge (q \wedge r) = (p \wedge q) \wedge r$.
By comparing the closure tables for $p \vee (q \vee r)$ and for $(p \vee q) \vee r$ it can be shown that they are identical.

Exercise 12h

By using closure tables prove the following; and draw diagrams of the different circuits:

1. $p \wedge (q \wedge r) = (p \wedge q) \wedge r$. Associative law.
2. $a \vee b = b \vee a$. The commutative law (no. 1).
3. $a \wedge b = b \wedge a$. The commutative law.
4. $a \vee (b \wedge c) = (a \vee b) \wedge (a \vee c)$. The distributive law (no. 3).
5. $a \wedge (b \vee c) = (a \wedge b) \vee (a \wedge c)$. The distributive law.
6. $(a \vee b)' = a' \wedge b'$. De Morgan's laws (Laws 10 and 11).
7. $(a \wedge b)' = a' \wedge b'$. De Morgan's laws.
8. $a \vee a = a$. Indempotent law (nos. 8 and 9).
9. $a \wedge a = a$. Idempotent law.
10. $a \vee a' = 1$. Complements (12–15).
11. $a \wedge a' = 0$.

A switch which is always open can be represented by 0, and a switch which is always closed by 1. The following then follow:

(i) $a \vee 1 = a$ (law 4)   (ii) $a \vee 0 = 0$ (law 5)
(iii) $a \wedge 1 = 1$ (law 6)   (iv) $a \wedge 0 = a$ (law 7)

Thus switching circuits obey all the laws required for a Boolean algebra.

Simplifying Switching Circuits

Consider the two circuits in Fig. 12-20. The Boolean functions are (a) $q \wedge p$ and (b) $(p \vee q) \wedge (p' \wedge q)(p \vee q')$ and the closure tables are as in Fig. 12-20.

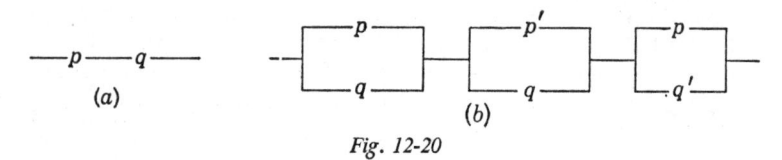

Fig. 12-20

SETS

p	q	p'	q'	p∨q	p'∨q	(p∨q)∧(p'∨q)	p∨q'	(p∨q)∧(p'∨q)∧(p∨q')	p∧q
0	0	1	1	0	1	0	1	0	0
0	1	1	0	1	1	1	0	0	0
1	0	0	1	1	0	0	1	0	0
1	1	0	0	1	1	1	1	1	1

(b)　　　　　　　　　　　(a)

From the closure tables it can be seen that the two circuits give the same results, that is they are equivalent. It is obviously useful, from an economic point of view, to obtain the simplest circuit, although this is not always a matter of obtaining the smallest number of switches. It is often possible to obtain a simpler circuit by treating the Boolean function as an algebraic expression and to simplify this by applying the laws of Boolean algebra.

Consider for example the above Boolean function:

(b) $= (p \vee q) \wedge (p' \vee q) \wedge (p \vee q') = [(p \vee q) \wedge (p' \vee q)] \wedge (p \vee q')$
$\qquad\qquad\qquad\qquad\qquad\qquad\qquad$ by associative law
$\qquad\qquad = q \vee (p \wedge p') \wedge (p \vee q')$
$\qquad\qquad\qquad\qquad\qquad\qquad\qquad$ by distributive law
$\qquad\qquad = q \vee 0 \wedge (p \vee q') \quad$ complements
$\qquad\qquad = q \wedge (p \vee q')$
$\qquad\qquad = (q \wedge p) \vee (q \wedge q')$
$\qquad\qquad\qquad\qquad\qquad\qquad\qquad$ by distributive law
$\qquad\qquad = (q \wedge p) \vee 0 \quad$ complement
$\qquad\qquad = (q \wedge p)$
$\qquad\qquad = $ (a)

Exercise 12j

Obtain the Boolean functions for the following circuits. In each case simplify circuit (i) and obtain circuit (ii) by using the laws of Boolean algebra, and thus show that each pair of circuits are equivalent. Check these equivalents by comparing the closure tables.

1. (i) $a \cdot (a+b)$ (ii) $a \cdot b$

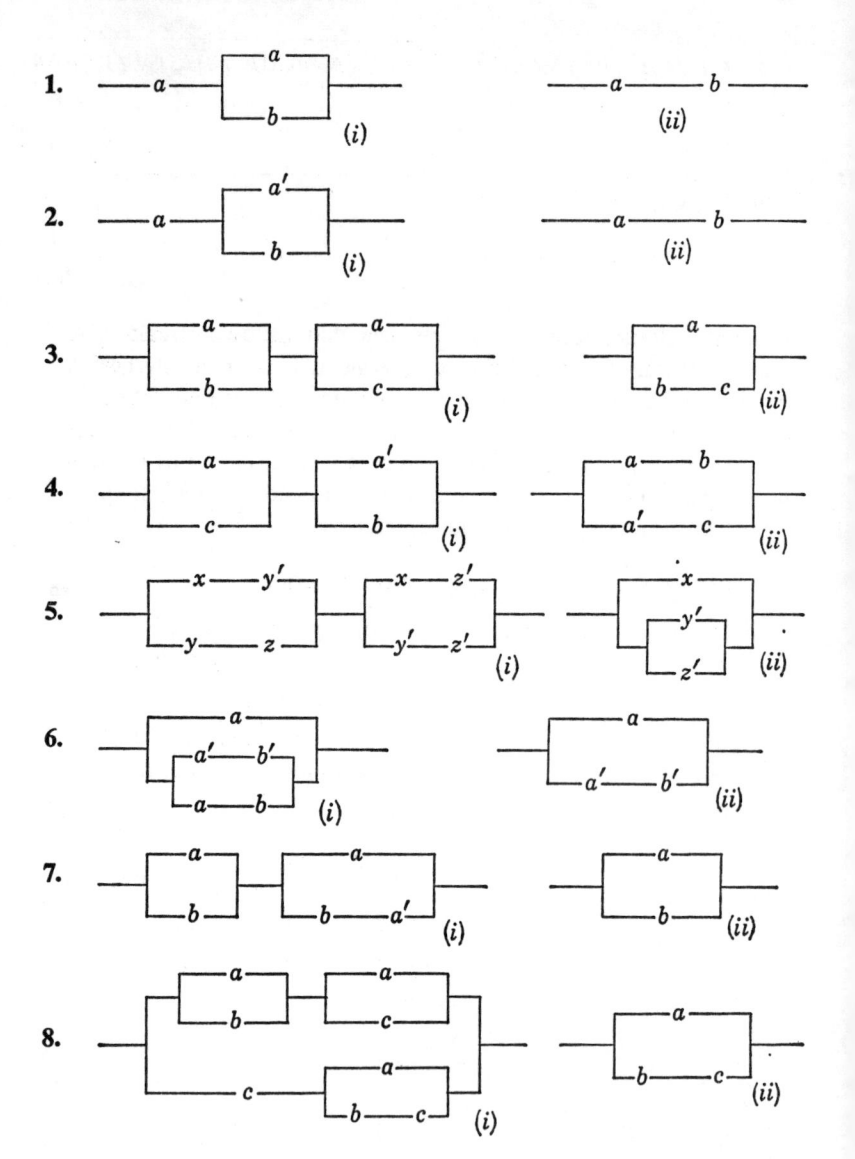

2. (i) $a \cdot (a'+b)$ (ii) $a \cdot b$

3. (i) $(a+b)(a+c)$ (ii) $a+bc$

4. (i) $(a+c)(a'+b)$ (ii) $ab+a'c$

5. (i) $(x+y'+z \cdot y)(x+z'+y' \cdot z')$ (ii) $x+y'+z'$

6. (i) $a + a'b' + ab$ (ii) $a + a'b'$

7. (i) $(a+b)(a+b+a')$ (ii) $a+b$

8. (i) $(a+b)(a+c) + c(a+bc)$ (ii) $a+bc$

13 Geometry

Polygons

What is a polygon?

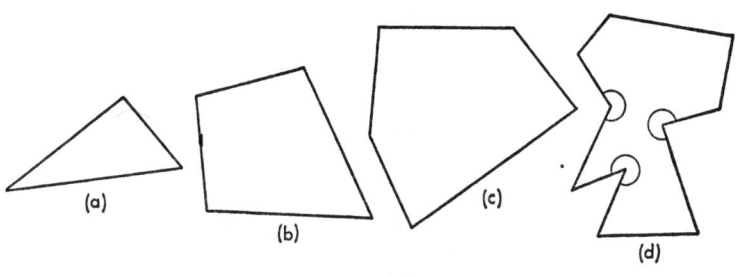

Fig. 13-1

All these figures are polygons.
What do they have in common?
They are all plane figures, i.e. they are drawn on a flat surface.
They are all closed figures, i.e. starting from any corner (or vertex) it is possible to travel right round the figure along the sides and to return to the starting point. They are all bounded by *straight* lines.
The marked interior angles in figure (d) are reflex angles (greater than 180°). Such a figure is called a re-entrant polygon.
Polygons whose interior angles are either acute or obtuse (less than 180°) are called convex polygons and the following work applies only to convex polygons.

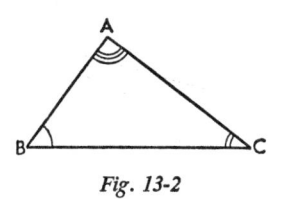

Fig. 13-2

The simplest polygon is a triangle.
The sum of the interior angles $\hat{A} + \hat{B} + \hat{C} = 180°$ or 2 right angles.

191

A four-sided polygon is called a quadrilateral.
Joint diagonal AC and the figure ABCD is divided into two triangles.

$\hat{D} + \hat{y} + \hat{z} = 180°$ (angle sum of a triangle)
$\hat{B} + \hat{x} + \hat{w} = 180°$ (,,   ,, ,, ,,   ,,)
Add $\hat{B} + \hat{D} + (\hat{x} + \hat{y}) + (\hat{z} + \hat{w}) = 360°$
$\therefore \hat{B} + \hat{D} + \hat{A} + \hat{C} = 360°$ or 4 right angles.

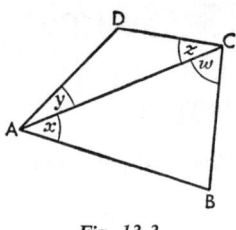

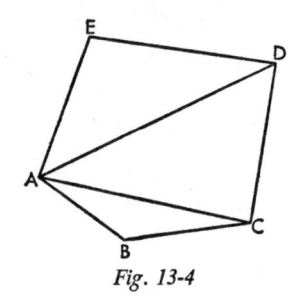

Fig. 13-3

A five-sided polygon is called a pentagon.
Join diagonals AC and AC of ABCDE.
How many triangles make up the figure? What is the total sum (in right angles) of the interior angles of a pentagon?

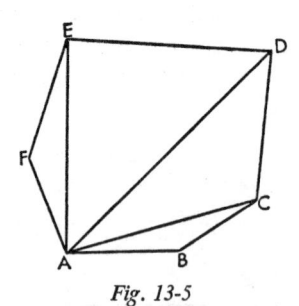

Fig. 13-5

A six-sided polygon is called a hexagon.
Join diagonals AC, AD, AE of ABCDEF. How many triangles make up the figure? What is the total sum (in right angles) of the interior angles of a hexagon?

GEOMETRY

Exercise 13a

1. By using the above information and by making suitable sketches, complete the following table.

NO. OF SIDES OF POLYGON	NO. OF DIAGONALS	NO. OF TRIANGLES	SUM OF INTERIOR ANGLES IN RIGHT ANGLES
3	0	1	2
4	1	2	4
5	2	3	6
6	3	4	8
7	4	5	10
8	5	6	12
9	6	7	14
10	7	8	16
11	8	9	18
12	9	10	20

2. Can you see a pattern in the above table?
If a polygon had n sides, how many diagonals will it have from one particular vertex? Into how many triangles will these diagonals divide the polygon? From this result state, in right angles, a possible expression for the sum of the interior angles of an n-sided polygon.

The result you obtain in Example 2 above has been obtained by *generalizing* a series of results. This is often a useful guide to a result, but it can be a dangerous process.

For example, at a large scout parade all the scouts (many hundreds of them) were wearing green berets. Is it possible to say that all scouts wear green berets? This might be true, but there is no *certainty* about the conclusion, unless there was a rule that all scouts must wear green berets. Even then this rule could be broken.

But the rules of mathematics are general rules which cannot be broken. They have to be proved from a general case and not generalized from a limited number of numerical cases.

To illustrate the danger of generalization take the formula of Father M. Mersenne (see Stage 2, p. 146) for prime numbers

$$M_p = 2^p - 1$$

Try
$p = 3$ $M_3 = 2^3 - 1 = 8 - 1 = 7$
$p = 5$ $M_5 = 2^5 - 1 = 32 - 1 = 31$
$p = 7$ $M_7 = 2^7 - 1 = 128 - 1 = 127$

Now 7, 31, 127 are all prime numbers.

We could generalize here and say that since for the odd values $p = 3$, $p = 5$, $p = 7$, M_p is a prime number then the value of $2^p - 1$ is prime for all odd values of p.

Try $p = 9$

$$M_9 = 2^9 - 1 = 512 - 1 = 511$$

But $511 = 7 \times 73$ and is therefore not prime (it has factors). From this example the dangers of generalization are evident.

Theorem

The sum of the interior angles of an n-sided convex polygon is $(2n - 4)$ right angles.

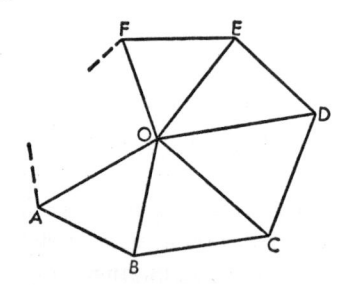

Fig. 13-6

Given. A convex polygon ABCDEF ... with n sides.

To prove that $\widehat{ABC} + \widehat{BCD} + \widehat{CDE} + \widehat{DEF} + \ldots = 2n - 4$ right angles.

Construction: Choose any point O *inside* the polygon and join AO, BO, CO, DO, EO, FO ...

Proof: In Triangle AOB

$\widehat{OAB} + \widehat{OBA} + \widehat{AOB} = 2$ right angles (angle sum of a triangle)

GEOMETRY

Similarly $\quad O\hat{B}C + O\hat{C}B + B\hat{O}C = 2$ right angles
$\qquad O\hat{C}D + O\hat{D}C + C\hat{O}D = 2$ right angles
and so on.

Since there are n sides to the polygon there are n triangles such as triangle AOB.

Adding all the angles of all the n triangles
$(A\hat{B}C + B\hat{C}D + C\hat{D}E + D\hat{E}F + \ldots)$
$\qquad\qquad + (A\hat{O}B + B\hat{O}C + C\hat{O}D + \ldots) = 2n$ right angles.

But
$(A\hat{O}B + B\hat{O}C + C\hat{O}D + \ldots) = 4$ right angles
$\qquad\qquad\qquad\qquad\qquad$ (sum of adj. angles at a point)
$\therefore (A\hat{B}C + B\hat{C}D + C\hat{D}E + D\hat{E}F + \ldots) + 4$
$\qquad\qquad\qquad\qquad = 2n$ right angles.
$\therefore A\hat{B}C + B\hat{C}D + C\hat{D}E + D\hat{E}F + \ldots = 2n - 4$ right angles.

Hence the sum of the interior angles of an n-sided convex polygon is $(2n - 4)$ right angles.

Note: The figure is deliberately incomplete and rows of dots are used in the proof because the exact value of n is unknown.

Look up the table you prepared for Exercise 13a, Example 1, and check your results by using the above formula.

Theorem

If the sides of a convex polygon are produced in order then the sum of the exterior angles so formed is 4 right angles.

Given: An n-sided convex polygon ABCDEFG ... with its sides produced in order to make exterior angles e_A, e_B, e_C, e_D, e_E, e_F ...
To prove that $e_A + e_B + e_C + e_D + e_E + e_F \ldots = 4$ right angles.

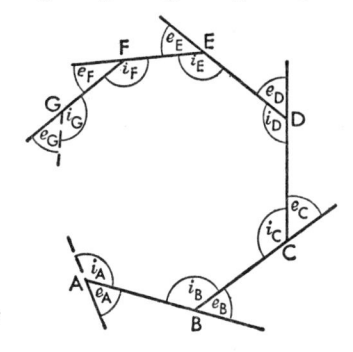

Fig. 13-7

Proof: Let the interior angles corresponding to e_A, e_B, e_C, etc., be respectively i_A, i_B, i_C, etc.

At A $\quad i_A + e_A = 2$ right angles (adj. angles on a straight line).
Similarly $\quad i_B + e_B = 2$ right angles
and $\quad i_C + e_C = 2$ right angles
and so on.

There are n vertices and hence there are n such sums as
$$i_A + e_A = 2 \text{ right angles}$$
∴ Adding all the angles at all the n vertices
$(i_A + i_B + i_C + i_D + \ldots) + (e_A + e_B + e_C + e_D + \ldots)$
$\hspace{6cm} = 2n$ right angles.
But $(i_A + i_B + i_C + i_D + \ldots) = 2n - 4$ right angles (sum of the
$\hspace{8cm}$ int. angles of a polygon)
∴ $(2n - 4) + (e_A + e_B + e_C + e_D + \ldots) = 2n$ right angles
∴ $(e_A + e_B + e_C + e_D + \ldots) \hspace{1.2cm} = 2n - (2n - 4)$
∴ $e_A + e_B + e_C + e_D + \ldots \hspace{1.5cm} = 4$ right angles

Hence the sum of the exterior angles of a convex polygon is 4 right angles. This sum is independent of the number of sides.

Regular Polygons

Regular polygons are polygons in which all the sides are equal and all the angles are equal.

NUMBER OF SIDES	NAME
4	Square
5	Pentagon
6	Hexagon
7	Septagon
8	Octagon
9	Nonagon
10	Decagon
12	Duodecagon

Certain regular polygons are named according to the number of sides (see table page 196). The calculation of interior and exterior angles is simplified for regular polygons.

Example

A regular polygon has 30 sides. Calculate its interior angle.

$$\begin{aligned} \text{Sum of the interior angles} &= (2n - 4) \text{ right angles where } n = 30 \\ &= 2(30) - 4 \\ &= 56 \text{ right angles} \\ \therefore \text{Each interior angle} &= \frac{56}{30} \text{ right angles} \\ &= \frac{56}{\cancel{30}_1} \times \overset{3}{\cancel{90}} \text{ degrees} \\ &= \underline{168^\circ} \end{aligned}$$

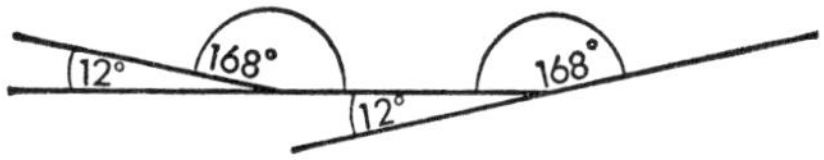

Fig. 13-8

Alternatively

$$\begin{aligned} \text{Sum of the exterior angles} &= 360^\circ \\ \therefore \text{Each exterior angle} &= \frac{360}{30} \\ &= 12^\circ \\ \therefore \text{Each interior angle} &= 180^\circ - 12^\circ \text{ (adj. angles on a straight line)} \\ &= \underline{168^\circ} \end{aligned}$$

Further. If the interior angle of a regular polygon is 170°, find the number of sides.

It is best here to work with the exterior angle.

The interior angle = 170°

∴ The exterior angle = 180° − 170° (adj. angles on a straight line)
= 10°

But the sum of the exterior angles of a polygon = 360°

∴ Number of exterior angles = $\dfrac{360}{10}$

= 36

∴ Number of sides = 36

Theorem

The exterior angle of a cyclic quadrilateral is equal to the interior opposite angle.

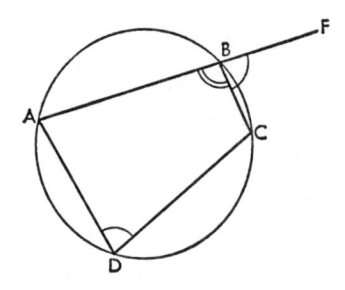

Fig. 13-9

Given. A cyclic quadrilateral ABCD with a side AB produced to F.

To prove that $F\hat{B}C = A\hat{D}C$

Proof:

$F\hat{B}C + A\hat{B}C = 180°$ (adj. angles on a straight line)

$A\hat{D}C + A\hat{B}C = 180°$ (opp. angles of a cyclic quad.)

∴ $F\hat{B}C = A\hat{D}C$

Exercise 13b

1. Copy out the table on page 196, adding *two* more columns headed exterior angle and interior angle. Calculate each of these angles for the regular polygons named, and complete the table.

GEOMETRY

2. Calculate the interior angles of regular polygons with (*a*) 15 sides, (*b*) 18 sides, (*c*) 20 sides, (*d*) 24 sides.

3. Calculate the number of sides of regular polygons whose exterior angles are (*a*) 30°, (*b*) 1°, (*c*) 4½°, (*d*) 6°.

4. Calculate the number of sides of regular polygons whose interior angles are (*a*) 120°, (*b*) 178°, (*c*) 171°, (*d*) 172½°.

5. Five of the interior angles of a hexagon are 146°, 78, 123°, 177°, 86°. Find the other interior angle.

6. Two interior angles of a quadrilateral are 97° and 103°. If the other two angles are equal, find them.

7. Seven of the interior angles of a nonagon (9 sides) are 171°, 147°, 158°, 166°, 173°, 121°, 89°. Find the sum of the other two interior angles. If their difference is 31°, find the two angles.

8. Calculate the size of angle $\widehat{ABC}$, Fig. 13-10.

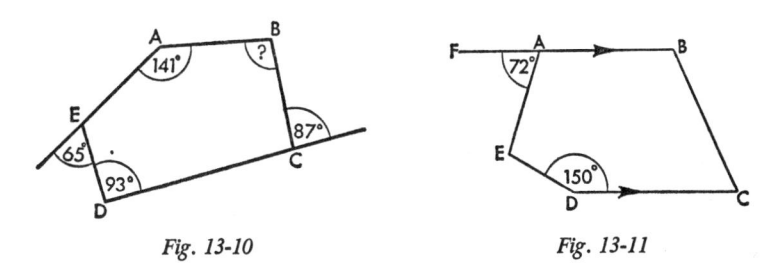

Fig. 13-10

Fig. 13-11

9. The angles of a hexagon are $x°$, $2x°$, $2x°$, $3x°$, $4x°$k and $3x°$. Find the value of x.

10. In the pentagon ABCDE, Fig. 13-11, AB is parallel to DC, $\widehat{FAE} = 72°$, $\widehat{EDC} = 150°$ and $\widehat{ABC} - \widehat{BCD} = 50°$. Find $\widehat{AED}$, $\widehat{ABC}$ and $\widehat{BCD}$.

11. In a regular polygon the interior angle is 8 times the exterior angle. How many sides has it?

12. In the pentagon ABCDE, (Fig. 13-12), AB = AE, $B\hat{A}E = B\hat{C}D$ = 90°, $A\hat{E}D = 100°$ and $E\hat{D}C = 125°$. Find $A\hat{B}C$ and prove that BE is parallel to CD.

Fig. 13-12

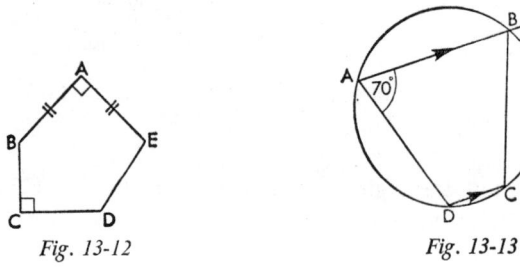

Fig. 13-13

13. In the cyclic quadrilateral ABCD, Fig. 13-13, AB is parallel to DC and $B\hat{A}D = 70°$. Calculate $C\hat{B}E$.

14.

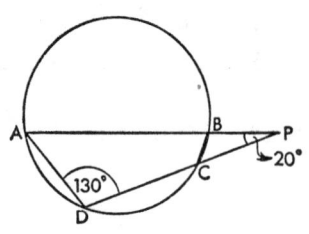

Fig. 13-14

In Fig. 13-14 if $A\hat{D}C = 130°$ and $B\hat{P}C = 20°$, calculate $B\hat{C}P$ and $B\hat{A}D$.

15. In Fig. 13-15 PB = PC. Prove that PA = PD and also that AD is parallel to BC.

16. If, in Fig. 13-16, $A\hat{C}D = 50°$ and $D\hat{B}C = 30°$, calculate $A\hat{D}E$. If $D\hat{A}F = 95°$, calculate $B\hat{P}A$.

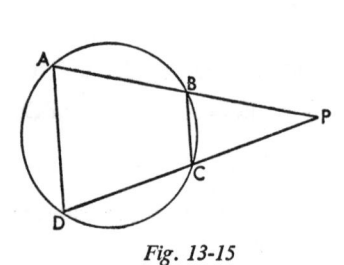

Fig. 13-15

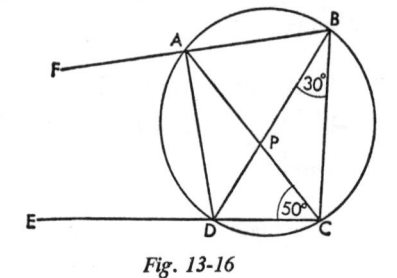

Fig. 13-16

GEOMETRY

17. If Fig. 13-17 $F\hat{A}B = 85°$. Calculate $D\hat{C}B$. What can you say about the lines AF and CD and why?

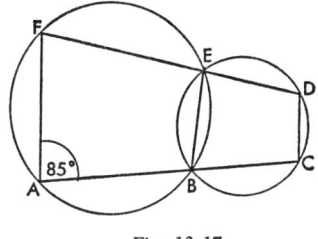

Fig. 13-17

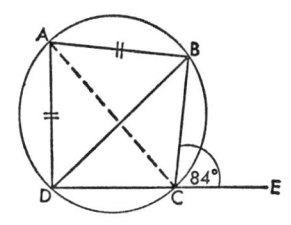

Fig. 13-18

18. In the cyclic quadrilateral ABCD (Fig. 13-18) AB = AD and $B\hat{C}E = 84°$. Find $A\hat{B}D$. Join AC and show that AC bisects $B\hat{C}D$.

19. In Fig. 13-19, if $B\hat{A}C = 25°$ and $A\hat{C}B = 42°$, calculate $A\hat{D}C$.

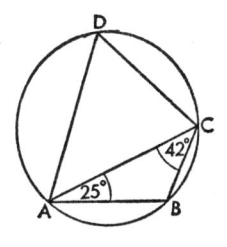

Fig. 13-19

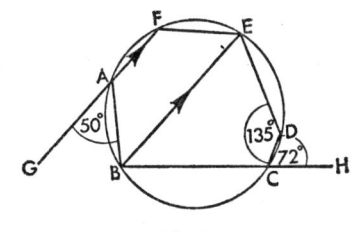

Fig. 13-20

20. In Fig. 13-20, AF is parallel to BE, $G\hat{A}B = 50°$, $H\hat{C}D = 72°$ and $E\hat{D}C = 135°$. Calculate (i) $F\hat{E}D$, (ii) $A\hat{B}C$.

21. In Fig. 13-21, O is the centre of the circle and $C\hat{O}A = 150°$. Find $E\hat{D}A$.

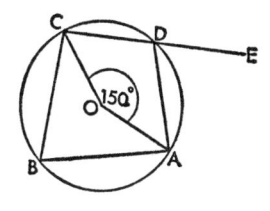

Fig. 13-21

201

LONGMAN MATHEMATICS

22. In Fig. 13-22, ABCD is a cyclic quadrilateral. $B\hat{A}D = 62°$ and $B\hat{E}C = 36°$. Calculate $A\hat{B}C$, $A\hat{D}C$ and $D\hat{F}C$.

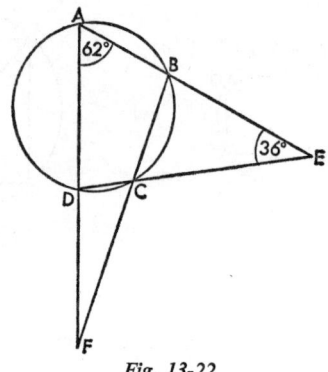

Fig. 13-22

23. In Fig. 13-23, $A\hat{B}D = 31°$, $B\hat{D}C = 27°$ and BE = EC. Calculate $B\hat{E}C$, $E\hat{C}B$, $A\hat{D}C$ and $B\hat{A}D$.

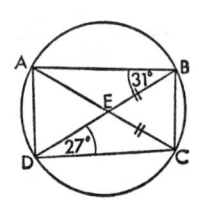

Fig. 13-23

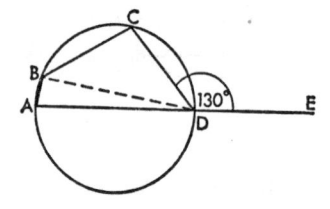

Fig. 13-24

24. In Fig. 13-24, AD is a diameter of the circle and $C\hat{D}E = 130°$. Calculate $D\hat{B}C$. If BC = CD, calculate $B\hat{A}D$.

25. In Fig. 13-25, $A\hat{B}E$ is a straight line. $G\hat{A}B = 70°$, $G\hat{E}B = 65°$. Prove that DCFG is a cyclic quadrilateral (i.e. that $D\hat{C}F$ and $D\hat{G}F$ are supplementary). If $A\hat{B}C = 120°$, calculate $A\hat{D}C$, $C\hat{F}E$ and $C\hat{D}G$. What do you notice about $C\hat{D}G$ and $C\hat{F}E$? Explain this last result in another way.

GEOMETRY

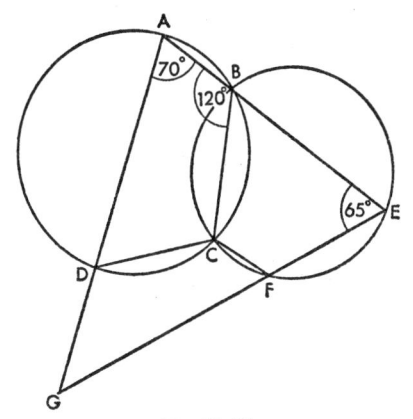

Fig. 13-25

26. Select the correct answers in the following statements
    (a) A regular polygon has 30 sides. The interior angles are each equal to (i) 12°, (ii) 56°, (iii) 168°, (iv) 120°.
    (b) A regular polygon has 16 sides. The exterior angles are each equal to (i) $22\frac{1}{2}°$, (ii) 155°, (iii) 25°, (iv) $157\frac{1}{2}°$.
    (c) The exterior angles of a regular polygon are each $7\frac{1}{2}°$. It has (i) 36 sides, (ii) 48 sides, (iii) 54 sides, (iv) 42 sides.
    (d) The interior angles of a regular polygon are each 177°. It has (i) 120 sides, (ii) 100 sides, (iii) 110 sides, (iv) 145 sides.

27.

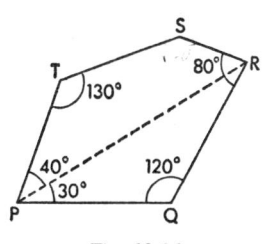

Fig. 13-26

In Fig. 13-26 PQRST is a polygon with the angles as marked. Are the following statements TRUE or FALSE?
   (a) The sum of the exterior angles is 540°
   (b) The sum of the interior angles is 540°
   (c) $\hat{P} + \hat{Q} + \hat{R} + \hat{T} = 390°$

203

(d) $\hat{S} = 140°$

(e) $\hat{TPR}$ and $\hat{TSR}$ are complementary

(f) PRST is cyclic quadrilateral

(g) PQ = QR

(h) PQR is an equilateral triangle

28.

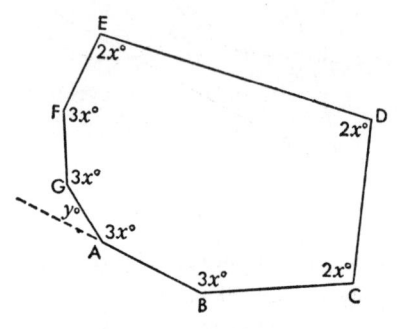

Fig. 13-27

In Fig. 13-27 the polygon ABCDEFG has angles as marked. Select the correct answers in the following statements.

(a) The figure is called (i) an octagon, (ii) a nonagon, (iii) a decagon, (iv) a septagon
(b) The sum of the interior angles is (i) 700°, (ii) 360°, (iii) 900°, (iv) 1080°
(c) The value of x is (i) 45°, (ii) 50°, (iii) 55°, (iv) 60°
(d) The exterior angle y (at A) is (i) 25°, (ii) 40°, (iii) 45°, (iv) 30°

29.

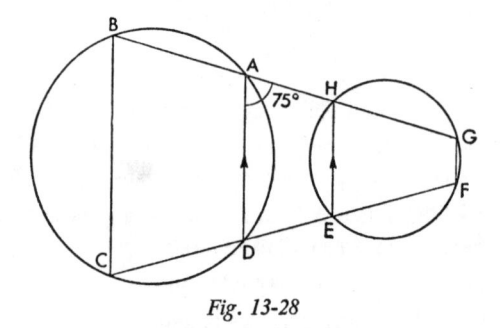

Fig. 13-28

In Fig. 13-28 AD is parallel to HE and $\hat{HAD} = 75°$

GEOMETRY

Say whether the following statements are TRUE or FALSE?
- (i) $G\hat{H}E$ is a corresponding angle to $H\hat{A}D$ ∴ $G\hat{H}E = 75°$
- (ii) AHED is a cyclic quadrilateral (exterior angle = interior opposite angle)
- (iii) $H\hat{A}D = B\hat{C}D = 75°$ (exterior angle cyclic quad. = interior opposite angle)
- (iv) $G\hat{H}E = B\hat{C}D = 75°$
- (v) BHEC is a cyclic quadrilateral
- (vi) $G\hat{F}E = 115°$ (opposite angles of a cyclic quad. are supplementary)
- (vii) $G\hat{F}C + B\hat{C}D = 180°$
- (viii) BC is parallel to GF
- (ix) $B\hat{A}D = 105°$ (adjacent angles or a straight line)
- (x) AGFD is a cyclic quadrilateral (exterior angle = interior opposite angle)

30.

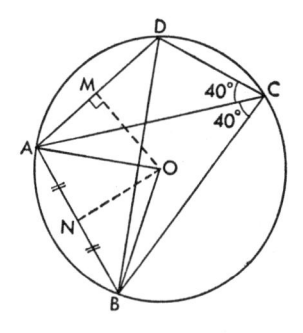

Fig. 13-29

In Fig. 13-29, ABCD is a cyclic quadrilateral in a circle centre O $D\hat{C}A = A\hat{C}B = 40°$, N is the mid-point of AB and OM is perpendicular to AD. Say whether the following statements are TRUE or FALSE?

- (i) $A\hat{D}B = 40°$
- (ii) $A\hat{O}B = 80°$
- (iii) $O\hat{B}A = 40°$
- (iv) $O\hat{A}B = 50°$
- (v) $D\hat{A}B = 110°$
- (vi) $A\hat{B}D = 40°$
- (vii) $A\hat{N}O = 80°$
- (viii) $A\hat{O}N = 40°$

205

(ix) $\widehat{OAD} = 50°$
(x) OM = ON
(xi) OMAN is not a cyclic quadrilateral
(xii) $\widehat{MON} = 80°$

Some Area Theorems

Here is a more formal treatment of the results obtained in Stage Three and some conclusions which follow from them.

Theorem. The area of a parallelogram is equal to the area of a rectangle on the same base and between the same parallels.

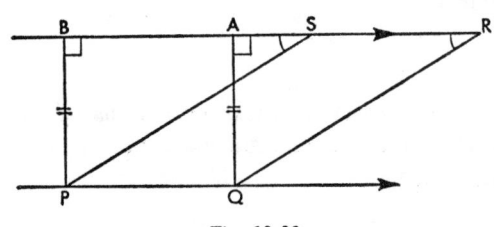

Fig. 13-30

Given: A parallelogram PQRS and a rectangle PQAB on the same base PQ and between the same parallels PQ and BASR.

To prove that   Area of PQRS = Area of PQAB.

Proof: In the triangles PBS, QAR

$$PB = QA \text{ (opp. sides parallelogram)}$$
$$\widehat{PBS} = \widehat{QAR} \text{ (corres. angles)}$$
$$\widehat{BSP} = \widehat{ARQ} \text{ (corres. angles)}$$

∴ Triangle PBS ≡ Triangle QAR (two angles, corres. side)

∴ Area of triangle PBS = Area of triangle QAR.

Quad. PQRB − triangle PBS = Quad. PQRB − triangle QAR
∴ Area of PQRS = Area of PQAB

From this result it follows that:

Area of parallelogram RQAB = Area of rectangle PQAB
$$= PQ \times PB$$
$$= \text{(base)} \times \text{(perpendicular height)}$$

Theorem. Parallelograms on the same base and between the same parallels are equal in area.

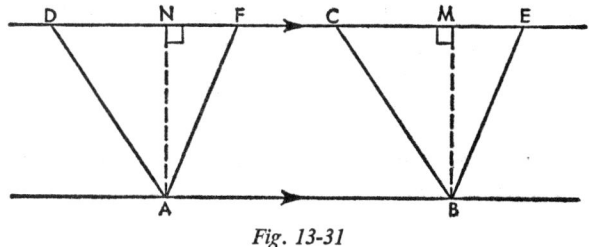

Fig. 13-31

Given: Two parallelograms ABCD, ABEF on the same base AB and between the same parallels AB and DFCE.

To prove that   Area ABCD = Area ABEF.

Construction: Draw rectangle ABMN on base AB and between parallels AB and DFCE.

Proof: Parallelogram ABCD = Rectangle ABMN
(on same base AB, between same parallels AB and DFCE)

Similarly   Parallelogram ABEF = Rectangle ABMN

∴ Area ABCD = Area ABEF

Theorem. Triangles on the same base and between the same parallels are equal in area. (Fig. 13-32.)

Given: Two triangles ABC, ABD on same base AB and between the same parallels AB and DC.

To prove that   Triangle ABC = Triangle ABD.

Construction: Draw AE and BF parallel to BC and AD respectively to complete parallelograms ABCE and ABFD.

Proof: triangle ABC = ½ parallelogram ABFD
(diagonal AC bisects parallelogram)

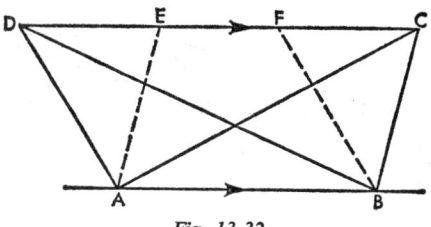

Fig. 13-32

Similarly   triangle ABD = ½ parallelogram ABFD
But   parallelogram ABCE = parallelogram ABFD
(on same base AB between same parallels AB and DC)
∴ triangle ABC = triangle ABD

It also follows that triangles on *equal* bases and between the same parallels are equal in area.

Note:
  Area parallelogram ABCE = (Base) × (perp. ht.)
    Area triangle ABC = ½ parallelogram ABCE
  ∴ Area triangle ABC = ½ (Base) × (perp. ht.)

Exercise 13c

1. In the triangle ABC (Fig. 13-33), D is the mid-point of AC. What can you say about the triangles ADB and DCB? Give reasons for your statement.

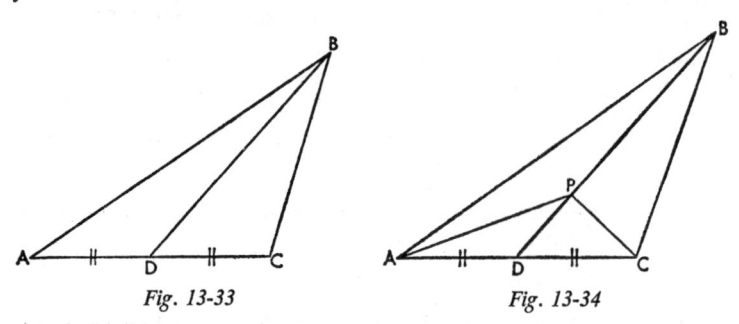

Fig. 13-33   *Fig. 13-34*

2. In Fig. 13-34 D is the midpoint of AC and P is any point on BD. Prove that the triangles APB and BPC are equal in area.

3. In Fig. 13-35 AB, DE and GF are parallel lines. DG is also parallel to AF. Prove that parallelogram ABCD is equal in area to parallelogram CEFG.

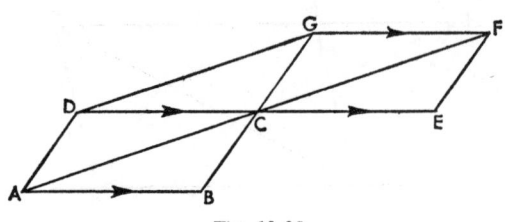

Fig. 13-35

GEOMETRY

4. In triangle ABC (Fig. 13-36), DE is parallel to BC. Show that triangles ABE and ADC are equal in area.

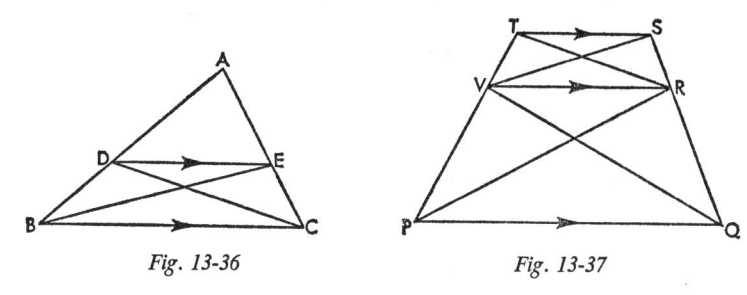

Fig. 13-36

Fig. 13-37

5. In Fig. 13-37 TS, VR and PQ are parallel lines. Prove that the triangles SVQ and TRP are equal in area.

6. In Fig. 13-38 ABCD is a rectangle. Show that parallelograms PQCD and ABRS are equal in area.

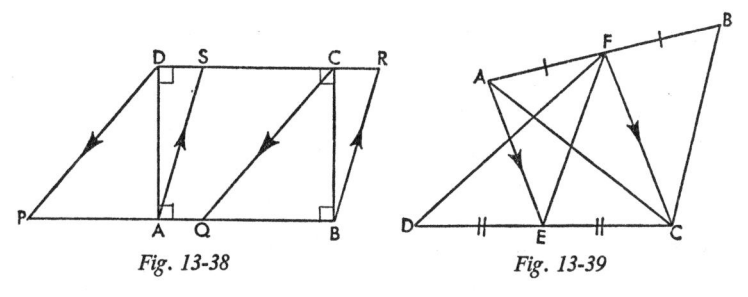

Fig. 13-38

Fig. 13-39

7. In Fig. 13-39 E and F are the mid-points of DC and AB respectively and AE is parallel to FC. Prove that triangles BFC and DEF are equal in area.

8. In Fig. 13-40, DB and CE are parallel. Prove that triangle ADE is equal in area to the quadrilateral ABCD.

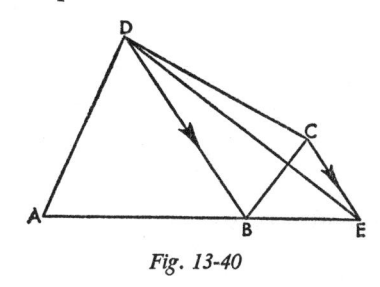

Fig. 13-40

209

A Useful Construction

To construct a triangle equal in area to a given quadrilateral.

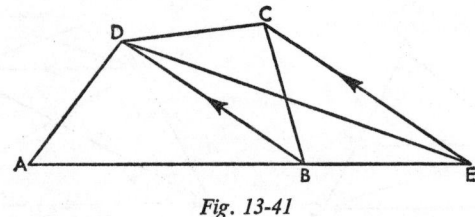

Fig. 13-41

Given: A quadrilateral ABCD.

To construct: A triangle whose area is equal to ABCD.

Construction: Join the diagonal BD and through C draw a line parallel to DB to cut AB produced at E. Join DE. Then AED is the required triangle equal in area to ABCD.

Proof: Triangle BDE = Triangle BDC (on same base DB and between the same parallels BD and CE)

Add triangle ABD to each of these.

∴ triangle BDE + triangle ABD = triangle BDC + triangle ABD

∴ triangle AED = quadrilateral ABCD

(*Note:* This proof was set as Question 8 in Exercise 13c.)

Exercise 13d

All these constructions are based on the area theorems above. Draw a rough sketch first before making an accurate drawing.

1. Draw an equilateral triangle ABC of side 5 cm. Construct a triangle ABD equal in area to triangle ABC such that $D\hat{A}B = 40°$. Measure BD.

2. Draw an isosceles triangle PQR in which PQ = 35 mm, PR = QR = 50 mm. Construct a triangle PQS equal in area to PQR such that PS = 75 mm. Measure QS and the angle $Q\hat{P}S$.

3. Draw triangle XYZ in which XY = 6·2 cm, XZ = 8·7 cm and YZ = 5 cm. Construct a triangle XPZ equal in area to triangle XYZ such that XP = YP. Measure YP.

GEOMETRY

4. Draw a parallelogram ABCD in which AB = 75 mm, AD = 37 mm and D$\widehat{A}$B = 50°. Construct a rectangle ABPQ equal in area to ABCD. Measure AQ and hence calculate the area of ABCD.

5. Draw a parallelogram PQRS in which PQ = 6·8 cm, PS = 3·6 cm and QS = 5 cm. Construct a parallelogram PQXY equal in area to PQRS such that PY = 2·4 cm. Measure Y$\widehat{P}$Q.

6. Draw a triangle ABC such that BC = 50 mm, AB = 75 mm and AC = 58 mm. Construct D, the mid-point of BC and join AD. On AD as base construct a triangle AQD with Q on the same side of AD as B such that DQ = AQ. Measure DQ. What can you say about the triangles QAD and ADC?

7. Construct a quadrilateral ABCD such that AB = 78 mm, AD = 50 mm, BD = 55 mm, BC = 42 mm and DC = 30 mm. Construct a point K on AB produced such that triangle AKD = quadrilateral ABCD. Construct DN perpendicular to AB and measure it. Hence calculate the area of quadrilateral ABCD.

8. Draw a parallelogram ABCD such that AB = 60 mm, AD = 32 mm and B$\widehat{A}$D = 45°. Construct a triangle equal in area to ABCD, and by measuring its perpendicular height calculate the area of the parallelogram.

9. Construct the quadrilateral PQRS in which PQ = 5 cm, QR = 2 cm., P$\widehat{Q}$R is a right angle, RS = 3 cm and PS = 3·8 cm. Construct a point A on PQ produced so that triangle PAS is equal in area to PQRS. Measure PA.

10. Draw a rectangle ABCD so that AB = 6 cm and AD = 4 cm. Construct a parallelogram ABPQ equal in area to ABCD such that AQ = 5 cm. On AQ construct a rhombus AQRS equal in area to ABPQ. Explain why AQRS is equal in area to ABCD. Measure angle Q$\widehat{R}$S.

11. Draw a parallelogram ABCD in which AB = 70 mm, AD = 42 mm and D$\widehat{A}$B = 55°. Construct a parallelogram ABXY equal in area to ABCD such that Y$\widehat{A}$B = 33°. On AY as base construct a rectangle equal in area to ABCD. Use this rectangle to calculate the area of ABCD.

12. Draw a convex pentagon PQRST in which PQ = 5 cm, PT =

211

3·7 cm, $T\hat{P}Q = 110°$, $P\hat{Q}R = 130°$, $QR = 2·5$ cm, $SR = 5$ cm and $TS = 4$ cm. By construction find a point X on PQ produced such that quadrilateral PXST is equal in area to pentagon PQRST. Further construct a triangle PYT, with Y on PX produced so that triangle PYT is equal in area to PQRST.

14 Series

In earlier work you have been introduced to some of the special numbers which can be built up into 'shapes', such as triangular numbers, square numbers, rectangular numbers, and cube numbers. Each number can be represented by dots in a particular shape of a particular size, and when the number of dots is counted it is found that it is in some definite relationship to the preceding smaller figure, and to the next larger figure. The numbers in fact form 'series'; a series can in fact be defined as a group of numbers, each of which is related to its two adjacent numbers, and thus to every other number in the series. The relationship between adjacent numbers can be formed in a great variety of ways.

Exercise 14a

1. Write down the 1st 5 terms in (*a*) the triangular number series, (*b*) the square number series, (*c*) the cubic number series.
2. Find how the following series are built up and give the 1st 5 terms in each series.

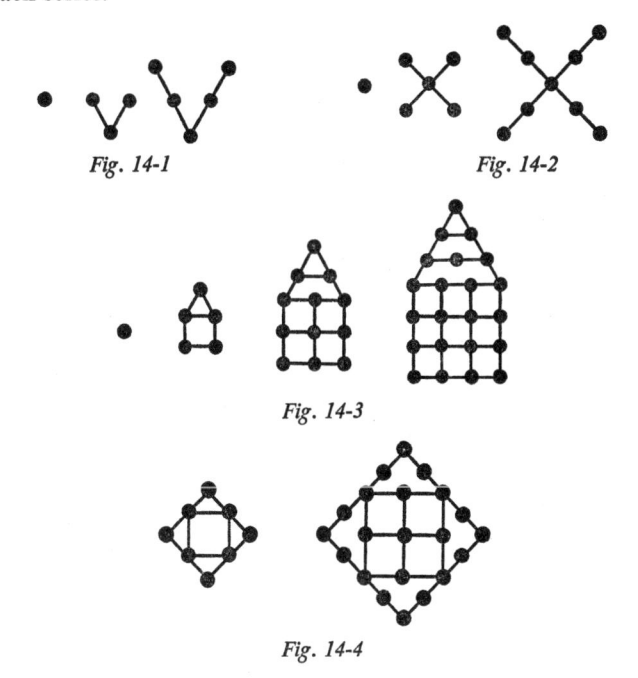

Fig. 14-1

Fig. 14-2

Fig. 14-3

Fig. 14-4

Fig. 14-5

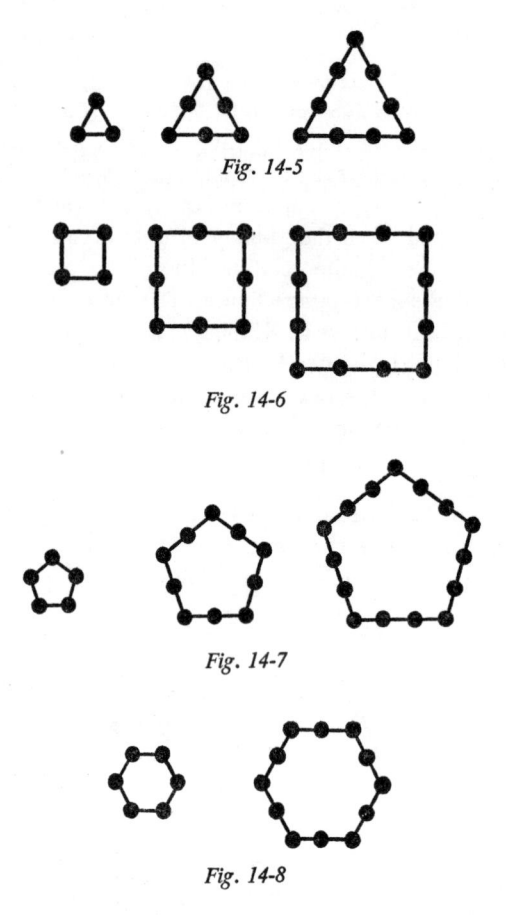

Fig. 14-6

Fig. 14-7

Fig. 14-8

Two of the main types of series are called ARITHMETICAL PROGRESSIONS and GEOMETRICAL PROGRESSIONS. The arithmetical progression (in future called an A.P.) is the simplest type of series; it is a series that moves from term to term in equal jumps, the difference between any two adjacent terms in the series being the same. The integers form an A.P. the difference between any two adjacent terms being 1. Note that the integers do in fact form 2 series.

(i) ... $-7, -6, -5, -4, -3, -2, -1, 0, 1, 2, 3, 4, 5$ ... and
(ii) ... $7, 6, 5, 4, 3, 2, 1, 0, -1, -2, -3, -4, -5, -6$ ...

The difference in (i) is 1, but the difference in (ii) is -1, since it is conventional to work always from left to right.

SERIES

Exercise 14b

1. Write out the four series formed from the integers when (*i*) the difference is 2, (*ii*) the difference is −2.

2. Write out the four smallest positive integers and the four largest negative integers in all the series formed having a common difference of 3.

3. Which of the series in Figs. 14-1 to 8 are A.P.s?

4. Which of the following are A.P.s? Give reasons for your answers:

(*i*) 10, 20, 40, 70, ...   (*ii*) 13, 18, 23, 28, 33, ...
(*iii*) The triangular numbers. (*iv*) The square numbers.
(*v*) $a, a + d, a + 2d, a + 3d, a + 4d ...$
(*vi*) $n + 1, n + 2, n + 3, n + 4, n + 5 ...$
(*vii*) $a + b + c, 2a + b + c, 3a + b + c, 4a + b + c ...$
(*viii*) $a, a + b, a + b + c, 2a + b + c, 2a + 2b + c,$
         $2a + 2b + 2c, ...$
(*ix*) $6 + q, 9 + q, 12 + q, 15 + q, ...$
(*x*) $a - 3, 2a - 3, 3a - 3, 4a - 3, ...$

Although many series have no common difference (e.g. the square numbers), the differences themselves sometimes form A.P.s; or even the differences between the differences! This can be shown simply by writing the series in a row, and then putting the differences between and below the terms to form a second row: and continuing this if necessary.

e.g.   2, 5, 11, 20, 32, 47
                 3   6   9   12   15
                  3   3   3   3

In Stage 3 the 'Binomial series' was obtained in a reverse way to the above—by adding two adjacent terms to form Pascal's triangle—

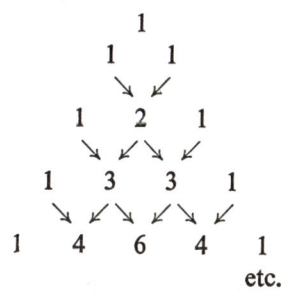

```
                1
              1   1
               ↘ ↙
             1   2   1
              ↘ ↙ ↘ ↙
           1   3   3   1
            ↘ ↙ ↘ ↙ ↘ ↙
         1   4   6   4   1
                              etc.
```

215

LONGMAN MATHEMATICS

Exercise 14c

1. Set out, with subsequent differences, all the series in Questions 1 and 2, Exercise 14a, that are not A.P.s.

2. (i) $y = 2x + 7$; $y = 3x - 5$ are examples of 'linear' equations since they give straight lines when plotted. By giving x values of 1, 2, 3, 4, ..., etc. form series for $2x + 7$ and $3x - 5$. Are these A.P.s? Will linear functions always give the same answer? Why?

   (ii) $y = x^2$; $y = 2x^2 + 7$ are examples of 'quadratic' equations, giving parabolas when plotted. By giving x values of 1, 2, 3, 4, ... etc. form series for x^2 and $2x^2 + 7$. Are these A.P.s? Can quadratics ever give A.P.s? Why? How many lines are necessary to reduce the differences to an A.P. series?

   (iii) $y = x^3$, $y = x^3/2 + 6$ are examples of 'cubic' equations. Obtain series as in (i) and (ii), for x^3, and $x^3/2 + 6$. Are these A.P.s? How many lines are necessary to reduce the differences to an A.P. series?

   (iv) The series 1, 16, 81, 256, 625, 1 296, 2 401, ..., is formed by the fourth powers (x^4) of 1, 2, 3, 4, etc. How many lines are necessary to reduce the differences to an A.P. series?

   (v) How many lines would be necessary to reduce the differences of x^5 to an A.P.? How many x^n? Using the series in (iv) above obtain the 5th powers of 1, 2, 3, 4, etc., and check your assumption.

3. Let the first term of an A.P. series be 'a_1', and the common difference be 'd'. Then if the 2nd term is a_2, this can be written $a_2 = a_1 + d$

   Similarly $\qquad a_3 = a_2 + d = a_1 + 2d$

   Continuing this $\qquad a_4 = a_3 + d = a_1 + 3d$
   $\qquad\qquad\qquad\qquad a_5 = a_4 + d = a_1 + 4d$
   $\qquad\qquad\qquad\qquad a_6 = a_5 + d = a_1 + 5d$

   Write in similar notation (i) a_7, (ii) a_9, (iii) a_{20}, (iv) a_{100}, (v) a_n. Discuss. The last result should be specially noted.

4. If $a_1 = 4$, $d = 3$ find the value of (i) a_6, (ii) a_7, (iii) a_{10}, (iv) s_{100}, (v) a_{120}.

5. A parachutist falls from a plane. He falls 6 m during the 1st second, 8 m during the 2nd second, 10 m during the 3rd second. If

SERIES

his fall continues in the same pattern how far does he fall during (*i*) the 5th second, (*ii*) the 8th second, (*iii*) the 20th second?

6. A boy is given a collection of 350 foreign stamps. He buys 15 stamps each week. How many will he have in (*i*) 9 weeks' time? (*ii*) in 13 weeks? (*iii*) in 20 weeks?

7. Find the 14th term of the series 11, 16, 21, 26, ...

8. Find the 75th term of the series 18, 25, 32, 39, ...

9. The following exercise refers to 'outline' figures as in Figs. 14-5, 6, and 7.
   (*i*) Find the 8th, 12th and 15th triangled numbers.
   (*ii*) Find the 5th, 10th and 20th squared numbers.
   (*iii*) Find the 6th, 9th and 12th pentagonal numbers.
   (*iv*) Continue the hexagonal numbers in Fig. 14-8 to obtain the 1st 6 terms of the series. Find the 10th, 15th and 20th hexagonal number.

10. Find the 10th, 18th, and 25th terms in the series $3\frac{1}{2}$, 5, $6\frac{1}{2}$, 8, ...

11. Find the 12th, 15th and 20th terms in the series $x - 3y$, $x - 2y$, $x - y$, x, ...

12. The 19th and 20th term of an A.P. are 57 and 60. Find d, a_1, a_{10}, a_{25}.

13. The 18th and 20th term of an A.P. are 78 and 86. Find d, a_1, a_{10}, a_{15}.

14. Find the 10th, 12th and 15th terms of the series 10, 7, 4, 1, ...

15. Find the 15th, 20th, and 25th terms of the series 4, $3\frac{1}{2}$, 3, $2\frac{1}{2}$, 2, ...

16. If the 10th and 16th terms of an A.P. are 9 and 12, find d_1, a_1, a_5 and a_{20}.

17. If the 5th and 11th terms of an A.P. are -5 and -8, find d_1, a_1, a_3, a_{10}, ...

18. If the 8th and 15th terms of an A.P. are 1 and 0 find d_1, a_1, a_5, and a_{20}.

To Sum an A.P.

In Stage 2 it was shown that the triangular numbers were formed by adding the integers, e.g. the 3rd $\triangle$ number is $1 + 2 + 3 = 6$: the 7th $\triangle$ number is $1 + 2 + 3 + 4 + 5 + 6 + 7 = 28$.

A quick method of evaluating each number was found by adding the first and last integers; the second and next-to-last integers, etc., as follows:

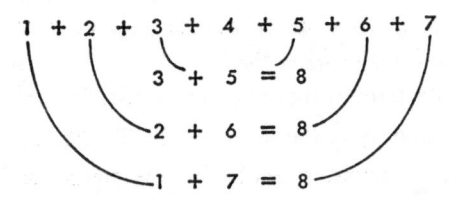

$$1 + 2 + 3 + 4 + 5 + 6 + 7$$
$$3 + 5 = 8$$
$$2 + 6 = 8$$
$$1 + 7 = 8$$

Since each △ number is the sum of an A.P. perhaps the same method can be used to sum any A.P.

Consider the A.P. 2, 4, 6, 8, 10, 12, 14. Adding the first term to the last; the second to the next to last, you obtain $2 + 14 = 4 + 12 = 6 + 10 = 16$.

Let the sum of the 1st 7 terms be written S_7 then
$$S_7 = 2 + 4 + 6 + 8 + 10 + 12 + 14$$
Re-writing in reverse $\quad S_7 = 14 + 12 + 10 + 8 + 6 + 4 + 2$
and adding the two $2 \times S_7 = 16 + 16 + 16 + 16 + 16 + 16 + 16$
Whence $2 \times S_7 = 7 \times 16$
$$S_7 = \frac{7 \times 16}{2}$$
$$= 56$$

Example

Find the sum of the first 10 terms of the A.P. 13, 18, 23, 28, 33, ...
$$S_{10} = 13 + 18 + 23 + 28 + 33 + 38 + 43 + 48 + 53 + 58$$
$$S_{10} = 58 + 53 + 48 + 43 + 38 + 33 + 28 + 23 + 18 + 13$$
By addition
$$2 \times S_{10} = 71 + 71 + 71 + 71 + 71 + 71 + 71 + 71 + 71 + 71$$
$$= 10 \times 71$$
$$\therefore S_{10} = 355$$

If you were asked to find the sum of the first 50 terms of some A.P. it would be far too tedious to write down the 50 terms, re-write them in reverse order, add up each pair and so arrive at the stage of line 4 in each example above. It is of course unnecessary. You can easily

SERIES

find the sum of each pair (how?) and you can know how many sums you will have to add together (how?).
When the sum of n terms is required the following general formula will be obtained from the above argument; $S_n = \dfrac{(a_1 + a_n)}{2} \times n$

where a_1 is the first term, a_n is the nth term and Sn is the sum of n terms. Discuss this formula in class so that you understand how it is obtained.

Example

Find the sum of the first 50 terms of the series $3\frac{1}{2}, 5, 6\frac{1}{2}, 8, 9\frac{1}{2}, \ldots$
First obtain the 50th term; $a_1 = 3\frac{1}{2}$, $d = 5 - 3\frac{1}{2} = 1\frac{1}{2}$

$$a_{50} = a_1 + (50 - 1)d = 3\frac{1}{2} + (49 \times 1\frac{1}{2})$$
$$= 77$$

Thus
$$S_{50} = \frac{(a_1 + a_{50})}{2} \times 50$$
$$= \frac{(3\frac{1}{2} + 77)}{2} \times 50$$
$$= 2\,012\frac{1}{2}$$

Example

Find the sum of the first 30 terms of the series $10, 7, 4, 1, -2, \ldots$
The 30th term is required; $a_1 = 10$, $d = -3$

$$\therefore a_{30} = 10 + (30 - 1)(-3)$$
$$= 10 - 87$$
$$= -77$$

Thus
$$S_{30} = \frac{(10 + (-77))}{2} \times 30$$
$$= -1\,005$$

Exercise 14d

1. Find the sum of the numbers 1–30 by (*i*) Starting with 1, and taking 30 terms and (*ii*) Starting with 0 and taking 31 terms.

2. Find the sum of the first n integers.

219

3. Find the sum of the following A.P.s. In each case find a_1; d and a_n first.

(i) $n = 15, a_1 = 5, a_n = 75$; (ii) $n = 9, a_1 = -14, a_n = 34$;
(iii) $n = 8, a_1 = 88, a_n = 32$; (iv) $n = 7, a_1 = 6, a_n = -6$;
(v) $n = 151, a_1 = 30, a_n = -170$;
(vi) $n = 10, a_1 = 5, d = 1\frac{1}{2}$; (vii) $n = 20, a_1 = 8, d = -2$;
(viii) $n = 8, a_1 = 12, d = \frac{1}{4}$; (ix) $n = 16, a_1 = 17, a_4 = -\frac{1}{2}$;
(x) $n = 25, a_1 = 10, a_5 = 6$;
(xi) $n = 30, a_2 = -1\,000, a_6 = -400$;
(xii) $n = 15, a_3 = -11, d = 4$;
(xiii) $n = 12, a_5 = -17, d = 4\frac{1}{2}$;
(xiv) $n = 18, a_4 = 5, a_8 = 6$;
(xv) $n = 24, a_5 = 6, a_{10} = 9\frac{3}{4}$;
(xvi) $n = 10, a_1 = x, a_n = x + 9$;
(xvii) $n = 20, a_1 = 2a, a_n = 2a + 57$;
(xviii) $n = 18, a_1 = x + 3y, a_n = x + 37y$;
(xix) $n = 12, a_1 = 2x + y, a_4 = 5x + 4y$;
(xx) $n = 10, a_1 = 5a, a_{10} = 5a + 96$

The Harmonic Series

A series closely associated with the Arithmetical series is the HARMONIC SERIES. In Chapter 1 the idea of a reciprocal was discussed; the Harmonic Series is derived by taking the reciprocals of the terms of an arithmetical series.

e.g.   1, 2, 3, 4, 5, 6, 7, ..., is an arithmetic series,
$\frac{1}{1}, \frac{1}{2}, \frac{1}{3}, \frac{1}{4}, \frac{1}{5}, \frac{1}{6}, \frac{1}{7}, \ldots$, is an harmonic series.

Arithmetic series are fairly common in everyday dealings, in elementary science and in scientific and mathematical theory, but examples of inverse proportion leading to harmonic series are much rarer. They are met in some branches of scientific research, for example in the study of selective breeding where certain strains are weeded out. The name of the series derives from the Greeks who discovered that the notes emitted by stretched strings harmonize when their lengths form the reciprocals of the whole number series, i.e. when they form a harmonic series.

A series is said to be harmonic when, in fractional form, the numerator remains constant, while the denominator increases (or decreases) by equal steps.

SERIES

e.g.   (i) $\frac{11}{1}, \frac{11}{3}, \frac{11}{5}, \frac{11}{7}, \frac{11}{9}, \frac{11}{11}, \ldots$
             (ii) $\frac{4}{3}, \frac{4}{8}, \frac{4}{13}, \frac{4}{18}, \frac{4}{23}, \frac{4}{28}, \ldots$

It is not always obvious that a series is in H.P. for example
         (i) $10, 3\frac{1}{3}, 2, 1\frac{3}{7}, 1\frac{1}{9}, \frac{10}{11}, \ldots$
         (ii) $\frac{4}{5}, \frac{2}{5}, \frac{4}{15}, \frac{1}{5}, \frac{4}{25},$

There are two methods which can be used to test a series for H.P.
    (i) Invert each term, and test to see if the resultant series is an A.P.
or (ii) Convert every term to a fraction, all having a common *numerator*, then test the denominators to see if they are in A.P.

Example

Method 1 $10, 3\frac{1}{3}, 2, 1\frac{3}{7}, 1\frac{1}{9}, \frac{10}{11}.$

Turn mixed numbers to improper fractions and invert each term.
$$10, \tfrac{10}{3}, 2, \tfrac{10}{7}, \tfrac{10}{9}, \tfrac{10}{11}.$$
$$\tfrac{1}{10}, \tfrac{3}{10}, \tfrac{1}{2} (= \tfrac{5}{10}), \tfrac{7}{10}, \tfrac{9}{10}, \tfrac{11}{10}$$

This is an A.P. common difference $\tfrac{2}{10}$.

Method 2   Step 1 $10, \tfrac{10}{3}, 2, \tfrac{10}{7}, \tfrac{10}{9}, \tfrac{10}{11}$
           Step 2 $\tfrac{10}{1}, \tfrac{10}{3}, \tfrac{10}{5}, \tfrac{10}{7}, \tfrac{10}{9}, \tfrac{10}{11}$

This is an H.P. since denominators are in A.P. and numerators are constant.

Exercise 14e

Which of the following series are in H.P.?

(a) $\frac{4}{5}, \frac{24}{35}, \frac{3}{5}, \frac{8}{15}, \frac{12}{25}, \ldots$
(b) $\frac{1}{4}, \frac{2}{7}, \frac{3}{10}, \frac{4}{13}, \frac{5}{16}, \frac{6}{19}, \ldots$
(c) $\frac{1}{3}, \frac{1}{4}, \frac{1}{2}, \frac{2}{3}, \ldots$
(d) $1\frac{3}{4}, 1\frac{1}{16}, \frac{7}{8}, \frac{7}{10}, \ldots$
(e) $\frac{1}{3}, \frac{1}{8}, \frac{4}{52}, \frac{3}{54}, \frac{2}{46}, \frac{2}{56}$
(f) $5, \frac{5}{8}, \frac{1}{3}, \frac{5}{22}, \frac{10}{58}, \ldots$
(g) $6, 5\frac{1}{7}, 4\frac{1}{2}, 4, 3, \frac{7}{10} \ldots$
(h) $6, 6\frac{6}{7}, 8, 7\frac{1}{5}, \ldots$
(i) $21, 6, 3\frac{1}{2}, 2\frac{8}{17}, 1\frac{10}{11}, \ldots$
(j) $1\frac{1}{16}, 1\frac{4}{11}, 1\frac{2}{5}, 1\frac{5}{9}, 1\frac{3}{4}, \ldots$

221

If there is an example in *a–j* above having one term out of H.P. give the correct term.

The Geometric Progression

Consider the series 1, 2, 4, 8, 16, 32, 64, ... Setting this out as was done with A.P.s and finding the differences you have

$$1, \quad 2, \quad 4, \quad 8, \quad 16, \quad 32, \quad 64, \ldots$$
$$1, \quad 2, \quad 4, \quad 8, \quad 16, \quad 32, \ldots$$
$$1, \quad 2, \quad 4, \quad 8, \quad 16, \ldots$$
$$\text{etc.}$$

Rather a strange result!

Try the same procedure with the following:

(*i*) 1, 3, 9, 27, 81, 243, 729.
(*ii*) 1, 4, 16, 64, 256, 1 024, 4 096.
(*iii*) 1, 5, 25, 125, 625, 3 125.

Discuss the results fully.

If you have examined the above series fully you should have discovered their structure, i.e. how the series are built up. You should also have noticed that the differences, and the differences of the differences, etc., have similar structures to the original series. Notice also the leading numbers to each row and their relationship to each other row.

Consider the series 1,   6,   36,   216,   1 296,   7 776.
the differences are   5,   30,   180,   1 080,   6 480.
                     25,   150,   900,   5 400,
                    125,   750,   4 500,
                    625,   3 750.
                           etc.

This can be written—

$6^0(6-1)^0 \quad 6^1(6-1)^0 \quad 6^2(6-1)^0 \quad 6^3(6-1)^0 \quad 6^4(6-1)^0$
$\qquad 6^0(6-1)^1 \quad 6^1(6-1)^1 \quad 6^2(6-1)^1 \quad 6^3(6-1)^1$
$\qquad\qquad 6^0(6-1)^2 \quad 6^1(6-1)^2 \quad 6^2(6-1)^2 \quad 6^3(6-1)^2$
$\qquad\qquad\qquad 6^0(6-1)^3 \quad 6^1(6-1)^3 \quad 6^2(6-1)^3$
$\qquad\qquad\qquad\qquad 6^0(6-1)^4 \quad 6^1(6-1)^4 \quad 6^2(6-1)^4$
$\qquad\qquad\qquad\qquad\qquad 6^0(6-1)^5 \quad 6^1(6-1)^5$
$\qquad\qquad\qquad\qquad\qquad\qquad \text{etc.}$

SERIES

Notice the indices are in A.P. Discuss this form of the series.

All the series dealt with in this section have been *geometric progressions* (G.P.s), each term in a G.P. series being the previous term multiplied by a common number, usually called the common ratio (or just the ratio). G.P.s are probably the most important of all series, they can be found in many everyday situations, and are used a great deal in scientific and mathematical theory.

If the first term in a G.P. is a_1 and the common ratio is r the series will be $a_1, a_1r, a_1r^2, a_1r^3, a_1r^4, a_1r^5, \ldots$

Exercise 14f

1. In the general series above write out:

(*i*) the 8th term; (*ii*) the 11th term; (*iii*) the 20th term; (*iv*) the 50th term; (*v*) the nth term.

2. In the general series above:
   (*i*) Divide the 2nd term by the 1st term.
   (*ii*) Divide the 3rd term by the 2nd term.
   (*iii*) Divide the 5th term by the 4th term.
   (*iv*) Divide the 8th term by the 7th term.
   (*v*) Divide the nth term by the $(n+1)$th term.

3. In the general series
   (*i*) Divide the 3rd term by the 1st term.
   (*ii*) Divide the 5th term by the 2nd term.
   (*iii*) Divide the 8th term by the 4th term.
   (*iv*) Divide the 16th term by the 11th term.

4. Write out the first five terms of the following series:
   (*i*) $a_1 = 8 \quad r = 4$ (*ii*) $a_1 = 8 \quad r = \frac{1}{2}$
   (*iii*) $a_1 = -8 \; r = 3$ (*iv*) $a_1 = 8 \quad 4 = -\frac{1}{2}$
   (*v*) $a_1 = 2 \; r = 10$ (*vi*) $a_1 = 2 \; r = -10$
   (*vii*) $a_1 = 12 \; r = 3$ (*viii*) $a_1 = 81 \; r = \frac{1}{3}$
   (*ix*) $a_1 = 81 \; r = -\frac{1}{3}$ (*x*) $a_1 = 1 \quad r = 0.1$

5. Find the ratio of the G.P. in which,
   (*i*) the 2nd term is 20 and the 4th term is 2 000
   (*ii*) ,, 1st ,, ,, 12 ,, ,, 3rd ,, ,, 108
   (*iii*) ,, 1st ,, ,, 12 ,, ,, 4th ,, ,, $1\frac{1}{2}$
   (*iv*) ,, 2nd ,, ,, 48 ,, ,, 4th ,, ,, 27
   (*v*) ,, 1st ,, ,, 12 ,, ,, 3rd ,, ,, $5\frac{1}{3}$

The geometric series are of such importance that a much deeper analysis will be made at a later stage.

The Fibonacci Series

It has already been noted that series can be formed in an unlimited number of different ways. For example the series 5, 13, 25, 41, 61, 85, ... is formed by taking the squares of two adjacent integers, e.g. $(1^2 + 2^2)$, $(2^2 + 3^2)$, $(3^2 + 4^2)$... Mathematicians have investigated all kinds of series, most of which are of no more than a

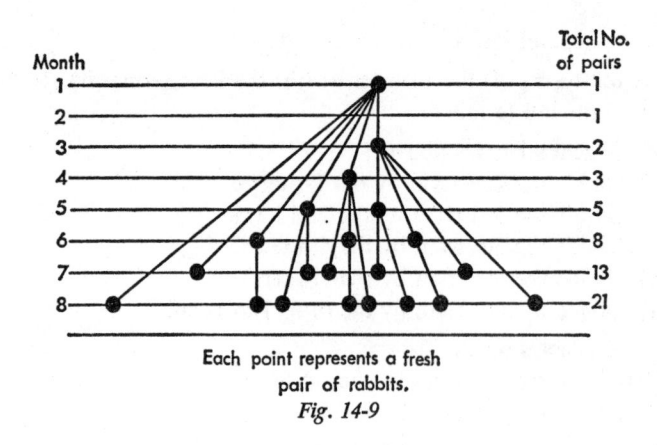

Each point represents a fresh pair of rabbits.
Fig. 14-9

passing interest, but a few have turned out to be of great significance. In one of the very few mathematical books of any value written during the Middle Ages, a period during which little progress was made in either mathematics or science, one mathematician, Leonardo of Pisa, nicknamed Fibonacci, poses and solves the following problem:

'Someone placed a pair of rabbits in a certain place to find out how many pairs of rabbits will be born in the course of one year; it being assumed that every month a pair of rabbits produces another pair, and that rabbits begin to bear young two months after their own birth.' The easiest method to solve this is by a diagram. Fig. 14-9 shows that the total number of pairs month by month is given by the series 1, 1, 2, 3, 5, 8, 13, 21 . . .

SERIES

Exercise 14g
1. Examine the series. How is it formed?
2. Continue the series for another four terms.
3. Write down five lines of differences. Discuss these.

The connection between any two terms in a series does not define the series. For example all the following are A.P.s with difference 3:

(*i*) 0, 3, 6, 9, ... (*ii*) 1, 4, 7, 10, ...
(*iii*) 2, 5, 8, 11, 14, ... (*iv*) $\frac{1}{2}$, $3\frac{1}{2}$, $6\frac{1}{2}$, $9\frac{1}{2}$, ...

The following are G.P.s with ratio 3:

(*i*) 1, 3, 9, 27, 81, ... (*ii*) 2, 6, 18, 54, ...
(*iii*) $1\frac{1}{2}$, $4\frac{1}{2}$, $13\frac{1}{2}$, $40\frac{1}{2}$, ...

Produce two new series which are developed by the same method as the series for the rabbits. The series obtained by Leonardo is of very special interest and is called the 'Fibonacci' series. The numbers have many special and interesting properties and start 1, 1, 2, 3, 5, ... the terms being called the Fibonacci numbers.

Exercise 14h

Here are a few of the properties of the Fibonacci numbers:

1. Take any 3 consecutive Fibonacci numbers. Multiply the 1st by the 3rd. Square the 2nd number. Compare the 2 answers. Repeat with other consecutive trios.

2. Any two adjacent Fibonacci numbers are 'co-prime', i.e. they have no common factor. Check this for the first 12 numbers.

Check the following properties with the first 24 numbers.

3. Fibonacci numbers are even only if the number of the term is divisible by 3. (Does this mean that every 3rd term is even?)

4. Fibonacci numbers are divisible by 3 only if the number of the term is divisible by 4.

5. Fibonacci numbers are divisible by 4 only if the number of the term is divisible by 6.

6. Fibonacci numbers are divisible by 5 only if the number of the term is divisible by 5.

While the Fibonacci numbers have many more interesting and more important properties than those above (the analysis of which is rather involved), the greatest significance of the series is found in its association with biological and botanical facts. For example by dividing each number by its right-hand neighbour a series of fractions is obtained:

$$\frac{1}{1}, \frac{1}{2}, \frac{2}{3}, \frac{3}{5}, \frac{5}{8}, \frac{8}{13}, \frac{13}{21}, \frac{21}{34}, \text{etc.}$$

These fractions are related to the growth of leaves and petals on plants. Moving along a stem from one leaf to the next leaf necessitates following a spiral path round the stem. The amount of turn from one leaf to the next is always some fraction of a complete rotation; this fraction is always one of the Fibonacci fractions!

You can check this practically; start with one particular leaf, move up the stem following the leaves round the stem until you reach a leaf directly above the first leaf. Count the number of complete turns taken around the stem and divide this number by the number of spaces between the leaves.

Pine cones, the centre of sunflowers and daisies are other examples of the Fibonacci series seen in nature.

Exercise 14j

1. Find out all you can about the GOLDEN SECTION, and its relation to the Fibonacci ratios.

2. Write out the first 15 Fibonacci ratios. Add one to each and change to improper fractions. What do you notice about your results?

3. Take the improper fractions obtained in question 2 and using a large scale, plot them against the number of each term, i.e. 1 to 15. What can you say about the numbers by considering the plottings?

15 The Number System and Fields

In earlier chapters you have been introduced to some new types of mathematical 'systems'. Pure Mathematics is very largely concerned with different systems or structures and their inter-relationships. For example, if a certain set system is being analysed, such questions as the following would be raised, 'How are the elements of a set related?'; 'Is there any order among the elements?'; 'What operations are valid?'; 'What properties are or are not involved in the operations?' etc.

The simplest system that you have so far considered has been the 'set', with most of the operations being concerned with similar or dissimilar sets. The work covered in set theory shows how a complete mathematical system can be developed without any necessary reference to numbers (although numbers have been introduced for the sake of easy examples). By placing restrictions on the elements in a set, a system of 'closed sets' was introduced; the restrictions were concerned with introducing an operation to combine elements, producing other elements in the set. Further restrictions produced the most important system so far discussed—the GROUP.

What are the properties of a group? (Revise.)

In Chapter 4 some introductory work has been done on still another mathematical system—the algebra of matrices. The most important system of all has not been analysed although you are fully aware of it—the system of numbers.

The Number System

You have been learning to use and manipulate numbers now for many years, but in this section a closer look will be taken at the set of laws which control the numbers. The laws, set out below, should be fully discussed and understood, and compared to systems whose elements do not obey the same laws. As you go through the laws revise the mathematical terms such as associative, commutative, distributive, identity, inverse, etc., and give examples of each law.

1. The set of elements is closed under addition.
2. The set of elements is closed under multiplication.
3. Addition of elements is associative.

4. Multiplication of elements is associative.
5. Addition of elements is commutative.
6. Multiplication of elements is commutative.
7. There is an identity element for addition.
8. There is an identity element for multiplication (with the exception of one element). Which is the exception?
9. There is an inverse for each element under addition.
10. There is an inverse for every element, except one, under multiplication. Which one?
11. Multiplication is distributive over addition for all elements.

Fields

You will probably never have met this formidable list of the 'laws of arithmetic' before, nevertheless, it has been behind all your work. Not only have you had to obey these laws, you have had to learn tables, money systems, weight systems, measure systems, etc.—no wonder arithmetic is found by many to be a very difficult subject; you will certainly have done well if you have understood all your previous work in arithmetic!!

Any mathematical system that obeys the eleven rules outlined above is called a FIELD. It was natural when mathematical systems were being explored, that a system to cover the numbers and their operations should be given a special place. The surprising thing to mathematicians was that other sets were found which also obeyed the eleven conditions of a field.

Exercise 15a

1. Check the set of positive and negative even numbers, plus zero, i.e. $\{0, \pm 2, \pm 4, \pm 6, \ldots\}$ against the laws of a field. Is the set a field? If not, which laws do not hold?

2. Repeat the above question for the set of positive and negative whole numbers, plus zero.

3. List the conditions for a group under addition that are present in the conditions for a field. What extra 'addition' law is present in a field?

THE NUMBER SYSTEM AND FIELDS

4. List the conditions for a group under multiplication that are present in the conditions for a field. What extra 'multiplication' law is present in a field?

+	O	E
O		
E		

×	O	E
O		
E		

Fig. 15-1

5. (*i*) Complete the two tables in Fig. 15-1 for the addition and multiplication of odd and even numbers.
  (*ii*) Is there an identity element for addition? i.e. does either O or E act as an identity?
  (*iii*) Is there an identity element for multiplication? Does either O or E act as an identity?
  (*iv*) Is there an addition inverse for each element? Can you complete the following equations?

  (*a*) O + ? = E
  (*b*) E + ? = E

  (*v*) Is there a multiplicative inverse for each element? Can you complete the following equations?

  (*a*) O × ? = O
  (*b*) E × ? = O

  (*vi*) Work through the remaining seven conditions for a field.
  (*vii*) Do O and E form a field? If not, why not?

Number Congruence

Suppose the time to be 10 hours after midnight; what time will it be in 16 hours?

You can obtain the answer by counting round the clock; you would get 10 + 16 = 2. If you did not tire you could count round to find how many hours after midnight it would be in 100 hours' time; this time you would get 10 + 100 = 14. No doubt however you have seen that an easier method would be to obtain the total of hours after midnight, divide by 24 (why?), and take the remainder as the required answer (why?).

229

If you add 76 hours on to a time of 10 hours after midnight, a time of 14 hours after midnight is obtained $\left(\text{since } \dfrac{76+10}{24} = 3 \text{ rem. } 14\right)$, the same as when 100 hours is added.

When numbers have the same remainder after division by 24 they are said to be CONGRUENT.

Exercise 15b

1. Find 4 other numbers congruent to 100, when divided by 24.

2. In what way are the differences between 100, 76 and the four numbers you found in question 1 related to each other?

The idea of congruence is not confined to dividing numbers by 24, you can choose any whole number that you like as a divisor. The number chosen is called the MODULUS. For example with modulus 3, the elements of the set of numbers $\{\ldots -9, -6, -3, 0, 3, 6, 9, \ldots\}$ are all congruent, since when any element in the set is divided by 3, the remainder is zero. This set is sometimes called the '0' set, modulus 3, or the residue class 0, modulus 3.

Similarly the elements of the set of numbers $\{\ldots -14, -11, -8, -5, -2, 1, 4, 7, 10 \ldots\}$ are congruent, the set being the '1' set, modulus 3, or the residue class 1, modulus 3. Note that the remainder is still $+1$, even when the negative elements in the set are divided by 3 (since, for example, $-11 = -12 + 1$).

Exercise 15c

1. Write out the set of numbers in the residue class 2, modulus 3, including 4 positive and 4 negative elements.

2. Are there any further residue classes modulus 3? If so what are they? If not, why not?

3. How many residue classes are there for modulus 4? Modulus 5? Modulus n?

4. Consider the elements of the residue class 0, modulus 3. What can be said about the difference between any *two* elements? What can be said about the difference between any two elements in residue class 1, modulus 3? In residue class 2, modulus 3? Why do you obtain the answer that you do?

THE NUMBER SYSTEM AND FIELDS

The congruence relationship is written 9≡12 mod 3 (read 9 is congruent to 12 modulus 3) or 4 ≡ 13 mod 3; 2 ≡ 14 mod 3.

Exercise 15d

1. Which of the following are true?
   (*i*) 11 ≡ 53 mod 7   (*ii*) 12 ≡ 22 mod 8
   (*iii*) 17 ≡ 35 mod 17   (*iv*) 21 ≡ 11 mod 10
   (*v*) 9 ≡ 54 mod 5

2. Find 3 numbers that are congruent to the following:
   (*i*) 4 mod 7; (*ii*) 3 mod 13; (*iii*) 5 mod 6.

3. Find the two lowest positive values of x that satisfy each of the following:
   (*i*) $x + 5 \equiv 2$ mod 3   (*ii*) $x + 4 \equiv 2$ mod 4
   (*iii*) $x + 6 \equiv 1$ mod 3   (*iv*) $x + 7 \equiv 3$ mod 4
   (*v*) $x + 5 \equiv 1$ mod 4

4. Repeat Question 3 above, finding the two largest negative numbers that satisfy the congruence relations.

5. Give all values, from the whole numbers 6 to 10, which satisfy the following congruence relations:
   (*i*) $x \equiv 0$ (mod 4)   (*ii*) $x \equiv 1$ (mod 4)
   (*iii*) $x \equiv 2$ (mod 4)   (*iv*) $x \equiv 6$ (mod 10)
   (*v*) $2x \equiv 3$ (mod 12)   (*vi*) $3x \equiv 51$ (mod 21)
   (*vii*) $4x \equiv 2$ (mod 22)   (*viii*) $2x + 7 \equiv 3$ (mod 9)
   (*ix*) $x^2 \equiv 1$ (mod 11)   (*x*) $x^2 \equiv 3$ (mod 13)

6. Give four values for x, in each of the following congruence relations, two of which will satisfy the relations, and two of which will not:
   (*i*) $12 \equiv 24$ (mod x)   (*ii*) $-10 \equiv 20$ (mod x)
   (*iii*) $18 \equiv 54$ (mod x)   (*vi*) $-7 \equiv -15$ (mod x)
   (*v*) $-7 \equiv -10$ (mod x)

7. Take any two elements from the residue class 0 modulus 3; add the elements. In which residue class modulus 3 do we find the sum element? Repeat with several other integers. Are all the 'sum-elements' in the same residue class modulus 3? Give a reason for your answer. Try if you can to show the reason algebraically.

8. Repeat Question 7, taking two elements from the residue class 1 modulus 3. Again give an algebraic explanation for your answer.

231

9. Repeat Questions 7 and 8, taking two elements from the residue class 2 modulus 3.

10. By considering any two elements, one from residue class 0 and one from residue class 1 modulus 3, find to which residue class their sum belongs. Try with different elements and finally give an algebraic proof of your result.

11. Repeat Question 10 first with elements from residue classes 0 and 2 then with elements from residue classes 1 and 2 modulus 3.

12. From the results obtained in Questions 7–11 you can now complete the addition table in Fig. 15-2 for the residue classes modulus 3.

×	0	1	2
0			
1			
2			

Fig. 15-2

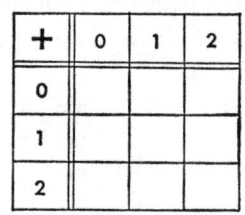

+	0	1	2
0			
1			
2			

Fig. 15-3

13. By using a similar method to that used in Questions 7–11, find the products of the residue classes modulus 3; giving an algebraic argument for your results. Copy out and fill in the multiplication table in Fig. 15-3.

14. (*i*) Is the set of residue classes (mod 3) closed under addition?
 (*ii*) Is the set closed under multiplication?
 (*iii*) Is addition of the residue classes associative?
 (*iv*) Is multiplication of the residue classes associative?
 (*v*) Is addition of the residue classes commutative?
 (*vi*) Is multiplication of the residue classes commutative?
 (*vii*) Is there an identity for addition? What is it?
 (*viii*) Is there an identity for multiplication? What is it?
 (*ix*) Has each residue class an inverse under addition? List them.
 (*x*) Has each residue class an inverse under multiplication? List them.
 (*xi*) Is multiplication distributive over addition for all residue classes?
 (*xii*) Is the set of residue classes a group under addition?
 (*xiii*) Is the set a group under multiplication? Would they be a group if the residue class 0 was excluded?
 (*xiv*) Is the set of residue classes a field?

THE NUMBER SYSTEM AND FIELDS

15. Repeat Questions 7–14 for the set of residue classes modulus 4.

16. The smallest number of elements a field can have is two—an addition identity and a multiplication identity. Taking these as 0 and 1 construct addition and multiplication tables as in the exercises above for residue classes modulus 2 and test whether these elements form a field.

17. Repeat Questions 7–14 for the set of residue classes modulus 5.

18. Repeat Questions 7–14 for the set of residue classes modulus 6.

19. Repeat Questions 7–14 for the set of residue classes modulus 7.

20. Compare the modulus numbers for those which give fields and those which do not give fields.

16 Chance in Mathematics

We frequently hear people using such phrases as 'I will take a chance on that', 'The chances are that you will be proved right', 'What chance did I have?', and so on. These are generally vague statements but, in fact, it is possible to calculate chance mathematically given certain conditions.

'Heads or Tails'

If you toss a coin then (assuming it does not rest on its edge!!) it must fall with either its head or its tail uppermost. Thus the *chance* that it will finish 'heads up' is one in two. Another way of expressing this is to say the *probability* of calling 'Heads' correctly is $\frac{1}{2}$. Suppose now we toss two coins simultaneously. If we examine every possibility we find these could fall as follows (note H = Head, T = Tail).

| HH | HT | TH | TT |

These are four possibilities and thus the *probability* of getting two heads (or no heads i.e. two tails) is $\frac{1}{4}$ or $(\frac{1}{2})^2$. We could put this result in the form of a frequency table thus

Number of 'Heads'	Frequency
0	1
1	2
2	1

from which we could plot a histogram as in Fig. 16-1.

If we toss three coins simultaneously then the possibilities are as follows

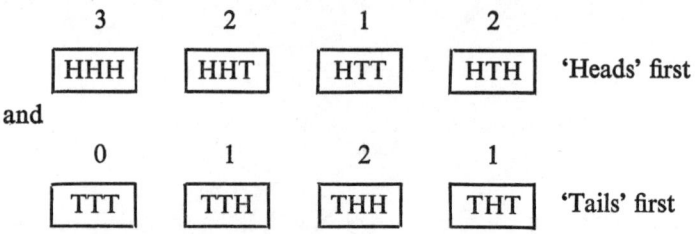

    3   2   1   2

| HHH | HHT | HTT | HTH | 'Heads' first

and

    0   1   2   1

| TTT | TTH | THH | THT | 'Tails' first

(*Note:* The figures over the 'boxes' give the number of 'Heads'.)

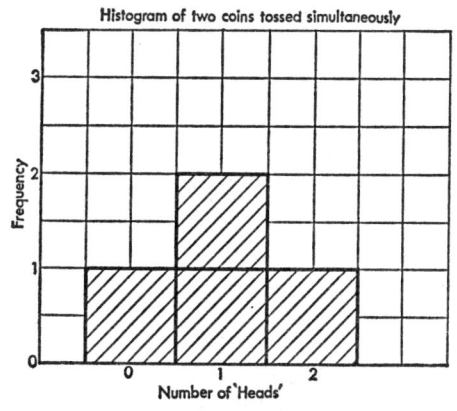

CHANCE IN MATHEMATICS

Histogram of two coins tossed simultaneously

Fig. 16-1

In this case there are eight possibilities and thus the *probability* of getting three heads (or no heads i.e. three tails) is $\frac{1}{8}$ or $(\frac{1}{2})^3$. As before we can make a frequency table and plot the corresponding histogram.

Number of 'Heads'	Frequency
0	1
1	3
2	3
3	1

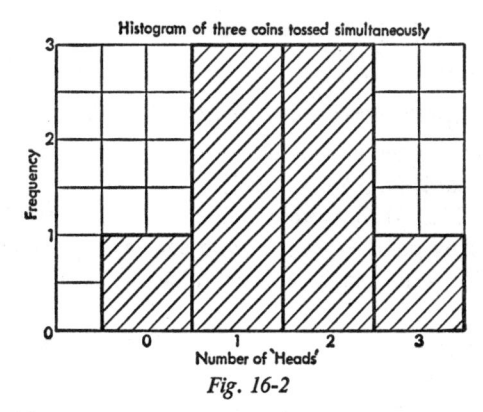

Histogram of three coins tossed simultaneously

Fig. 16-2

Exercise 16a

1. Following the method shown above estimate the probability of getting 4 heads or 4 tails when four coins are tossed simultaneously.

235

Check this result by writing out all the possible arrangements in 'boxes'. From your results construct a frequency table and draw the corresponding histogram.
What is the probability of getting (a) one 'head'?; (b) two 'heads'?; (c) three 'heads'?

2. Two similar dice have numbers 1 to 6 marked on their faces. They are thrown simultaneously. Taking each number from 1 to 6 on the first dice write down every possible combination of numbers on the two dice. Make a table showing the total of the numbers in each throw. From this result construct a frequency table of these totals and draw the corresponding histogram.
   (a) What is the probability of throwing two sixes?
   (b) What is the most likely total to be thrown, i.e. the mode of distribution?

3. There are 4 candidates in an election: Mr Green (Conservative), Mr Brown (Labour), Mr White (Liberal), Mr. Black (Independent). By using suitable symbols to represent each of these candidates and writing out all possibilities, estimate the probability that the final order at the election will be (1) Mr Brown, (2) Mr Green, (3) Mr White, (4) Mr Black.
(*Note:* You need only be concerned about finding the probability that Mr Brown, Mr Green and Mr White are respectively 1st, 2nd and 3rd, because Mr Black will then necessarily be 4th.)

Exercise 16b
Practical Experiments Concerned with Probabilities

1. You can solve Exercise 16a, Question 3, by a practical experiment thus: Take 4 cards (e.g. an Ace, a King, a Queen, a Jack or 4 cards numbered 1, 2, 3, 4) to represent the four candidates and arrange these in as many possible ways as you can, noting the arrangement each time. You will then be able to calculate the probability quite easily.
Check your results against the results of the calculation $4 \times 3 \times 2 \times 1$. This number is sometimes written as 4! (spoken factorial 4).

2. Take two sets of cards numbered respectively 1, 2, 3, 4, 5 and 2, 4, 6, 8, 10. Taking one card from each set find all the possible totals of the two cards taken together. Construct a frequency table of the totals and draw the corresponding histogram.

CHANCE IN MATHEMATICS

Find
  (a) the probability that the total will be 11.
  (b) the probability that the total will be an even number.
  (c) the most likely total.

3. Design an experiment to find the probability that in a family of five children the second and third are girls.

4. Design suitable experiments to find
  (a) the probability of forecasting correctly the results of two football matches out of two games;
  (b) the probability of forecasting correctly the results of four football matches out of four games;
  (c) the probability of forecasting correctly the results of six football matches out of six games.

Can you estimate the probability of forecasting 8 correct results out of 8 games?

5. Suppose that the following 8 soccer teams are left in the quarter finals of the F.A. Cup:

  Tottenham Hotspur   Liverpool
  Everton   Sheffield Wednesday
  Manchester United   Arsenal
  West Ham United   Aston Villa

find by experiment the probability that
  (a) Tottenham Hotspur and Aston Villa will be opponents in the next round.
  (b) Sheffield Wednesday will play Arsenal at home.

This short chapter on the introduction of the Theory of Probability shows that this section of Mathematics is closely related to Statistics and to a section of mathematics dealing with Permutations and Combinations.

Using the mathematical laws and processes of Probability, which we shall investigate more fully in Stage 5, we can predict accurately the chance or probability of a particular result. Note that probability is always measured as a fraction or a ratio. Thus, if the probability is 1 then the result is a certainty; if the probability is 0 then the result is an impossibility—any other degree of probability is between 0 and 1.

237

17 Revision Exercises

Paper R.1

1. Using log. tables find the value of:

(a) $(0.38)^2 \times \dfrac{1}{0.06821}$

(b) $\dfrac{3.142 \times (0.78)^2 \times 2.5}{36}$

2. The straight line distance between two points on a map is 3·125 cm. A boy measures this distance and writes it down as 3 cm. What percentage error has he made? If the scale of the map was 1 cm to 6 km, find the actual error he made, giving your answer in kilometres.

3. Two ships leave a certain spot at midnight. One sails NW.(315°) at a speed of 12 km/h and the other NE. (045°) at 18 km/h. How far are they apart at 15.00? Give your answer in kilometres.

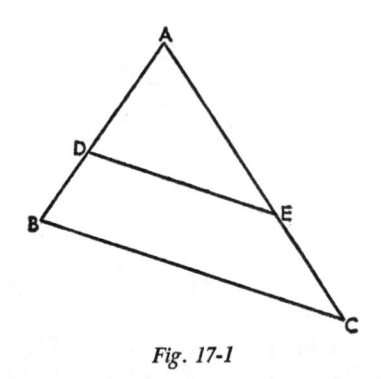

Fig. 17-1

4. The triangles ABC and ADE are similar. Prove that DE is parallel to BC. If $\dfrac{AD}{AB} = \dfrac{3}{4}$ find the length of BC given that DE = 12 cm.

5. Construct an equilateral triangle ABC in which each side is 5 cm long. Cut this triangle out and place it on a piece of squared paper so that the side BC is horizontal and A is above BC. By placing a pin through the point B rotate the triangle ABC until it is completely

REVISION EXERCISES

inverted (see Fig. 17-2) marking eight different positions of C during the rotation. What is the locus of C?

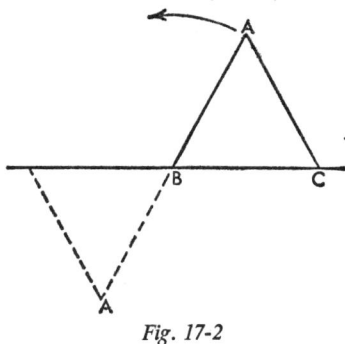

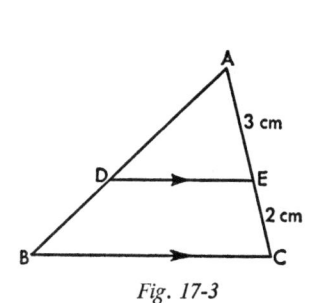

Fig. 17-2

Fig. 17-3

6. What is the solution of the equation:
$$42 - 21x = 14?$$
A $x = 8\frac{1}{3}$
B $x = 0$
C $x = 1\frac{1}{3}$
D $x = 18\frac{2}{3}$

Paper R.2

1. In Fig. 17-3 DE is parallel to BC. AE = 3 cm, EC = 2 cm. If the area of the triangle ABC is $12\frac{1}{2}$ cm² what is the area of triangle ADE? *(Cambridge)*

×2. Plot the graph of the equation if
$$y = -x^2 + 3x + 4 \text{ from } x = -2 \text{ to } x = 5$$
From your graph find
   (a) the values of x when $y = 0$;
   (b) the value of x when y is a maximum.

3. Use logs. to find the value of
   (a) $38 \cdot 26 \times (0 \cdot 026\ 25)^2$
   (b) $\sqrt{0 \cdot 941\ 5}$

4. A sum consists of a number of 10 p pieces, an equal number of 5 p pieces and twice the number of 2 p pieces. If the total amount is £3·42 how many 2 p pieces are there? *(J.M.B.)*

239

LONGMAN MATHEMATICS

5. I pay a standing charge of a pence per quarter plus a charge of b pence for each unit of electricity used. When I used 108 units in one quarter my bill was £1·70, and when I used 240 units my bill was £2·36. Find the values of a and b.

6. If $\cos x = \frac{1}{3}$ and x is an acute angle then which is the value of $\sin x$?

    A $\frac{2}{3}$

    B $\frac{2\sqrt{2}}{3}$

    C $\frac{2}{3\sqrt{2}}$

    D $\frac{2}{2\sqrt{3}}$

Paper R.3

✦1. A railway carriage is 15 m long and 2·25 m wide. A scale model is made 2·5 cm long. Find
    (a) the width of the model;
    (b) the height of the real carriage if the height of the model is 40 mm.   (U.E.I.)

2. Using a graphical method solve the quadratic equation
$$x^2 - 3x + 1 = 0$$
    (U.E.I., adapted)

3. Draw a circle of radius 4 cm and mark a point distant 7 cm from the centre of the circle. Construct the tangents from P to the circle, showing your construction lines clearly.

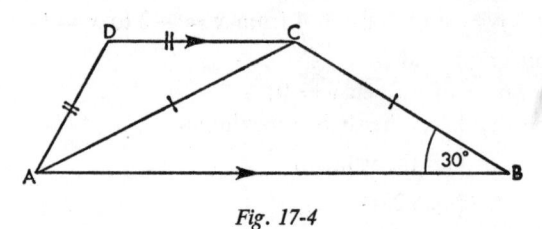

Fig. 17-4

4. In Fig. 17-4 ABCD is a trapezium with AB parallel to DC. If $AC = BC$ and $AD = DC$ and $CBA = 30°$, find the angles of the trapezium.

240

REVISION EXERCISES

*5. A body starts from rest and travels for 6 s. Its distance S m from the starting point after t s is given by the equation $S = t^2(9 - t)$. Draw the distance-time graph for values of x from 0 to 6.

*6. After all reliefs have been considered a man's taxable income amounts to £660·00. Assuming that the first £160·00 is taxed at 30% and the remainder at 41·25% how much tax does he pay?
    A £78·00
    B £165·00
    C £243·00
    D £400·00

Paper R.4

1. A set of saucepans of similar shape are of internal diameter 10 cm, 15 cm, and 20 cm. The smallest holds a litre. Find how much each of the others will hold. (Let smallest height be $5x$ cm.)
    (U.E.I. adapted)

*2. From an aircraft flying at a steady altitude of 5 000 m the angle of depression of an aerodrome in the direct line of flight was 16° 45', and 1¾ min. later the aircraft was vertically above the aerodrome. Calculate the speed of the aircraft in km/h.   *(A.E.B. adapted)*

*3. Two ships leave a certain point at midnight. One travels on a course 015° at 12 km/h and the other on a course 072° at 8 km/h. By drawing a suitable diagram, find the distance between the two ships at 03.00 and the bearing of the second ship from the first at that time.

4. A householder has a choice of two tariffs for electricity. He may pay either 3 p for each unit concerned or he may pay £1·40 per quarter and 1 p for each unit consumed. What is the number of units consumed when the charge is the same in either case?

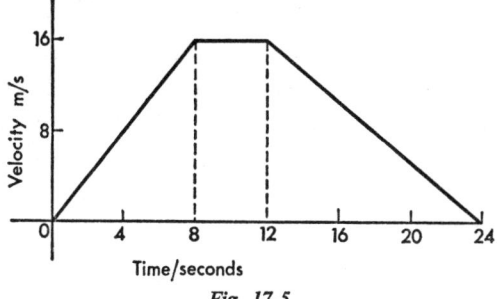

Fig. 17-5

5. The graph in Fig. 17-5 shows the variation of velocity with time for a moving body. Find
   (a) the total distance travelled by the body;
   (b) the acceleration after 4 s.

6. A man pays £160·50 income tax in one year. If the first £78 of tax represents the first £260·00 of taxable income and the remainder is taxed at 41·25 p in the pound, what is his taxable income?
   A £260·00
   B £460·00
   C £520·00
   D £780·00

Paper R.5

1. Two objects have the same shape. The linear dimensions of one are 4 times larger than the corresponding linear dimensions of the other. Calculate
   (a) the ratio of the surface areas of the two objects;
   (b) the ratio of their volumes.

2. The formula for the volume of a sphere is $V = \frac{4}{3}\pi r^3$. Find the volume of a steel ball bearing whose radius is 0·025 cm. (Take $\pi = 3·14$.)

3. A man owns a house whose rateable value is assessed at £175. If the local rate is 49 p in the £1, how much does he pay in each *half yearly* instalment?

4. The estimated product of a penny rate is £52 000. If the Annual Rate is 52½ p in the pound how much is collected in rates during this particular year?

5. The total amount collected in rates in a certain borough was £2 250 000. Of this amount £1 500 000 was spent on education. If the total annual rate for the borough was 51 p in the pound, calculate the amount of the rate which was used for educational purposes.

6. A man cycles 6 km at an average speed of 20 km/h and a further 8 km at an average speed of 16 km/h. What is his average speed for the whole journey?
   A 17 km/h
   B 17·5 km/h
   C 18 km/h
   D 18·5 km/h

REVISION EXERCISES

Paper R.6

This paper consists of either (*a*) Alternative Choice or (*b*) Multiple Choice, answers to questions. You are required to select the correct answer in each case, giving reasons for your choice.

1. I wish to find the area of a circle the length of whose diameter I know, I should

A multiply the diameter by π;
B divide the diameter by two to find the radius and multiply this value by π^2;
C find the radius, square it and multiply this value by π;
D perform some entirely different processes from any of these.

2. I am required to find the centre of the inscribed circle of a given triangle. Should I

A bisect two of the angles of the given triangle and find the point where these bisectors meet, or
B bisect two of the sides of the given triangle and find the point where these bisectors meet?

3. ABC is an equilateral triangle. Has the triangle in its plane,

A one axis of symmetry,
B two axes of symmetry;
C three axes of symmetry;
D four axes of symmetry;
E more than four axes of symmetry?

Illustrate your answer by a diagram.

4. Two solids have the same shape. One has linear dimensions 50 times larger than the other. Will the ratio of their volume be

A 1:2 500
B 1:125 000
C 1:500 000
D none of these?

5. Chief Wallamaloo has developed a coinage system of his own. There are only two kinds of coin, one silver and one copper. On pay day his soldiers are told they may take no more than 40 coins. For every silver coin they take, they must take four copper coins (i.e. 1 silver coin $=$ 4 copper coins in value). For every silver coin chosen over the correct number each soldier must give back 4 copper coins.

243

LONGMAN MATHEMATICS

What is the correct number of silver coins to choose for maximum value

A 5 silver coins;
B 6 silver coins;
C 7 silver coins;
D 8 silver coins;
E 9 silver coins;
F none of these?

6. If $y = x^2 - 5x - 2$ and $x = -3$, what is the corresponding value of y?

A -26
B -8
C 22
D 24

Paper R.7

1. Find the lengths of AB and BC in Fig. 17-6.

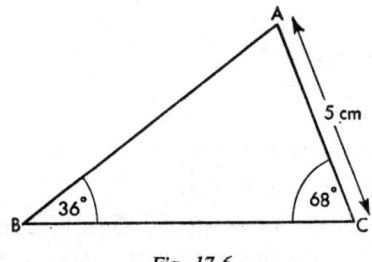

Fig. 17-6

✗ 2. Use logs. to find the value of
(a) $(0{\cdot}365\ 2)^3$
(b) $\sqrt{0{\cdot}758\ 2}$

✓ 3. Find the amount of Income Tax which will be paid by Mr Jones whose gross income is £1 250. You may assume that Mr Jones can claim a total relief of £500 and that the first £260 is taxed at 30 p in the pound and the remainder at 41·25 p in the pound.

✗ 4. In one quarter I use 120 units of electricity. If my house occupies a floor area of 140 m² and the 'standing charge' is £1·52, how much

REVISION EXERCISES

will I have to pay for my electricity given that each unit costs 0·85 pence?

5. A surveyor wishes to find the height of a flag-pole on an inaccessible tower. He finds that the angle of elevation of the top of the flag-pole from a certain point is 25°. Walking 3 m nearer to the foot of the tower, he now finds that the angle of elevation is 32° (see Fig. 17-7). Find the height of the flag-pole.

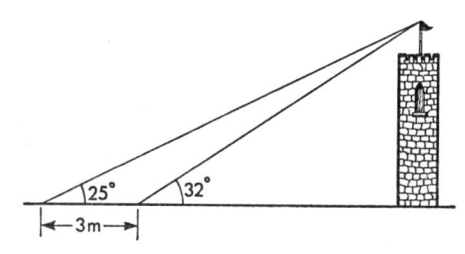

Fig. 17-7

6.

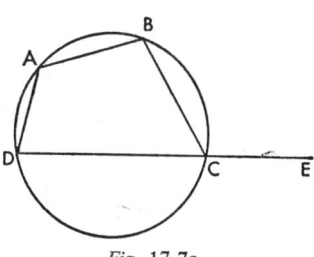

Fig. 17-7a

In the figure above (not drawn to scale) BCE = 120° and ADE = DAB. What is the value of ABC?

    A 60°
    B 90°
    C 120°
    D 140°

Paper R.8

1. A man travelled a distance of 6 km, running for part of the way at 18 km/h and walking the rest at 6 km/h. If he had run the distance he walked and walked the distance he ran he would have taken a quarter of an hour less. How far did he run?

2. A body starts from rest and travels for 6 s. Its distance s m from the starting point after t s is given by the equation
$$s = t^2(9 - t)$$
Draw the distance-time graph for values of t from 0 to 6.
From your graph find
  (a) after how long the body is 70 m from the starting point
  (b) the speed of the body after 2 s   (*A.E.B.*)

×**3.** Last week my joint of beef weighed 1·4 kg. This week the price of beef has risen by 12 per cent. What is the weight of a joint of beef which I should now get for the same money as last week?
(*University of London*)

×**4.** A rural district council requires a rate of 47 p in the pound. If a man pays £23·5 in rates each *half* year what is the rateable value of his house?

×**5.** Mr Smith, Mr Jones and Mr Robinson all live in the same street. They try to catch the 08.00 train to London each morning, but they either just catch it or just miss it. Design an experiment to find the probability:
  (a) that Mr Smith only will catch the train
  (b) that Mr Jones and Mr Robinson will catch the train.
  (c) They will all catch the train.

6. A regular polygon has each internal angle equal to 135°. Which polygon is it?

  A a hexagon (6 sided)
  B a heptagon (7 sides)
  C An octagon (8 sided)
  D a nonagon (9 sided

Paper R.9

1. (a) If a, b and c are any real numbers except zero, which of the following statements are true and which are false? (Set out your answer by writing down the numbers (*i*), (*ii*), (*iii*), (*iv*), (*v*) with TRUE or FALSE against each
  (*i*) $a \times (b + c) = (a \times b) + (a \times c)$
  (*ii*) $a + (b \times c) = (a + b) \times (a + c)$

REVISION EXERCISES

    (iii) $a \times b = b \times a$
    (iv) $(a - b) - c = a - (b - c)$
    (v) $(a \, W \, b) \, W \, c = a \, W \, (b \, W \, c)$

(b) How many axes of symmetry in the plane has
    (i) An isosceles triangle?
    (ii) An equilateral triangle?
    (iii) A rhombus?
Which of the above figures have centres of symmetry?

(L.C.C., L.S.S.E.)

2. On my journey each morning I pass 5 sets of traffic lights within a distance of 1 km. Assuming they can either be red or green and that they are unaffected by weight of traffic, design an experiment to find the probability that I shall find them all showing the green light at the same time.

3. A theodolite 135 cm high is placed 15 m from a tree and the angle of elevation of the top of the tree is found to be 21°. Calculate the height of the tree to the nearest centimetre. *(U.E.I., adapted)*

4. (a) A triangle ABC is inscribed in a circle, centre O. Angle AOB = 128°, angle BOC = 106°. Find the value of angle ABC.

(b) ABCD is a cyclic quadrilateral: the diagonal BD bisects the angles at B and D. Show that angle BAD is a right angle. What is the line BD in relation to the circle?

(U.E.I., adapted)

5. (a) Find the value of $64^2 - 58^2$.
(b) Solve the equation $x^2 - x - 20 = 0$

Paper R.10

1. A body starts from rest and its velocity v m/s at a time t s is given by the following table

t	0	0·5	1	2	3	4	5
v	0	12	19·5	29·5	34	31	19·8

LONGMAN MATHEMATICS

Draw a graph showing the connection between t and v and use it to find

(i) the distance travelled in the 5 seconds;
(ii) the acceleration at the instant when $t = 2$. (A.E.B.)

2. 100 candidates recently sat an examination and the results graded in ranges of 5 marks are shown in the following table

Mark Range	0–4	5–9	10–14	15–19	20–24
Number of Candidates	8	24	38	27	3

Draw the cumulative frequency graph and find the median value of the marks.

3. A particle moves in such a way that after t s its velocity, v m/s, is given by the equation $v = 12t - \frac{3}{4}t^2$.

Taking values of t from 0 to 16 (even numbers only) find the corresponding values of v and plot the velocity/time graph. From your graph find the distance travelled by the particle during the 16s before it comes to rest.

4. One method of helping to decide the author of the 'Dead Sea Scrolls' recently discovered was to find the 'most fashionable' length of word; in other words, finding the *mode* of the frequency distribution. Look at the following passages in St Mark's and St John's gospels.

St Mark, Chapter VI, verse 43:

'And they took up twelve baskets full of the fragments, and of the fishes.' (Miracle of feeding the five thousand.)

St Mark, Chapter VIII, verse 8:

'So they did eat and were filled and they took up of the broken meat that was left seven baskets.' (Miracle of feeding the four thousand.)

St John, Chapter VI, verse 13:

'Therefore they gathered them together and filled twelve baskets with the fragments of the five barley loaves, which remained over and above unto them that had eaten.' (Miracle of feeding the five thousand.)

REVISION EXERCISES

Make frequency tables of the number of letters per word in each of these passages, grading them as follows:

(1 to 3); (4 to 6); (7 to 9); (10 to 12)

and find the mode in each case.

Do you find this method helps you to identify the author?

6. The value of $\dfrac{\bar{3}\cdot 982\,6}{2}$ is:

A $\bar{1}\cdot 491\,3$
B $\bar{1}\cdot 991\,3$
C $\bar{2}\cdot 491\,3$
D $\bar{2}\cdot 991\,3$

Paper R.11

1. A body starts from rest and its velocity after t s is given by the equation

$$v = \tfrac{1}{10}(20t - t^2)$$

Taking values of t from 0 to 5 plot the velocity/time graph and, using any suitable method, find from your graph the distance travelled in 5 s.

2. Describe in your own words the relation which exists between x and y in the following cases. Where possible also express the relation in the form

$$y \propto x \text{ or } y \propto \frac{1}{x}$$

(i) $y = $ Time taken in travelling between London and York.
   $x = $ The speed of travelling.

(ii) $y = $ The time taken to work a test paper.
   $x = $ The number of children working it.

(iii) $x = $ The number of school dinners ordered today.
   $y = $ The money paid for them.

(iv) $y = $ the market value of a car.
   $x = $ The number of years it has been in use.

(N.B. the sign $\propto$ means 'is proportional to'.)   (U.E.I.)

3. The accompanying histogram Fig. 17-8 shows the number of emergency calls for ambulances received each hour from 09.00 to 21.00 on a particular day (each square represents one case). Find

LONGMAN MATHEMATICS

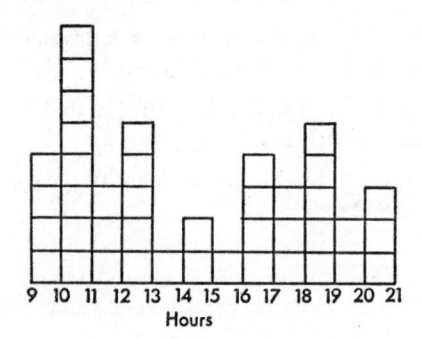

Fig. 17-8

Hours: 9 10 11 12 13 14 15 16 17 18 19 20 21

  (i) the total number of calls made;
  (ii) the number of calls per hour which were (a) the mean (b) the mode. *(L.C.C., L.S.S.E., adapted)*

4. (a) XY is a fixed line of length 10 cm. What is the locus of the point Z if angle XZY is 90°?

  (b) In Fig. 17-9, 0 is the centre of the circle, CB is parallel to OA, angle OAC = 35°. Find the number of degrees in the angle AOB.
  (University of London, adapted)

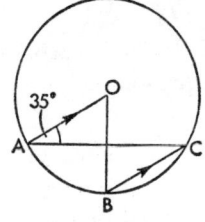

Fig. 17-9

5. In the recent Little World Cup series, the soccer teams of four countries, England, Brazil, Argentina and Portugal, were competing. Each team played each other team once. Find
  (a) how many games were played in all;
  (b) the probability that England would play Brazil in the first round assuming all four teams were 'put in the hat' together.

6.

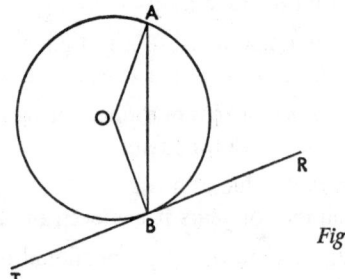

Fig. 17-9a

In the above figure O is the centre of the circle and TBR is the tangent at B. $\hat{OAB} = 21°$, what is the value of the angle $\hat{ABR}$?

250

REVISION EXERCISES

A 21°
B 69°
C 42°
D 111°

Paper R.12

1. Find the area of the irregular figure shown in Fig. 17-10. AK = 30 mm, BH = 47·5 mm, CG = 37·5 mm, DF = 17·5 mm and the perpendicular distance between successive parallel lines is 12·5 mm.

(A.E.B.)

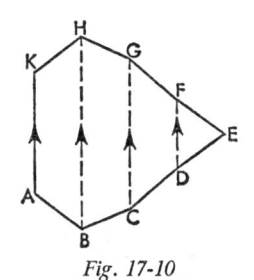

Fig. 17-10

2. A man's income for the year is £1 746 on £726 of which no tax was charged. Tax was charged on the remainder as follows: 30 p in the pound on the first £260, and the remainder at 41·25 p in the pound. During the year £400 was deducted under P.A.Y.E. Calculate by how much the tax was underpaid or overpaid.

(A.E.B., adapted)

3. A model of a ship is made to a scale of 1 cm to 10 m. If the volume of the model is 1 cm³ calculate the volume of the ship.

4. The heights of 200 boys were measured and are given in the following table

Height /cm	120	122	124	126	128	130	132	134	136	138	140	142	144	146
No. of boys	3	5	8	9	8	7	12	13	15	14	11	10	12	10

Height/cm	148	150	152	154	156	158	160	162	164	166
No. of boys	11	12	8	7	5	9	5	3	2	1

LONGMAN MATHEMATICS

Using ranges of 6 cm in heights, i.e. (120–124), (126–130), etc., construct a frequency table and calculate the arithmetic mean of this distribution using the method of the assumed mean.

5. From the frequency table in Question 4 construct a cumulative frequency table and calculate the median of this distribution. Check your result by drawing the cumulative frequency graph (or ogive) and measuring the median.

6. A rectangular block has a volume of 216 cm³. What is the volume of a similar block in which the linear dimensions are 3 times as large?

    A 648 cm³
    B 194 4 cm³
    C 5 832 cm³
    D 17 496 cm³

Paper R.13

1. (a) Solve the equation $\dfrac{x+3}{4} = \dfrac{5x-12}{2}$

  (b) Factorize completely (i) $3x - 9xy$
                                 (ii) $9a^2 - 4b^2$
                                 (iii) $t^2 - 5t - 6$ (C.O.P.)

2. (i) If $y = mx + c$ express x in terms of y, m and c.
  (ii) Express 1 260 as a product of prime factors.
  (iii) If $\dfrac{1}{R} = \dfrac{1}{x} + \dfrac{1}{y}$ calculate R if x is 2 and y is 3.   (R.S.A.)

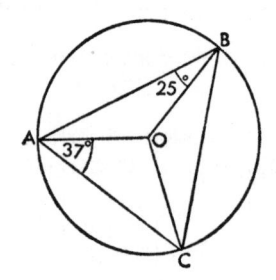

Fig. 17-11

3. Fig. 17-11 shows a circle with centre O and radius 7·5 cm; the angle OBA = 25° and the angle OAC = 37°. Calculate

REVISION EXERCISES

  (*i*) the size of angle OBC;
  (*ii*) the area of triangle ABC. (*A.E.B.*)

4. At the corner A of a rectangular courtyard ABCD, where A, B, C and D all lie on the same horizontal plane, a vertical flagpole is erected. The sides AB and BC are of length 60 metres and 25 metres respectively. Use mathematical tables to find:
  (*i*) the height of the pole if the angle of elevation of the top of the pole from B is 16°. Give your answer in feet correct to the nearest foot.
  (*ii*) the angle of elevation of the top of the pole from C. Express your answer correct to the nearest degree. (*C.O.P.*)

5. (*a*) If p and q are any even numbers and r and s are any odd numbers
  (*i*) is $pr + qs$ even or odd?
  (*ii*) is $(p + q)(r + s)$ even or odd?
  (*iii*) is $pqrs$ always divisible by 6?
  (*iv*) is $pq(r + s)$ always divisible by 8?
  (*v*) is $p + r$ always prime?
 (*b*) (*i*) Express the denary number 26 in the binary scale.
   (*ii*) Add together the binary numbers 10 011 and 1 010, giving your answer in the binary scale.
   (*iii*) Multiply the binary number 1 010 101 by the denary number 8, giving your answer in the binary scale.
  (*L.C.C.*)

6. Select the correct answer in each case.
  (*a*) The difference between 92½ p and £1·02 is (*i*) 89½ p, (*ii*) 9½ p.
  (*b*) The product of 0, 0·2, 0·4 and 0·6 is (*i*) 1·2, (*ii*) 0·36, (*iii*) 0·036, (*iv*) 0
  (*c*) The result of dividing 0·063 by 0·7 is (*i*) 0·009, (*ii*) 0·09, (*iii*) 0·9, (*iv*) 9
  (*d*) The value of the cube root of 0·008 is (*i*) 0·02, (*ii*) 0·002 6, (*iii*) 0·2, (*iv*) 0·002.

Paper R.14

1. (*a*) Find the value of $\dfrac{(2\frac{2}{5} - 1\frac{1}{3})}{(3\frac{3}{4} + \frac{7}{8})}$
  (*b*) Find four numbers (less than 50), each of which, when divided by 2, 3 or 4, will always give a remainder of 1.

(c) Express 0·312 5 as a fraction in its lowest terms.

(R.S.A., 1962)

2. In each of the diagrams (Figs. 17-12, 13 and 14) below (which are not accurately drawn), 0 is the centre of the circle. In Fig. 17-13, PT is a tangent to the circle at T. In each case calculate the size, in degrees, of the angle marked $x°$ and explain your reasoning.

(C.O.P.)

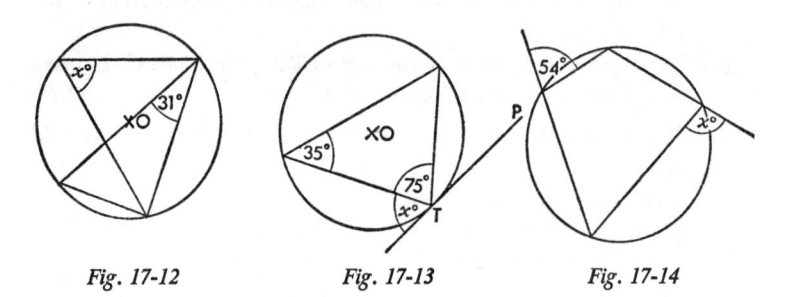

Fig. 17-12   Fig. 17-13   Fig. 17-14

3. In a quadrilateral ABCD the sides AB and DC are parallel. The diagonal AC = 46 mm, AB = 65 mm, AD = 30 mm and the angle BAC = 32°. Calculate

(i) the perpendicular distance from C to AB;
(ii) the length of BC;
(iii) the two possible sizes of the angle $A\hat{D}C$. (A.E.B.)

4. (a) From the formula $S = \pi (r^2 + rl)$ express l in terms of the other symbols.

(b) In a rhombus ABCD, AB = 9 cm and the angle A is 110°. Calculate the area of the rhombus. (A.E.B.)

5. (a) One of the following numbers is exactly divisible by 18. Which?

(i) 9 700 200 050 080
(ii) 97 002 000 100 701
(iii) 97 002 000 100 800

(b) (i) Express the denary number 27 in the binary scale.
(ii) Express the binary number 111 111 in the denary scale.
(iii) Add the following binary numbers and give your answer in the binary scale.
11 101 + 11 101 + 11 101 + 11 101 (L.C.C.)

REVISION EXERCISES

6. Are the following statements TRUE or FALSE?
- (i) $\frac{1}{3} + \frac{1}{7} + \frac{1}{10} = \frac{3}{20}$
- (ii) $2\frac{1}{2} - 1\frac{1}{3} = 1\frac{1}{6}$
- (iii) $2\frac{1}{2} \times 1\frac{1}{3} = 2\frac{1}{6}$
- (iv) $2\frac{1}{2} \div 1\frac{1}{3} = 1\frac{7}{8}$
- (v) $\frac{3}{4}$ of $\frac{8}{9} = \frac{2}{3}$
- (vi) $\frac{2}{3}$ of $76\frac{1}{2}$ p $= 51$ p
- (vii) $0\cdot 1 \times 0\cdot 2 \times 3 = 0\cdot 06$
- (viii) If $0\cdot 6x = 2\cdot 13$ then $x = 3\cdot 55$
- (ix) If $\dfrac{3x}{5} = \dfrac{9}{10}$ then $x = 6$
- (x) If $\dfrac{7}{9} = \dfrac{4}{3x}$ then $x = 1\frac{5}{7}$

Paper R.15

1. Calculate with the aid of tables:
- (i) $27\cdot 35 \times 8\cdot 75$
- (ii) $3\cdot 864 \div 0\cdot 075\ 9$
- (iii) $(4\cdot 75)^2$
- (iv) $\sqrt[3]{0\cdot 865}$ (R.S.A.)

2. Solve the following equations:
- (i) $\dfrac{x}{2} + \dfrac{x}{3} = 1 - \dfrac{x}{4}$
- (ii) $5x + 3y = 1;\ 2x - y = 7$
- (iii) $2x^2 - x - 15 = 0$ (R.S.A.)

3. Draw the graph of $y = x^2 - 2x - 3$ from $x = 4$ to $x = -2$. From your graph solve the equations:
- (i) $x^2 - 2x - 3 = 0$
- (ii) $x^2 - 2x = 4$
- (iii) $x^2 - 2x = 2$ (R.S.A.)

4. A straight pole 10 metres long rests against the vertical wall of a building and makes an angle of 64° with the horizontal ground. Calculate the distance of the foot of the pole from the wall. A rope is stretched taut from the bottom of the pole to a point on the wall 2·7 metres above the ground and directly behind the pole. Calculate the angle the rope makes with the wall.   (R.S.A.)

5. Fig. 17-15 shows three adjacent sides of a regular 20-sided polygon

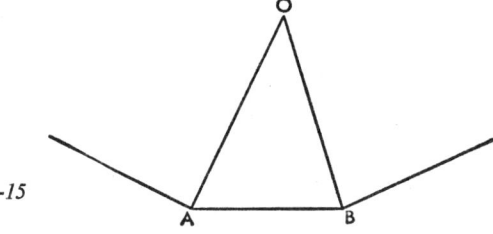

Fig. 17-15

with centre O. Calculate the internal angle of the polygon and the angles $\widehat{OAB}$ and $\widehat{AOB}$. If AB = 6 cm calculate the area of triangle OAB. Hence find the area of the polygon.

6.

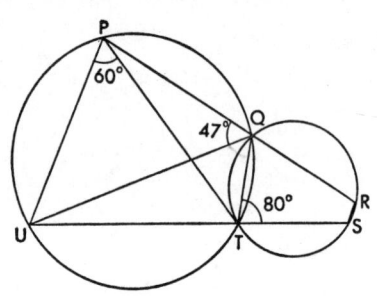

Fig. 17-16

In Fig. 17-16 two circles intersect as shown. $\widehat{UPT} = 60°$, $\widehat{PQU} = 47°$ and $\widehat{QTS} = 80°$. Are the following statements TRUE or FALSE?

(i) $\widehat{UQT} = 60°$
(ii) $\widehat{RST} = 53°$
(iii) $\widehat{PUT} = 35°$
(iv) PU is parallel to RS
(v) $\widehat{TQR} = 53°$
(vi) $\widehat{TPQ} = 20°$
(vii) $\widehat{TPQ} + \widehat{PTQ} = 53°$
(viii) $\widehat{QTP} = 47°$

Paper R.16

1. Using tables, calculate

(a) $\dfrac{3\cdot 46 \times \sqrt{79\cdot 02}}{0\cdot 034\ 1}$

(b) $\dfrac{1}{0\cdot 367} + \dfrac{1}{0\cdot 083}$

(c) $\sqrt{0\cdot 008\ 61}$

2. (a) Factorize (i) $5x^2 - 20$
(ii) $2a^2 + 21bc + 6ab + 7ac$
(iii) $x^2 - 4x - 21$

(b) Simplify $\dfrac{3x}{x^2 - 1} + \dfrac{2}{x + 1} - \dfrac{3}{x - 1}$ (R.S.A.)

3. Figs. 17-17, 17-18 and 17-19 are not accurately drawn. In each case O is the centre of the circle and in Fig. 17-17, PT is the tangent to

REVISION EXERCISES

the circle at T. Calculate in each case the size of the angle marked $x°$ and explain your reasoning.

(C.O.P.)

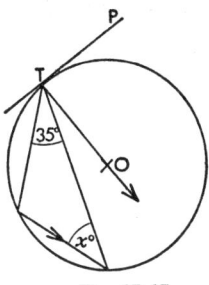

Fig. 17-17 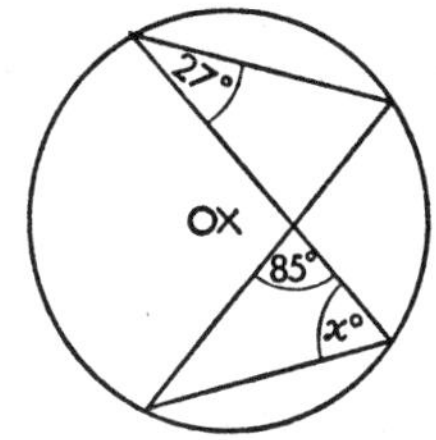   *Fig. 17-18* 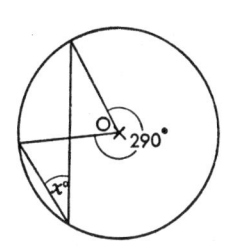   *Fig. 17-19*

4. (a) A cyclist travels a distance of 77 km in 2 hours 56 minutes. Cycling at the same average speed how long will it take him to travel 112 km allowing 22 minutes for stoppages?

   (b) Calculate the simple interest payable on a loan of £550 for eight months at a rate of 7 per cent per annum, giving your answer correct to the nearest new penny.

(C.O.P.)

5. $2n + 1$, $2n + 3$ and $2n + 5$ are consecutive odd numbers provided n is any positive whole number. Show that
   (a) their sum is always divisible by 3;
   (b) their sum is always odd;
   (c) the middle number is the average of the first and third numbers;
   (d) the difference between the square of the middle number and the product of the first and last numbers is the same whatever the value of n;
   (e) the sum of three times the first number, twice the second number and the third number is always even.

6. Select the correct answers in each part.
   (a) The solution of $\frac{2y}{3} - 7 = 5$ is (i) $y = -3$; (ii) $y = 6$; (iii) $y = 12$; (iv) $y = 18$
   (b) The solution of $\frac{3a}{4} - \frac{2a}{3} - 1 = 0$ is (i) $a = 1$; (ii) $a = 12$; (iii) $a = -1$; (iv) $a = -12$

(c) The solutions of $\left.\begin{array}{l}2p + 3q = 7 \\ q - p = 4\end{array}\right\}$ are
(i) $p = -3, q = 1$;
(ii) $p = 2, q = 1$;
(iii) $p = 1, q = 3$;
(iv) $p = -1, q = -2$

(d) The solution of $\dfrac{1}{2x} + \dfrac{2}{x} = \dfrac{5}{6}$ is (i) $x = 1\frac{1}{5}$; (ii) $x = 3$; (iii) $x = 1\frac{4}{5}$; (iv) $x = 2$

Paper R.17

1. (i) Simplify $\dfrac{(6\frac{2}{5} - 4\frac{3}{4})}{(2\frac{3}{4} \times 1\frac{3}{5})}$

   (ii) Express $\frac{3}{16}$ as a decimal fraction.

   (iii) Three men, A, B and C share the profits of a business. A gets $\frac{5}{8}$ of the profit, B gets $\frac{1}{3}$, and C gets £100. What were the total profits of the business? (R.S.A.)

2. (a) Find, without using logarithms, the value of
   (i) $13·7 \times 28·4 + 13·7 \times 17·6$
   (ii) $227·342 \div 0·71$

   (b) Simplify $(2x - y)(3x + y) - x(5x - y)$. (A.E.B.)

3. (a) Find the average of 2·36 kg, 0·47 kg, 5·04 kg, 7·82 kg, 4·07 kg and 6·80 kg, giving your answer correct to 2 decimal places.

   (b) Find the value of $a^2 - ab + bc$ when $a = -1$, $b = -2$, and $C = -3$.

   (c) Factorize $a^2 - b^2 + a - b$. (A.E.B.)

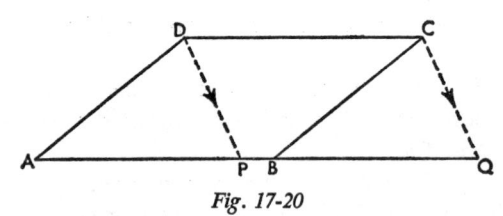

Fig. 17-20

4. In the parallelogram ABCD, Fig. 17-20, P is any point on AB. CQ is drawn parallel to DP. Prove that DPQC is a parallelogram. Prove also that triangles ADP and BCQ are congruent and use this fact to show that the areas ABCD and DPQC are equal.

5. Prove that in any triangle ABC:
$$\dfrac{a}{\sin A} = \dfrac{b}{\sin B} = \dfrac{c}{\sin C}$$

REVISION EXERCISES

In a triangle ABC, B = 42° 12', A = 70° 56' and b = 223 mm. Calculate c and the radius of the circumcircle.

6. Are the following statements TRUE or FALSE?
   (a) $46(_7) = 34(_{10})$
   (b) $693(_{10}) = 2\,011(_7)$
   (c) $445(_7) + 236(_7) = 1\,014(_7)$
   (d) The difference between $264(_7)$ and $300(_7)$ is 3
   (e) $423(_7) \times 6 = 3\,504(_7)$
   (f) $3\,442(_7) \div 5 = 516(_7)$
   (g) $35(_7) = 11\,110(_2)$
   (h) $35(_7) + 45(_7) = 2\,021(_3)$

Paper R.18

1. (a) A rectangular lawn 16 m by 13 m has a rectangular rose bed 4 m by 2·6 m cut from it. Express the area of the bed as a fraction of the area of the lawn remaining.
   (b) Factorize $4x^3 - x$.
   (c) In Fig. 17-21 XY is parallel to ZW. Calculate the angle YPW.

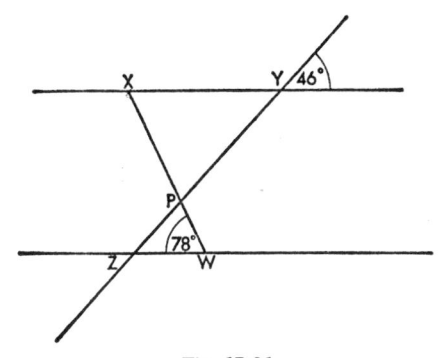

Fig. 17-21

(A.E.B.)

2. (a) Reduce to a single fraction in its simplest form
$$(7\tfrac{1}{2} - 5\tfrac{5}{8}) \div 3\tfrac{1}{3}$$
   (b) Find the exact values of
   (i) $73·06 \times 0·32$
   (ii) $4·207 \div 0·35$ (C.O.P.)

3. Write out the '4 times' multiplication table in the 'base 5' notation as far as 4×10. Use this table to multiply 342 by 44 in. in 'base 5'

notation. Check your answer by converting 342 and 44 into denary notation and multiplying out. Add the digits in the multiplication table you first wrote down. What do you notice? Write down a simple rule to find which numbers in the 'base 5' system are divisible by 4. Which of the following 'base 5' numbers are divisible by 4? 220, 321, 413, 1 111, 401.

4. From an aircraft A a cruiser C is 10 km away on a bearing 214° (S.34°W.) and a destroyer D is 15 km away on a bearing 139° (S.41°E.). Calculate how far the destroyer is (*i*) East (*ii*) South of the cruiser. Hence or otherwise calculate the bearing of the destroyer from the cruiser. (Neglect the height of the aircraft.) (*A.E.B.*)

5. If $a = \frac{1}{2}$, $b = 2$, $c = -3$ find the values of:

(*i*) $ab + c^2$; $3ab^2c$; $\dfrac{b}{a} + \dfrac{c}{b}$

(*ii*) Express as a single fraction $\dfrac{2}{x+1} - \dfrac{1}{x}$

(*iii*) If $\dfrac{1}{a} = \dfrac{1}{b} + \dfrac{1}{x}$ express x in terms of a and b. (*R.S.A.*)

6.

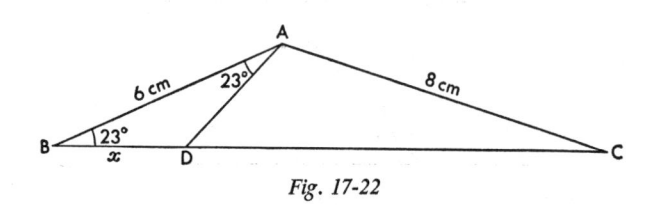

Fig. 17-22

In Fig. 17-22, $\widehat{ABD} = \widehat{BAD} = 23°$, AB = 6 cm and AC = 8 cm. Are the following statements TRUE or FALSE?

(*i*) AD = x (*vi*) $\widehat{ACB} = 17° 2'$
(*ii*) $x = 3 \cos 23°$ (*vii*) $\widehat{BAC} = 140° 58'$
(*iii*) $x = 3 \cdot 259$ cm (*viii*) $\widehat{DAC} = 116° 58'$
(*iv*) $\dfrac{6}{\sin ACB} = \dfrac{8}{\sin 23°}$ (*ix*) BC = 13·16 cm
 (*x*) CD = 16·42 cm
(*v*) $\sin ACB = \dfrac{8 \sin 23°}{6}$

REVISION EXERCISES

Paper R.19

1. Draw the graph of $y = 4x - x^2$. Take values of x from -1 to 5. On the same axes draw the graph of $y = 0.5x + 1$. Give the values of x at the points where the two graphs intersect. *(R.S.A.)*

2. A field ABCDE, Fig. 17-23, is boarded by five straight fences. A surveyor lays out the straight line XCYZE where BX, DY and AZ are all perpendicular to XE. He obtains the following measurements in metres:

$$\begin{aligned} XC &= 31 & BX &= 22 \\ CY &= 9 & DY &= 48 \\ YZ &= 10 & AZ &= 60 \\ ZE &= 82 \end{aligned}$$

Calculate the area of the field in square metres.

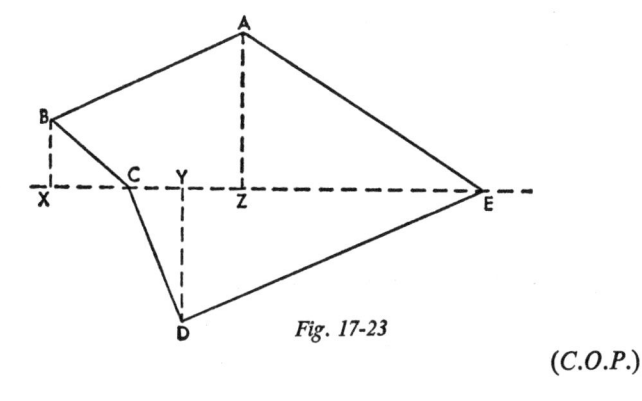

Fig. 17-23

(C.O.P.)

3. The maximum mark given for a test was 10. The graph on p. 262, Fig. 17-24, shows the number of children obtaining each mark.
  (*a*) How many children were tested?
  (*b*) Find the marks which are (*i*) the median, (*ii*) the mode, (*iii*) the mean.
  (*c*) Which of the answers to part (*b*) corresponds to the average mark? *(L.C.C.)*

4. (*i*) How many times does a wheel of 42 cm diameter revolve in travelling 1 088 m?
  (*ii*) Calculate the diameter of a circular lawn whose area is 242 m². *(R.S.A.)*

261

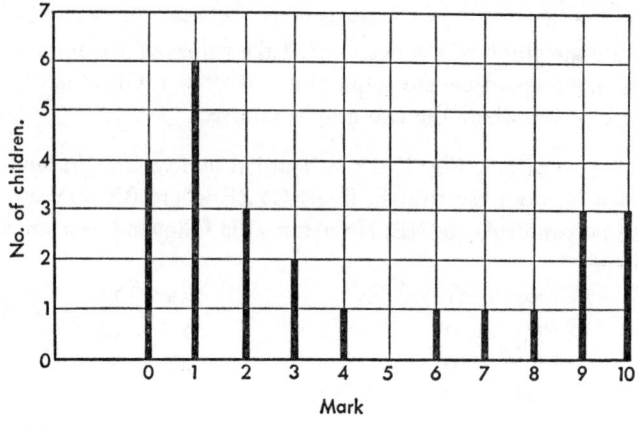

Fig. 17-24

5. A garage is allowed a 12½ per cent trade discount on the retail price of a car and a 15 per cent trade discount on the retail price of a motor scooter. Find the total price paid by the garage, after the discount has been deducted, when it orders three cars at the retail price of £656 each and four scooters at the retail price of £120 each.

(*C.O.P.*)

6. Select the correct answer for each part. If $a = -1$, $b = 2$, $c = 0$ and $d = -3$
   (*a*) The value of $abcd$ is (i) -6 (ii) $+6$ (iii) 0 (iv) $+12$
   (*b*) The value of $ad + bc$ is (i) $+3$ (ii) $+5$ (iii) -5 (iv) -3
   (*c*) The value of $a^2b^2 - c^2d^2$ is (i) $+13$ (ii) -5 (iii) $+5$ (iv) $+4$
   (*d*) The value of $\dfrac{bc}{ad}$ is (i) $\frac{2}{3}$ (ii) 0 (iii) $-\frac{2}{3}$ (iv) $1\frac{1}{2}$
   (*e*) The value of $\dfrac{abd + bd}{c - bd}$ is (i) -1 (ii) 2 (iii) -2 (iv) $+1$

Paper R.20

1. (*a*) Simplify $(16\frac{1}{3} - 8\frac{5}{6}) \div 3\frac{3}{4}$.
   (*b*) Use tables to find $\sqrt{40 \cdot 58}$.
   (*c*) A cartwheel has 15 spokes and is being decorated for a carnival. One spoke is painted red, the next spoke is painted white, the next blue, and the pattern is repeated until all the

REVISION EXERCISES

spokes are painted. Find the angle between one red spoke and the next red spoke. (*A.E.B.*)

2. (*a*) Solve the equations
$$\frac{x}{2}+\frac{y}{3}=6, \quad \frac{3x}{2}-\frac{2y}{3}=3$$

(*b*) A man bought 18 kg of copper at £x per kg and 19 kg of copper at £y per kg. What was the average price per kg of the copper?

(*c*) Draw a line AB of length 75 mm and by geometrical construction find a point P in AB such that AP:PB = 2:5. Measure the length of AP. (*A.E.B.*)

3. (*a*) A factory chimney of height 56 m casts a shadow of length 100 m on level ground. Calculate the angle of inclination of the sun.

(*b*) In Fig. 17-25 ABCD is a rectangle, not drawn to scale, AD = 9·2 cm, AE = 6·4 cm, BF = 4·8 cm and the angle ADE is equal to the angle BEF. Calculate

(*i*) the length of EB;

(*ii*) the value of $\dfrac{\text{area of triangle ADE}}{\text{area of triangle BEF}}$ (*A.E.B.*)

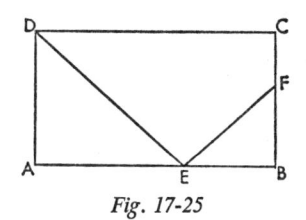

Fig. 17-25

4. VABCDEF is a pyramid whose vertex is V and whose horizontal base is a regular hexagon ABCDEF with sides each 5 cm in length. The slant edges through V are all 10 cm long. Calculate

(*i*) the vertical height of the pyramid;
(*ii*) the angle between the face VAB and the base;
(*iii*) the angle between the edge VA and the base. (*A.E.B.*)

5.

Marks obtained	0	1	2	3	4	5	6	7	8	9	10
No. of pupils	4	6	3	7	9	10	12	8	6	6	1

The table shows the results of a Mathematics test, and the number of pupils who scored each mark between 0 and 10.
 (a) Draw a histogram to represent these results.
 (b) How many pupils took the test?
 (c) Find the number of marks which were (i) the mean.
                                        (ii) the mode.

6.

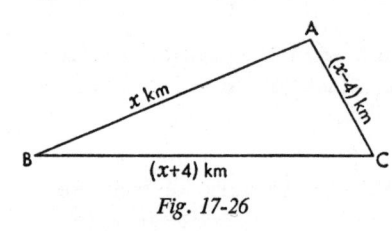

Fig. 17-26

In Fig. 17-26, A, B and C are three towns and their distances apart are shown. A man cycles from A to B at 10 km/h, from B to C at 12 km/h and from C to A at 16 km/h. His total times for the whole journey is 5 hours.

Are the following statements TRUE or FALSE?

(i) The average speed $= \dfrac{10 + 12 + 16}{3} = 12\frac{2}{3}$ km/h

(ii) Time for AB is $\dfrac{x}{10}$ h, for BC is $\dfrac{(x+4)}{12}$ h and for CA is $\dfrac{(x-4)}{16}$ h.

(iii) Total time $= \dfrac{3x}{38}$ h.

(iv) $\dfrac{x}{10} + \dfrac{x+4}{12} + \dfrac{x-4}{16} = 5$

(v) $59x = 1\,180$

(vi) $x = 20$

(vii) AB $= 16$ km, BC $= 20$ km and AC $= 24$ km

(viii) The total distance is 60 km

(ix) The average speed $= \dfrac{60}{5} = 12$ km/h

Paper R.21

1. (a) Use tables to calculate the values of the following expressions correct to three significant figures.

  (i) $32\cdot08 \times 2\cdot034$ (ii) $\dfrac{1}{0\cdot342} - \dfrac{1}{4\cdot96}$

REVISION EXERCISES

(b) In each of the following diagrams, Figs. 17-27, 28, and 29, which are not accurately drawn, O represents the centre of the circle. Calculate the values of x, y and z. (L.C.C.)

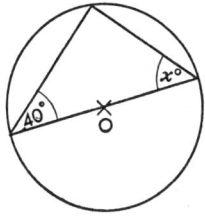

Fig. 17-27 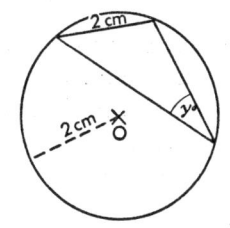   Fig. 17-28 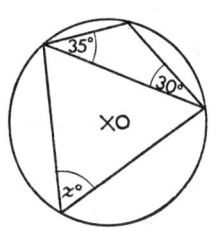   Fig. 17-29

2. (a) If A square units is the area of a trapezium, whose parallel sides are of lengths a units and b units at a distance h units apart, then $A = \frac{1}{2}(a + b)h$
   (i) Find an expression of h in terms of A, a and b.
   (ii) One of the parallel sides of a trapezium is 3 cm long and the distance between the parallel sides is 7 cm. If the area of the trapezium is 28 cm², find the length of the other parallel side.

(b) If $x = \dfrac{1}{y^2} - 3$
   (i) Find the value of x when $y = \frac{1}{2}$.
   (ii) Find the value of y when $x = 13$. (C.O.P.)

3. (a) Find the exact value of $\dfrac{1\cdot 2 \times 0\cdot 006}{0\cdot 36 \times 0\cdot 04}$
   (b) Calculate the total gas bill for a house when 24 therms of gas, at 10·42 p per therm, are used and a meter charge of 15 p is included in the bill. Express your answer correct to the nearest penny. (C.O.P.)

4. Solve the following equations:
   (i) $\dfrac{y+6}{2} - \dfrac{y-2}{5} = \dfrac{y+9}{3} - 1$
   (ii) $\left. \begin{array}{l} 4x + 3y = 41 \\ 9x - 3y = 24 \end{array} \right\}$
   (iii) $10x^2 - 19x = 56$ (Solve by factorizing.) (R.S.A.)

5. Construct a quadrilateral ABCD so that AB = 75 mm, AD = 35 mm, BD = 67 mm, BC = 52 mm and CD = 45 mm. Construct a

point P on BA produced so that triangle PCB is equal in area to quadrilateral ABCD. Measure PB and the perpendicular distance of C from AB, and hence calculate the area of the quadrilateral ABCD.

6. Are the following statements TRUE or FALSE?
    (i) 0·01 is a closer estimate to the value of $(0·2)^3$ than 0·001
    (ii) 4·099 5 = 4·1 (correct to 2 significant figures)
    (iii) 0·099 5 = 0·010 (correct to 3 decimal places)
    (iv) $\sqrt{2·25}$ is closer to 1·3 than to 1·6
    (v) 700 is a closer approximation to 3^6 than 1 000

Paper R.22

1. (a) Express £1·35 as a percentage of £6.
   (b) An emery wheel of diameter 28 cm runs at 1 200 revolutions per minute. Calculate, in metres per second, the speed of a point on the circumference. (Take π as $3\frac{1}{7}$.)
   (c) Simplify the expression $a^2 - b^2 - (a - b)^2$.   (A.E.B.)

2. A shopkeeper bought x pencils for £10 and offered them for sale so that he would make a profit of 1 p on each pencil. At the end of the month he had 50 pencils left and had taken £9. Write down an expression for the selling price of a pencil in pence. Hence form an equation for x and, by solving it, find the price for which the shopkeeper sold each pencil.   (A.E.B.)

3. (a) Fig. 17-30, not drawn to scale, represents a plot of land. AB is due North. Using a scale of 2 cm to represent 10 m make an accurate plan of the plot when:
   AR = 4 m; PQ = 17 m;
   RE = 15 m; QD = 15 m;
   RP = 5 m; QB = 6 m;
   PC = 11 m.
   (b) On your plan measure CD to the nearest millimetre.

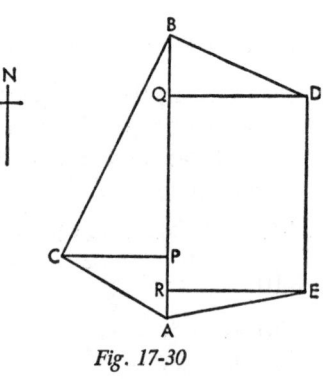

   Fig. 17-30

   How many metres does this represent on the plot?
   (c) Find the bearing of C from A correct to the nearest degree.
   (d) Calculate the total area of the plot in square metres. (L.C.C.)

REVISION EXERCISES

4. A man walks 100 metres along a road which slopes upwards at 20° to the horizontal. The slope of the road now increases and is 23° to the horizontal. The man then walks another 200 metres. Calculate how far he is (*i*) horizontally, (*ii*) vertically, from his starting point. (*R.S.A.*)

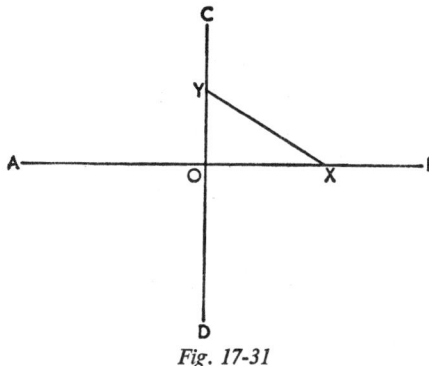

Fig. 17-31

5. Fig. 17-31 represents two fixed perpendicular straight lines AOB and COD. XY is a straight line of *fixed* length which may take up any position provided that X is on AB and Y is on CD. The envelope of all possible positions of XY has a centre of symmetry at O and is called an astroid.

(*a*) How many axes of symmetry has an astroid?

(*b*) If P and Q are points on the perimeter of an astroid and the straight line PQ passes through O, then PQ may be called a diameter of the astroid. By calculation, or by drawing and measurement find the ratio between the lengths of the longest and shortest diameters of an astroid. (*L.C.C.*)

6. In Fig. 17-32, ABCDE is a regular pentagon inscribed in a circle centre O, radius 3 cm. XBY is the tangent at B. Are the following statements TRUE or FALSE?

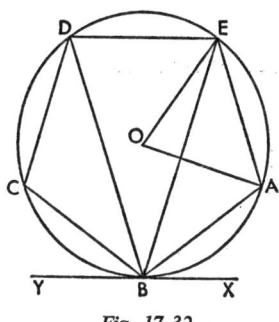

(*i*) $A\hat{B}C = 108°$

(*ii*) $A\hat{B}Y + C\hat{B}Y = 62°$

(*iii*) $B\hat{D}C = 36°$

(*iv*) $C\hat{B}D = 36°$

(*v*) $A\hat{B}D = 82°$

Fig. 17-32

267

(vi) $E\hat{B}A = 36°$ (vii) $E\hat{O}A = 72°$
(viii) Area AOEA $= 3 \times 3 \times \sin 72°$ cm²
(ix) Area ABCDE $= 45 \sin 72°$ cm²
(x) Area ABCDE $= 21{\cdot}4$ cm²

Paper R.23

1. (a) If the postage rate for newspapers is increased from 1 p to $1\frac{1}{2}$ p each, what is the weekly increase in cost to a publisher who sends 5 000 copies of his paper by post each week?

   (b) The piece of string attached to a tie-on luggage label is 22 cm long. How many such labels can be completed from 100 metres of string?   (R.S.A.)

2. (i) If $a = 3$, $b = 4$, $c = -2$, find the value of $\dfrac{a-b-c}{a+b+c}$

   (ii) Factorize $4x^2 - 36$.

   (iii) Make h the subject of the formula $v = \sqrt{2gh}$.
        (R.S.A.)

3. At a certain library the numbers of books issued weekly for six successive weeks are 1 826, 2 154, 2 267, 2 092, 1 951 and 2 550.

   (a) What was the average weekly issue?

   (b) By how much do the maximum and minimum issues differ from the average? Express these differences as a percentage of the average.

   (c) How many books would the librarian expect to issue in a year of 52 weeks?   (R.S.A.)

4. ABCD is a cyclic quadrilateral. AB is produced to E. If angle CBE = 130° and angle DAC = 30°, calculate angles ACD and DBC.

5. The results shown below may be called 'expansions'.

$$\begin{aligned}
2 &= 1 + 1 \\
2^2 &= 1 + 2 + 1 \\
2^3 &= 1 + 3 + 3 + 1 \\
2^4 &= 1 + 4 + 6 + 4 + 1 \\
2^5 &= 1 + 5 + 10 + 10 + 5 + 1 \\
2^6 &= 1 + 6 + 15 + 20 + 15 + 6 + 1 \\
2^7 &= \dots\dots\dots\dots\dots\dots\dots\dots\dots
\end{aligned}$$

Write out the expansion of 2^7.

REVISION EXERCISES

The first four numbers in the expansion of 2^n are:
$$1 + n + \frac{n(n-1)}{1 \times 2} + \frac{n(n-1)(n-2)}{1 \times 2 \times 3}$$
Find these four numbers when $n = 20$.   (L.C.C.)

6. Select the correct answer to the following. There may be more than one correct answer in parts (a) and (b)
   (a) 30 976 is exactly divisible by (i) 8 (ii) 7 (iii) 11 (iv) 9
   (b) 1 101 010$_{(2)}$ is (i) odd (ii) even (iii) exactly divisible by 110$_{(2)}$ (iv) exactly divisible by 110 101$_{(2)}$
   (c) The value of $17^2 - 9^2$ is (i) 8^2 (ii) 26^2 (iii) 208 (iv) 198
   (d) The value of $32 \cdot 4 \div 0 \cdot 024$ is (i) 1·35 (ii) 0·013 5 (iii) 135 (iv) 1 350

Paper R.24

1. (a) Factorize completely:
      (i) $3x - 27x^2$
      (ii) $\pi R^2 - \pi r^2$
      (iii) $4x^2 + 4x - 3$
   (b) Solve the simultaneous equations
   $$3x - 5y = 7$$
   $$4x = 7y + 2$$ (C.O.P.)

2. The flight of a stone thrown vertically upwards with an initial velocity of 15 metres per second is described by the equation
$$S = 15t - 5t^2$$
where S is the distance of the stone from the ground in metres and t the time of flight in seconds. Values of S corresponding to certain values of t are given below.

t/s	$\frac{1}{2}$	$1\frac{1}{2}$	2
S/m	6·25	11·25	10

Plot these values on a graph. Calculate sufficient extra values to allow you to draw an accurate graph from $t = \frac{1}{2}$ to $t = 2\frac{1}{2}$. From your graph read off as accurately as possible:
   (a) the maximum height of the stone above the ground, and
   (b) the two values of t when the stone is 7 metres above the ground.   (C.O.P.)

3. The diagrams below, Figs. 17-33 and 34, are not accurately drawn. In each case O is the centre of the circle. In Fig. 17-34 P is the point from which the tangents to the circle are drawn. In each case calculate the size, in degrees, of the angle marked $x°$.

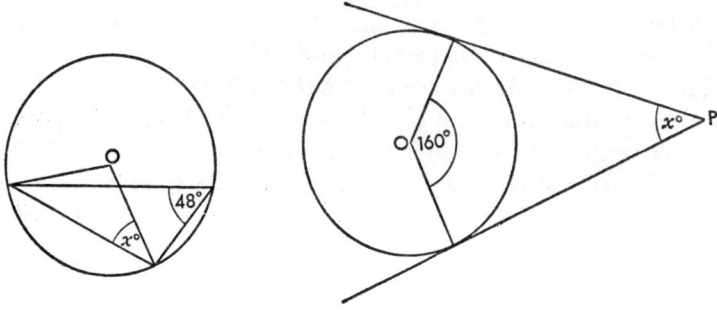

Fig. 17-33   *Fig. 17-34*

4. A stone column is in the form of a cylinder surmounted by a cone. The diameter of the cylinder and of the base of the cone is 70 cm, the height of the cyclinder is 3·5 m and the height of the cone 66 cm Find the volume of stone in the column. What is the weight of the whole column if a cubic metre of stone weighs 700 kg? Take π as $\frac{22}{7}$.
(*R.S.A.*)

5. Draw the graphs of $y = x^3 + 2$ and $y = \frac{3}{2}x + 2$ for values of x between -2 and $+2$ using the same scales and axes. Show, by vertical shading, the area inside which are the points for which y is greater than $x^3 + 2$ and less than $\frac{3}{2}x + 2$; and by horizontal shading, those points for which y is less than $x^3 + 2$ and greater than $\frac{3}{2}x + 2$.
(*A.E.B.*)

6. $A = 3x + 2y$, $B = 4x - y$, $C = 6x + 4y$
   Select the correct answer to the following:
   (*a*) The value of $A - B$ is (*i*) $x + 3y$ (*ii*) $3y - x$ (*iii*) $7x + y$ (*iv*) $x - 3y$
   (*b*) The value of $B + C$ is (*i*) $10x - 3y$ (*ii*) $2x + 5y$ (*iii*) $2x - 5y$ (*iv*) $10x + 3y$
   (*c*) The value of $A \times B$ is (*i*) $12x^2 + 2y^2$ (*ii*) $12x^2 - 5xy + 2y^2$ (*iii*) $12x^2 + 5xy - 2y^2$ (*iv*) $12x^2 - 2y^2$
   (*d*) If $A = 2$ and $B = 10$, the solutions of the resulting simultaneous equations are (*i*) $x = 2$, $y = -2$ (*ii*) $x = 3\frac{3}{5}$, $y = 4\frac{2}{5}$ (*iii*) $x = -2$, $y = +2$ (*iv*) $x = 4\frac{2}{5}$, $y = 7\frac{3}{5}$

REVISION EXERCISES

(e) If $A = 2$ and $C = 4$, the solutions of the resulting simultaneous equations are (i) $x = 0$, $y = 0$ (ii) $x = \frac{1}{3}$, $y = \frac{1}{2}$ (iii) $x = 4$, $y = -5$ (iv) there is no one pair of values which satisfy them.

Paper R.25

1. (a) Simplify $\dfrac{(7\frac{2}{5})^2 - (3\frac{4}{5})^2}{(7\frac{2}{5} + 3\frac{4}{5})}$

   (b) If $S = ut + \frac{1}{2} ft^2$, find u when $S = 30$, $t = 3$ and $f = 8$.

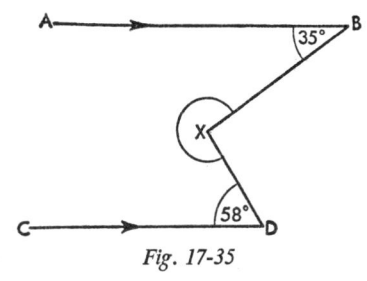

   Fig. 17-35

   (c) Calculate the reflex angle BXD, marked in Fig. 17-35 given that AB and CD are parallel. (*A.E.B.*)

2. (a) Reduce to a single fraction in its lowest terms
   $$\frac{4x - 3}{5} - \frac{6 + 2x}{15}$$

   (b) By selling his car for £425 the owner would lose 15 per cent on his cost price. Find the price at which he must sell it in order to gain 20 per cent on his cost price. (*C.O.P.*)

3. In Fig. 17-36 ABC is a triangle and AD is the perpendicular from A to BC. AB is 15 cm long; AC is 13 cm long; AD is 10 cm long. Calculate the length of BC. Calculate the value of BAD to the nearest minute. (*R.S.A.*)

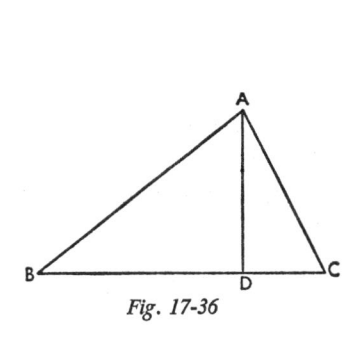

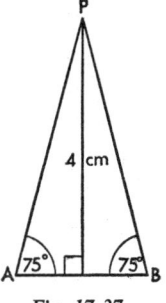

Fig. 17-36

Fig. 17-37

4. A number of triangles identical with the triangle APB shown in Fig. 17-37 are placed so that they completely surround point P to form a regular polygon.
   (a) How many sides has this regular polygon?
   (b) Calculate the length in centimetres of AB to two places of decimals.
   (c) Find the area of the polygon to the nearest square centimetre.
   (L.C.C.)

5. Fig. 17-38 (not drawn to scale) shows a plot of land APBQ. AB is 100 metres long and A is due North of B.
   (a) Taking 1 centimetre to represent 10 metres, make an accurate scale drawing of the plot.
   (b) Find to the nearest metre, the length of each of the four sides of the plot.
   (c) Find to the nearest 100 square metres, the area of the plot.
   (d) What is the bearing of (i) P from B, (ii) Q from A?
   (L.C.C.)

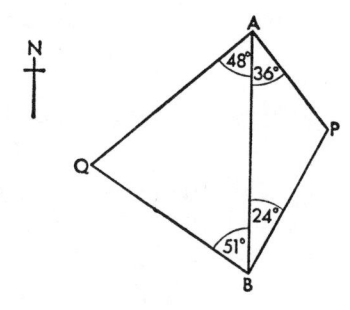

Fig. 17-38

6. Select the correct answers to the following. In part (c) there may be more than one correct statement.
   (a) If $\sin x = 0.6732$, x is (i) 42° 18′, (ii) 42° 19′, (iii) 42° 17′ (iv) 43° 19′.
   (b) If $\cos x = 0.3294$, x is (i) 70° 46′, (ii) 70° 70′, (iii) 70° 44′, (iv) 70° 38′.
   (c) Angle A is greater than angle B where A and B are both acute angles. (i) $\sin A$ is greater than $\sin B$, (ii) $\cos A$ is greater than $\cos B$, (iii) $\tan A$ is less than $\tan B$, (iv) A and B are both less than 90°, (v) $(A + B)$ is greater than 90°.
   (d) In Fig. 17-39 PQ is a wire tie fixed to a telegraph pole PR, QR = 3 metres. The length of PR is
      (i) $3\sqrt{3}$ m (ii) $\dfrac{3}{\sqrt{3}}$ m (iii) 1·5 m (iv) 6 m.

(e) In Fig. 17-39 the length of PQ is (i) $\dfrac{3}{\sqrt{3}}$ m, (ii) $\sqrt{3}$ m, (iii) 1·5 m, (iv) 6 m.

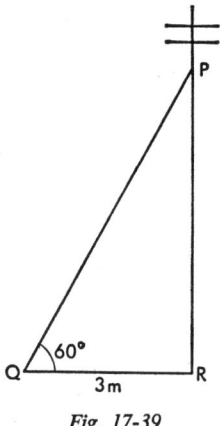

Fig. 17-39

Paper R.26

1. (a) Divide 0·087 5 by 2·85 until you have five decimal places in your answer. Give the answer
   (i) correct to three decimal places;
   (ii) correct to three significant figures.
(b) Simplify $2x(x - y + z) - x(3x - 2y - 4z) + x(x + y + 2z)$
(c) In an isosceles triangle ABC, AB = AC and the angle A is 44°. The bisectors of the angles A and B intersect at 1. Calculate the angle AIB. *(A.E.B.)*

2. On a sheet of graph paper draw two axes at right angles to one another. Scale the x axis from -20 to $+20$ and the y axis from -30 to $+30$, using scales of 2 cm to represent 10 units on each axis.
   (a) Plot the following points:
      A($-$ 15, 18); B(11, 18); C(15, $-$20); D($-$15, $-$12).
   (b) Draw the line through the origin parallel to DC. Give as accurately as you can the coordinates of the point where this line crosses BC.
   (c) What is the size of the angle DAB? *(L.C.C.)*

3. Fig. 17-40 represents a circle of radius one unit together with two squares. The vertices of the smaller square lie on the circumference of the circle and the sides of the larger square are tangents to the circle. Taking π as $3\frac{1}{7}$ find the difference between the area of the circle and the *average* area of the two squares, and express this difference as a fraction of the area of the circle. (*L.C.C.*)

Fig. 17-40

4. (*a*) The legs of a step ladder are opened at an angle of 30°. If the legs are each 2·6 m long, how high is the top of the step ladder above the ground?

   (*b*) A flagstaff casts a shadow 15 m long. At the same time the length of the shadow cast by a vertical stick of length 2·5 m is 1 m. Calculate the height of the flagstaff. (*R.S.A.*)

5. Three candidates took part in an election. The winning candidate had a majority of 7 400, one fifth of all the votes cast, over the second candidate, and the last candidate polled 1 750 votes. How many votes did the winning candidate receive?

6. Are the following statements TRUE or FALSE?

   (*a*) One factor of $6x^2 + 11x - 7$ is $(2x + 1)$.

   (*b*) The other factor of $6x^2 + 11x - 7$ is $(3x + 7)$.

   (*c*) The roots of the equation $6x^2 + 11x = 7$ are $x = -\frac{1}{2}$ or $x = 2\frac{1}{3}$.

   (*d*) If x is greater than $1\frac{1}{2}$, $(3x - 2)$ is positive (greater than 0).

   (*e*) If x is greater than 5, $(x - 5)$ is negative (less than 0).

   (*f*) $(3x - 2)(x - 5) = 3x^2 - 17x + 10$.

   (*g*) If x is greater than 5, $3x^2 - 17x + 10$ is negative.

   (*h*) If x is less than $1\frac{1}{2}$, $3x^2 - 17x + 10$ is positive.

   (*i*) If x is less than 5, $(x - 5)$ is negative.

   (*j*) If x lies between $1\frac{1}{2}$ and 5, $3x^2 - 17x + 10$ is negative.

   (*Hint:* For parts (*d*) to (*j*) a rough sketch of the function $y = 3x^2 - 17x + 10$ will be useful.)

REVISION EXERCISES

Paper R.27

1. Given that S is the set $\{1, 5, 7, 11\}$ write down the multiplication table (mod 12) for the elements of S.
   If x and y are two elements of S such that $5x \equiv 7$ (mod 12) and $xy \equiv 5$ (mod 12), find x and y. *(J.M.B.)*

2. Plot on the same axes the graphs of $y = \dfrac{1}{x}, y = \dfrac{2}{x}, y = \dfrac{3}{x}$ for values of x from -4 to $+4$.

3. A spherical solid 'cap' is cut from a 26-cm diameter sphere. If the cap is 8 cm deep what is the area of the circular plane surface?

4. (*a*) In the quadrilateral ABCD, AB is parallel to CD, AB = AC and the angle ACD is 38°. Calculate the sizes, in degrees, of the angles BAC and ABC.
   (*b*) In Fig. 17-41 DF = FE. Find the value of c in terms of a and b. *(C.O.P.)*

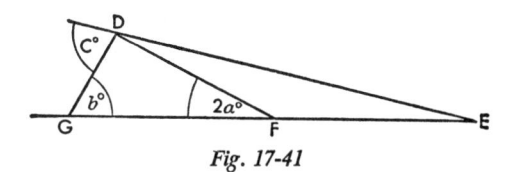

Fig. 17-41

5. (*a*) Reduce to a single fraction in its lowest terms
   $$\frac{5}{x-4} - \frac{3x+8}{x(x-4)}$$
   (*b*) Solve the equation $x^2 - 3x = 4$ *(C.O.P.)*

6. The logarithm to the base ten of $(0.07)^2$ is approximately:
   A $\bar{3}\cdot690$ B $\bar{2}\cdot690$
   C $\bar{2}\cdot845$ D $\bar{1}\cdot146$
   E $\bar{1}\cdot423$ *(J.M.B.)*

Paper R.28

1. Write down the next two numbers in the sequences:
   (*a*) 2, 3, 5, 8, 12, ...
   (*b*) 2, 3, 5, 8, 13, ...
   (*c*) 2, 3, 5, 9, 16, ...
   (*d*) 2, 3, 5, 9, 17, ...
   (*e*) 2, 3, 5, 10, 20, ...

2. (*i*) The length and breadth of a rectangular swimming pool differ by 12 metres. Find by algebra the lengths of the sides if the area is 160 square metres.
   (*ii*) Solve $6x^2 + x - 2 = 0$.
3. Find the residues congruent to the first fifteen square numbers, modulus 9. Comment on the results. Compare the results to the digital sum of the square number.
4. (*i*) Write out the multiplication table for residues 1, 2, 3 and 4, modulus 5.
   (*ii*) Write out the table of rotations of a square about its centre.
   (*iii*) Compare the tables.
   (*iv*) Reconstruct table (*i*) interchanging the 3 and 4. Now compare the two tables.
5. Construct the multiplication table for residues 1, 5, 7, and 11, modulus 12. What group conditions are obeyed?
6. If $x = A \cap B'$ which of the following is true
   A $x' = A' \cap B'$ **B** $x' = A' \cap B$
   C $x' = A' \cup B$ **D** $x' = A' \cup B'$
   E $x' = A \cup B'$ (*J.M.B.*)

Paper R.29

1. Express as fractions
   (*a*) the area of a sphere over the area of the containing cube,
   (*b*) the volume of a sphere over the volume of the containing cube.
2. Two octahedra are used as dice, having their faces marked with the number 1 to 8. By throwing the dice together totals from 2 to 16 can be obtained. Show graphically the frequency of the totals, and calculate the probability of throwing a 10.
3. Find the radius of the parallel of latitude 27°N., on the earth, assuming that the radius of the earth is 6 300 km.
Two ships are both in latitude 27°N., and their longitudes are 20°W. and 70°W.
Find the distances between the two ships measured along the parallel of latitude 27°N.
4. Two ships A and B leave port at the same time, A sailing in a direction 127° (S.53°E.) at 10 km/h and B in a direction 217° (S.37°W.) at 12 km/h. Find the bearing of A and B after one hour (*a*) by means of a scale drawing, (*b*) by calculation.   (*R.S.A.*)

REVISION EXERCISES

5. (a) The 2 long sides of a right-angled triangle measure 21 cm and 29 cm in length. Calculate the remaining side and find the size and tangent of the smallest angle in the triangle.
   (b) ABC is an isosceles triangle with AB = AC. D is a point in AC and BD = BC. If BDC = 81°, find the value of ABD.

6. If $x = yz$, and if y increases by 20% of its original value, and z also increases by 20% of its original value, then the increase of x over its original value is given by
   A 56%   B 44%   C 40%   D 20%   E 400%   (*J.M.B.*)

Paper R.30 (*Congruences*)

1. Sets A, B, C, and D are the four residue sets 0, 1, 2, and 3, modulus 4. If $a \in A$, $b \in B$, $c \in C$, $d \in D$:
   (i) form an addition table for a, b, c, and d.
   (ii) form a multiplication table for a, b, c, and d.

2. Consider the residue class 1, modulus 3, i.e. ... 1, 4, 7, 10, ... from these elements are formed the congruent relationships, $4 \equiv 1$ (mod 3): $7 \equiv 1$ (mod 3): etc. By a rearrangement the congruent sign gives way to an equals sign.
   e.g. $4 \equiv 1$ (mod 3) → $4 - 1 = 3$
             $7 \equiv 1$ (mod 3) → $7 - 1 = 2(3)$
             $10 \equiv 1$ (mod 3) → $10 - 1 = 3(3)$ etc.
   (i) Does this form of equality exist between any 2 members of the set?
   (ii) If $a \equiv b$ (mod 3) write an equation connecting a and b.
   (iii) If $c \equiv d$ (mod m) write an equation connecting c, d and m.
   (iv) If $a \equiv$ zero (mod m) write an equation connecting a, m, and 0.

3. (i) Express $a \equiv b$ (mod m) as an equation.
   (ii) Express $c \equiv d$ (mod m) as an equation.
   (iii) By adding the equations from (i) and (ii) show $(b + d) = (a + c)$ mod m.
   (iv) By subtraction show $(b - d) = (a - c)$ mod m.

4. Let $x \equiv y$ (mod 6), where $x =$ (prime numbers less than 100).
   (i) Find y if $y \in$ (residues, mod 6) for all elements x.
   (ii) Which residues (mod 6) are missing in (i)?
   (iii) Which residues occur once only?

277

(*iv*) By substituting the missing residues for y in the equation formed from the congruence $x \equiv y \pmod{6}$ find reasons why y cannot take the values when x is prime.

(*v*) If $x \in \{\text{prime numbers greater than } 100\}$, what values can y take?

5. Let $x \equiv y \pmod 7$ where $x \in \{\text{all prime numbers}\}$.
   (*i*) Let $x \equiv y \pmod 7$ where $x \in \{\text{all prime numbers}\}$.
   (*i*) By substituting for x (starting with 1), find all possible values for y, where $y \in \{\text{residues, mod } 7\}$.
   (*ii*) Compare your answer to that obtained in Question 4 above; give reason for any differences. (Form equations if necessary.)

6. Given that S is the set $\{1, 3, 4, 5, 9\}$ write down the multiplication table (mod 11) for the elements of S.
Use the table to find elements of S satisfying the following congruences:
   (*i*) $5x \equiv 1 \pmod{11}$ (*ii*) $x^2 \equiv 3 \pmod{11}$ (*J.M.B.*)

Paper R.31 (*Mappings*)

1. Plot the points (1, 1) (1, 2) (1, 3) (1, 4) (1, 5) (1, 6)
   (*i*) What happens when the points are transformed by the matrix $\begin{bmatrix} 1 & 0 \\ 0 & 1 \end{bmatrix}$?
   (*ii*) Transform each point by the matrix $\begin{bmatrix} 1 & 1 \\ 0 & 1 \end{bmatrix}$
   (*iii*) Transform each point by the matrix $\begin{bmatrix} 1 & 2 \\ 0 & 1 \end{bmatrix}$
   (*iv*) Transform each point by the matrix $\begin{bmatrix} 1 & 3 \\ 0 & 1 \end{bmatrix}$
   (*v*) What happens in the mapping to the 'y' values of each ordered pair? Why?
   (*vi*) Describe what happens in the mapping to the 'x' values, and why. The effect is termed a 'shear'.

2. Plot the points (1, 1) (2, 1) (3, 1) (3, 2) (3, 3) (2, 3) (1, 3) (1, 2)
   (*i*) Find the area of the figure.
   (*ii*) Transform each point by the matrix $\begin{bmatrix} 1 & 1 \\ 0 & 1 \end{bmatrix}$
   (*iii*) Find the area of the new figure.
   (*iv*) Repeat with the transform $\begin{bmatrix} 1 & 2 \\ 0 & 1 \end{bmatrix}$

REVISION EXERCISES

(v) What do you expect from the transform $\begin{bmatrix} 1 & 3 \\ 0 & 1 \end{bmatrix}$? Check by plotting the transformed points and finding the new area.

3. Plot the points (1, 1) (1, 2) (1, 3) (1, 4) (1, 5) (1, 6)
   (i) Transform each point by the following matrices:

      (a) $\begin{bmatrix} 1 & 0 \\ 1 & 1 \end{bmatrix}$ (b) $\begin{bmatrix} 1 & 0 \\ 2 & 1 \end{bmatrix}$ (c) $\begin{bmatrix} 1 & 0 \\ 3 & 1 \end{bmatrix}$

   (ii) What happens in the mapping to the '*x*' values? Why?
   (iii) What happens in the mapping to the '*y*' values? Why?

4. (i) Plot the points (1, 1) (2, 1) (3, 1) (3, 2) (3, 3) (2, 3) (1, 3) (1, 2).
   (ii) Transform each point by the matrix $\begin{bmatrix} 1 & 0 \\ 1 & 1 \end{bmatrix}$.
   (iii) Find the area of the new figure.
   (iv) Repeat with the transform $\begin{bmatrix} 1 & 0 \\ 2 & 1 \end{bmatrix}$.
   (v) What would you expect from $\begin{bmatrix} 1 & 0 \\ 3 & 1 \end{bmatrix}$? Check by plotting the new figure and finding its area.

5. (i) Plot (a) the triangle (2, 2) (3, 5) (6, 4);
       (b) the quadrilateral (4, 2) (4, 5) (6, 6) (9, 3).
   (ii) Find the areas of the figures.
   (iii) Find the areas when the 2 figures are transformed by

      (a) $\begin{bmatrix} 2 & 0 \\ 0 & 2 \end{bmatrix}$ (b) $\begin{bmatrix} 3 & 0 \\ 0 & 3 \end{bmatrix}$ (c) $\begin{bmatrix} \frac{1}{2} & 0 \\ 0 & \frac{1}{2} \end{bmatrix}$.

6. Find the images of $\begin{bmatrix} 1 \\ 0 \end{bmatrix}$ and $\begin{bmatrix} 0 \\ 1 \end{bmatrix}$ under the transformations with the following matrices: $A = \begin{bmatrix} 1 & 0 \\ 0 & -1 \end{bmatrix}$ (ii) $B = \begin{bmatrix} 0 & 1 \\ 1 & 0 \end{bmatrix}$
   (iii) $C = AB$.

Describe each transformation in geometrical terms.

(J.M.B.)

Paper R.32

1. (i) Plot (a) the triangle (1, 3) (3, 6) (6, 1)
       (b) the quadrilateral (1, 1) (7, 3) (5, 6) (2, 5)
   (ii) Find the areas of the figures.
   (iii) Find the areas when the 2 figures are transformed by

      (a) $\begin{bmatrix} 1 & 0 \\ 1 & 1 \end{bmatrix}$ (b) $\begin{bmatrix} 1 & 1 \\ 0 & 1 \end{bmatrix}$ (c) $\begin{bmatrix} 1 & 2 \\ 0 & 1 \end{bmatrix}$ (d) $\begin{bmatrix} 1 & 0 \\ 2 & 1 \end{bmatrix}$

2. By considering the multiplication table of residue classes mod. 4, show that if m is an integer then $m^2 \equiv 0$ or 1 (mod. 4).

3. By considering the multiplication table of residue classes mod. 8, show that if m is an integer then $m^2 \equiv 0$, or 1, or 4 (mod. 8).

4. If $y = x^2 - 3x$, the table below gives values of x and some of the corresponding values of y. Complete the table and plot the graph of $y = x^2 - 3x$ using scales of 1 inch for 1 unit for x and $\frac{1}{2}$ inch for 1 unit for y.

x	-2	-1	0	1	2	3	4
y	10		0		-2		

(a) From your completed graph read off as accurately as possible the minimum value of $x^2 - 3x$ and the value of x for which this occurs.

(b) Use the graph to solve the equations (I) $x^2 - 3x = 0$; (II) $x^2 - 3x = 4$. *(C.O.P.)*

5. An officer on a ship observes that the angle of elevation of the top of a cliff is 12°. The ship is one kilometre from the foot of the cliff. Use trigonometrical tables to calculate

(a) the height of the cliff, to the nearest metre.

(b) If the ship sails towards the cliff to a point where the angle of elevation of the top of the cliff is 63°, find the length of a straight line from the top of the cliff to the boat, correct to the nearest metre. *(C.O.P. adapted)*

6. If log $(x^2) = \bar{1} \cdot 701\ 2$ then the value of x is approximately
A 0·22 **B** 0·25 **C** 0·50 **D** 0·71 **E** 0·93 *(J.M.B.)*

Paper R.33

1. A variable circle (i.e. a circle whose diameter varies) moves so that its centre always lies on a fixed circle radius 3 cm, and its

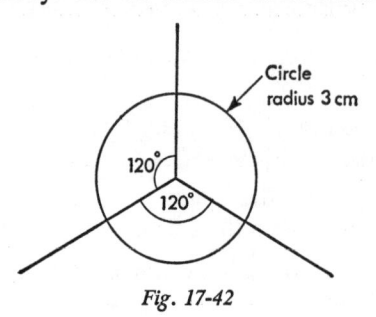

Fig. 17-42

REVISION EXERCISES

circumference always *touches* one of three lines which are drawn from the centre of the fixed circle and are at an angle of 120° with each other, Fig. 17-42. Find the envelope formed by the variable circle.

2. Can the sum of an even number of even numbers plus an odd number of odd numbers ever be the same as the sum of an even number of odd numbers plus an odd number of even numbers? Give reasons for your answer.

3. 'a' is a sphere, diameter 10 m: 'b' is a cylinder 9 m high 9 m diameter; 'c' is a cone, base 12 m diameter, height 12 m; 'd' is a regular tetrahedron each side being 15 m; 'e' is an 8 m cube and 'f' is a squared pyramid base side and height being 11 m.
   (*i*) Arrange these in ascending order by their total surface area.
   (*ii*) Arrange them in ascending order by volume.

4. (*i*) Draw out Fig. 17-43, each square having a side of 2 cm. Cut the area into 4 pieces so that they can be reassembled to form a square.
   (*ii*) Repeat with Fig. 17-44.

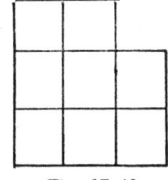

Fig. 17-43 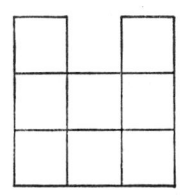   *Fig. 17-44*

5. (*a*) Can Fig. 17-45 be drawn in one continuous line? If so draw it. Do not 'close' corners but leave a small gap to show continuity of line.
   (*b*) Repeat with Fig. 17-46 putting in one extra line yourself if necessary.

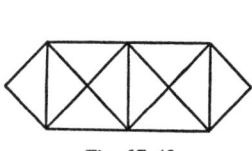

Fig. 17-45 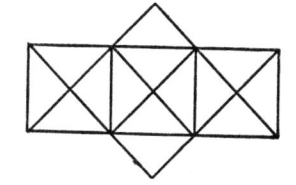   *Fig. 17-46*

6. If $u = x^2 - \dfrac{y}{z}$ which of the following is correct?

A $y = x^2 - uz$ B $y = \dfrac{x^2 - u}{z}$ C $y = x^2z - uz$
D $y = uz - x^2z$ E $y = x^2z - u$? (*J.M.B.*)

Paper R.34
1. Draw a circle diameter 7 cm, and draw in a diameter. Mark the diameter at every ½ cm and draw chords at these points perpendicular to the diameter. With the intersections of the chords and the diameter as centres, draw circles having the chords as diameters. What is the envelope of the circles?
2. A pedestrian walking at 8 km/h passes a milestone at noon. At 13·30 a cyclist, travelling at 24 km/h in the same direction, passes the same milestone. Find graphically at what time the cyclist overtakes the pedestrian. Use scales of 4 cm to the hour on the time axis and 1·5 cm to 1 km on the distance axis. (*R.S.A., adapted*)
3. Solve (*i*) $\dfrac{x-4}{3} = \dfrac{x-2}{7} + 1$ (*ii*) $\begin{array}{l} 6a - b = 5 \\ 2a + 3b = 10 \end{array}$
   (*iii*) $x^2 + x = 12$ (*R.S.A.*)
4. What is the length of the longest straight wire which can be fastened in a room measuring 10 m × 12 m × 15 m?
5. Draw an accurate diagram to illustrate the following extract from a surveyor's notebook and calculate the area of the property ABCDEFA. (All distances are in metres.)

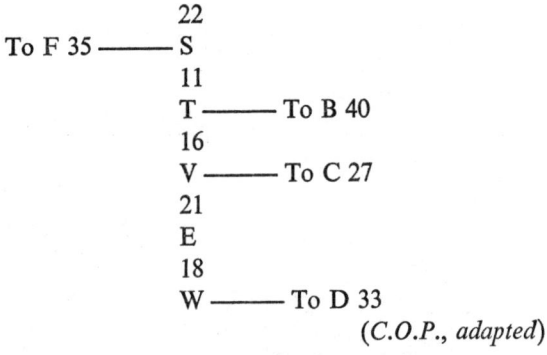

```
                    A
                    22
        To F 35 ——— S
                    11
                    T ——— To B 40
                    16
                    V ——— To C 27
                    21
                    E
                    18
                    W ——— To D 33
```
(*C.O.P., adapted*)

6. Is it TRUE or FALSE that the following figures are cyclic (i.e. a circle can be drawn passing through their vertices)?
   (*a*) any triangle
   (*b*) any quadrilateral

REVISION EXERCISES

(c) any square
(d) any parallelogram
(e) a quadrilateral with internal angles of 43°, 106°, 137°, 74° in that order. (A.E.B.)

Paper R.35

1. A lifeboat searching for a raft sails from base along a bearing 316° (N.44°W.) for 20 km, then changes course to N.68°W. and continues this course for 18 km when the raft is found. How far is the lifeboat now from base and what is the bearing on which it must sail to arrive back?

2. At 12.00 a tourist leaves town A by bicycle and travels directly towards town B, 60 km distant from A, at a constant average speed of 25 km per hour. At 13.00 a traveller sets out by car from town B to travel directly to town A and moving at a constant average speed of 30 km per hour.
Represent the above information on a distance-time graph using scales of 1 cm to represent 5 km on the distance axis, and 5 cm to represent 1 hour on the time axis. From your graph find:
   (a) At what time and at what distance from B do the tourist and traveller meet? Give answer to nearest minute and nearest kilometre.
   (b) If the tourist stopped for 27 minutes at 13.00 at what average speed, in km/h, correct to 2 sig. figs., would he have to travel to arrive in town B by 14.15? (C.O.P.)

3. Construct accurately, without the use of protractor or set square, triangle ABC such that BC = 6 cm; AB = 5 cm and angle ABC 60°. Measure length AC. On the same figure construct the locus of a point P which moves so that it is always equidistant from AB and BC. Mark the locus carefully. (All construction lines must be clearly shown; and results should be in centimetres to the nearest tenth.)
(C.O.P.)

4. In Fig. 17-47 AB = AC and angle BAC = 30°. P and R are points on the sides AC and AB so that angle PBC is 45° and angle BCR is 30°. BP and CR intersect at Q. Prove
(i) AP = PB; (ii) BR = BQ.
(Oxford)

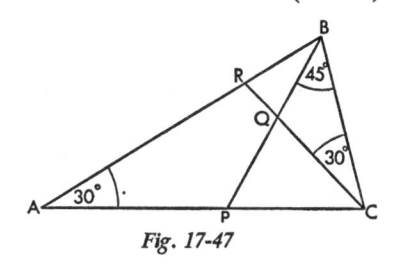

Fig. 17-47

5. (a) If $2x = 5y$ find the numerical value of $\dfrac{x-y}{x+y}$
  (b) A train takes 14 minutes to travel a distance of 10·5 kilometres. Find its average speed in kilometres per hour.

6. Is it TRUE or FALSE that the representation of any number which is a multiple of 4 (base 10):
  A ends in 0 when the base is 2
  B ends in 1 when the base is 3
  C ends in 0 when the base is 4
  D never ends in 0 when the base is 5? *(A.E.B.)*

Paper R.36

1. A motorist's car will travel 2·5 km on one litre of petrol. On holiday in France he travels 3 200 kilometres, and petrol costs 0·80 francs per litre. Calculate the cost of petrol for this holiday in English money. (£1 = 13·80 francs.) *(R.S.A., adapted)*

2. A wire is bent into the form of a circle of radius 28 cm. If it had been bent into the form of a square what would have been the length of the side of the square? (Use $\pi = \tfrac{22}{7}$.) *(R.S.A.)*

3. (a) A bakery made and sold 125 000 loaves every day. What was the increase in its daily takings when the price of bread was raised from 5 p to 5½ p per loaf?
  (b) 500 watches were distributed for repair among 23 workmen so that each man received either 21 or 22 watches. How many men repaired 21 watches and how many repaired 22?
  (R.S.A.)

4. Calculate by logarithms
  (i) $\dfrac{31\cdot83 \times 1\cdot296 \times 0\cdot058\,7}{9\cdot216 \times 0\cdot008\,5 \times 6\cdot284}$ (ii) $\sqrt{3\cdot26 \times 0\cdot018\,2}$
  (R.S.A.)

5. A solid white wooden cube has sides 8 cm long. On each face a black circular disc, six centimetres in diameter, is painted. What is the total area of white surface left on the cube? *(R.S.A.)*

6. Is it TRUE or FALSE that the following conditions imply that the triangle ABC is congruent to the triangle DEF?
  (a) angle A = angle D; AB = DE; AC = DF

REVISION EXERCISES

(b) angle A = angle D; angle B = angle E; angle C = angle F
(c) angle A = angle D; angle B = angle E; AB = DE
(d) angle A = angle D; AB = DE; BC = EF.   (A.E.B.)

Paper R.37

1. A cyclindrical piece of wood is sharpened at one end to a conical shape, as shown in Fig. 17-48.
What volume of wood is cut away in this operation?
(*Hint:* find the remaining volume in 2 parts.)
   (*R.S.A., adapted*)

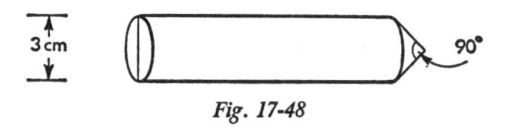

Fig. 17-48

2. In an airing cupboard a housewife keeps a small electric lamp alight. What did the electricity cost to light this lamp for the year 1963 if a unit of electricity costs $2\frac{1}{2}$ p and will light this lamp for 50 hours?   (*R.S.A.*)

3. (a) State the method of determining whether a number is divisible exactly by three.
   (b) Write down in words the number next after a million which is exactly divisible by three.
   (c) Find the prime factors of 1 764, and hence or otherwise find its square root.   (*R.S.A.*)

4. A housewife has a rectangular piece of pastry of uniform thickness. From it she cuts out circular pieces for tarts. The length of the rectangle is 30 cm and the breadth is 20 cm. Each tart has a diameter of 5 cm. How many of these circular pieces can she cut out?

She gathers the remaining pieces of pastry and after squeezing them together rolls the pastry out to form a circle of the same thickness of pastry as before. What is the radius of this circle, correct to one decimal place? (Take π as $\frac{22}{7}$.)   (*R.S.A.*)

5. (a) Draw a Venn diagram to illustrate three non-empty sets A, B, and C, subsets of a universal set, which satisfy

$$A' \cap B = \varphi, \quad B' \cap C \subset A, \quad B \cap C \neq \varphi$$

(b) Verify by means of a Venn diagram that for any two sets, A and B, subsets of a universal set $\mathscr{E}$,
$$(A \cap B)' \cap (A \cup B)' = A' \cap B'.$$
(The part of the Venn diagram corresponding to each of the expressions in brackets should be distinctly shaded and labelled.)
Identify each of the sets A', B', $A \cap B$, $(A \cap B)'$, $A \cup B$ and $(A \cup B)'$ when $\mathscr{E}$ is the set of integers, A is the set of multiples of 2 and B is the set of multiples of 3. *(A.E.B.)*

6. This question concerns the least remainders modulo 6 (i.e. the numbers 0, 1, 2, 3, 4, 5 only). State whether the following are TRUE or FALSE.
   (a) $(2 \times 4) + 4 = 0$.
   (b) The solution of $(5 \times x) + 1 = 5$ is $x = 5$.
   (c) The equation $(4 \times x) + 4 = 0$ has two different solutions.
   (d) The equation $x^2 = 2$ has two different solutions.
   (e) The equation $x^3 = x$ has six different solutions.
   (Met. C.S.E.)

Paper R.38

1. Find the weight of a piece of brass tubing 8 cm long, of outside diameter 2·9 cm and 1 mm thick (1 cm³ weighs 8 g). *(R.S.A.)*

2. A lathe spindle revolves at 156 r.p.m. and the lead screw causes the carriage to move 0·4 mm for each revolution of the spindle. How long would it take the carriage to move 12 cm along the bed?

3. Three hydraulic presses A, B, and C are used to produce the same kind of stampings. A produces 46 per hour, B produces 40 per hour and C produces 34 per hour. If the value of the output of the three presses for a day's working of 8 hours is £400, what are the earnings of each press? *(R.S.A.)*

4. (a) A circular piece of metal of 2 cm diameter has a hole of 1½ cm diameter punched out in the middle. What area of metal remains? Take π as $\frac{22}{7}$. *(R.S.A.)*
   (b) A cylindrical jar of diameter 8 cm and depth 14 cm is full of water. If this water is poured into an empty cylindrical vessel of diameter 6 cm find the depth of the water. *(R.S.A.)*

5. A steel tool, over-all length 6¼ cm and diameter 0·5 cm is in the form of a 6 cm cylinder and a right cone of 0·25 cm height. What is

REVISION EXERCISES

the weight of the tool if steel weighs 8·17 g per cubic centimetre?
(Take π as $\frac{22}{7}$.)

6. This question refers to three sets $A = \{a, b, c, d, e, f, g, h\}$, $B = \{a, g, h, i, j, k\}$ and $C = \{a, c, d\}$
   (i) Which of the following statements is true?
   (a) $A \subset C$; (b) $C \subset A$; (c) $A \subset B$; (d) $B \subset A$
   (ii) Which of the following statements is true?
   (a) $A \cap B = C$; (b) $A \cup B = B$; (c) $A \cap C = C$; (d) $A \cap C = A$
   (iii) Which of the following statements is true?
   (a) $n(A) = n(B)$; (b) $n(A) + n(B) + n(C) = n(A \cup B \cup C)$;
   (c) $n(A) + n(B) = n(A \cap B) + n(A \cup B)$; (d) $n(A) + n(B) = n(C)$
   (iv) Which of the following satisfies the equation $A \cap X = C$?
   (a) $X = A$; (b) $X = A \cup B$; (c) $X = B$; (d) $X = C$
   (v) Which of the following sets is equal to the set $A \cup (B \cap C)$?
   (a) $\{a, g, h\}$ (b) $\{i, j, k\}$ (c) C (d) A (*Met. C.S.E.*)

Paper R.39

1. A man left his property to be divided as follows: $\frac{1}{2}$ to his wife: $\frac{1}{3}$ of the remainder to each of his 2 sons: and the rest to be shared equally by his 5 daughters. If each daughter received £175
   (a) What did each son receive?
   (b) What did his wife receive? (*R.S.A. adapted*)

2. (a) What will be the cost of excavating a trench 60 m long, 1·25 m wide, and 1·75 m deep at 2½ p per cubic metre? (*R.S.A.*)
   (b) Use the above answer to find the cost of excavating a trench 26 m long, 3·5 m wide and 1·5 m deep at the same cost per cubic metres. (*R.S.A.*)

3. (a) How many times will a garden roller, of outside diameter 33·6 cm, revolve whilst rolling one length of a garden 66 metres long? (Take $\pi = 3\frac{1}{7}$.)
   (b) Calculate the length of a slant edge of a right pyramid on a rectangular base, the height of the pyramid being 12 cm and the length and breadth of the base being 8 cm and 6 cm respectively. (*C.O.P.*)

4. (a) A certain plastic material is produced by mixing 3 powders A, B and C in the proportion of 4:2:3 by weight. Calculate the weight of each powder used in producing 425·7 g of plastic.

(b) if $\frac{1}{f} = \frac{1}{v} + \frac{1}{u}$, find the value of v when $f = 5$ and $u = 6$.

(C.O.P.)

5. If A and B are subsets of a universal set $\mathscr{E}$, the set C is defined by $C = (A \cap B') \cup (A' \cap B)$
   (i) Draw a Venn diagram to illustrate C, carefully marking the sets $A \cap B'$ and $A' \cap B$
   (ii) If $\mathscr{E}$ is the set of all integers, A is the set of multiples of 3 and B is the set of multiples of 4 what is the set C? (A.E.B.)

6. If a number x, when corrected to 2 sig. figs. becomes 1·2 then which of the following could x^2 be?
   A less than 1·3
   B greater than 1·5
   C equal to 1·53 correct to 3 sig. figs. (A.E.B.)

Paper R.40

1. (a) A man erects a fence around his property which is in the shape of a sector of a circle, as shown in Fig. 17-49. The arc of the circle subtends an angle of 60° at the centre of the circle. If the radius of the circle is 105 m calculate:
   (i) the total length of the fence;
   (ii) the cost of the fencing if one metre of the material costs 60 p.
   (Take $\pi = 3\frac{1}{7}$.)

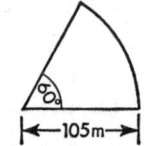

   Fig. 17-49

   (b) Reduce to a single fraction in its simplest form $(4\frac{1}{3} - 1\frac{1}{8}) \times \frac{6}{11}$.
   (c) Find $4\frac{1}{2}$ per cent of £3 250. (C.O.P.)

2. It is estimated that out of every £1 earned, 9 p is saved. Calculate how much more a man who earns £1 200 per annum should save in a year than a man who earns £720 per annum. (Oxford)

3. From a roll of cloth 14 m long a dealer sells 5·75 metres at £·55 per metre, 4 metres at £·52 per metre and the rest at £·40 per metre. Calculate the total amount he receives for the roll.

(Oxford)

REVISION EXERCISES

4. The top of an open tank is a horizontal rectangle ABCD, 10 m wide and 24 m long. The ends ADSP and BCRQ are vertical rectangles, 10 m by 6 m, and 10 m by 18 m respectively. The base is a sloping plane and the other two sides are vertical. The depth of water is measured along QB from Q (Fig. 17-50).

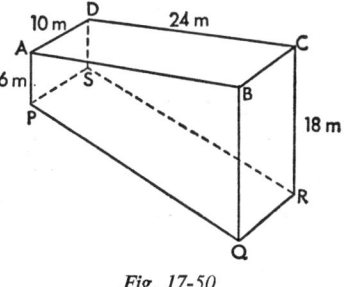

Fig. 17-50

(*i*) Calculate the number of cubic metres of water in the tank when the water is 6 m deep.

(*ii*) With this amount of water in the tank, calculate how much water must be added to raise the depth to 17 m.

(*iii*) If the water is 6 m deep and 850 m³ of water is added, calculate the new depth of water. (*Oxford*)

5. Calculate the local rates paid on a house of net rateable value £28 when the rates are at £1·11 in the £.

If the same amount in rates is paid on a house where the local rate is £0·75 in the £, calculate the net rateable value of the house.

(*Oxford*)

6. If x and y are non-zero numbers and $x + y = 0$ state whether the following are TRUE or FALSE

(*a*) x is negative
(*b*) x or y is negative
(*c*) xy is negative
(*d*) $x^2 + y^2 = -2xy$
(*e*) $x^2 - y^2 = 2xy$ (*A.E.B.*)

Answers

Exercise 1a
1. 68·29 2. 4 881 3. 653·1 4. 37 860 5. 0·116 5
6. 0·008 395 7. 0·000 001 563 8. 0·769 6 9. 0·000 012 17
10. (a) 1 963 cm^2 (b) 1·039 cm^2

Exercise 1b
1. 2·374 2. 5·602 3. 2·654 4. 29·93 5. 5·394
6. 2·828 7. 6·931 8. 31·32 9. 2·859 10. 4·547 cm

Exercise 1c
1. 0·180 3 2. 0·990 8 3. 0·200 8 4. 0·793 6
5. 0·032 01 6. 0·498 7 7. 0·215 4 8. 0·577 3
9. 1·214 cm^3 10. 1·447

Exercise 1d
1. 0·156 8 2. 4·000 3. 0·009 561 4. 939·7
5. 6·390 6. 1·44

Exercise 1e
1. 1·5 2. 0·961 3. 17·9 4. 200 5. 114 6. 4·82
7. 81·6 8. 1·297 9. 5·543 10. 126·6 cm^2
11. 11·05 cm 12. 1 596 cm^3

Exercise 2a
2. 0·454 0, 0·965 9, 0·707 1, 0·225 0, 0·500 0, 0·998 6, 0·898 8, 0·275 6, 0·309 0, 0·934 2, 0·813 1, 0·614 3, 0·894 2, 0·894 9, 0·583 5, 0·518 7, 0·965 2, 0·574 5, 0·081 1, 0·801 6, 0·949 5
3. 45°, 16°, 83°, 41°, 1°, 13° 24′, 81° 42′, 54° 54′, 24′, 31° 6′, 49° 14′, 6° 59′, 32° 21′, 78° 40′, 68° 47′, 14° 49′, 61° 31′, 28° 52′, 9° 31′, 34° 57′

Exercise 2b (Correct to 2 significant figures)
1. 9·56 cm 2. 2·96 m 3. 5·54 cm 4. 1·92 cm
5. 357 mm 6. 4·05 m 7. 105 cm 8. 637 mm
9. 7·10 cm 10. 13·3 m 11. 30·1 m 12. 43·6 m
13. 43·9 mm 14. 96·2 mm 15. 6·81 cm, 5·51 cm 16. 13·2 cm

ANSWERS

Exercise 2c
1. 48° 36' 2. 51° 3' 3. 33° 4' 4. 22° 20' 5. 40° 46'
6. 39° 54' 7. 49° 50' 8. 28° 23' 9. 47° 35' 10. 44° 36'
11. 8° 13' 12. 44° 26' 13. 39° 24', 9·74 cm 14. 23° 2',
21·17 cm (*correct to 2 decimal places*) 15. 26° 23', 8·06 cm

Exercise 2d
2. 0·358 4, 0·034 9, 0·500 0, 0·998 6, 0·960 3, 0·840 6, 0·290 7,
0·644 1, 0·991 2, 0·109 7, 0·856 0, 0·696 8, 0·252 4, 0·942 4,
0·762 5, 0·211 6, 0·999 4, 0·063 0, 0·643 4, 0·787 8
3. 18°, 45°, 31° 42', 76° 24', 58° 54', 86° 12', 2° 24', 82° 30',
83° 31', 68° 32', 15° 29', 78° 2', 58° 17', 37° 38', 23° 31', 77° 56',
28° 19', 58° 27', 83° 25', 54° 35'

Exercise 2e (*Correct to 3 significant figures*)
1. 7·99 cm 2. 10·6 cm 3. 1·66 cm 4. 1·22 cm
5. 10·3 m 6. 13·6 cm 7. 22·6 cm 8. 30·5 m
9. 780 mm 10. 151 m 11. 1·55 m 12. 1·69 cm
13. 24·9 cm 14. 192 m 15. 24·8 km 16. 6·89 m

Exercise 2f
1. 44° 25' 2. 31° 48' 3. 64° 37' 4. 51° 32' 5. 38° 56'
6. 36° 32' 7. 51° 28' 8. 54° 3' 9. 69° 20' 10. 52° 30'
11. 31° 48' 12. N. 40° 38' W. or S. 40° 38' W. 13. 33° 34'
14. 36° 52' 15. 48° 20'

Exercise 2g
1. 15 m, $15\sqrt{3}$ m 2. $7\sqrt{2}$ cm 3. 5 cm, $5\sqrt{3}$ cm
4. $5\sqrt{3/3}$ cm, $10\sqrt{3/3}$ cm 5. $7\sqrt{2}$ cm 6. $2\sqrt{3}$ m
7. $3\sqrt{3}$ cm 9 cm 8. 5 m 9. 7 cm, 14 cm
10. $2\sqrt{6}$ cm, $3\sqrt{2}$ cm

Exercise 2h (*Correct to 3 significant figures*)
1. 45° 35', 7·14 cm 2. 48° 36', 2·65 m 3. 23° 58', 9·85 cm
4. 9·61 cm 5. 9·21 m 6. 28·7 mm 7. 13·6 cm
8. 40° 45', 49° 15' 9. 30° 10. 16 11. 29·4 m
12. N. 59° 2' E, 23·3 km 13. 56° 13', 43° 47', 7·20 cm

14. 7·120 m **15.** 6·52 m, 2·55 m **16.** 17·0 m **17.** 25·26 m
18. 6·92 km **19.** 605 m, 214 m, 73·7 m, 151 m, 10° 39′
20. 26° 34′, 45°, 15·7 m, 9·9 m, 6·26 m, 4·95 m
21. 3·81 cm, 0·922 cm, 3·41 cm

Exercise 2i

1. 20·3 cm, 15·2 cm   **2.** 2·07 cm, 2·02 cm
3. 75·9 mm, 115 mm   **4.** 10 cm, 8·26 cm
5. 4·34 cm, 2·92 cm   **6.** 3·24 cm, 7 cm
7. 443 mm, 381 mm   **8.** 33·8 m, 23·7 m
9. 49·3 km, 53·4 km, 47·6 km   **10.** 11·7 m   **11.** 5·22 cm
12. 35·1 m   **13.** 5·70 m   **14.** 3·86 cm
15. 49·64 m, 456·4 m, 200·6 m, 469 m
16. (i) true, (ii) true (iii) false (iv) false (v) true (vi) false
17. (i) true (ii) false (iii) false (iv) true (v) false (vi) false
18. (a) (i) true (ii) false (iii) false
  (b) (i) true (ii) true
  (c) (i) false (ii) false (iii) true (iv) true (v) false
19. (a) (iii) (b) (iv) (d) (iv)
20. (i) false (ii) false (iii) false (iv) true (v) true (v) true

Exercise 3e

1.
$$A - \begin{array}{c|ccccc|c} & 1 & 2 & 3 & 4 & 5 & \\ \hline & 1 & 0 & 0 & 0 & 0 & 1 \\ & 1 & 0 & 0 & 1 & 0 & 2 \\ & 0 & 0 & 0 & 1 & 0 & 3 \\ & 1 & 0 & 0 & 0 & 1 & 4 \\ & 1 & 0 & 1 & 1 & 0 & 5 \end{array}$$

2. 1, 0, 0, 1, 1, 0

3. $A^* = \begin{bmatrix} 1 & 1 & 0 & 1 & 1 \\ 0 & 0 & 0 & 0 & 0 \\ 0 & 0 & 0 & 0 & 1 \\ 0 & 1 & 1 & 0 & 1 \\ 0 & 0 & 0 & 1 & 0 \end{bmatrix}$

4.

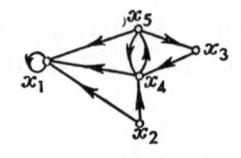

All directions reversed

Exercise 4a

1. (i) (15, 18) (ii) (12, 21) (iii) (6, 3) (iv) (−6, −3) (v) (6, 12)
2. (i) (2, 2) (ii) (−2, 2) (iii) (−2, 2) (iv) (2, −2)

ANSWERS

3. (i) (0, 2) (ii) (4, 4) (iii) (8, 6) (iv) (12, 8) (v) (16, 10)
  (vi) (20, 12)
4. $x-2y+2=0$ 5. No points remain unchanged
7. $x_n = 0x + 0y$
  $y_n = 0x + 0y$

Exercise 4c

1. $\begin{bmatrix} -3 \\ 9 \end{bmatrix}$ $\begin{bmatrix} -12 \\ 12 \end{bmatrix}$ $\begin{bmatrix} 1 & 5 \\ 1 & 2 \end{bmatrix}$ $\begin{bmatrix} 0 \\ 21 \end{bmatrix}$ $\begin{bmatrix} -3 \\ 0 \end{bmatrix}$

2. A $\begin{bmatrix} 0 \\ 2 \end{bmatrix}$ $\begin{bmatrix} 4 \\ 4 \end{bmatrix}$ $\begin{bmatrix} 8 \\ 6 \end{bmatrix}$ $\begin{bmatrix} 12 \\ 8 \end{bmatrix}$ $\begin{bmatrix} 16 \\ 10 \end{bmatrix}$ $\begin{bmatrix} 20 \\ 12 \end{bmatrix}$

   B $\begin{bmatrix} -1 \\ 1 \end{bmatrix}$ $\begin{bmatrix} 0 \\ 4 \end{bmatrix}$ $\begin{bmatrix} 1 \\ 7 \end{bmatrix}$ $\begin{bmatrix} 2 \\ 10 \end{bmatrix}$ $\begin{bmatrix} 3 \\ 13 \end{bmatrix}$ $\begin{bmatrix} 4 \\ 16 \end{bmatrix}$

   C $\begin{bmatrix} -3 \\ 2 \end{bmatrix}$ $\begin{bmatrix} -2 \\ 6 \end{bmatrix}$ $\begin{bmatrix} -1 \\ 10 \end{bmatrix}$ $\begin{bmatrix} 0 \\ 14 \end{bmatrix}$ $\begin{bmatrix} 1 \\ 18 \end{bmatrix}$ $\begin{bmatrix} 2 \\ 22 \end{bmatrix}$

   D $\begin{bmatrix} 2 \\ 1 \end{bmatrix}$ $\begin{bmatrix} 6 \\ 6 \end{bmatrix}$ $\begin{bmatrix} 10 \\ 11 \end{bmatrix}$ $\begin{bmatrix} 14 \\ 16 \end{bmatrix}$ $\begin{bmatrix} 18 \\ 21 \end{bmatrix}$ $\begin{bmatrix} 22 \\ 26 \end{bmatrix}$

   E $\begin{bmatrix} 0 \\ 3 \end{bmatrix}$ $\begin{bmatrix} 0 \\ 8 \end{bmatrix}$ $\begin{bmatrix} 0 \\ 13 \end{bmatrix}$ $\begin{bmatrix} 0 \\ 18 \end{bmatrix}$ $\begin{bmatrix} 0 \\ 23 \end{bmatrix}$ $\begin{bmatrix} 0 \\ 28 \end{bmatrix}$

   F $\begin{bmatrix} 1 \\ 0 \end{bmatrix}$ $\begin{bmatrix} -4 \\ 0 \end{bmatrix}$ $\begin{bmatrix} -9 \\ 0 \end{bmatrix}$ $\begin{bmatrix} -14 \\ 0 \end{bmatrix}$ $\begin{bmatrix} -19 \\ 0 \end{bmatrix}$ $\begin{bmatrix} -24 \\ 0 \end{bmatrix}$

Exercise 4d

1. (i) $\begin{bmatrix} 3 \\ 6 \end{bmatrix}$ (ii) $\begin{bmatrix} 2 \\ 1 \end{bmatrix}$ (iii) $\begin{bmatrix} 4 \\ 5 \end{bmatrix}$

Exercise 4e

1. (i) $\begin{bmatrix} 2 & -2 \\ 2 & 2 \end{bmatrix}$ (ii) $\begin{bmatrix} 2 & -2 \\ 2 & 2 \end{bmatrix}$ (iii) $\begin{bmatrix} -1 & 1 \\ 3 & 3 \end{bmatrix}$

   (iv) $\begin{bmatrix} 3 & 1 \\ 3 & -1 \end{bmatrix}$ (v) $\begin{bmatrix} -1 & -3 \\ 1 & 3 \end{bmatrix}$ (vi) $\begin{bmatrix} 0 & 0 \\ 4 & 2 \end{bmatrix}$

   (viii) $\begin{bmatrix} -4 & 1 \\ 5 & 4 \end{bmatrix}$ (ix) $\begin{bmatrix} 0 & 0 \\ -3 & 1 \end{bmatrix}$ (x) $\begin{bmatrix} 1 & 3 \\ 0 & 0 \end{bmatrix}$

   (xi) $\begin{bmatrix} 2 & 4 \\ 4 & 2 \end{bmatrix}$ (xii) $\begin{bmatrix} 2 & 4 \\ 4 & 2 \end{bmatrix}$

2. (i) $\begin{bmatrix} 2 & 0 \\ 0 & 2 \end{bmatrix}$ (ii) $\begin{bmatrix} 1 & -1 \\ 1 & 1 \end{bmatrix}$ (iii) $\begin{bmatrix} 2 & -3 \\ 1 & 2 \end{bmatrix}$

   (iv) $\begin{bmatrix} 1 & 2 \\ 2 & 1 \end{bmatrix}$ (v) $\begin{bmatrix} 0 & 0 \\ 1 & 3 \end{bmatrix}$ (vi) $\begin{bmatrix} -3 & 1 \\ 0 & 0 \end{bmatrix}$

LONGMAN MATHEMATICS

(vii) $\begin{bmatrix} 1 & 0 \\ 0 & 1 \end{bmatrix}$ (viii) $\begin{bmatrix} 1 & -1 \\ 1 & 1 \end{bmatrix}$ (ix) $\begin{bmatrix} 2 & -3 \\ 1 & 2 \end{bmatrix}$

(x) $\begin{bmatrix} 1 & 2 \\ 2 & 1 \end{bmatrix}$

3. (i) $\begin{bmatrix} -2 & 0 \\ 0 & 2 \end{bmatrix}$ (ii) $\begin{bmatrix} -1 & -1 \\ -1 & 1 \end{bmatrix}$ (iii) $\begin{bmatrix} -2 & -3 \\ -1 & 2 \end{bmatrix}$

(iv) $\begin{bmatrix} -1 & 2 \\ -2 & 1 \end{bmatrix}$ (v) $\begin{bmatrix} 0 & 0 \\ -1 & 3 \end{bmatrix}$ (vi) $\begin{bmatrix} 3 & 1 \\ 0 & 0 \end{bmatrix}$

(vii) $\begin{bmatrix} -2 & 0 \\ 0 & 2 \end{bmatrix}$ (viii) $\begin{bmatrix} -1 & 1 \\ 1 & 1 \end{bmatrix}$ (ix) $\begin{bmatrix} -2 & 3 \\ 1 & 2 \end{bmatrix}$

(x) $\begin{bmatrix} -2 & 2 \\ 2 & 1 \end{bmatrix}$ (xi) $\begin{bmatrix} 0 & 0 \\ 1 & 3 \end{bmatrix}$ (xii) $\begin{bmatrix} 3 & -1 \\ 0 & 0 \end{bmatrix}$

4. (i) $\begin{bmatrix} 2 & 0 \\ 0 & -2 \end{bmatrix}$ (ii) $\begin{bmatrix} 1 & 1 \\ 1 & -1 \end{bmatrix}$ (iii) $\begin{bmatrix} 2 & 3 \\ 1 & -2 \end{bmatrix}$

(vi) $\begin{bmatrix} 1 & -2 \\ 2 & -1 \end{bmatrix}$ (v) $\begin{bmatrix} 0 & 0 \\ 1 & -3 \end{bmatrix}$ (vi) $\begin{bmatrix} -3 & -1 \\ 0 & 0 \end{bmatrix}$

(vii) $\begin{bmatrix} 2 & 0 \\ 0 & -2 \end{bmatrix}$ (viii) $\begin{bmatrix} 1 & -1 \\ -1 & -1 \end{bmatrix}$ (ix) $\begin{bmatrix} 2 & -3 \\ -1 & -2 \end{bmatrix}$

(x) $\begin{bmatrix} 1 & 2 \\ -2 & -1 \end{bmatrix}$ (xi) $\begin{bmatrix} 0 & 0 \\ -1 & -3 \end{bmatrix}$ (xii) $\begin{bmatrix} -3 & 1 \\ 0 & 0 \end{bmatrix}$

5. (i) $\begin{bmatrix} -2 & 0 \\ 0 & -2 \end{bmatrix}$ (ii) $\begin{bmatrix} -1 & 1 \\ -1 & -1 \end{bmatrix}$ (iii) $\begin{bmatrix} -2 & 3 \\ -1 & -2 \end{bmatrix}$

(iv) $\begin{bmatrix} -1 & -2 \\ -2 & -1 \end{bmatrix}$ (v) $\begin{bmatrix} 0 & 0 \\ -1 & -3 \end{bmatrix}$ (vi) $\begin{bmatrix} 3 & -1 \\ 0 & 0 \end{bmatrix}$

(vii) $\begin{bmatrix} -2 & 0 \\ 0 & -2 \end{bmatrix}$ (viii) $\begin{bmatrix} -1 & 1 \\ -1 & -1 \end{bmatrix}$ (ix) $\begin{bmatrix} -2 & 3 \\ -1 & -2 \end{bmatrix}$

(x) $\begin{bmatrix} -1 & -2 \\ -2 & -1 \end{bmatrix}$ (xi) $\begin{bmatrix} 0 & 0 \\ -1 & -3 \end{bmatrix}$ (xii) $\begin{bmatrix} 3 & -1 \\ 0 & 0 \end{bmatrix}$

6.

	I	II	III	IV
I	I	II	III	IV
II	II	I	IV	III
III	III	IV	I	II
IV	IV	III	II	I

ANSWERS

Exercise 4f

1. (−10, −10); (−10, −9); (−10, −7); (−10, −5); (−8, −4); (−6, −3); (−4, −2); (−2, −1); (0, 0); (2, 1); (4, 2); (6, 3); (8, 4); (10, 5); (10, 7) (10, 9); (10, 10)

2. (0, 3); (1, 4); (2, 5); (3, 6); (4, 5); (3, 4); (2, 3); (1, 2); (0, 3); (−1, 4); (−2, 5); (−3, 6); (−4, 5); (−3, 4); (−2, 3); (−1, 2)

5.

	I	II	III	IV	V	VI	VII	VIII
I	I	II	III	IV	V	VI	VII	VIII
II	II	I	IV	III	VII	VIII	V	VI
III	III	IV	I	II	VI	V	VIII	VII
IV	IV	III	II	I	VIII	VII	VI	V
V	V	VI	VII	VIII	I	II	III	IV
VI	II	V	VIII	VII	III	IV	I	II
VII	VII	VIII	V	VI	II	I	IV	III
VIII	VIII	VII	VI	V	IV	III	II	I

Exercise 5a

1. 15 km/h, 0 km/h, 12 km/h
2. 4 km/h, 0 km/h, 2·67 km/h (to 2 decimal places)
3. 40 km/h, 30 km/h, 0 km/h, 24 km/h
4. 32 km/h, 40 km/h, 0 km/h, 50 km/h

Exercise 5b

1. 6 m/s, 16 m/s, 10 m/s
2. 7·2 m/s going up, 7·2 m/s going up
3. (a) 14·4 m/s (b) 28·8 m/s

Exercise 5c

1. 11·11 m/s² (to 2 decimal places)
2. (a) 3·81 m/s² (to 2 decimal places)
   (b) 13·72 km/h² (to 2 decimal places)
3. 1·67 m/s² (to 2 decimal places)

Exercise 5d (to 2 decimal places)
1. $1 \cdot 33 \, \text{m/s}^2$ 2. $0 \cdot 80 \, \text{m/s}^2$ 3. (i) $0 \cdot 44 \, \text{m/s}^2$ (ii) $0 \cdot 44 \, \text{m/s}^2$
4. $5 \, \text{m/s}$ 5. (a) 21 (km/h)/s (b) 5 (km/h)/s

Exercise 5e
1. 2 km   2. $0 \cdot 82$ km (to 2 decimal places)

Exercise 5f
1. $167 \cdot 5$ m   3. $0 \cdot 133$ km   4. (i) $24 \, \text{m/s}^2$, 667 m

Exercise 6a
1. (a) $76 \cdot 8 \, \text{cm}^2$ (b) 4 cm
2. (i) equilateral (ii) $625\sqrt{3} \, \text{mm}^2$ (iii) $3750\sqrt{3} \, \text{mm}^2$
3. (i) $\dfrac{625}{4}\sqrt{3} \, \text{mm}^2$ (ii) $150\,000\sqrt{3} \, \text{mm}^2$
4. (a) 5:2 (b) $350\sqrt{11}$ mm by $200\sqrt{11}$ mm
5. (a) 1:2 (b) parallel (c) 1:4

Exercise 6b
1. $0 \cdot 75 \, \text{m}^3$ 2. $625\sqrt{3} \, \text{mm}^3$, $1406 \cdot 25\sqrt{3} \, \text{mm}^3$
3. $40 \cdot 07$ mm, $48 \cdot 48$ mm, $80 \cdot 14$ mm, $96 \cdot 96$ mm
$\dfrac{AP}{PQ} = \dfrac{BC}{QR} = \dfrac{AC}{PR} = \dfrac{1}{2}$ yes
4. 43° 50′, 76° 10′, 43° 50′, 76° 10′

Exercise 6c
4. $7 \cdot 5$ cm   5. 18 m

Exercise 7a
1. £135·75   2. £259·50   3. £340, £560, £735
4. £37·13 (to nearest p)   5. £19·80   6. £239·79
7. (a) £1 016·36 (b) £1 198·00   8. £333·75

Exercise 7b
1. £46·75   2. (a) £3 240 000, (b) £2 200 000   3. 60 p
4. £260   5. 1963, £9

Exercise 7c
1. (a) £7·55 (b) £6·42½   2. heavy duties rate 82½ p

ANSWERS

Exercise 7c
1. (*a*) £3·46 (*b*) £7·50   2. £6·07   3. Flat rate 64p
4. £15·10½

Exercise 8a
48%

Exercise 8b
64·5%; 74%

Exercise 8c
1. (*a*)

Marks	No in set A
20–24	1
25–29	3
30–34	2
35–39	0
40–44	0
45–48	0
50–54	0
55–59	1
60–64	3
65–69	2
70–74	6
75–79	2
80–84	7
85–89	1
90–94	2
95–99	3
100–104	1

(*b*)

Maths Marks	No in set A
Not more than 25	1
" " " 30	4
" " " 35	6
" " " 40	6
" " " 45	6
" " " 50	6
" " " 55	6
" " " 60	7
" " " 65	10
" " " 70	12
" " " 75	18
" " " 80	20
" " " 85	27
" " " 90	28
" " " 95	30
" " " 100	33
" " " 105	34

297

2. English Marks

(a)

Marks	No in set B		
30–34	2		
35–39	6		
40–44	5		
45–49	6		
50–54	4	3	Modal Range →
55–59	7	0	
60–64	4	3	
65–69	0		
70–74	1		

(b)

Marks	No in set B
Not more than 25	2
,, ,, ,, 40	8
,, ,, ,, 45	13
,, ,, ,, 50	19
,, ,, ,, 55	23
,, ,, ,, 60	30
,, ,, ,, 65	34
,, ,, ,, 70	34
,, ,, ,, 75	35

3. Cumulative Frequency Table

Marks	No in set
Not more than 5	8
,, ,, ,, 10	32
,, ,, ,, 15	70
,, ,, ,, 20	97
,, ,, ,, 25	100

Median $12\frac{1}{2}$

ANSWERS

Exercise 8d

1. Cumulative Frequency Table

Marks				No in set
Not more than			15	5
,,	,,	,,	20	21
,,	,,	,,	25	45
,,	,,	,,	30	84
,,	,,	,,	35	134
,,	,,	,,	40	195
,,	,,	,,	45	263
,,	,,	,,	50	326
,,	,,	,,	55	398
,,	,,	,,	60	463
,,	,,	,,	65	511
,,	,,	,,	70	543
,,	,,	,,	75	568
,,	,,	,,	80	586
,,	,,	,,	85	601
,,	,,	,,	90	610
,,	,,	,,	95	619
,,	,,	,,	100	624

Median ←occurs at $312\frac{1}{2}$

2. (*i*) 157·78 cm

(*ii*) Cumulative Frequency Table

Height in cm	No in set
150	2
152	2
154	17
156	46
158	71
160	83
162	93
164	97
166	100

(*iii*) 156·2, 154·8, 158·8

3.

Marks			No in set
Less than		5	1
,,	,,	10	3
,,	,,	15	8
,,	,,	20	8
,,	,,	25	10
,,	,,	30	13
,,	,,	35	18
,,	,,	40	24
,,	,,	41	41
,,	,,	50	51
,,	,,	55	58
,,	,,	60	72
,,	,,	65	82
,,	,,	70	92
,,	,,	75	98
,,	,,	80	101
,,	,,	85	103
,,	,,	90	104
,,	,,	95	105
,,	,,	100	105

52, $63\frac{1}{2}$, 41

Exercise 8e

1. English Mode: 57
   Maths Mode: 77

2. (*i*) 440·3 (*ii*) 440 (*iii*) 437·5

ANSWERS

Exercise 9a

1. $x = 3$ 2. $y = -2$ 3. $x = -1$ 4. $x = 1\frac{1}{2}$
5. $x = -7$ 6. $b = -9$ 7. $y = 1$ 8. $x = -2$
9. $x = 1, y = -2$ 10. $x = \frac{1}{2}, y = \frac{1}{3}$ 11. $x = -1, y = 3$
12. $a = -\frac{2}{3}, b = 1\frac{1}{2}$ 13. $c = 9\frac{6}{7}, d = 14\frac{6}{7}$ 14. $x = 6, y = 4$
15. $x = -2, y = -3$ 16. $2a^2+a-21$ 17. $a^3-a^2b+ab^2-b^3$
18. $18p^2-45pq+28q^2$ 19. $2x^2+2xy+11x-3y-21$
20. $a^2-2b^2-3c^2+ab-5bc+2ac$ 21. $(y+5)^2$
22. $(a+7)(a-3)$ 23. $(x+2y)(x+y)$ 24. $(14+a)(5-a)$
25. $(2x+1)(x-9)$ 26. $(2y+3)(15y+2)$ 27. $3(4a+b)/(4a-b)$
28. $9(5+m)(5-m)$ 29. $6(xy+6a^2b^2)(xy-6a^2b^2)$
30. $(a+3b)(a-6)$ 31. $(x-7)(3+y)$ 32. $(3a+b)(2x-5y)$
33. $(2x-9y)(7x-3y)$ 34. $(2p-3q)(p+20q)$
35. $(x+y)(3x^2-4y)$ 36. $x = 5$ or 7 37. $y = 1\frac{1}{2}$ or -11
38. $a = \frac{1}{2}$ or $-5\frac{1}{2}$ 39. $p = -1\frac{1}{2}$ or $\frac{1}{3}$ 40. $x = 2\frac{1}{2}$ or $-\frac{1}{3}$
41. $x = 0$ or $\frac{1}{3}$ 42. $a = 0$ or 5 43. $x = 0$ or $\frac{1}{3}$
44. $x = -1\frac{1}{2}$ 45. $p = -$ or $3\frac{1}{2}$ 46. $x = 3$ or -1
47. $x = 0$ or 4 48. $x = 10$ or -2 49. $x = 1$ or $-1\frac{3}{10}$
50. $x = 3\frac{1}{2}$ or -1 51. 3 or -6 52. 9 and 13
53. $3\frac{1}{2}p$ or $2\frac{1}{2}p$ 54. $x = 5, y = 7$ 55. $x = 3$
56. $a = 8, b = 2$ 57. 6 cm   58. $10\frac{3}{4}$ and $12\frac{1}{4}$ 59. 5 and 11
60. $x-1, x+1$

Exercise 9b

1. $L = A/B$ 2. $M = V/LB$ 3. $Y = x+z-3$
4. $y = 6bx/5a$ 5. $m = (y-c)/x$ 6. $x = (a+ab)/b$
7. $B = p/2-L$ 8. $h = 2A/(x+y)$ 9. $x = (2A-hy)/h$
10. $a = (L-x)/TX$
11. $S = a+b+c/2, S-b = c+a-b/2, S-C = a+b-c/2$
12. $t = \sqrt{(A/\pi)}, r = 0.9217$ cm   13. $h = 3V/\pi r^2, r = \sqrt{(3V/\pi r)}$
14. $h = 4\pi^2 I/MgT^2$ 15. $f = (v-u)/t$ 16. $f = 2(s-ut)/t^2$
17. $h = (A/2\pi r)-r$ 18. $c = 2\Delta/b \sin A$ 19. $u = (2s/t-v)$
20. $h = E/mg - v^2/2g, v = \sqrt{2E/m-2gh}$
21. $x = (2y-3)/(1+y), x = 1\frac{1}{3}$ 22. $v = uf/u-f$
23. $R_1 = R_2 R/(R_2-R)$ 24. $h = 2r-(3V/4\pi r^2)$
25. $\cos A = (b^2-c^2-a^2)/2bc, A = 26° 20'$
26. $l = h\sqrt{l/u^2+l}$ 27. $y = (2\frac{1}{2}E/p)-x$
28. $x = L-\sqrt{2M/W}$ 29. $L = \sqrt{121/M-3r^2}$

301

30. $h = a^2/12x - a/2$ 31. $y = v^2/2g - x^2g/2v^2$
32. $g = a[(3\pi+4)/2T]^2$ 33. $M = m/3(R^2-1)$
34. $T_2 = T_1 - 33\,000H/V$, $T_2 = 748$
35. $p = (F_1\pi d^2/4F_2t) + d$, $p = 278 \cdot 5$ (to 1 decimal place)

Exercise 9c

1. 72 km/h 2. 3 hr 20 min 3. 2 hr 30 min, 100 km/h
4. 80 km/h 5. 82·11 km/h 6. 160 km/h
7. $\dfrac{T+\frac{1}{2}}{T}$ hr, $\frac{1}{2}$ hr 8. $7x/24$ hr, 6·86 km/h (to 2 decimal places)
9. $(15x+19y)/xy$ h, $(xy+4\,800)/80y$ h, $\dfrac{80xy+4\,800y}{xy+4\,800}$ km/h

Exercise 9d

1. 180 km 2. 32 km 3. 36 km from A, $1\frac{1}{2}$ h
4. 28 km, 14·00 h 5. 40 km 6. 20 km 7. 10 km
8. $x = 80$, $y = 40$ 9. 90 km 10. 60 km/h, 30 km/h
11. 60, 70 km/h 12. 8, 12 km/h 13. 400, 500 km/h
14. 8, 9 km/h, 18 km from 1 town 15. 30 km/h
16. 112, 80 km/h 17. $1\frac{1}{4}$ h, 80 km
18. 56 km/h, 48 km/h (or 24, 16 km/h) 19. 120 km/h, 100 km/h
20. 80 km/h 21. (*i*) true (*ii*) false (*iii*) false (*iv*) true (*v*) false (*vi*) true (*vii*) false (*viii*) true (*ix*) true (*x*) false
22. (*i*) false (*ii*) true (*iii*) true (*iv*) false (*v*) true
23. (*i*) false (*ii*) true (*iii*) false (*iv*) false (*v*) true (*vi*) true
24. (*a*) (*iv*) (*b*) (*iii*) (*c*) (*ii*) (*d*) (*iv*)
25. (*i*) true (*ii*) false (*iii*) false (*iv*) true (*v*) false (*vi*) false (*vii*) false (*viii*) true

Exercise 10c

1. $V = \frac{3}{4}\pi r^3$, $A = 4\pi r^2$

Exercise 10d

1. 110 km
2. 39 600, 39 000, 37 200, 34 300, 30 300, 25 500
4. (*i*) 1 650 km (*ii*) 19 800 (*iii*) 1 100 km
5. 4 070 km 6. 1 650 km, 37° W (to nearest degree)

ANSWERS

7. 8 920 km **8.** $r = \dfrac{V}{\pi h^2} + \dfrac{h}{3}$ (i) 22 cm (ii) 386·57 cm² (to 2 decimal places)
9. 30½°W, longitude approximately 4°S

Exercise 11a

1. $A = 007°$, N7°E $B = 097°$, 5081°E., $C = 195°$, S15°W
   $D = 303°$, N57°W.
2. 123° **3.** 141° **4.** 198° **5.** 354° **6.** 189°
7. 360° **8.** 285° **9.** 98° **10.** 180° **11.** 320°
12. 234° **13.** 225° **14.** 157½ **15.** 157½° **16.** 070°
17. 310° **18.** 185° **19.** 357° **20.** 030° **21.** 250°
22. 070° **23.** 152° **24.** 270° **25.** 082½°

Exercise 11b

1. 9·24 km; 3·83 km   **2.** 10·23 km, 10·97 km
3. 14·9 km, 10·07 km   **4.** 964 m, 470 m (to nearest m)
5. 053° 8′, 5 km   **6.** 209° 44′, 16·1 km   **7.** 333° 5′, 14·81 km
8. 122° 47′, 86·83 km   **9.** 060° 21′, 57·87 km, 237° 6′, 60·75 km,
   214° 7′, 108·7 km   **10.** 143° 12′, 54·70 km
11. 051° 21′, 6 043 m   **12.** 052° 7′, 292° 37′, 017° 32′
13. 137° 9′, 173·7 km   **14.** 15·19 km, 14·73 km, 9·96 km
15. 148° 17′, 11·94 km   **16.** 10·1 km, 218° 26′
17. 293 m, 214 m 21 448 m² (to nearest m)
18. 214° 14′, 169·8 km

Exercise 11c

1. 11·92 m, 24° 48′   **2.** 29° 3′   **3.** 23° 32′, 45° 77′, 30° 35′
4. 24° 16′, 26° 34′   **5.** 36° 52′, 46° 41′   **6.** 13·56 cm, 57° 57′, 66° 8′
7. 26° 10′, 42° 28′   **8.** 68·74 m, 217·9 m, 110·9 m
9. 4·59 m, 65° 12′   **10.** 74·73 m   **11.** 344·8 m, 37° 28′
12. 23° 41′, 52° 7′   **13.** 54° 44′, 72√3 cm²   **14.** 21·13 m, 12° 12′
15. 85·78 m, 52° 50′   **16.** 11·08 cm, 67° 24′, 78° 13′
17. (*a*) true (*b*) false (*c*) false (*d*) true (*e*) true
18. (*a*) true (*b*) false (*c*) true (*d*) true (*e*) true (*vi*) false (*vii*) true
   (*viii*) false (*ix*) true (*x*) false
19. (*a*) false (*b*) true (*c*) false (*d*) true (*e*) true (*f*) *true* (*g*) false
   (*h*) true (*i*) true
20. (*a*) (*ii*), (*b*) (*i*), (*c*) (*ii*), (*d*) (*ii*), (*e*) (*ii*), (*f*) (*ii*)

Exercise 12a
1. 9   2. 4   3. 21%   4. 75   5. 84

Exercise 12b
1. 76; 13; 16; 15
2. The Headmaster was right. At least 26 boys study chemistry
3. 95   4. 50%, 10%, 30%   5. 14
6. (a) 10 (b) (i) 3 (ii) 26   7. (a) 26 (b) 5 (c) 2 (d) 41 (e) 41
8. 400, 50   9. 51   10. 225, 297, 333
11. (i) $n(S_1)+n(S_2)+n(S_3) = n(A \vee B)$ $n(S_1) = n(A \wedge B')$
$n(S_2) = n(A \wedge B)$
$n(S_3) = n(B' \wedge A)$
(ii) $n(A')+n(B')+n(C') = n(A \vee B \vee C)'$

Exercise 12d
2.

$\vee$	0	1
0	0	1
1	1	1

$\wedge$	0	1
0	0	0
1	0	1

′	
0	1
1	0

Exercise 12e

p	q	$p \wedge q$
0	0	0
0	1	0
1	0	0
1	1	1

p
$\wedge$	0	1
0	0	0
1	0	1
q

a	a'
1	0
0	1

v	
1	0
0	1

Exercise 12f
1. (i) ⊏ $\begin{matrix}a\\b\end{matrix}$ ⊐   (ii) —a—b—   (iii) ⊏ $\begin{matrix}a\\b\\c\end{matrix}$ ⊐

ANSWERS

(iv) $-a-b-c-$ (v) $-\boxed{\begin{smallmatrix}a\\b-c\end{smallmatrix}}-$ (vi) $-\boxed{\begin{smallmatrix}a\\b\end{smallmatrix}}-c-$

(vii) $-a-\boxed{\begin{smallmatrix}b\\c\end{smallmatrix}}-$ (viii) $-\boxed{\begin{smallmatrix}a-b\\c\end{smallmatrix}}-$ (ix) $-\boxed{\begin{smallmatrix}a-b\\c-d\end{smallmatrix}}-$

(x) $-\boxed{\begin{smallmatrix}a\\b\end{smallmatrix}}-\boxed{\begin{smallmatrix}c\\d\end{smallmatrix}}-$ (xi) $-a-\boxed{\begin{smallmatrix}b\\a'\end{smallmatrix}}-$ (xii) $-\boxed{\begin{smallmatrix}a\\a'-b'\\a-b\end{smallmatrix}}-$

2. (i) $x \lor y \land z$ (ii) $x' \lor (x \land y) \lor z$ (iii) $(x \land y) \lor (x' \land y')$
(iv) $(u \lor v) \land (x \lor y)$ (v) $a \land (b \lor c) \land d$
(vi) $(a \lor b) \land (c \lor d) \land (e \lor f)$ (vii) $x \lor (x' \lor y)$
(viii) $(a \land b) \lor (b' \lor a')$ (ix) $[(z \lor x') \land y'] \lor [(y \lor x) \land z']$
(x) $[(x \lor y) \land (x \lor z)] \lor [x' \lor z']$

Exercise 12g

(i)

a	b	$a \lor b$
0	0	0
0	1	1
1	0	1
1	1	1

(ii)

a	b	$a \land b$
0	0	0
0	1	0
1	0	0
1	1	1

(iii)

a	b	c	$a \lor b$	$b \lor c$	$a \lor c$
0	0	0	0	0	0
0	0	1	0	1	1
0	1	0	1	1	0
1	0	0	1	0	1
0	1	1	1	1	1
1	1	0	1	1	1
1	1	1	1	1	1
1	0	1	1	1	1

(iv)

a	b	c	a ∧ b ∧ c
0	0	0	0
0	0	1	0
0	1	0	0
0	1	1	0
1	0	0	0
1	0	1	0
1	1	0	0
1	1	1	1

(v)

a	b	b ∧ c	a	a ∨ (b ∧ c)
0	0	0	1	1
0	1	0	1	1
1	0	0	0	0
1	1	1	0	1

(vi)

a	b	c	a ∨ b	(a ∨ b) ∧ c
0	0	0	0	0
0	0	1	0	1
0	1	0	1	0
0	1	1	1	1
1	0	0	1	0
1	0	1	1	1
1	1	1	1	1
1	1	1	0	1

ANSWERS

(*vii*)

a	b	c	b ∧ c	a ∧ (b ∨ c)
0	0	0	0	0
0	0	1	1	0
1	0	1	1	1
1	0	0	0	1
0	1	0	1	0
1	1	0	1	1
1	1	1	1	1
0	1	1	1	1

(*viii*)

a	b	c	a ∧ b	(a ∧ b) ∨ c
0	0	0	0	0
0	0	1	0	1
0	1	0	0	0
0	1	1	0	1
1	0	0	0	0
1	0	1	0	1
1	1	0	1	1
1	1	1	1	1

(ix)

a	b	c	d	$a \wedge b$	$c \wedge d$	$(a \wedge b) \vee (c \wedge d)$
0	0	0	0	0	0	0
0	0	0	1	0	0	0
0	0	1	0	0	0	0
0	0	1	1	0	1	1
1	0	0	0	0	0	0
1	0	0	1	0	0	0
1	0	1	0	0	0	0
1	0	1	1	0	1	1
0	1	0	0	0	0	0
0	1	0	1	0	0	0
0	1	1	0	0	0	0
0	1	1	1	0	1	1
1	1	0	0	1	0	1
1	1	0	1	1	0	1
1	1	1	0	1	0	1
1	1	1	1	1	1	1

ANSWERS

(x)

a	b	c	d	a ∨ b	c ∨ d	(a ∨ b) ∧ (c ∨ d)
0	0	0	0	0	0	0
0	0	0	1	0	1	0
0	0	1	0	0	1	0
0	0	1	1	0	1	0
1	0	0	0	1	0	0
1	0	0	1	1	1	1
1	0	1	0	1	1	1
1	0	1	1	1	1	1
0	1	0	0	1	0	0
0	1	0	1	1	1	1
0	1	1	0	1	1	1
0	1	1	1	1	1	1
1	1	0	0	1	0	0
1	1	0	1	1	1	1
1	1	1	0	1	1	1
1	1	1	1	1	1	1

(xi)

a	b	a'	b ∨ a'	a ∧ (b ∨ a')
0	0	1	1	0
0	1	1	1	0
1	0	0	0	0
1	1	0	1	1

(xii)

a	b	a'	b'	a'∧b'	a∨(a'∧b')	(a∧b)	a∨(a'∧b')∨(a∧b)
0	0	1	1	1	1	0	1
0	1	1	0	0	0	0	0
1	0	0	1	0	1	0	1
1	1	0	0	0	1	1	1

(i)

x	y	z	x∨y	(x∨y)∧z
0	0	0	0	0
0	0	1	0	0
0	1	0	1	0
0	1	1	1	0
1	0	0	1	0
1	0	1	1	1
1	1	0	1	0
1	1	1	1	1

(ii)

x	y	x'	z	x∧y	x'∨(x∧y)	x'∨(x∧y)∧z
0	0	1	0	0	1	0
0	0	1	1	0	1	1
0	1	1	0	0	1	0
0	1	1	1	0	1	0
1	0	0	0	0	0	0
1	0	0	1	0	0	0
1	1	0	0	1	1	0
1	1	0	1	1	1	1

ANSWERS

(iii)

x	y	x'	y'	$x \wedge y$	$x' \wedge y'$	$(x \wedge y) \vee (x' \wedge y')$
0	0	1	1	0	1	1
0	1	1	0	0	0	0
1	0	0	1	0	0	0
1	1	0	0	1	0	1

(iv)

u	v	x	y	$u \vee v$	$x \vee y$	$(u \vee v) \wedge (x \vee y)$
0	0	0	0	0	0	0
0	0	0	1	0	1	0
0	0	1	0	0	1	0
0	0	1	1	0	1	0
1	0	0	0	1	0	0
1	0	0	1	1	1	1
1	0	1	0	1	1	1
1	0	1	1	1	1	1
0	1	0	0	1	0	0
0	1	0	1	1	1	1
0	1	1	0	1	1	1
0	1	1	1	1	1	1
1	1	0	0	1	0	0
1	1	0	1	1	1	1
1	1	1	0	1	1	1
1	1	1	1	1	1	1

(v)

a	b	c	d	$b \lor c$	$a \land (b \lor c)$	$a \land (b \lor c) \land d$
0	0	0	0	0	0	0
0	0	0	1	0	0	0
0	0	1	0	1	0	0
0	0	1	1	1	0	0
1	0	0	0	0	0	0
1	0	0	1	0	1	0
1	0	1	0	1	1	1
1	0	1	1	1	0	0
0	1	0	0	1	0	0
0	1	0	1	1	0	0
0	1	1	0	1	0	0
0	1	1	1	1	0	0
1	1	0	0	1	1	0
1	1	0	1	1	1	1
1	1	1	0	1	1	0
1	1	1	1	1	1	1

ANSWERS

(vi) From exercise (iv)
$(a \vee b) \wedge (c \vee d) \wedge (e \vee f) = 1$, only if $a = 1$ or if $b = 1$, or if a and $b = 1$ and

c	d	e	f
1		1	
1			1
1		1	1
	1	1	
	1		1
	1	1	1
1	1	1	
1	1		1
1	1	1	1

(vii)

x	x'	y	x' ∨ y	x ∨ (x' ∨ y)
0	1	1	1	1
1	0	0	0	1
0	1	0	1	1
1	0	1	1	1

(viii)

a	b	a'	b'	a ∧ b	a' ∨ b'	(a ∧ b) ∨ (a' ∨ b')
0	0	1	1	0	1	1
0	1	1	0	0	1	1
1	0	0	1	0	1	1
1	1	0	0	1	0	1

313

(ix)

x	y	z	x'	y'	z'	$(z \vee x')$	$(z \vee x') \wedge y'$	$(y \vee x)$	$(y \vee x) \wedge z'$	$(z \vee x') \wedge y' \vee (y \vee x) \wedge z'$
0	0	0	1	1	1	1	1	0	0	1
0	0	1	1	1	0	1	1	0	0	1
0	1	0	1	0	1	1	0	1	1	1
0	1	1	1	0	0	1	0	1	0	0
1	0	0	0	1	1	0	0	1	1	1
1	0	1	0	1	0	1	1	1	0	1
1	1	0	0	0	1	0	0	1	1	1
1	1	1	0	0	0	1	0	1	0	0

ANSWERS

x	y	z	x'	z'	$x \vee y$	$x \vee z$	$(x \vee y) \wedge (x \vee z)$	$x' \vee z'$	$(x \vee y) \wedge (x \vee z) \vee (x' \vee z')$
0	0	0	1	1	0	0	0	1	1
0	0	1	1	0	0	1	0	1	1
0	1	0	1	1	1	0	0	1	1
0	1	1	1	0	1	1	1	1	1
1	0	0	0	1	1	1	1	1	1
1	0	1	0	0	1	1	1	0	1
1	1	0	0	1	1	1	1	1	1
1	1	1	0	0	1	1	1	0	1

(x)

315

Exercise 12h

1. $-p-q-r$
2. $-a-b-$ (parallel a,b), $-b-a-$ (parallel b,a)
3. $-a-b-$, $-b-a-$
4. $-a-b-c-$ (parallel), $-a-b-a-c-$
5. $-a-b-c-$, $-a-b-a-c-$
6. $[-a-b-]'$
7. $[-a-b-]'$, $-a'-b'-$
8. $-a-a-$
9. $-a-a-$
10. $-a-a'-$
11. $-a-a'- = 0$

Exercise 12j

1. $a \wedge b$
2. $a \wedge b$
3. $a \vee c$
4. $(a \wedge b) \vee (a' \wedge c)$
5. $x \vee (y' \vee z)$
6. $a \vee (a' \wedge b')$
7. $a \vee b$
8. $a \vee (b \wedge c)$

Exercise 13a

1.

3	0	1	2
4	1	2	4
5	2	3	6
6	3	4	8
7	4	5	10
8	5	6	12
9	6	7	14
10	7	8	16
11	8	9	18
12	9	10	20

2. $(n-3)$ diagonals: $(n-2)$ triangles; $(2n-4)$ right angles

ANSWERS

Exercise 13b

1.

4	90°	90°
5	72°	108°
6	60°	120°
7	$51\frac{3}{7}°$	$128\frac{4}{7}°$
8	45°	135°
9	40°	140°
10	36°	144°
11	$32\frac{8}{11}°$	$147\frac{3}{11}°$
12	30°	150°

2. (a) 156° (b) 160° (c) 162° (d) 165°
3. (a) 12 (b) 360 (c) 80 (d) 60 **4.** (a) 6 (b) 180 (c) 40 (d) 48
5. 110° **6.** 80°, 80° **7.** 102°, 133° **8.** 98° **9.** 48°
10. 102°, 115°, 65° **11.** 18° **12.** 135° **13.** 110°
14. 30° **16.** 80°, 75° **17.** 95° **18.** 48° **19.** 67°
20. (i) 122° (ii) 95° **21.** 75° **22.** 98°, 82°, 20°
23. 58°, 61° **24.** 40°, 80° **25.** 60°, 120°, 120°
26. (a) (i), (b) (i), (c) (ii), (d) (i)
27. (a) false (b) true (c) false (d) true (e) false (f) true (g) true (h) false
28. (a) (iv), (b) (ii), (d) (iv)
29. (i) true (ii) false (iii) true (iv) true (v) true (vi) false (vii) true (viii) false (ix) true (x) true
30. (i) true (ii) true (iii) false (iv) true (v) false (vi) true (vii) false (viii) true (ix) true (x) true (xi) false (xii) true

Exercise 13d

1. 3·75 cm **2.** 79 mm (ii) 76° 30′ **3.** 3·7 cm
4. 2 125 mm² **5.** 57° or 123° **6.** 38·75 mm
7. 1 991 mm² **8.** 1 357·63 mm² **9.** 6·9 cm **10.** 74°
11. 1 686·38 mm²

Exercise 14a
1. (a) 1, 3, 6, 10, 15 (b) 1, 4, 9, 16, 25 (c) 1, 8, 27, 64, 125
2. (i) 1, 3, 5, 7, 9 (ii) 1, 5, 9, 13, 17 (iii) 15, 12, 22, 35
   (iv) 8, 21, 40, 65, 96 or (8, 21, 36, 53, 72) (v) 3, 6, 9, 12, 15
   (vi) 4, 8, 12, 16, 20 (vii) 5, 10, 15, 20, 25 (viii) 6, 12, 18, 24, 30

Exercise 14b
1. (i) ... $-8, -6, -4, -2, 0, 2, 4, ...$; ... $-7, -5, -3, -1, 1, 3, 5, ...$ ... $8, 6, 4, 2, 0, -2, -4, ...$; ... $7, 5, 3, 1, -1, -3, -5$
2. 1, 4, 7, 10; $-10, -7, -4, -1$; 2, 5, 8, 11 $-11, -8, -5, -2°, 0, 3, 6, 9$; $-12, -9, -6, -3$
3. all except Figs. 3 and 4
4. (ii), (v), (vi), (vii), (ix), (x)

Exercise 14c

```
1    3    6    10   15        1    4    9    16   25
   2    3    4    5              3    5    7    9
     1    1    1                   2    2    2

1    8    27   64   125       1    5    12   22   35   51
   7    19   37   61             4    7    10   13   16
     12   18   24                  3    3    3    3
        6    6

1    8    21   40   65   96   8    21   36   53   72
   7    13   19   25   31       13   15   17   19
     6    6    6    6              2    2    2
```

2. (i) 9, 11, 13, 15, 17 ... AP
   -2, 1, 4, 7, 10 ... AP
   (ii) 1, 4, 9, 16, 25 ... not an AP
   9, 15, 25, 39, 57 ... not an AP
   (iii) 18, 27, 64, 125 ... not an AP; two
   (iv) three (v) four; $n-1$

ANSWERS

3. (i) $a_7 = a_1+6d$ (ii) a_1+8d (iii) a_1+19d (iv) a_1+99d
   (v) $a_1+(n-1)d$
4. (i) 19 (ii) 22 (iii) 31 (iv) 301 (v) 361
5. (i) 14 (ii) 20 (iii) 44
6. (i) 485 (ii) 545 (iii) 650   7. 76   8. 536
9. (i) 24, 36, 45 (ii) 20, 40, 80 (iii) 30, 45, 60
   (iv) 6, 12, 18, 24, 30, 36, 60, 90, 120   10. 17, 29, $39\frac{1}{2}$
11. $x+8y, x+11y, x+16y$ 12. 3, 3, 30, 75   13. 4, 10, 46, 66
14. $-17, -23, -32$ 15. $-3, -5\frac{1}{2}, -8$ 16. $\frac{1}{2}, 4\frac{1}{2}, 6\frac{1}{2}, 14$
17. $-\frac{1}{2}, -3, -4, -7\frac{1}{2}$ 18. $-\frac{1}{7}, 2, 1\frac{3}{7}, -\frac{5}{7}$

Exercise 14d

1. 465   2. $\dfrac{(1+n)n}{2}$

3. (i) 600 (ii) 90 (iii) 480 (iv) 0 (v) $-10\,570$ (vi) $117\frac{1}{2}$ (vii) -220
   (viii) 103 (ix) -428 (x) -50 (xi) 30 750 (xii) 135 (xiii) -123
   (xiv) $114\frac{3}{4}$ (xv) 279 (xvi) $10x+45$ (xvii) $40a+570$
   (xviii) $18x+360y$ (xix) $90x+78y$ (xx) $50a+480$

Exercise 14e

(a) yes (b) no (c) no; substitute $\frac{2}{5}$ for $\frac{1}{4}$ (d) no; substitute $1\frac{1}{6}$ for $1\frac{1}{16}$
(e) yes (f) yes (g) no; substitute $3\frac{3}{5}$ for $3\frac{7}{10}$ (h) no; substitute
$9\frac{3}{5}$ for $7\frac{1}{5}$ (i) yes (j) no; substitute $1\frac{3}{11}$ for $1\frac{4}{11}$

Exercise 14f

1. (i) $a_1 r^2$ (ii) $a_1 r^{10}$ (iii) $a_1 r^{19}$ (iv) $a_1 r^{49}$ (v) $a_1 r^{n-1}$
2. (i) r (ii) r (iii) r (iv) r (v) r
3. (i) r^2 (ii) r^3 (iii) r^4 (iv) r^5
4. (i) 8, 32, 128, 512, 2048 (ii) 8, 4, 2, $1\frac{1}{2}$ (iii) $-8, -24, -72, -216,$
   -648
   (iv) $8, -4, 2, -1, \frac{1}{2}$ (v) 2, 20, 200, 2000, 20 000
   (vi) $2, -20, 200, -2000, 20\,000$ (vii) 12, 36, 108, 324, 972
   (viii) 81, 27, 9, 3, 1 (ix) $81, -27, 9, -3, 1$
   (x) 1, 0·1, 0·01, 0·001, 0·000 1
5. (i) 10 (ii) 3 (iii) $\frac{1}{2}$ (iv) $\frac{3}{4}$ (v) $\frac{2}{3}$

Exercise 14g
2. 34, 55, 89, 144

Exercise 15a
1. not a field; no identity element or inverses under multiplication
2. not a field, no inverses under multiplication
3. commutativity   4. commutativity
5. (i)

+	O	E
O	E	O
E	O	E

×	O	E
O	O	E
E	E	E

(ii) E (iii) O (iv) yes; O, E (v) not for E
(a) O (b) no (vii) no; there is no multiplication inverse

Exercise 15b
1. 76, 52, 28, 4, −20 ...   2. common difference 24

Exercise 15c
1. ... −10, −7, −4, −1, 2, 5, 8, 11, ...
2. no   3. four, five, n 4. difference is always a multiple of 3

Exercise 15d
1. (i), (iv), (v)
2. (i) 11, 18, 25, etc (ii) 16, 29, 42, etc. (iii) 11, 17, 23, etc.
3. (i) 3, 6 (ii) −2, −6 (iii) −2, −5 (iv) −4, −8 (v) −4, −8
4. (i) −3, −6 (ii) −2, −6 (iii) −2, −5 (iv) −4, −8 (v) −4, −8
5. (i) 8 (ii) 9 (iii) 6, 10 (iv) 6 (v) none (vi) 10 (vii) 6 (viii) 7 (ix) 10 (x) 9
6. possible answers (i) 1, 2, 5, 7; (ii) 2, 5 4, 7; (iii) 4, 6 5, 8
7. $(3a)+(3a+3) = (6a+3) \in$ residue class 0 modulus 3
8. $(3a+1)+(3a+4) = (16a+5) \in$ residue class 2 modulus 3
9. $(3a+2)+(3a+5) = (16a+7) \in$ residue class 1 modulus 3
10. $(3a)+(3a+1) = (6a+1) \in$ residue class 1 modulus 3
11. $(3a) + (3a+2) = (6a+2) \in$ residue class 2 modulus 3
    $(3a+1)+(3a+2) = (6a+3) \in$ residue class 0 modulus 3

ANSWERS

12.

+	0	1	2
0	0	1	2
1	1	2	0
2	2	0	1

13. $(3a) \times (3a+3) = 9a^2+9a \in$ residue class 0 modulus 3
$(3a+1) \times (3a+4) = 9a^2+15a+4 \in$ residue class 1 modulus 3
$(3a+2) \times (3a+5) = 9a^2+21a+10 \in$ residue class 1 modulus 3
$(3a) \times (3a+1) = 9a^2+3a \in$ residue class 0 modulus 3
$(3a) \times (3a+2) = 9a^2+6a \in$ residue class 0 modulus 3
$(3a+1) \times (3a+2) = 9a^2+9a+2 \in$ residue class 2 modulus 3

×	0	1	2
0	0	0	0
1	0	1	2
2	0	2	1

14. (*i*) yes (*ii*) yes (*iii*) yes (*iv*) yes (*v*) yes (*vi*) yes (*vii*) yes 0 (*viii*) yes 1 (*ix*) yes 0, 2, 1 (*x*) no 0 has no inverse (*xi*) yes (*xii*) yes (*xiii*) no, yes (*xiv*) yes if the residue class 0 is excluded

15.

+	0	1	2	3
0	0	1	2	3
1	1	2	3	0
2	2	3	0	1
3	3	0	1	2

×	0	1	2	3
0	0	0	0	0
1	0	1	2	3
2	0	2	0	2
3	0	3	2	1

16.

+	0	1
0	0	1
1	1	0

×	0	1
0	0	0
1	0	1

A field

Residue classes 0 and 2 modulus 4 have no inverse under multiplication; not a field

17.

+	0	1	2	3	4
0	0	1	2	3	4
1	1	2	3	4	0
2	2	3	4	0	1
3	3	4	0	1	2
4	4	0	1	2	3

×	0	1	2	3	4
0	0	0	0	0	0
1	0	1	2	3	4
2	0	2	4	1	3
3	0	3	1	4	2
4	0	4	3	2	1

A field

321

LONGMAN MATHEMATICS

18.

+	0	1	2	3	4	5
0	0	1	2	3	4	5
1	1	2	3	4	5	0
2	2	3	4	5	0	1
3	3	4	5	0	1	2
4	4	5	0	1	2	3
5	5	0	1	2	3	4

×	0	1	2	3	4	5
0	0	0	0	0	0	0
1	0	1	2	3	4	5
2	0	2	4	2	2	4
3	0	3	0	3	0	3
4	0	4	2	0	4	2
5	0	5	4	3	2	1

Residue classes 0, 2, 3, 4 modulus 6 have no inverse under multiplication; not a field

19.

+	0	1	2	3	4	5	6
0	0	1	2	3	4	5	6
1	1	2	3	4	5	6	0
2	2	3	4	5	6	0	1
3	3	4	5	6	0	1	2
4	4	5	6	0	1	2	3
5	5	6	0	1	2	3	4
6	6	0	1	2	3	4	5

×	0	1	2	3	4	5	6
0	0	0	0	0	0	0	0
1	0	1	2	3	4	5	6
2	0	2	4	6	1	3	5
3	0	3	6	2	5	1	4
4	0	4	1	5	2	6	3
5	0	5	3	1	6	4	2
6	0	6	5	4	3	2	1

A field

20. Prime modulus numbers give fields; non-prime numbers do not give fields

Exercise 16a

1. $\frac{1}{16}$ (a) $\frac{1}{4}$ (b) $\frac{3}{8}$ (c) $\frac{1}{4}$ 2. (a) $\frac{1}{36}$ (b) 7   3. $\frac{1}{24}$

Exercise 16b

2. (a) $\frac{3}{25}$ (b) $\frac{2}{5}$ (c) 7, 9 or 11   3. $\frac{1}{4}$ 4. (a) 13^2 (b) $\frac{1}{34}$ (c) $\frac{1}{36}$
   (d) $\frac{1}{38}$ 5. (a) $\frac{1}{7}$ (b) $\frac{1}{14}$

Revision Exercises

R.1
1. (a) 2·116 (b) 0·1327   2. 4%, 0·75 km   3. 324 km
4. 16 cm   5. semi-circumference   6. (C)

R.2
1. 4·5 cm²   2. 4 and −1 (b) $x = 1\frac{1}{2}$ 3. (a) 0·026 36
   (b) 0·97   4. 36   5. (a) £1·16 (b) ½p   6. (B)

322

ANSWERS

R.3
1. (a) 3·75 cm (b) 24 m   2. $x = 2·618$ or $0·382$
4. $A = 60°$, $B = 30°$, $\widehat{C} = 150°$, $\widehat{D} = 120°$ 6. (C)

R.4
1. 3·375 litres, 8 litres   2. 797·52 km/h   3. 30·51 km, 153° 43′
4. 70   5. (a) 224 m (b) 2 ms^2 6. (B)

R.5
1. 16:1, 64:1   2. $0·00006545$ cm^3 3. £42·88
4. £2 730 000   5. 34p   6. (B)

R.6
1. (C)   2. (A)   3. (C)   4. (B)   5. (D)   6. (C)

R.7
1. 7·888 cm, 8·253 cm   2. (a) 0·048 7 (b) 0·087 08
3. £257·62½   4. £2·4   5. 5·513 m   6. (D)

R.8
1. 4·125 km   2. (a) 3·6 s (b) 24 ms   3. 1·25 kg   4. £100
5. $\frac{1}{8}$; $\frac{1}{4}$; $\frac{1}{8}$ 6. (C)

R.9
1. (a) (i) true (ii) false (iii) true (iv) false (v) false
   (b) (i) 1 (ii) 3 (iii) 2: the equilateral triangle only
2. $\frac{1}{32}$ 3. 5·894 m   4. (a) 63° (b) diameter
5. (a) 732 (b) $x = 5$ or -4

R.10
1. $\simeq 128$ m; $\simeq 0·75$ m/s^2 3. 512 m   6. (D)

R.11
1. $20\frac{5}{6}$ units   2. (i) y or $\propto 1/x$ (ii) no relationship (iii) $y \propto x$
   (iv) $y \propto 1/x$
3. (i) 41 (ii) (a) $3\frac{34}{41}$ (b) 3
4. (a) a circle on XY as diameter (b) 70°   5. (a) 6 (b) $\frac{1}{3}$
6. (B)

R.12
1. $1468{\cdot}75\,\text{cm}^2$ 2. £8·50 overpaid   3. $1000\,\text{m}^3$
4. 141   5. 141·4   6. (C)

R.13
1. (a) $x = 3$ (b) (i) $3x(1-3y)$ (ii) $(3a+2b)(3a-2b)$ (iii) $(t-6)(t+1)$
2. (i) $x = (y-c)/m$ (ii) $2^2 \times 3^2 \times 5 \times 7$ (iii) $R = 1\frac{1}{5}$
3. (i) 28° (ii) $71{\cdot}9\,\text{cm}^2$ 4. (i) 52 m (ii) 15°
5. (a) (i) even (ii) even (iii) no (iv) yes (v) no (b) (i) 11 010
   (ii) 11 101 (iii) 1 010 101 000
6. (a) (ii) (b) (iv) (c) (ii) (d) (iii)

R.14
1. (a) $\dfrac{128}{555}$ (b) 13, 25, 37, 49 (c) $\tfrac{5}{16}$
2. 59°, 70°, 126°
3. (i) 24·38 mm (ii) 35·63 mm (iii) 54° 21′ or 125° 39′
4. (a) $(S/\pi r) - r$ (b) $76{\cdot}1\,\text{cm}^2$ [correct to 3 significant figures]
5. (a) 97 002 000 100 800 (b) (i) 11 011 (ii) 63 (iii) 1 110 100
6. (i) false (ii) true (iii) false (iv) true (v) true (vi) true (vii) true
   (viii) true (ix) false (x) true

R.15
1. (i) 239·3 (ii) 50·93 (iii) 22·56 (iv) 0·952 8
2. (i) $\tfrac{12}{13}$ (ii) $x = 2, y = -3$ (iii) $x = 3$ or $-2\tfrac{1}{2}$
3. (i) $x = 3$ and -1 (ii) 3·236 and 1·236 (iii) $x = 2{\cdot}732$ and $-0{\cdot}732$
4. 4·384, 31° 38′   5. 162°, 81°, 18°, $56{\cdot}8\,\text{cm}^2$ [correct to 3 significant figures], $1136{\cdot}5\,\text{cm}^2$ [correct to 1 decimal place]
6. (i) true (ii) false (iii) false (iv) true (v) false (vi) true (vii) false
   (viii) false

R.16
1. (a) 901·8 (b) 14·775 (c) 0·092 79
2. (a) (i) $5(x+2)(x-2)$ (ii) $(2a+7c)(a+3b)$ (iii) $(x+3)(x-7)$
   (b) $2x - 5/x^2 - 1$
3. $27\tfrac{1}{2}°$, 68°, 35°   4. (a) 4h 38 min (b) £25·66
6. (a) (iv), (b) (ii), (c) (iii), (d) (iii)

ANSWERS

R.17
1. (i) $\frac{3}{8}$ (ii) 0·1875 (iii) £2400   2. (a) (i) 630·2 (ii) 32·2 (b) x^2-y^2
3. (a) 4·43 kg (b) 5 (c) $(a-b)(a+b+1)$ 5. 305 mm, 1·66 mm
6. (a) true (b) false (c) true (d) true (e) true (f) false (g) false (h) false

R.18
1. (a) $\frac{1}{9}$ (b) $x(2x+1)(2x-1)$ (c) 124°
2. (a) $\frac{9}{16}$ (b) (i) 23·3792 (ii) 12·02
3. $4\times1 = 4$ $4\times6 = 44$ 33303, 220, 413, 1111
   $4\times2 = 13$ $4\times7 = 103$
   $4\times3 = 22$ $4\times8 = 112$
   $4\times4 = 31$ $4\times9 = 121$
   $4\times5 = 40$ $4\times10 = 130$
4. (i) 15·4 km (ii) 3·03 km, 101° 7′
5. (i) 10; -18; $2\frac{1}{2}$ (ii) $(x-1)/x(x+1)$ (iii) $ab/(b-a)$
6. (i) true (ii) false (iii) true (iv) true (v) false (vi) true (vii) false (viii) true (ix) true (x) false

R.19
1. 0·31 and 3·18   2. 6593
3. (a) 25 (b) (i) 5 (ii) 1 (iii) 4 (c) (iii)   4. (i) $8\frac{8}{33}$ (ii) 77 m
5. £2130   6. (a) (iii), (b) (i), (c) (ii), (d) (ii), (e) (i)

R.20
1. (a) 2 (b) 2·524 (c) 72°
2. (a) $x = 6$, $y = 9$ (b) $18x+19y/37$ (c) 21·43 mm [correct to 2 decimal places]   3. (a) 29° 15′ (b) (i) 6·9 cm (ii) $1\frac{7}{9}$
4. (i) 8·662 cm (ii) 63° 26′ (iii) 60°   5. (b) 72 (c) 5, 6
6. (i) false (ii) true (iii) false (iv) true (v) true (vi) true (vii) false (viii) true (ix) true

R.21
1. (a) (i) 65·24 (ii) 2·7224 (b) $x = 50°$, $y = 30°$
2. (a) (i) $h = A/a+b$ (ii) 5 cm (b) (i) 1 (ii) $\pm\frac{1}{4}$
3. (a) $\frac{1}{2}$ (b) 265p
4. (i) $y = 42$ (ii) $x = 5$, $y = 7$ (iii) $x = 3\frac{1}{2}$ or $-1\frac{3}{5}$
5. 2026·4 mm   6. (i) true (ii) true (iii) false (iv) false (v) true

LONGMAN MATHEMATICS

R.22
1. (a) 22·5% (b) 1·76 m/s (c) $2b(a-b)$ 2. 6p
3. (b) 31·06 m (c) 309° 17′ (d) 581 m^2
4. (i) 278 m (ii) 112 m (to 3 significant figures)
5. (a) 4 (b) 2:1
6. (i) true (ii) false (iii) true (iv) true (v) false (vi) true (vii) true (viii) true (ix) true (x) false

R.23
1. (a) £25 (b) 454 2. (i) $\frac{1}{8}$ (ii) $4(x+3)(x-3)$ (iii) $h = v^2/2g$
3. (a) 2 140 (b) 410, 314; 19·1%, 14·7% (c) 111 280 4. 20°, 30°
5. $1+7+21+35+35+121+7+1$; $1+20+190+1140$
6. (a) (i), (iii) (b) (ii), (iv) (c) (iii) (d) (iv)

R.24
1. (a) (i) $3x(1-9x)$ (ii) $\pi(R+r)(R-r)$ (iii) $(2x+3)(2x-1)$
   (b) $x = 39, y = 22$
2. (a) 11·25 m (b) 0·6s, 2·4s 3. 42°, 20° 4. 5·72 88 m^3; 4010·16 kg
6. (a) (ii) (b) (iv) (c) (iii) (d) (i) (e) (iv)

R.25
1. (a) $3\frac{3}{5}$ (b) -2 (c) 267° 2. (a) $(2x-3)/3$ (b) £600
3. 19·5 cm [to 3 significant figures]; 48° 12′
4. (a) 12 (b) 2·14 cm (c) 51 cm^2
5. (b) AP = 47 m; PB = 68 m; BQ = 75 m; QA = 79 m;
   (c) 4 300 m^2 (d) (i) 024° (ii) 228°
6. (a) (ii) (b) (i) (c) (i), (iv) (d) (i) (e) (iv)

R.26
1. (a) (i) 0·031 (ii) 0·030 7 (b) xy (c) 124°
2. (b) $x = 13·5, y = -3·6$ (c) 90°
3. $\frac{1}{7}$ square unit $\frac{1}{22}$ 4. (a) 2·511 m (b) 37·5 m 5. 21·325
6. (a) false (b) true (c) false (d) true (e) false (f) true (g) false (h) true (i) true (j) true

R.27

	1	5	7	11
1	1	5	7	11
5	5	1	11	7
7	7	11	1	5
11	11	7	5	1

$x = 11, y = 7$

ANSWERS

3. 452·5 cm² **4.** (a) 38°, 71° (b) $c = a+b$
5. (a) $2/x$ (b) $x = 4$ or $x = -1$ **6.** (A)

R.28
1. (a) 17, 23 (b) 21, 34 (c) 27, 43 (d) 33, 65 (e) 37, 63
2. (i) 20 m, 8 m (ii) $x \pm \frac{1}{2}$ or $-\frac{2}{3}$
3. 1, 4, 0, 7, 7, 0, 4, 1, 0, 1, 4, 0, 7, 7, 0

4. (i)

×	1	2	3	4
2	2	4	1	3
3	3	1	4	2
4	4	3	2	1

(ii)

	POSITION
	1 2 3 4
R 90°	2 3 4 1
O	
T 180°	3 4 1 2
A	
T 270°	4 1 2 3
I	
O 360°	1 2 3 4
N	

(iv)

	1	2	3	4
1	1	2	3	4
2	2	3	1	4
3	4	1	3	2
4	3	4	2	1

→

	1	2	3	4
1	1	2	3	4
2	2	3	4	1
3	3	4	1	2
4	4	1	2	3

→

2	3	4	1
3	4	1	2
4	1	2	3
1	2	3	4

5.

	1	5	7	11
1	1	5	7	11
5	5	1	11	7
7	7	11	1	5
11	11	7	5	1

1. closure
2. associativity
3. existence of identity elements
4. existence of inverses

6. (C)

R.29
1. (a) $\pi/6$ (b) $\pi/6$ **2.** $\frac{7}{64}$ **3.** 5613 km, 4900 km
4. 76° 48′ **5.** (a) 20 cm, 43° 36′, $\frac{20}{31}$ (b) 63° **6.** (B)

R.30

+	a	b	c	d
a	a	b	c	d
b	b	c	d	a
c	c	d	a	b
d	d	a	b	c

×	a	b	c	d
a	a	a	a	a
b	a	b	c	d
c	a	c	a	c
d	a	d	c	b

2. (i) yes (ii) a−b = 3n (iii) c−d = mn (iv) a−o = mn
3. (i) a−b = ms (ii) c−d = mt
4. (i)

x	2	3	5	7	11	13	17	19	23	29	31	37	41	43	47	53	59
y	2	3	5	1	5	1	5	1	5	5	1	1	5	1	5	5	5

61	67	71	73	79	83	89	97
1	1	5	1	1	5	5	1

(ii) 0,4 (iii) 2,3 (v) 1,5

5. (i) 0,1,2,3,4,5,6
6.

×	1	3	4	5	9
1	1	3	4	5	9
3	3	9	1	4	5
4	4	1	5	9	3
5	5	4	9	3	1
9	9	5	3	1	4

(i) x = 9
(ii) x = 5

R.31

1. (ii) (2,1) (3,2) (4,3) (5,4) (7,6) (iii) (3,1) (5,2) (7,3) (9,4) (11, 5)(13,6)
   (iv) (4,1) (7,2) (10,3) (13,4) (16,5) (19,6)
2. (i) 4 units² (ii) (2,1) (3,1) (4,1) (5,2) (6,3) (5,3) (4,3) (3,2)
   (iii) 4 units² (iv) (3,1) (4,1) (5,1) (7,2) (9,3) (8,3) (7,3) (5,2)
3. (i) (a) (1,2) (1,3) (1,4) (1,5) (1,6) (1,7)
   (b) (1,3) (1,4) (1,5) (1,6) (1,7) (1,8)
   (c) (1,4) (1,5) (1,6) (1,7) (1,8) (1,9)
4. (ii) (1,2) (2,3) (3,4) (3,5) (3,6) (2,5) (1,4) (1,3) (iii) 4 units²
   (iv) (1,3) (2,5) (3,7) (3,8) (3,9) (2,7) (1,5) (1,4) (v) 4 units²
5. 5 units², 12 units² (a) 20 units² 48 units²
   (b) 45 units 108 units
   (c) $1\frac{1}{4}$ units 3 units

ANSWERS

R.32
1. (*ii*) 95 units², 16·5 units² (*iii*) (*a*) 9·5 units², 16·5 units²
   (*b*) 9·5 units² (*c*) 9·5 units², 16·5 units² (*d*) 0 units², 0 units²
   16·5 units²
4.

x	-2	-1	0	1	2	3	4
y	10	4	0	-2	-2	0	4

   (*a*) $-2\frac{1}{4}$ when $x = -1$
5. (*a*) 213 m (*b*) 239 m
6. D

R.33
2. no   3. (*i*) a, c, b, e, d, f (*ii*) d, f, c, e, a, b
5. (*a*) yes; start top or bottom centre
   (*b*) Line to join 2 end corners necessary
6. (C)

R.34
2. 14·15   3. (*i*) $x = 10\frac{3}{4}$ (*ii*) $a = 1\frac{1}{4}$; $b = 2\frac{1}{2}$ (*iii*) $x = 3$ or -4
4. 21·66 m   5. 3 294 m²
6. (*a*) false (*b*) false (*c*) true (*d*) false (*e*) true

R.35
1. 37·16 km, 304° 39′   2. (*a*) 13·05; 33 km (*b*) 44 km/h
3. 5·568 cm   5. (*a*) $\frac{3}{7}$ (*b*) 45 km/h
6. (*a*) true (*b*) false (*c*) true (*d*) false

R.36
1. £7·42   2. 44 cm   3. (*a*) £625 (*b*) 6 and 17
4. (*i*) 4·945 (*ii*) 0·243 5   5. 214·3 cm²
6. (*a*) true (*b*) false (*c*) true (*d*) false

R.37
1. 7·073 cm³   2. £4·38
3. (*a*) the sum of its digits is divisible by 3
   (*b*) one million and two
   (*c*) $2^2 \times 3^2 \times 7^2$; 42
4. 20, 13·4 cm

5. (a)

(b)

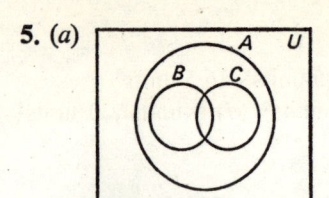

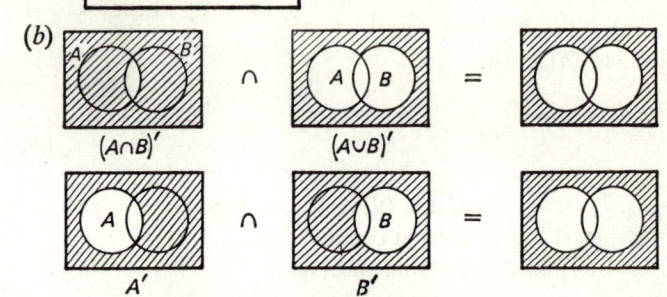

areas named are shaded

6. (a) true (b) false (c) true (d) false (e) true

R.38
1. 56·32 g **2.** $1\frac{12}{13}$ min. **3.** £153·33 **4.** (a) 1·375 cm (b) 24·89 (to 2 decimal places)
5. 97·66 g **6.** (i) (b) (ii) (c) (iii) (c) (i) (d)

R.39
1. (a) £875 (b) £2 625 **2.** (a) 52·5p (b) £1·36$\frac{1}{2}$
3. (a) $66\frac{2}{3}$ (b) 13 cm **4.** (a) 189·2 g, 94·6 g, 141·9 g (b) 30
5.

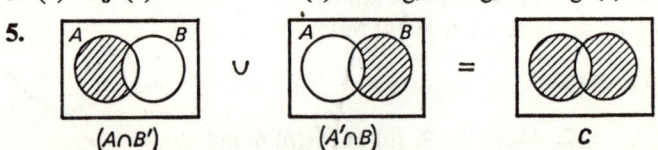

(ii) set of multiples of 3 and 4 excluding those that are common to both sets A and B (3+12n; 4+12n; 6+12n; 8+12n) n=0, 1, 2, 3.....
6. A or B

R.40
1. (a) (i) 320 m (ii) £192 (b) $1\frac{3}{4}$ (c) £146·25
2. £43·2 **3.** £6·94 (to nearest p) **4.** (i) 360 m³ (ii) 2 280 m³ (iii) 11 m
5. £31·08, £41·44 **6.** (a) unknown (b) true (c) true (d) true